Husserl, Intentionality, and Cognitive Science

⅃Ь *Bradford Books*

Edward C. T. Walker, Editor. *Explorations in* THE BIOLOGY OF LAN-GUAGE. 1979. The M.I.T. Work Group in the Biology of Language: Noam Chomsky, Salvador Luria, *et alia.*

Daniel C. Dennett. BRAINSTORMS: *Philosophical Essays on Mind and Psychology.* 1979.

Charles E. Marks. COMMISSUROTOMY, CONSCIOUSNESS AND UNITY OF MIND. 1980.

John Haugeland, Editor. MIND DESIGN. 1981.

Fred I. Dretske. KNOWLEDGE AND THE FLOW OF INFORMATION. 1981.

Jerry A. Fodor. REPRESENTATIONS: *Philosophical Essays on the Foundations of Cognitive Science.* 1981.

Ned Block, Editor. IMAGERY. 1981.

Roger N. Shepard and Lynn A. Cooper. MENTAL IMAGES AND THEIR TRANSFORMATIONS. 1982.

John Macnamara. NAMES FOR THINGS: *A Study of Human Learning.* 1982.

Hubert L. Dreyfus, Editor in Collaboration with Harrison Hall. HUSSERL, INTENTIONALITY AND COGNITIVE SCIENCE. 1982.

Husserl
Intentionality
and
Cognitive Science

HUBERT L. DREYFUS, EDITOR

in collaboration with
Harrison Hall

A Bradford Book

The MIT Press
Cambridge, Massachusetts
London, England

Library of Congress Cataloging in Publication Data
Main entry under title:

Husserl, intentionality, and cognitive science.

    1. Husserl, Edmund, 1859-1938——Addresses, essays,
lectures.   I. Dreyfus, Hubert L. II. Hall, Harrison, 1945-
B3279.   H94H87.   193   81-17183.
ISBN 0-262-04065-4   AACR2.

This book was set in IBM Baskerville
by Horne Associates, Inc.
and printed in the
United States of America.

Contents

Husserl, Intentionality, and Cognitive Science

Introduction

It often takes several generations—sometimes even centuries—before an original philosopher is sufficiently understood that the work of critical interpretation can begin. Thus, we have barely begun to put Frege, Wittgenstein, Merleau-Ponty, and Heidegger into proper perspective for evaluation. Husserl, however, is in much worse shape. His students and followers have tirelessly been producing books, articles, and anthologies appraising every aspect of his philosophy, as if the job of appropriating his central insight and taking over his technical terminology had already been accomplished. Yet Husserl felt that none of his students, from the most loyal to the most critical,[1]* had understood the nature and significance of what he considered his most important discovery: the special realm of entities revealed by the transcendental phenomenological reduction. And although the misunderstandings are largely his fault, Husserl was, regrettably, right. The reduction has been performed and pronounced unperformable, and existence has been bracketed and declared unbracketable, by an army of Husserl exegetes, all without a clear explanation in non-Husserlian terms of what the reduction is, what it reveals, and why according to Husserl one must perform it in order to do philosophy.

It took an analytic philosopher and logician, Dagfinn Føllesdal,

*Notes which contain something more than, or other than, textual citations have been marked with an asterisk throughout the volume.

influenced by the study of Frege, to see what Husserl considered
to be his greatest achievement: a general theory of the contents of
intentional states which accounted for the directedness of all mental activity. As Føllesdal explains more fully in the papers included
in this volume, the phenomenological reduction is Husserl's way of
describing the turning of attention away from both objects in the
world and psychological activity to the mental contents which
make possible the reference of each type of mental state to each
type of object.

In his most fully worked-out account of intentionality, Husserl
called the abstract structure by virtue of which the mind is directed towards objects a *noema*. Following Føllesdal, a new generation
of Husserl interpreters has been working out what the noema is
and what view of mind and reference it implies. Thanks to this
work, Husserl has finally begun to be recognized as the precursor
of current interest in intentionality—the first to have a general
theory of the role of mental representations in the philosophy of
language and mind. As the first thinker to put directedness of
mental representations at the center of his philosophy, he is also
beginning to emerge as the father of current research in cognitive
psychology and artificial intelligence.

The purpose of this anthology is to make the papers of these
new Husserl interpreters available to analytic philosophers, cognitive scientists, and all who want to understand the central notions
of phenomenology. Once Husserl's account of the pervasiveness of
intentionality has been grasped, along with the complexity of the
representational content which makes intentionality possible, Husserl interpreters will, we hope, carry through the tasks of reexamin-
ing Husserl's work on logic, language, psychology, other minds,
history, and the social sciences. We would have liked to include papers showing the relevance of Husserl's analysis of intentionality
in each of these areas, but the approach to Husserl put forth here
is new and its availability has thus far been restricted to scattered
journal articles, so that many of the specific areas in which he applied his basic insight remain to be effectively explored.

Once we have a fuller picture of the scope and plausibility of
Husserl's "strict science," we will be able to appreciate his growing
sense of the difficulties of his approach. We will then be in a better
position to evaluate the insights of investigators like Martin Heidegger and Maurice Merleau-Ponty, who developed their views in
opposition to Husserl's insistence on the philosophical priority of

the analysis of the representational content of individual intentional states.

A better understanding of the phenomenological movement is only part of what can be gained. Besides contributing to Husserl studies, such a new approach can contribute directly to current research in cognitive science, by providing concepts, analyses, and guidelines for further work as well as by raising questions concerning the possible limitations of all attempts to ground meaning and intelligibility in abstract mental structures.

To try to fill out what Husserl scholarship will look like once the reduction is understood would be to write the next Husserl anthology. However, it is already possible to show in some detail how Husserl's concerns and concepts can be used to illuminate current philosophical and psychological research, and vice versa. To show these parallels here, we will first have to sketch briefly the development of Husserl's account of intentionality. Since this account is the subject of several of the papers included in this anthology, to avoid repetition the presentation must be concise. Those interested in a more detailed account of Husserl's early view can turn to Chapter 5, below. Those seeking further details concerning Husserl's final worked-out theory may consult Chapters 1, 4, and 6. In general, since the papers in this anthology are presupposed, and at best only partially explained, in this introduction, it might also be profitable to read it as an epilogue showing how the papers included here relate to one another and to the rapidly growing discipline Husserl called cognitive science.

I. The Development of Husserl's Theory of Intentionality

Husserl's theory of intentionality developed through two stages. The first stage corresponds exactly to what Jerry Fodor, in his article on methodological solipsism, calls the representational theory of mind, and, we shall argue, the second stage may be linked to what Fodor calls the computational theory of representations. In 1900, in his *Logical Investigations* (*L.I.*), Husserl noted that several mental states (which he calls "acts") with the same object can have different contents if each state is directed toward the object under a different aspect.[2*] Moreover, he held that since numerically different mental states can have the same content, the content of the act cannot be identical with the specific occurring act but must be an abstraction of some sort. As Richard Aquila points out, at this stage Husserl conceives the relation of content to act on the model of the relation of a universal to the particulars which instantiate it.

> On Husserl's view . . . the self-identical meaning which several acts may share stands to those acts, or at least to some component of those acts, in the relation of a universal to the particulars which instaniate that universal:
>> Meaning is related to varied acts of meaning . . . just as Redness *in specie* is to the slips of paper which lie here, and which all "have" the same redness. Each slip has, in addition to other constitutive aspects (extension, form, etc.), its own individual redness, i.e., its instance of this colour species.   (*L.I.* p. 330)
>
> One way to put this point would be to say that Husserl's ontology of meaning commits us to no more than mental acts (and their constituents) and their universal properties. Accordingly, the difference between two thoughts which refer to the same object, and yet which differ in content, lies in the fact that each, or a part of each, instantiates a different meaning —which is to say that the two thoughts are, at least in one respect, different thoughts. And what two thoughts which share the same content have in common is simply the fact that those two thoughts are, at least in one respect, qualitatively the same. Since these would appear to be propositions which any theory of mental acts is bound to grant, we may thus say that Husserl's early ontology is, with respect to meanings, an economical one. It commits us to no more than mental acts and their properties, and this is something to which we are committed anyway.[3]

Husserl further held that the representational content of an act, its "meaning-essence" has two components: (1) the "matter" of the act which represents an object under a particular aspect, and (2) the "quality" of the act which represents the relation of the subject to the represented object—that is, whether the object specified by the content is perceived, believed, doubted, desired, and so forth. It is important to reiterate, however, that in *L.I.* Husserl has no ontological commitment to how the intentional content of an act is realized in the mind or brain, nor has he a view of what job the content performs other than that of individuating types of mental acts by describing the objects to which each type purportedly refers.

An example of current philosophical research which has deep affinities with Husserl's early account, including strikingly Husserlian distinctions, is John Searle's work on the philosophy of language and on intentionality. Early on, J. N. Mohanty saw the Husserlian conceptualization implicit in Searle's analysis of speech acts. In a footnote to a paper published in 1977—before Searle himself published the account of intentionality included in this volume—Mohanty remarked:

There is a use of "proposition" in the context of speech acts according to which the sentences "Sam is smoking," "Is Sam smoking?," "Sam may be smoking," and "Sam should not smoke" express the same propositional content, consisting of the same referring and predicating acts but with different illocutionary forces. (See John Searle, *Speech Acts,* Cambridge: Cambridge University Press, 1969, esp. p. 30.) Husserl's "act-matter" may correspond to what Searle calls "propositional content," and Husserl's "act-quality" to "illocutionary force."[4*]

Searle develops these distinctions in his paper "What is an Intentional State? ":

Intentional states represent objects and states of affairs in exactly the same sense that speech acts represent objects and states of affairs. . . . In the . . . speech acts cases there is an obvious distinction between the propositional content *that you will leave the room* and the illocutionary force with which that propositional content is presented in the speech act. . . . Equally in . . . Intentional states, there is a distinction between the representative content *that you will leave the room,* and the psychological mode, whether belief or fear or hope or whatever, in which one has that representative content.[5*]

Just as in *L.I.* Husserl began with the analysis of language and then in the course of his subsequent work applied the distinctions he made there to a general theory of intentionality which is supposed to account for all meaningful activity, including the use of language, so Searle states:

By explaining Intentionality in terms of linguistic acts, I do not mean to suggest that Intentionality is somehow essentially linguistic. The analogy between speech acts and Intentional states is drawn as an expository device, as a heuristic for explaining Intentionality. Once I have tried to make the nature of Intentionality clear, I will argue that the direction of dependence is precisely the reverse. Language is derived from Intentionality, and not conversely. The direction of *pedagogy* is to explain Intentionality in terms of language. The direction of *analysis* is to explain language in terms of Intentionality.[6*]

There are further parallels. For Husserl an act of perception has two components: an interpretive sense and an intuitive sense. The act is said to be *filled* if these two senses *coincide.* The total perceptual act is *verified* if, in the course of further experience, these components continue to coincide. The act successfully refers, however, only if there is in fact an object with properties exactly as intended. For example, my act of taking something to be a house is *filled* if I have the visual experience of a house; it is *verified* if anticipations of inside and back continue to be filled; it truly refers, however, if and only if there is in fact such a house. On this point Husserl is adamant:

> It need only be said to be acknowledged *that the intentional object of a presentation is the same as its actual object . . . and that it is absurd to distinguish between them . . .* 'The object is merely intentional' does not, mean that it exists, but only in an intention, of which it is a real *(reelles)* part, or that some shadow of it exists. It means rather that the intention, the reference to an object so qualified, exists, but not that the object does. If the intentional object exists, the intention, the reference, does not exist alone, but the thing referred to exists also. [7]

In Searle's terms, each mental state involves a representation of its conditions of satisfaction—the conditions under which the specification of its content would be satisfied and objective reference attained. And, as Searle notes: "just as the conditions of satisfaction are internal to the speech act, so the conditions of satisfaction of the Intentional state are internal to the Intentional state." [8]

In light of this theory of intentionality the phenomenological reduction assumes the central importance Husserl attributed to it. It is a special act of reflection, in which we turn our attention *away from* the object being referred to (and *away from* our psychological experience of being directed toward that object), and turn our attention *to* the act, more specifically to its intentional content, thus making our representation of the conditions of satisfaction of the intentional state our object. [9*]

At this point the parallel between the theory of language and the theory of intentionality in Husserl and Searle helps us understand one of Husserl's most obscure and misunderstood claims, viz. that the evidence given to phenomenological reflection is indubitable. Searle points out that we do not need some special sort of evidence to find out what we mean, what would satisfy our intentions, or in general what our intentional states represent. Just as we know what would count as an order being obeyed or a belief being confirmed, we simply know—i.e., are able to recognize—the condition of satisfaction of any of our intentional states. As Searle puts it, an intentional state just *is* a representation of its conditions of satisfaction. In exactly the same vein Husserl takes it for granted that phenomenological reduction gives "apodictic evidence" of the intentional content of our current mental state.

Since the conditions of satisfaction of an intentional state are internal to the intentional state they define, phenomenological analysis need not concern itself with whether or not the object aimed at by the intentional state exists. So Husserl can claim that phenomenological reflection amounts to a bracketing of objective existence which, at the same time, opens up for analysis *"an infinite realm of being of a new kind."*[10] And, since the subject must necessarily know what would count as satisfying his intentional state, the phenomenological reduction gives the subject a field of "ultimate evidences [the subject] has [him]self produced."[11]

Husserl, both early and late, was so impressed with the indubitability of one's knowledge of one's own intentional states that he thought an examination of the structures involved would at last provide an ultimate foundation for all knowledge. For us, however, that is the most dated and least interesting aspect of Husserl's achievement. What is important to contemporary psychology and philosophy of mind is the way Husserl changed his account of intentionality around 1908. By the time he published *Ideas,* thirteen years after the *Logical Investigations,* he had moved to a stronger view of what the intentional content is and how it works. He argued that an act of consciousness or *noesis* does not, on its own, do the work of representing an object and its relation to the subject; rather, the act has intentionality only by virtue of an "abstract form" or noema correlated with the act.

The noema, as conceived by Husserl, is a complex entity that has a difficult—perhaps impossibly difficult—job to perform. It must account for the mind's directedness towards objects. Therefore it must contain three components. One component must pick out a particular object outside the mind, another component must provide a "description" of that object under some aspect, and a third component must add a "description" of the other aspects which the object picked out could exhibit and still be the same object. In short, the noema must "refer," "describe," and "synthesize."

For early Husserl in *Logical Investigations* (and for Searle) the representational content simply does the job. In *Ideas,* however, Husserl bravely tries to explain how the job gets done. According to this later account, reference is provided by predicate-*senses* which, like Fregean *Sinne,* just have the remarkable property of picking out objects. These predicates, which presumably refer to atomic properties, are combined into complex "descriptions" of complex objects, as in Russell's theory of descriptions. Furthermore, the noema contains a component which determines which other possible descriptions can also apply to the same object and in what order the other aspects so described can appear. This is like the account worked out by C. I. Lewis, for whom the "meaning in mind" contains something like a list of all further compatible experiences. For Husserl, who is close to Kant on this point, however, the noema is not a list but a hierarchy of rules. There is a rule determing the ordered set of predicate-senses which describe what the object looks like, and higher-order rules that determine which other predicates can be expected to apply, i.e. what other appearances can count as appearances of the same object. This is clearly a sketch of a powerful, if perhaps ultimately untenable, cognitivist theory of mental activity as the rule-governed ordering of elements. Husserl's decisive step in the direction of cognitivism can be highlighted by one last comparison between Husserl and Searle, this time with an eye to their differences.

In *Ideas* Husserl generalized his purely descriptive account of the content of intentional states developed in *L.I.* by introducing abstract meanings (Sinne) and their rule-governed combination. Searle, on the other hand, develops his theory of intentionality by generalizing an account of intentional content very close to the one Husserl held in *L.I.,* viz. that the representational content of a mental state is simply whatever conditions of satisfaction those mental states which pick out the same object in the same respect have in common.[12] So, whereas later Husserl commits himself to the view that the content of intentional states is a complex abstract structure built up of primitives, especially those he calls predicate-senses, Searle, like early Husserl, contends that one can determine the logical properties of intentional states without taking a stand on how the representational content is realized. Searle's account of intentionality thus remains neutral on whether a representation plays its role in producing intentionality by virtue of its abstract form or whether the representation has no abstractable structure but must be directly instantiated as an organization of neurons,[13*] while Husserl explicitly opts for a level of description in terms of rules.

This decisive difference between Searle and Husserl, or between early and later Husserl himself, gives rise to opposed answers to two interrelated crucial questions: (1) What is the role of the representational content? Granted it is an essential feature of intentional states, does it have a functional role in making intentionality possible as well? (2) How much of our meaningful activity involves intentional content? Granted one always knows what one means, can all human understanding be analyzed in terms of intentional content?

We shall now see how a positive answer to question *one* leads Husserl to a theory of mental activity he calls transcendental idealism, which makes him an important precursor of cognitive science, while Searle's negative answer, stopping short at the representational theory of mind, leaves Searle, like early Husserl, a direct realist, and leads to a criticism of cognitivism. We will then show how a positive answer to question *two* leads Husserl to the claim that all mental life, even our awareness of practical activity and our sense of existing in a shared world, must be a form of object-directedness and so have intentional content; while a negative answer, as worked out by Heidegger and sketched by Searle, suggests that the attempt to analyze all meaning and intelligence solely in terms of mental representations is so misguided as to be doomed from the start.

II. Husserl's Anticipation of Cognitive Psychology

When Husserl embraced the view that an act refers by virtue of its being correlated with a sense, he not only accepted the Fregean theory that the representational content is realized as an abstract entity—the noema—but also adopted a Kantian or cognitivist view that the mind structures our experience of reality. Husserl calls the job that the *noemata* perform in unifying experience, and in making intentionality possible, "constitution," and, true to his Kantian heritage, calls his theory of constitution "transcendental idealism." Husserl, however, is an idealist in only a minimal sense. As Harrison Hall explains in his paper, Husserl is no empirical idealist—he does not subscribe to the phenomenalist view that objects are the sum of their appearances—nor does he hold with the absolute idealists that objects are ultimately mind dependent. He takes no stand on these metaphysical issues. Rather, in *Ideas* and all subsequent works, he calls himself a transcendental idealist, because he holds that mental activity plays an essential role in making reference possible and in determining the sorts of objects to which we can refer.[14]* As he later puts it:

> We then understand ourselves, *not as a subjectivity which finds itself in a world ready-made . . . but a subjectivity bearing within itself, and achieving all the possible operations to which this world owes its becoming.* In other words, we understand ourselves . . . *as transcendental subjectivity*, where by "transcendental", nothing more is to be understood than a regressive inquiry concerning the ultimate source of all cognitive formation . . .[15]   Exp & Jud p99

Later Husserl's account of these mental operations is straight-forwardly Kantian or cognitivist. Since the description of an object as, say, a house as opposed to a façade, already implies that it must have an inside and back, there is no way to separate the Fregean or descriptive aspect of the noema as an ordered set of predicate-senses from the more Kantian version of the noema as a rule for organizing further possible experiences. Or, to put it another way, borrowing from Roderick Firth, the appearance of the front of a house presents itself as one member of a family of appearances of other aspects of the house. If it did not so present itself, it would be the appearance of a façade, not of a house from the front. Thus the noema which enables us to perceive an object as a house must already imply the ordered appearance of the other perspectives. For these reasons Husserl holds that the representational content or noema is a "rule," and that the job it performs is to "synthesize" the manifold of experiences (moments of time, aspects of objects, etc.) into a unified experience of a unified object. Husserl's important step beyond Kant, whom he considered vague and speculative, is his attempt to spell out in detail the structural features of the constitutive rules not only for the form, but also for the content, of experience. To study the possibility of objective reference one must analyze the noema essentially correlated with each intentional state, isolate the component "predicate-senses," and determine their hierarchical relations of dependence and other structural features. This long-term effort, which always attracted Husserl but which in the end reduced him almost to despair, makes Husserl the ambivalent father of cognitive science.

Whether in fact Husserl held what Fodor calls the computational theory of mind—that is, whether according to Husserl, unlike Frege, the predicate-senses do their job of representing objects under aspects, and of unifying diverse experiences of the same objects, strictly on the basis of their shapes (i.e. as a syntactic system independent of any interpretation)—cannot be so easily determined. There is, however, considerable evidence, as we shall see, that Husserl thought of the noemata as complex *formal* structures, since even without the digital computer to supply a model for his intuitions, he thought of a noema as a "*strict* rule (*feste regel*) for possible syntheses."[16] And, to turn the issue around, there is no evidence which suggests that he ever thought of the rules he was concerned with as *semantic*. They have no *ceteris paribus* conditions, nor is there any question of interpretation involved in their application. They function, rather, as we shall see in detail, as layer upon layer of operations, ultimately based on primitive operations which organize sensory data into the elements over which the higher order rules operate.

Once Husserl moved from the view of intentional content as a logical property of intentional states to the view of the content as a noema or rule governing the operations which make intentionality possible, he opened up a whole new field for phenomenological investigation. Since *"any object whatever ... points to a struc-* *ture ... that is governed by a rule,"*[17] one has to investigate the rules governing all mental activity directed at objects. Naturally, all these mental operations must form a complex structured system. As Husserl notes: "transcendental subjectivity is not a chaos of intentional processes."[18] Rather, it requires "a *universal constitutive* *synthesis* in which all syntheses function together in a definitely ordered manner ... "[19] Thus "an enormous task is foreshadowed, which is that of transcendental phenomenology as a whole: the task of *carrying out all phenomenological investigations* within the unity of a systematic and all-embracing order by following, as our mobile clue, a system to be found out level by level ... "[20]

Husserl threw himself into this project and spent a great deal of effort trying to spell out the *noematic* structures, especially those involved in the perception of objects. We will have occasion to look at his specific account of the general features of these structures when we turn to his contribution to artificial intelligence. Here, first, it is important to consider certain of Husserl's methodological assumptions, as well as his account of the basic operations presupposed by his theory.

Husserl calls his method a phenomenological explication of the transcendental ego. The constant reference of all mental operations back to their source in the constitutive activities of the transcendental ego might seem to suggest that for him consciousness plays some crucial role in the organization of experience and in the production of intentionality. If this were indeed the case, Husserl's phenomenology would be the extreme opposite of a computational theory of representational contents which treats the rules it postulates as programs that could run on any "device," whether it be a mind or a nonconscious computer. But, in fact, for Husserl, like Kant, the notion of mental activity is so broadened that it does not require consciousness at all. Indeed, Kant and Husserl are precursors of cognitivism precisely because their rules operate like programs totally independently of the awareness of a conscious subject.

There is one essential role for consciousness or subjectivity in Husserl—and in this way he differs from Kant and also from most contemporary cognitive psychologists. It concerns his evidence for his alleged mental operations. Kant claimed that the mind did not have direct access to its synthesizing activity but could know it only by a transcendental deduction. Husserl objected that this made Kant unscientific. According to Husserl, in order to be considered psychologically real, the rules must be available to consciousness. He maintained that the only evidence we have that our minds or transcendental egos are performing mental operations involving rule-like structures of primitive elements is our direct access to the content of our own mental states. As we have already seen, both early Husserl and Searle insist that we must in principle have access to the representational content of our intentional states. For Searle the representational content is internal to the mental state: so, for example, to have a conscious belief is ipso facto to be conscious of its conditions of satisfaction, although for Searle, whether all representations are in fact retrievable is an empirical question. Husserl takes the stronger view that we *must in fact* have direct and indubitable access to our noemata if they are, indeed, the way intentional content is realized. According to him, intentionality has a "structure I can at any time *consult.*"[21] Indeed, "I must consult it, if I intend to understand what is actually the case here: that nothing exists for me otherwise than by virtue of the *actual and potential performance of my own consciousness* . . . [T]his indicates certain performances which cohere synthetically thus and so, which . . . I can explicate and which I can also freely bring about . . . not a multiplicity demanded or postulated from some superior standpoint, but one that, although hidden at first, can be uncovered."[22]

What one uncovers, besides the general structures we will soon discuss, are the primitives which make up the more complex structures. An example of such primitives—though presumably not the only one—is what Husserl calls predicate-senses. It might seem at first that the intentional content of the mental states which are directed to objects under certain aspects is too holistic to be analyzed into predicates. Husserl, indeed, was the first to describe the "pre-predicative" aspects of experiences, such as the woolly-redness of the carpet, which on the face of it do not seem to be combinations of primitive context-free predicates. Although the woolly-red can be matched by a chip on a color chart which can be named by the predicate red and which can in turn be matched to fire engines and cherries, still such a reduction to an isolable predicate would seem to leave out an essential phenomenological characteristic of the original datum, precisely its woolly-redness. How is this to be reconciled with the thesis that the *noema* is built up out of *predicate*-senses?

Husserl does not hesitate to bring his descriptive account into line with his cognitivist assumptions. In fact, it is typical of him to describe phenomena which seem to be counterexamples to his general theory and then, with a total conviction that he has "consulted" the original "hidden" phenomenon, to argue that the recalcitrant phenomena vanish in the light of what is uncovered by analytic reflection. We will have occasion to see in Part V below that Husserl deals with the problem of cultural background practices and bodily skills in this same fashion, and Izchak Miller's paper on Husserl's account of temporality can be read as showing how Husserl tries to fit time into a theory committed to analyzing even temporal passage into a combination of durationless instants. In each case, phenomena which do not on the face of it seem amenable to the sort of analysis Husserl's theory requires are, nonetheless, treated as a rule-governed synthesis of isolable elements.

Here at the lowest level of anaysis, where Husserl needs some sort of primitives to get his hierarchical *noematic* analysis off the ground. He claims that transcendental consciousness relates data "passively" and "unconsciously" according to rules governing similarity, association, etc. Such organization presupposes some already structured but non-intentional material (hyletic data).[23*] Whatever is responsible for this organization: bodily receptors, analogue processes, or algorithms operating on sensory inputs, these processes fall outside the analysis of the content of intentional states and so outside the discipline of transcendental phenomenology. This non-noematic organization—what might now be called "pre-processing"—produces the basic elements of perception represented by the basic components of the noema. McIntyre and Smith in Chapter 5 argue that Husserl held that these noematic components of perception form part of a language of thought; the meanings expressed in language being just those noematic Sinne which underlie acts of thought and perception. Thus, appearances notwithstanding, the basic elements of perceptual noemata are predicate senses—i.e., they are the sort of isolated meanings which could be dealt with in the predicate calculus. Moreover, such elements are supposed to be hidden but efficacious all along in thought and perception. Gurwitsch puts this point succinctly when, after claiming that for Husserl perceived objects appear to us with generic determinations and in a certain typicality, he adds: "[t] hematization [then] consists in unfolding and articulating a . . . *noema* into its constituents. The latter which before thematization were *imbedded* in the initial . . . *noema* and had *implicit efficacy* . . . are now unraveled and displayed."[24]* Husserl's conviction that "preconstituted" *identical* predicates underly the perception of *similarity* anticipates the cognitive psychologist's conviction that the perception of similarity must be explained in terms of a combination of identical features and that, in general, there must be elementary operations whose rule-governed combination account for higher-level intelligent behavior, whether we are initially aware of these structures or not. Such a conviction is essential for the computational account of mental activity.

Whether the basic elements and higher order structures can be discovered by directly consulting one's own experience—i.e., by asking oneself what we have in mind in each case—is not crucial for cognitive psychology. It is, however, necessary for Husserl's brand of foundationalism. But, as we shall now see, Husserl himself suggests that in doing phenomenological *psychology* we could as well consult a test subject as consult ourselves, and it seems equally possible that we could just as well hypothesize the elements and structures or deduce them from overt behaviour. What is essential to phenomenological *psychology* is that there be an autonomous realm whose rule-like operation can be understood without reference to the activity of the brain, without asking whether anything is actually causally affecting our sense organs, without deciding whether the natural world is or is not the way science tells us it is, without asking whether any of our intentional states are actually satisfied, and, most generally, without taking a stand on whether anything at all exists for our mental states to be satisfied by. The job of the phenomenological psychologist is to examine the activity that makes reference *possible* while remaining uncommitted as to whether, in any given case, or even in general, reference is in fact achieved. This abstention, which Husserl calls the *phenomenological epoche* or the bracketing of existence, has, he insists, important methodological implications for psychology.

III. Husserl's Methodological Solipsism

In *Crisis* Husserl introduces a restricted form of phenomeno-logical reduction or *epoche* as the methodological basis for a new pure psychology:

> In pure psychology, that is, in the true sense, descriptive psychology, the epoche is the means for making experienceable and thematizable, in their own essential purity, the conscious subjects which in natural worldlife are experienced and experience themselves as standing in intentional-real rela-tions to objects that are also real in the mundane sense. Thus, for the abso-lutely disinterested psychological observer, the subjects become "phenom-ena" in a peculiarly new sense—and this reorientation is called, here, the phenomenological-psychological reduction. [25]

In Hilary Putnam's terminology, taken over by Fodor, this bracketing of the concerns of naturalism, along with the implicit denial of the relevance of the causal component of reference, makes Husserl a methodological solipsist. Indeed, Fodor's argu-ments for methodological solipsism as a research strategy in psychology are strikingly similar to Husserl's arguments for his phenomenological reduction as the basis of a "pure intentional psy-chology"—the scientific psychology Husserl struggled unsuccess-fully to substitute for the naturalistic psychology of his day. Since history seems to be repeating itself, we can, by comparing Husserl and Fodor, gain a deeper appreciation of each as well as some foresight concerning the problems in store for Fodor's "Thorough-ly modern mentalist."

From Husserl's point of view, Fodor is rediscovering a very im-portant discipline: the phenomenological theory of cognition, which Hume and Kant saw dimly and which Husserl brought into its own.

> Psychological theory of cognition has a legitimate sense—when understood simply as a name for work done on the manifold problems that cognizing, as a function in human psychic life, sets for psychology as the science of this psychic life. . . . The restriction of psychological judging to intentional mental processess . . . yields a *psychologico-phenomenological* judging. It may even be said that the result is a self-contained *psychological phenom-enology.* . . . [26]

This new "cognitive psychology" (*Erkenntnispsychologie*) is pre-cariously situated between naturalism and transcendental phe-nomenology in that it takes the psyche to be situated in the world and in causal interaction with the environment, but it makes no use of this assumption in its purely descriptive investigations.

> [I]n this psychologico-phenomenological judging, a *psychological* appercep-
> tion is performed, though what is intentionally coposited by this appercep-
> tion, namely *the relation to the organism* and thus to something worldly,
> *does not enter expressly into the conceptual content* of the judging.[27]

Fodor holds that the cognitive psychologist must make precisely this "epochē," and he contends that the cognitive psychologist must be content with a solipsistic psychology, since he will never have the final story on the physical world and thus on what is causally affecting the psyche, and since even if he could have a final physical theory, there might well be no theory of the complicated social and psychological interactions which determine reference. Husserl, however, is unwilling to stop at this point. He insists that a thoroughgoing cognitive psychology must finally develop into a transcendental phenomenology. That is, even if the psychologist cannot have, and does not need, a finished naturalistic psychology, he does need and must have an account of all cognitive operations, including those involved in imputing causal interaction.

> Certainly I am in psychophysical causal connexion with the outside world
> —that is to say: I, this human being, a man among men and brutes, among
> other realities too all going together to make up the world. But the world
> with all its realities, including my human real being, is a universe of consti-
> tuted transcendencies—constituted in mental processes and abilities of my
> ego;.. accordingly, this constituted world is preceded by my ego, as the
> ultimately constitutive subjectivity.[28]

In this demand that an intentional psychology account even for our experience of natural causality and the natural world, Husserl's common-sense realism and his transcendental idealism come clearly into focus and fit together coherently:

> [A] radical, psychological unfolding of my apperceptive life and of the par-
> ticular world appearing in it, in respect to the *how* of the particular ap-
> pearances . . . in the transition to the transcendental attitude, would im-
> mediately have to take on transcendental significance as soon as I now, at
> the higher level, constantly take into account the meaning-conferring ac-
> complishment . . . through which the world-representation has the sense of
> something really existing—the life in which everyone has his world-
> representations, finds himself as existing, representing, acting according to
> purposes in the world.[29]

But once the transcendental phenomenologist allows that he must account for *all* experience, even everyday realism, he runs into the problems raised by Smith and McIntyre in Chapters 11 and 12 respectively, namely how to integrate into *noematic* analysis the contextual character of indexical and other kinds of singular reference. Whether Husserl, as extended by Smith, can solve this problem depends upon whether the total context can be taken up into the noema. We will return to this question at the end of this introduction. For the moment we need only note that for Searle a "presentational" intentional state like perception can have as part of its content the specification of a particular object as the cause of that particular intentional state.[30] But this simple realism is not taken advantage of by either Fodor or Husserl. For, as we have seen, Fodor wants to rule out all concern with causality and reference from his methodological solipsism, and Husserl wants to take up the whole causal story into what he sometimes calls "my concrete being as a monad."[31]

Husserl's commitment to building the whole story of how human beings relate to one another and to objects into his transcendental phenomenology makes his final project more ambitious than Searle's and more comprehensive than cognitive psychology as Husserl and Fodor define it. Indeed, in his attempt even to integrate all pragmatic and contextual considerations into his account, rather than attempting to bracket them out, Husserl's view resembles the ambitious project of artificial intelligence.

IV. Husserl's Anticipation of Artificial Intelligence

Husserl's transcendental phenomenology is related to work in artificial intelligence in two ways. First, as we have just seen, Husserl is committed to much more than working out the role of mental structure in what Fodor calls the job of type-individuating intentional states. He is committed to capturing the intentional structure and mental operations involved in *all* forms of intelligent behavior, even pragmatic, contextual interactions with objects and people in the physical and social world.

Second, Husserl's actual account of the complex formal structures involved in the "constitution" of the objective world has anticipated and perhaps even directly contributed to the most promising proposals in current AI research. In 1972, drawing on Husserl's phenomenological analysis, I pointed out in my book *What Computers Can't Do* that it was a major weakness of AI that no programs made use of expectations. I noted that instead of modeling intelligence as a passive receiving of context-free facts, Husserl thought of intelligence as a context-determined goal-directed activity—as a search for anticipated facts.[32] For him the mental representation of any type of object had to provide a context or "horizon" of expectation or "predelineations" for structuring the incoming data: a "rule governing *possible* other consciousness of [the object] as identical—possible, as exemplifying essentially predelineated types."[33]

As Husserl spells it out:

> [T]here is no experience, in the simple and primary sense of an experience of things, which, grasping a thing for the first time and bringing cognition to bear on it, does not already "know" more about the thing, than is in this cognition alone . . . This preknowledge is indeterminate as to content, or not completely determined, but it is never completely empty; and were it not already manifest, the experience would not at all be experience of this one, this particular thing . . . [T]his horizon in its indeterminateness is copresent from the beginning as a spectrum (*Spielraum*) of possibilities, as the prescription of the path to a more precise determination, in which only experience itself decides in favor of the determinate possibility it realizes as opposed to others.[34]

Husserl illustrates as follows:

> The predelineation itself, to be sure, is at all times imperfect; yet, with its *indeterminateness*, it has a *determinate structure*. For example: [This] die leaves open a great variety of things pertaining to the unseen faces; yet it is already "construed" in advance as a die, in particular as colored, rough, and the like, though each of these determinations always leaves further particulars open. This leaving open, prior to further determinings (which perhaps never take place), is a moment included in the given consciousness itself . . . [35]

The predelineations are, of course, not magical precognitions but are based on past experience which has led to the formation of representations of prototypical objects.

> The factual world of experience is experienced as a *typified world*. Things are experienced as trees, bushes, animals, snakes, birds; specifically, as pine, linden, lilac, dog, viper, swallow, sparrow, and so on. The table is characterized as being familiar and yet new. What is given in experience as a new individual is first known in terms of what has been genuinely perceived; it calls to mind the like (the similar). But what is apprehended *according to type* also has a horizon of possible experience with corresponding prescriptions of familiarity and has, therefore, *types* of attributes not

yet experienced but expected. When we see a dog, we immediately anticipate its additional modes of behavior: its typical way of eating, playing,
running, jumping, and so on. We do not actually see its teeth; but we know
in advance how its teeth will look—not in their individual determination
but *according to type,* inasmuch as we have already had previous and frequent experience of "similar" animals, of "dogs," that they have such
things as "teeth" and of this typical kind. [36]

The *noema,* then, contains a rule describing all the features
which can be expected with certainty in exploring a certain
type of object—features which remain "inviolably the same: as
long as the objectivity remains intended as *this* one and of this
kind." [37] The rule also prescribes "predelineations" of properties that are possible but not necessary features of this type of object: "Instead of a completely determined sense, there is always,
therefore, a *frame of empty sense* (leerer Sinnesrahmen) . . ." [38]

In 1973 Marvin Minsky proposed a new data structure remarkably similar to Husserl's for representing everyday knowledge:

A *frame* is a data-structure for representing a stereotyped situation, like
being in a certain kind of living room, or going to a child's birthday
party . . .
    We can think of a frame as a network of nodes and relations. The top
levels of a frame are fixed, and represent things that are always true about
the supposed situation. The lower levels have many *terminals*—slots that
must be filled by specific instances or data. Each terminal can specify conditions its assignments must meet . . .
    Much of the phenomenological power of the theory hinges on the inclu-
sion of expectations and other kinds of presumptions. *A frame's terminals
are normally already filled with "default" assignments.* [39]

In Minsky's model of a frame, the "top level" is a developed version of what in Husserl's terminology "remain inviolably the same"
in the representation, and Husserl's predelineations have become
"default assignments"—additional features that can normally be
expected. The result was a step forward in AI techniques from a
passive model of information-processing to one which tries to take
account of the interactions between a knower and his world. The
task of AI thus converges with the task of transcendental phenomenology. Both must try to explicate the prototypes in various
domains which determine the possible default assignments.

V. Husserl's (and AI's) Problems

Husserl thought of his method of investigating transcendental-
phenomenological constitution—i.e., "explicating" the noema for

all types of objects, as the beginning of progress toward a new "rigorous science," and Patrick Winston hailed Minsky's frame paper as the "ancestor of a wave of progress in AI."[40] But Husserl's project ran into serious trouble, and there are signs that Minsky's has too.

During twenty-five years of trying to spell out the components of the noema of everyday objects, Husserl found that he had to include more and more of a subject's common-sense understanding of the everyday world:

> To be sure, even the tasks that present themselves when we take single types of objects as restricted clues prove to be extremely complicated and always lead to extensive disciplines when we penetrate more deeply. That is the case, for example, with a transcendental theory of the constitution of a spatial object (to say nothing of a Nature) as such, of psycho-physical being and humanity as such, culture as such.[41]

He spoke of the noema's "huge concreteness"[42] and of its "tremendous complication,"[43] and he sadly concluded at the age of seventy-five that he was a perpetual beginner and that phenomenology was an "infinte task."[44]

There are hints in the frame paper that Minsky has embarked on the same "infinite task" that eventually overwhelmed Husserl:

> Just constructing a knowledge base is a major intellectual research problem . . . We still know far too little about the contents and structure of common-sense knowledge. A "minimal" common-sense system must "know" something about cause-effect, time, purpose, locality, process, and types of knowledge . . . We need a serious epistemological research effort in this area.[45]

Minsky's naivetë and faith are astonishing. Transcendental phenomenology *is* just such a research effort. Indeed, philosophers from Plato to Husserl, who uncovered all these problems and more, have carried on serious epistemological research in this area for two thousand years without notable success. Moreover, the list Minsky includes in this passage deals only with natural objects, and their positions and interactions. As Husserl saw, intelligent behavior also presupposes a background of cultural practices and institutions. Observations in the frame paper such as: "Trading normally occurs in a social context of law, trust, and convention. Unless we also represent these other facts, most trade transactions will be almost meaningless"[46] show that Minsky has understood this too.

It was Heidegger who forced Husserl to face precisely these problems. He pointed out that there are other ways of "encountering" objects than relating to them as objects of perception or predication. When we use a piece of equipment like a hammer, Heidegger claims, we actualize a bodily skill (which cannot be represented in the mind) in the context of a socially organized nexus of equipment, purposes, and human roles (which cannot be represented as a set of facts). This context and our everyday ways of skillful coping in it are not something we *know* but, as part of our socialization, form the way that we *are*. As Heidegger put it later, using the term "clearing" for what a Wittgensteinian would call the background of practices: "the clearing in which present beings as such . . . can be discerned by man . . . is not an object of mental representation, but is the dominance of usage (*Brauch*)."[47] Heidegger draws the consequences in his lectures of 1927 aimed largely at Husserl's students:

> The appeal to the intentionality of comportment toward things does not make comprehensible the phenomenon occupying us . . . The sole characterization of intentionality hitherto customary in phenomenology proves to be inadequate. . . . This leads first of all to the . . . task . . . of *interpreting more radically the phenomenon of intentionality* . . . With this task of bringing to view a basic determinant of human existence we run up against a central problem which has remained unknown to all previous philosophy.[48]

In *Being and Time* Heidegger attempts to show that Husserlian intentionality is not self-sufficient. He claims to give a "concrete demonstration" that the interconnected totality of equipment and social practices which he calls significance (*Bedeutsamkeit*) is a condition of the possibility of abstract meanings, such as Husserl's noemata, which Heidegger, following Husserl, calls significations (*Bedeutungen*). Heidegger concludes: "in significance itself, with which human beings are always familiar, there lies the ontological condition which makes it possible for beings . . . to disclose such things as 'significations' . . ."[49]

A similar account of the importance of the practical background and a similar criticism of any theory of intentionality that tries to analyze all meaning solely in terms of the structures of the content of intentional states has been sketched by John Searle. Searle has been led by the logic of his own position to see the importance of the nonrepresentable background and thus to face the problem Heidegger posed for Husserl. In his paper "Literal Meaning" Searle takes the philosopher's favorite assertion, "The cat is on the mat," and proceeds to show, in a series of amusing examples, how in some cases this assertion may not determine truth conditions at all, as in the case of a cat floating in contact with a mat in outer space, and how it may, nonetheless, be given truth conditions even under these strange circumstances—when, for example, after observing that cat-mat pairs come in two orientations with respect to the rocket ship window, an astronaut reports, concerning the current case, that this time the cat is on the mat. Searle uses such examples to argue (against the traditional philosophical account of sentence meaning) that, first, the truth conditions of an assertion are always relative to a background, and, second, that this background does not form part of the semantic content of the sentence:

> There is no constant set of assumptions that determine the applicability of the notion of literal meaning, rather the sentence may determine different truth conditions relative to different assumptions in ways that have nothing to do with ambiguity, indexical dependence on context, presupposition failure, vagueness or change of meaning as these notions are traditionally conceived. Furthermore, our examples suggest that the assumptions are not specifiable as part of the semantic content of the sentence, or as presuppositions of the applicability of that semantic content, for at least two reasons. First, they are not fixed and definite in number and content; we would never know when to stop in our specifications. And second, each specification of an assumption tends to bring in other assumptions, those that determine the applicability of the sentence used in the specification. [50]

Searle then generalizes this problem to all speech acts and finally to all intentional states, arguing that in general the representational contents of intentional states only determine conditions of satisfaction relative to a background of practices. He then asks the crucial question for AI:

> But even assuming we could not do a sentence by sentence specification of the assumptions behind the understanding and application of each sentence, could we do a completely general specification of all the assumptions, all the things we take for granted, in our understanding of language? Could we make our whole mode of sensibility fully explicit? [51]

His answer is agnostic—less optimistic than Husserl's and Minsky's, but not as conclusively discouraging as Heidegger's.

> It seems to me that the arguments in this article don't determine the answer to that question one way or the other. The fact that for each of a large range of sentences the assumptions are variable and indefinite and that the specification of one will tend to bring in others does not by itself show that we could not specify an entire set which would be independent

of the semantic analysis of individual sentences but which taken together would enable us to apply the literal meaning of the sentences. The practical difficulties in any such specification would of course be prodigious, but is there any theoretical obstacle to the task? In order to show that there was we would have to show that the conditions under which sentences can represent were not themselves fully representable by sentences. Perhaps that claim is true, but it has not been the aim of my discussion to show that it is true. [52]

Searle thus takes the issue precisely up to the splitting of the ways between Husserl and AI on the one hand, and Heidegger and those who deny the possibility of cognitive science on the other. The crucial question becomes: Can the taken-for-granted everyday common-sense background presupposed in assigning satisfaction conditions to every intentional state be treated as a belief system which can be analyzed in terms of the intentional content of each of its constituent beliefs? Or is the background rather a combination of skills, practices, discriminations, etc., which are not intentional states, and so, a fortiori, do not have the sort of intentional content which could be explicated in terms of formal rules?

Husserl's response to Heidegger's objection—like the AI community's response to Searle—has been the "imperturbable" conviction that the everyday background or pre-given life-world is, of course, a belief system—what else could it be?—and all that is needed to spell it out is more research grants and more work. Husserl thus accepts Heidegger's argument that each noema functions only against the practical horizon of the life-world, and then claims that these background practices themselves are really a set of "sedimented" background *assumptions,* each of which has its own noematic content, which need only be "reactivated" by the phenomenologist. Husserl thus in effect treats the background as a system of frames.

Husserl presented this answer to Heidegger's critique in his posthumously published *Crisis of the European Sciences.* After developing at length Heidegger's idea that all cognition depends on a world in which we are involved and which can never be made explicit as an object, Husserl then introduces the transcendental *epochē* as a total change from this involved "natural attitude."

Now how can the pregivenness of the life-world become a universal subject of investigation in its own right? Clearly, only through a *total change* of the natural attitude, such that we no longer live, as heretofore, as human beings within natural existence . . . The life which effects world-validity in natural world-life does not permit of being studied from within the attitude of natural world-life. What is required then, is a *total* transformation of attitude, a *completely unique, universal epochē.*[53]

The idea is that whatever we experience must be taken by us as something—i.e., it must fit into a noema or frame. How else could it have coherence and intelligibility? So we must rediscover what counts as world for us, and how it came to have that "validity" (*Geltung*). Or, as Husserl says elsewhere, we must discover the "intentional history" of what we now simply take for granted. The suggestion is that as we came to understand the world, we once had to make sense of it in terms of specific hypotheses—and that this early intentional content, although unconscious and habitual, still plays a functional role. Husserl explains:

> In order to gain a conception of how this total transformation of attitude is to be carried out, let us consider again the style of natural, normal life. There we move in a current of ever new experiences, judgments, valuations, decisions. In each of these acts the ego is directed toward *objects* in its surrounding world, dealing with them in one way or another. It is of them that we are conscious in these acts themselves, sometimes simply as actual, sometimes in modalities of actuality (for example, as possible, as doubtful, etc.). None of these acts, and none of the validities involved in them is isolated: in their intentions they necessarily imply an infinite horizon of inactive validities which function with them in flowing mobility. The manifold acquisitions of earlier active life are not dead sediments; even the background . . . of which we are always concurrently conscious but which is momentarily irrelevant and remains completely unnoticed, still functions according to its implicit validities.[54]

Since the thesis still holds that we always have access to the content of our intentional states, it follows for Husserl that we must also have access to this dormant intentionality.

> [T]he particular object of our active consciousness, and correlatively the active, conscious having of it, being directed toward it, and dealing with it —all this is forever surrounded by an atmosphere of mute, concealed, but cofunctioning validities, a *vital horizon* into which the active ego can also direct itself voluntarily, reactivating old acquisitions . . . Because of this constantly flowing *horizonal character,* then, every straight-forwardly performed validity in natural world-life always presupposes validities extending back, immediately or mediately, into a necessary subsoil of obscure but occasionally available reactivatable validities. . . .[55]

Thus we can understand intentionality as "a complex of performances, which are included as *sedimented history* in the currently constituted intentional unity . . .—a history *that one can always uncover by following a strict method.*"[56]

The argument has a certain plausibility. Much of what we do seems to involve sedimented beliefs. As I dash out of the door of my office, for example, I do not consciously entertain the belief that the floor continues on the other side, but if you stop me and ask me whether, when I charged confidently through the door, I believed the floor continued on the other side, I would have to respond that, indeed, I did. Likewise, even for a skill like swimming which seems, once acquired, to run off as an autonomous pattern of muscular contractions, if I am stopped in mid stroke and asked what I am doing, I would have to give the reply that I am, for example, moving my arm into position to enter the water—so even habitual actions seem, on inspection, to have their intentional content.

The question that must be asked, however, is whether this is not again—as in the case of the discovery of primitive predicates underlying prepredicative perception—a case of retroactive illusion? It might be that in walking out the door of my office I am simply engaging in a bit of motor activity, which may (or may not) once have been accompanied by the idea "there is more floor out there," but which takes place now without such a belief playing any functional role. Likewise, when a skilled performer is asked how he does what he does, he often tells you the only thing he knows, viz., the sequence of operations he once followed in acquiring the skill, but that does not mean he now follows those steps or any others, and the flexibility and success of the skill suggests that rules no longer play a functional role.[57*]

This general issue takes us back to the second of the important differences between early Husserl and Searle, on the one hand, and later Husserl and the cognitivists, on the other. All agree that intentional states have as their content a representation of their conditions of satisfaction. For Searle, however, this simply means that when my desires are satisfied, or my orders obeyed, etc., I will be able to recognize that my intentional state has been appropriately satisfied. As Searle's "Literal Meaning" article shows in detail, it does not mean and cannot mean that I already know in advance what would count and what could fail to count as satisfaction. To take one of Searle's examples: If I command you to close the door and you tear it from the wall, bring it to the middle of the room, and then swing it so the latch clicks into place, have you obeyed my command? There is no obvious answer until the pragmatic context is more fully filled in, and I can only ask myself in each particular case, has my order been obeyed?

Husserl, on the other hand, along with the introduction of his Kantian theory of the content of intentional states—namely that the content is a strict rule—also commits himself to the view that what will count as satisfying my intentional state is either definite and so can be spelled out in advance by consulting my own mental content, or is still open, but in such a rule-like way that even this indefiniteness can, in principle, be filled in by an infinite set of default assignments.

> In the clarification of this typical generality in the form of determinate "possibilities" . . . the realm (*Spielraum*) for these possibilities is given as the explicit "extension" of the indeterminate generality of anticipation. [58]

Thus for Husserl there is either no answer to the question whether my command was obeyed when the door was moved into the frame in the middle of the room, or there is an answer and my recognizing this act as obeying or disobeying my command shows that that answer was dictated by a component of a rule in my noema which I could have consulted all along. It is this conviction that all non-arbitrary—i.e., intelligible—behavior must be specified *in advance* in the noema (not the stronger condition that I can always uncover this specification) which underlies the conviction that no matter how intractable the phenomenon may appear, it must always be amenable to cognitivist analysis.

The critic of cognitivism who questions this conviction is always confronted with the question: what else could account for the unity, order, and intelligibility of our behavior but the appropriate mental operations? Moreover, if these operations are to do the job without a regress of *ceteris paribus* conditions, they must be computations. This answer seems more and more self-evident as the cognitivist position descends from Hume to Kant, to Husserl, to Fodor. A different response, however, which is philosophically safer, if less challenging, is to stick to the pure phenomena as do early Husserl and Searle, simply describing language and intentional states and the logical conditions required by intentionality, while taking no stand on what makes intentionality possible. A further, more dramatic countermove is to change the subject altogether and ask about the intelligibility, unity, and order of *public behavior* rather than *private experiences;* answering this question in terms of shared practices, goals, roles, etc. This is the response of Heidegger, Dewey, and Wittgenstein. Heidegger calls it *existential* as opposed to *transcendental* phenomenology.

Of course, some processes must provide the causal basis for the organization of experience, but all we know about those processes is that they must be in the brain. Whether in addition to the public phenomenon and brain processes there is a *mental* (formal) level of description in which as-yet-undiscovered complex rules organize as-yet-undiscovered mental primitives, remains to be seen. One thing is clear: despite Heidegger's warnings, Husserl struggled with these issues to the end. His insights and his problems are now the legacy of cognitive science.

I

Historical Background

1

Brentano and Husserl on Intentional Objects and Perception

Dagfinn Føllesdal

In order to shed some light upon the relationship between Brentano and Husserl, I shall discuss briefly their views on intentional objects and on perception. I have chosen to focus my comments on these two themes partly because the themes were central to their relationship and partly because they are also interconnected in a certain way that we shall look at. I will begin by saying a little about Brentano's view on intentionality and some of the problems associated with it. I will then explain how Husserl tried to solve these problems. Afterwards I will go on to discuss some features of Brentano's view of perception, and I will finally show how Husserl here too starts out from Brentano, but modifies Brentano's ideas in such a way as to create a quite different theory.

Let us first consider intentionality. Brentano, as you know, held that intentionality is characterized by a certain kind of directedness. We encounter problems when we try to characterize it, and you will remember that in his early writings Brentano simply said that the directedness is characterized by there being some object which is always there, which the act is directed toward. Brentano's phrase is that the object "intentionally inexists" in our act. This immediately gave rise to various misunderstandings. The problems came up because if one tries to clarify this notion—and his students certainly did not find it quite clear—one seems immediately to be faced with a dilemma: on the one hand one might try to emphasize the fact that there is always some object there, and then the problem is that if this is going to be the case, that object has to be a rather watered down kind of object. It is something that in a certain way exists only in our consciousness. This also was suggested by the phrase "intentional inexistence," and this led to various interpretations of Brentano that he himself later found necessary to guard himself against. There are several letters from Brentano to various of his students in which he complains bitterly that people have taken him to hold that the intentional object is some kind of object in our mind. Brentano wants to make clear that this is an untenable position, and he has various arguments to show that it is untenable. One argument consists in pointing out various differences between the real physical object and the object of thought. These are two different things, and in fact Brentano is not the first one who has emphasized their difference. We find the same observation made, for example, by Frege, and before him by Bolzano. One might, for example, hold that when a person is thinking about Pegasus, then really what he is thinking about is just his idea of Pegasus. Frege rejected this, saying that if that were the case then clearly with the same ground we could say that when somebody is thinking about the moon, what he is really thinking about is just his idea of the moon. And clearly an idea of the moon is quite a different thing from the moon itself.[1] Brentano makes pretty much the same point arguing against the view that the intentional object is something in our mind. Another of his remarks is that "it is paradoxical in the highest degree to say that what a man promises to marry is an *ens rationis* and that he keeps his word by marrying a real person."[2] There has to be some connection between the object to whom you give the promise, and the person whom you later marry. These are examples of the kind of difficulties that Brentano finds in that view. For that reason he rejects the attempt to save the theory of intentionality by saying that the object should be part of our own conciousness.

Brentano then goes on to insist that the object is a real full-fledged physical object. But of course that gives rise to other difficulties.

Brentano was aware of them, and so were his students. One very simple and straightforward way out is to do what Meinong did, viz. to hold that the object is a real full-fledged physical object, but that in cases where there is no such thing, the object has the

property of nonexistence. The difficulties involved in treating existence as a predicate and in holding that some objects do not exist
are well known, and one might wonder whether Brentano ever
held such a view. Clearly there are passages in Brentano where he
says in so many words that in some cases the object of our act
does not exist. One might claim that he never intended this very
seriously, but he clearly says it. Another problem is that he also
uses pronouns all the time to talk about it and he also even uses
demonstratives, saying that *this* object does exist. So, he says
things like this. On the other hand it is quite clear that he is not
very happy with it, because he also says: "I admit that I am unable
to make any sense at all out of this distinction between being and
existence."[3] There are people, he says, who make it, and it is
clear that Meinong is one of the people he has in mind, and
Meinong's students. Not being able to make any sense of such a
distinction, Brentano returns again and again to the problem of
the status of the intentional object. He tries repeatedly to clarify
what is meant, and it is quite clear what side he is on: he insists
that the object of the act is a full-fledged physical object, not
something in our mind.

One proposal hinted at in some of the texts is for a translation
theory. Brentano suggests that when we say that a mental reference refers to an object, we speak improperly. We speak that way
just for convenience, and what we say should be regarded only as
convenient shorthand for something else, more clumsy and incon-
venient, which does not involve reference to anything nonexisting.

In Brentano's own words: "for every sentence which seems to
have one of the things mentioned as its subject or predicate, (one)
can form an equivalent in which subject and predicate are re-
established as real entities."[4] Brentano gives credit to Leibniz for
this idea of what Brentano calls "a translation," an idea which
"removes a host of subtle and abstruse debates which have per-
plexed metaphysics and logic."[5] These fictions should not be
avoided, he thinks. Thus, for example, they may facilitate logic,
by simplifying expression and even thought itself. Likewise,
mathematicians use with advantage the fictions of numbers less
than zero, and many others.

One weakness of Brentano's proposal is that, unlike Russell
when he presented his theory of definite descriptions, Brentano
does not give any directions or outlines of how this translation is
to be performed. Another even more serious difficulty is that it
might seem to jeopardize his whole idea of intentionality as

directedness. What happens to the mental phenomena and their directedness when our talk about them has been thus translated into talk where no intentionally inexisting object is referred to? When we perform such a translation, do we find that our thinking that the mental phenomenon contained an object intentionally in it was fallacious?

And what about the cases in which the object referred to does exist—as, for example, when somebody thinks of the moon? Why should we not also in that case perform the translation and end up saying that the object of this thought is not the moon after all? Brentano does not answer these questions.

The intentional object hence seems to be a problem for Brentano—one that, in my view, he never solved properly, and I think that this is the main reason why so many of his students deviated from him. They all agreed that the notion of intentionality was very important in philosophy, and also that directedness was a main characteristic of intentionality. But Brentano never quite succeeded in clarifying this notion of directedness to their satisfaction. I suspect that Brentano was not satisfied himself and that this, too, was a reason why he turned to it again and again. The contexts where he returns to it are always complaints that his students misunderstood his view. He then tries to make clear what his own view is, but every time he tries, he ends with something which, in my view at least, is not very clear.

One wonders, is there any way of getting around these problems? One way that has been suggested is to say that the directedness in question is not a genuine relation, but a kind of one-place predicate, a property of people. This serves well as far as it goes, but the problem with this approach is that it eliminates a lot that we would like to keep. Another way of handling the problems has been proposed by Richard Arnaud in "Brentanist Relations" in the *Festschrift* for Chisholm.[6] Arnaud suggests that statements concerning intentional objects should be construed as statements that are indicative of propositional attitudes. When one says that somebody is afraid of something, this should be paraphrased into something to the effect that he is afraid that so and so. Thereby one avoids direct-object constructions in such contexts.

However, this does not seem to me a satisfactory approach. There are several reasons why neither the predicate solution nor the solution by propositional attitudes is satisfactory. One has to do with learnability. That is one of the arguments that Arnaud in his article uses against the predicate view. However, as long as we do not have a theory of propositional attitudes that explains how the truth values of propositional attitude statements depend upon the constituent parts of these statements, there are related problems about the logical relationships between sentences of this form. These relationships tend to disappear if you treat the whole thing as one monadic predicate, and they are not properly taken care of if you treat the whole thing as propositional attitudes, since we lack a theory of propositional attitudes which interconnects them in the proper way.

There is another problem that I consider far more important—there are certainly cases in which we would like to quantify into contexts of this kind. We may want to say, for example, that there is something which we believe to be so and so, or of which we are afraid. These constructions cannot be handled at all if they are treated as composite monadic predicates or as expressions of propositional attitudes. And it seems to me that we need quantificational phrases of that kind. I do not think all our use of such phrases is due to confusion. We therefore need some way of handling them—that is, we need a way of quantifying into such phrases. We do not get that if we treat them as composite monadic predicates, because there is no place appropriate for quantification there. There seems to be no idea in Brentano that solves this problem for us.

It seems to me that Husserl's way of handling the problem retains the virtue of our being able to quantify into such contexts and produce all the constructions that we would want. The basic difference between Husserl and Brentano is that while Brentano tried all the time to deal with these problems by appealing only to the two notions of the subject and the object, Husserl uses a third, intermediary notion, what he calls the *noema,* which is introduced to account for the directedness of the mental phenomena. While Brentano had tried to characterize directedness by talking about the object towards which the act is directed, Husserl instead characterizes the directedness by the introduction of this entity, the noema. This notion is closely parallel to Frege's notion of sense. I do not claim that he got it from Frege, because Husserl also studied several other philosophers who had similar notions, like Bolzano; Bolzano's notion of an objective idea (*Vorstellung an sich*) is quite similar to Frege's notion of sense. However, among the philosophers whom Husserl had read before he developed his own treatment of intentionality, Frege was the one who had developed the idea of sense most systematically. Frege was also the only one who had used the notion of sense to analyze contexts involving verbs for mental activities, like "believes" etc.

There are many remarks in Bolzano that also point in the direction that Husserl took. Now, of course Brentano also knew Bolzano. We might wonder why Brentano did not make use of Bolzano's ideas in his treatment of intentionality. However, although Brentano esteemed Bolzano very highly, he tells us that he cannot find any particular point where he learned from him. It seems that Brentano had never studied Bolzano's *Wissenschaftslehre* carefully. He had read little by Bolzano apart from his *Paradoxes of the Infinite.* But Husserl, particularly in the 1890s, seriously sat down and worked through the *Wissenschaftslehre,* in addition to studying Frege, and he tells us that he was very impressed by Bolzano's notion of ideas in themselves. Husserl also says that earlier he had not been interested in the *Wissenschaftslehre,* because he had regarded it as a kind of obscure metaphysics, but upon the second reading in the 1890s he discovered that these four volumes contained extremely important philosophical ideas.

By help of a trichotomy between the acting subject, the noema, and the object, Husserl is able to both retain Brentano's idea of the directedness of mental phenomena and overcome the difficulties where there are no corresponding objects. While Brentano kept insisting that the directedness of the act should be accounted for by means of some object toward which the act is directed, and got into all his problems, Husserl's view is that the directedness of the act should be accounted for not by some object toward which the act is directed, but by a certain structure of our consciousness when we are performing an act. This structure Husserl calls the noema.

Now, what is important is that this object which is introduced to account for the directedness of the consciousness is *not* that towards which our consciousness is directed. That is the little point that makes all the difference between Brentano and Husserl. What our consciousness is directed towards will always be a normal, full-fledged object—that is, a physical object or whatever else we are conscious of. In many cases there is no such thing. However, we still have directedness—that is, our consciousness is always *as if* there were an object. The point of the noema is to explain what this "as if" amounts to. That is to say, studying the noema is to study the different features of consciousness to see how they all fit together, so that they seem to be features of one object.

Artificial Intelligence Corporation
200 Fifth Ave
Waltham, Mass   02254
     617   890   8400

Through this theory Husserl preserves Brentano's (I think very correct) intuition that our acts should be as if directed towards normal full-fledged physical objects. And he is able to preserve this even in cases where there is no such object. So here we have seen one point where Husserl seems to have overcome a problem in Brentano by separating what is in consciousness as a structure of it and what is in the world outside us.

This idea of separating these two things occurs also in Husserl's treatment of perception, as we shall see in a moment. But before we leave the intentional object, I should like to note that by introducing the notion of the noema, Husserl is able to preserve also those features of act-contexts that make it possible to quantify into such contexts. One can work out the logic of this in a proper way without getting into the difficulties that are normally encountered in such intentional contexts. It seems to me that the best way of doing it is by using not the usual modal logics that have been proposed for perception, but the ideas of Alonzo Church, who has worked out systematically Frege's view on sense and reference. Hence it seems to me, if one wants to work out a Husserlian theory of acts, and of perception in particular, the best logical starting point would be Church's logic of sense and denotation. [7] By treating perception and intentionality in that way, one can salvage quantification into such contexts, and one salvages all the logical interrelations one would want between the different features of the object of our act.

But now to perception. Here also Husserl, especially in his *Ideas*, takes Brentano as a starting point, and then shows why one should modify him. Husserl first discusses the distinction that Brentano makes between mental and physical phenomena.

We have so far talked mainly about the mental phenomena, and we have seen that Husserl retains Brentano's basic idea of the directedness of mental phenomena, but that he modifies it by using a distinction relating to Frege's and Bolzano's distinction between sense and reference. Husserl has no further complaint about the category of mental phenomena. However, he thinks that Brentano went wrong when he discussed physical phenomena. Husserl claims that, in discussing physical phenomena, Brentano has lumped together two things that should be carefully separated. The two things that should be separated are, according to Husserl, what he calls the objective and the material phases of our experience. We shall take a look at this with the help of the following diagram, which I shall explain and comment on as we go.

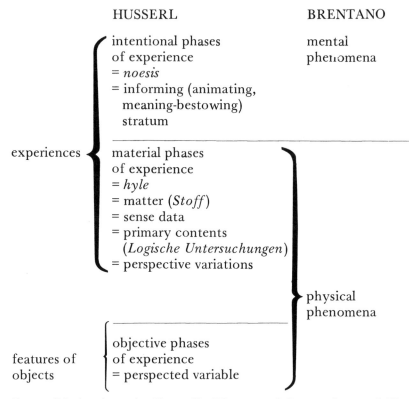

Some Distinctions in Husserl's Theory of Perception and How
They Compare with Brentano's Distinction between Mental and
Physical Phenomena

What are the material and the objective phases of experience
that should be separated according to Husserl? Husserl discusses
various of Brentano's examples of physical phenomena. Brentano
cites as examples colors and sounds. He also unfortunately includes
in one place landscape, but that is clearly a slip, and many of Brentano's followers complained that Husserl focused too much on
that one example.[8] We will leave it out, because it is a slip and because Husserl's criticism is independent of that unfortunate example. While Brentano held that physical phenomena exist *only*
intentionally (sharing thereby the view of many philosophers that
secondary sense qualities do not exist independently of their being
perceived), Husserl held that they exist in the same way that physical objects do. Husserl maintained that in addition to physical objects and shapes and so on, there are also colors and sounds in the

external world. Like all objects in the external world, these objects can be experienced from different perspectives. An example he gives is the sound of an orchestra playing in a concert hall. That sound is experienced differently depending on where you are sitting in the hall or, if you are late, whether you are standing outside and hear it through closed doors. It is the same sound, but it sounds different. The objective phases of experience for Husserl are therefore shapes, sounds, colors, and so on. In the case of shapes, it is easy to follow him. We all know from epistemology the example of a round table top. The shape is round but appears different, depending on where we are located relative to the top. Now Husserl claims that the same thing holds for sounds and colors and so on.

The example of colors may seem a little strange, but Husserl insists that while an object may be of a certain color, this color may appear differently, depending, e.g., on light conditions, on what kind of glasses we wear, and so on. In spite of these variations there is an objective color (which might of course change from time to time) and there are different ways of experiencing that color. Other phrases that Husserl uses to distinguish the color from our experience of it is the "perspected variable" of the color and the "perspective variations" of our experience.

Now we come to the material phases of our experience. These phases are, Husserl says, experiences that we undergo when our sensory organs are affected. When we see some object, or see the shape of it or the color, we are affected in certain ways, and the experiences that we undergo are what he calls material phases of our experience. Another word he uses for this is *hyle*. He simply takes over the Aristotelian word for matter and says that the hyle are not objects that we perceive, or features of such objects—for example, colors. The hyle are experiences that we undergo when we see these objects, their colors, their shapes, etc. So again he has a distinction between what is the object of our act, and what goes on in us. The material phases are things that go on in us, they have temporal coordinates—they start at a certain time and end at a certain time. But these temporal coordinates need not coincide with the temporal coordinates of the objective phase of which they are experiences. The color may remain there long after we have stopped observing it, so that the temporal features of the color are different from those of the hyle we have. I will not go into this, but in Husserl's lectures on internal time-consciousness, he has additional criticisms of Brentano, because he finds the distinction between mental and physical phenomena in Brentano not adequate to account for the fact that we can experience something that lasts through a long period of time, so that the object that we experience has this long duration, although our experience of it has only a short duration. Now, one unfortunate thing in Husserl is that he uses the phrase "sense data" (in German *Empfindungsdaten*) for the hyle. This, I think, has caused a good deal of misinterpretation. Sense data, in most theories, are things that we see or hear, but for Husserl they are not, they are merely experiences, and we do not see them. This is, of course, a very odd use of sense data, but I think it is a much better notion to use in epistemology than the traditional notion of sense data. That Husserl used "sense datum" for what he had in mind indicates that he was very poor at reading other philosophers and adapting his own terminology and exposition to the current terminology of his time. The price he had to pay was that he was very often misunderstood.

So, what happens when we experience and perceive, according to Husserl, is that there is some object that impinges causally upon our sensory organs. We then have some hyle. These hyle are animated by what Husserl calls a meaning-bestowing stratum. This stratum he calls the *noesis*. The noesis, then, informs the hyle so as to give us an act that is directed towards the appropriate object. We could make these notions clearer by taking first a case of imagining. If you just imagine things, you can have pretty much whatever noesis you want. However, when you perceive things, the hyle you have will serve as boundary conditions, and they will eliminate the possibility of lots of noeses. The hyle do not shrink the possibilities to one; there are still different possibilities. However, the function of the hyle is to eliminate certain possibilities. At any one time you will have one particular noesis. As your experience goes forward and you get more hyle, those hyle you get do perhaps not fit the noesis you had originally. You will then say that you misperceived, and you will take on some other noesis compatible with both the hyle you had originally and the later hyle that forced you to give up the original noesis.

I said very briefly that the hyle are brought about when the physical object irritates our sensory organs. Husserl does not say much about the hyle. But it seems to me that the so-called causal theory of perception could be accommodated very well to Husserl's view of perception. It would be a restriction on the way in which you can structure the world that you experience, viz. the restriction that whatever object you perceive has to be placed in such a position in the world that it causally affects your sensory organs. However, there is no necessity to interpret Husserl this way. He has really not gone into the problem, and I point out that it would be compatible with his view to have a causal theory of perception. Maybe he would have done it quite differently himself.

It seems to me that Husserl has found a rather interesting way of handling perception. It is remarkable that Husserl compared our sensory experiences to Aristotelian matter, which was not some object perceived, according to Aristotle, but nevertheless plays a role in our perception, while Brentano, although he was an expert on Aristotle, never got the idea of comparing the physical phenomena to matter. I think there are good reasons for this, since Brentano lumped so many different things together and called them physical phenomena that he would not be likely to compare all of them to Aristotelian matter. Having divided Brentano's physical phenomena into two groups, Husserl found that one of these groups came close to the Aristotelian notion of matter and could appropriately be called hyle. Husserl therefore propounds a kind of hylomorphism. What corresponds to Aristotle's "form" or *morphe,* could, in a first approximation, be called the noesis, which informs the hyle. However, the noema that I talked about at the beginning of this paper is an even better counterpart to the form; the noesis is simply the temporal counterpart to the abstract noema. Hence, to sum up, the noema should be compared to the form, the noesis to the informing part of the consciousness, and the hyle to the boundary conditions which limit the range of noemata that we can have in a given case of perception. Neither the noema nor the noesis (nor the hyle) are objects of the acts whose noema, noesis, or hyle they are. However, they are the features through whose interplay our consciousness has the directedness towards objects, the intentionality, that Brentano claimed it to have.

2

Husserl and Frege: A New Look at Their Relationship

J. N. Mohanty

Husserl's explicit rejection of psychologism as a theory of the origin of the logico-mathematical entities and his advocacy of a conception of pure logic as a science of objective meanings were first expounded in the *Prolegomena to Pure Logic* (1900), and Husserl tells us that the *Prolegomena,* in its essentials, is a reworking of lectures he had given at Halle in the year 1896.[1] Føllesdal, in his careful study of the relation between Frege and Husserl during these years, asks the question, at what time between 1890 (the year of publication of the *Philosophie der Arithmetik*) and 1896 did this change in Husserl's mode of thinking take place?[2] The papers published during 1891-1893 do not, according to Føllesdal, bear testimony to any such change. In the paper, "Psychologische Studien zur Elementaren Logik" of the year 1894, Husserl still believes that the foundations of logic can be clarified with the help of psychology. Accordingly, the change must have occurred between the years 1894 and 1896. Frege's famed review of the *Philosophie der Arithmetik* appeared in 1894. Føllesdal therefore conjectures that it is Frege's review which must have led Husserl to a complete revision of his prior mode of thinking.[3] This view of the Frege-Husserl relationship is shared by many writers. A recent writer even speaks of Husserl's "traumatic encounter with Frege."[4]

In this paper I wish to argue that the basic change in Husserl's
mode of thinking which by itself could have led to the *Prolegomena* conception of pure logic had taken place by 1891. This change
may be discerned in Husserl's review of Schröder's *Vorlesungen
über die Algebra der Logik.* [5] It also underlies the program of *Inhaltslogik* worked out in "Der Folgerungskalkül und die Inhaltslogik" of the same year. [6] If pure logic is defined in the *Prolegomena* in terms of the concept of ideal objective meanings, [7] then the
1891 review of Schröder's work contains this concept. If the major burden of Frege's 1894 review of the *Philosophie der Arithmetik* is the lack of distinction, in that work, between the subjective
and the objective, [8*] between *Vorstellung* and *Begriff* and between
both and the object, then Husserl had already come to distinguish
between *Vorstellung* as meaning and as object in his 1891 review.
If this be so, then another historical judgment—connected with the
above—needs to be revised. It has been held by many authors that
Husserl's distinction, in the *Logische Untersuchungen,* between
meaning and object of an expression originates with Frege. Thus,
for example, Hubert Dreyfus writes: "Husserl simply accepted and
applied Frege's distinctions . . . The only change Husserl made in
Frege's analysis was terminological." [9*] Now, if Husserl's review of
Schröder already contains that distinction, then it surely antedates
the publication of Frege's celebrated paper "Über Sinn und Bedeutung" of 1892, and Husserl must have arrived at it independently of Frege.

Referring to Schröder's distinction between univocal and equivocal names, Husserl writes:

> . . . he lacks the true concept of the meaning of a name. That requirement
> of univocity is also expressed in the form: "The name shall be of a . . .
> constant meaning." (48) However, according to the relevant discussions on
> pages 47-48, the author identifies the meaning of the name with the repre-
> sentation (*Vorstellung*) of the object named by the name, from which the
> striking consequence follows, to be sure, that all common names are equiv-
> ocal. It is not as if the author had overlooked the distinction between
> equivocal and common names—and besides, who could overlook it! But to
> see a distinction and to apprehend its essence are two different things.
> Moreover, he uses the term "meaning" (*Bedeutung*) itself equivocally, and
> that in an already intolerable degree. In the above quotation, in spite of
> mutually opposed and false explanations, what is intended is the ordinary
> sense. On another occasion, however, what is actually meant is the object
> named by the name; how otherwise, e.g., could, in verbal contradiction
> with the above mentioned requirement, the common names be as such

characterized as being such that "several meanings are true of them with the same right and justification!" (69) And even that is not enough; the class corresponding to the common name is also called its meaning (69fn.). It is therefore understandable that the author is not able to formulate the essence of equivocation precisely . . . It is further connected with unclarity in the concept of meaning that Schröder regards names such as "round square" as meaningless (*unsinnige*) and sets them apart from univocal and equivocal names. Obviously he confuses here two different questions: (1) whether there belongs to a name a meaning (*ein "Sinn"*); and (2) whether an object corresponding to a name exists. [10]

This paragraph clearly shows that Husserl did distinguish, as early as 1891, between:

(1) the sense or meaning of a term (for which he is using both '*Bedeutung*' and '*Sinn*', though in the *Logische Untersuchungen* he will prefer '*Bedeutung*'),

(2) the object (*Gegenstand*) which the name may designate in case the object exists,

(3) the representation (*Vorstellung*) of such an object.

Representations may vary, but the meaning or *Sinn* may remain the same. Furthermore, there may be no object that is designated, and yet a name may have meaning. Even when there are objects that are designated, the multiplicity of objects does not imply multiplicity of meanings. He therefore has a clear distinction between *Vorstellung, Gegenstand,* and *Bedeutung* or *Sinn.*

It is true that these remarks do not contain the thesis of the *ideal* objectivity of meanings, but they certainly do not confuse meaning with *Vorstellung* and therefore testify to an awareness of the *objectivity* of meanings as contrasted with the subjectivity of the *Vorstellungen.*

Could Husserl have derived this threefold distinction from any of Frege's earlier writings? If anywhere in Frege's writings before 1891, we are to look for it in *Die Grundlagen der Arithmetik* (1884). But Frege writes in his letter to Husserl of May 24, 1891, that in the *Grundlagen* he had not yet drawn the distinction between meaning and reference. [11*] It is unlikely, then, that Husserl took it from him. It is more likely that both arrived at the distinction independently, for Husserl writes back to Frege: "I also notice that in spite of essential points of divergence, our points of view have many things in common. Many observations which forced themselves on me, I find had been expressed by you many years earlier." That seems in principle to be a true account of their relationship at this stage, though it would seem that on this point, i.e. the distinction between meaning and reference, Husserl and Frege must have arrived at it about the same time and independently of each other.

What is of importance for our present purpose, however, is that Husserl's overcoming of subjectivism in favor of an objective theory of meaning and the consequent theory of logic is already foreshadowed in the 1891 review of Schröder's work and three years prior to Frege's review of the *Philosophie der Arithmetik*. The other 1891 paper, i.e. the one on *Inhaltslogik* more clearly brings this out.

II

Amongst the major theses which Husserl puts forward, insofar as his conception of logic at this point is concerned, we may mention the following:

(1) A calculus qua calculus is not a language: "the two concepts are fundamentally different. Language is not a method of systematic-symbolic inference, calculus is not a method of systematic-symbolic expression of psychic phenomena."[12]

(2) A logic qua logic is not a calculus. A calculus is a technique, a *Zeichentechnik*. Logic is concerned not with mere signs but with conceptual contents.[13]

(3) Deductive logic is not the same as a technique of inference, nor is it exhausted by a theory of inference. There are deductive operations other than inferring. A deductive science does not consist merely of inferences. It may involve, e.g., the operation 'computing' (*Rechnen*), which is not inferring.[14]

(4) It is not true that only an extensional calculus of classes is possible. A calculus of conceptual contents, or intensions, is also possible.[15]

(5) An *autonomous* extensional logic of classes is not possible, for every extensional judgment (*Umfangsurteil*) is, in truth, an intensional judgment (*Inhaltsurteil*). The concept of class presupposes the concepts of 'conceptual content' and 'object of a concept.'[16]

(6) Every judgment has two aspects: logical content and 'algorithmic content.'[17] The logical content is the judged content (*Urteilsgehalt*)—i.e., that which it states (*das, was sie behauptet*). Reducing a categorical judgment to a relation of subsumption

among classes brings out its algorithmic content. The two are equivalent but not always identical. They are identical when the judgment is a judgment about classes.

(7) A judgment by itself is directed not toward classes or conceptual contents, but toward objects of concepts (*Begriffs-gegenstände*).[18]

(8) Geometrical thinking is not operations with signs or figures. The signs are mere 'supports' for the 'conception of the truly intended operations with concepts and with respective objects of those concepts.'[19]

Most of these theses are retained, with modifications and shifts in emphasis no doubt, in the *Prolegomena* and the *Investigations*. Pure logic is the science of meanings. "Everything that is logical falls under the two correlated categories of meaning and object."[20] Algorithmic methods spare us genuine deductive mental work by "artificially arranged mechanical operations on sensible signs"[21] and "their sense and justification depend on validatory thought."[22] Certainly, Husserl has now, in the *Prolegomena,* much more sympathetic understanding of the "mathematicising theories of logic" and he has come to regard the mathematical form of treatment as the only scientific one which offers us "systematic closure and completeness."[23] But he is still cautioning us that "the mathematician is not really the pure theoretician, but only the ingenious technician, the constructor, as it were, who, looking merely to formal interconnections, builds up his theory like a technical work of art."[24] But this note of warning is mollified by the assurance that what makes science possible is not essential insight but "scientific instinct and method,"[25] and that philosophical investigation should not meddle in the work of the specialist but should seek to "achieve insight in regard to the sense and essence of his achievements as regards method and manner."[26] The thesis that extension of a concept presupposes its intension is developed in the Second Investigation, though there is more explicit emphasis on the ideal objectivity of meanings and there is talk of the *Inhalt* as a *species*.

III

Husserl sent copies of his 1891 papers to Frege. We know of this from the correspondence between the two men. It is worthwhile therefore to find out what Frege's responses to the Husserl papers were. In his letter of May 24, 1891, after acknowledging receipt of Husserl's *Philosophie der Arithmetik* and the papers on Schröder and *Inhaltslogik,* Frege emphasizes that the two have many ideas in common, and renews his decision to write down his own thoughts on Schröder's book.[27] He agrees with some of Husserl's criticisms of Schröder, e.g. of Schröder's definitions of '0', '1', 'a+b' and 'a−b'. Referring to the *Philosophie der Arithmetik,* Frege hopes that sometime in the future, time permitting, he may reply to Husserl's criticisms of his own theory of number. He draws attention to one major difference between them, and that concerns how a common name relates to its objects. Frege illustrates his own view with the help of a schema (see below).

Sentence	Proper name	Common name
↓	↓	↓
Sinn of the sentence (*Gedanke*=Thought)	*Sinn* of the proper name	*Sinn* of the common name
↓	↓	↓
Bedeutung of the sentence (its truth-value)	*Bedeutung* of the proper name (*Gegenstand*)	*Bedeutung* of the common name (=concept)→ object which falls under the concept

In the case of common names—according to Frege—one step more is needed to reach the object than in the case of proper names. Furthermore, in the case of common names, the concept may be empty—i.e., unless there is an object, the concept ceases to be scientifically useful. In the case of proper names, however, if a name does not name anything—i.e., lacks an object—it is scientifically useless. This refers to Frege's well-known and controversial thesis that concepts constitute the reference, not the Sinn, of common names. Frege contrasts with this Husserl's view that the Sinn, (or, in Husserl's language, the Bedeutung) of a common name is the concept expressed by it and its reference is constituted by the object or objects falling under the concept. The letter makes it clear that Frege does recognize that Husserl made a distinction between *Sinn* and *Gegenstand,* only he does *not* here ascribe to Husserl a distinction between *Vorstellung* and *Sinn.*

Husserl writes back to Frege on July 18, 1891. He admits the great intellectual stimulus he has received from Frege's theories and goes on to express his views about the many points of agreement between them—to which reference has been made earlier. Among these points of agreement, Husserl refers to his own distinction between 'language' (*Sprache*) and 'calculus,' which he now finds in Frege's 1883 paper "Über den Zweck der Begriffsschrift,"[28] where he distinguishes between the concept of "calculus ratiocinator" and the concept of "lingua characteristica." It appears to him that the *Begriffsschrift* is intended to be a lingua characteristica and not a "sign language constructed in imitation of the arithmetical." He concludes the letter by expressing agreement with Frege's rejection of "formal arithmetic" as a *theory* of arithmetic, however important it may be as an extension of the arithmetical technique. Husserl is referring to Frege's "Über formale Theorien der Arithmetik,"[29] whose copy Frege had just sent him. The sense of 'formalism' in which Frege rejects it as a theory of arithmetic is that according to which the signs for numbers like '1/2,' '2/3,' 'π' are empty, meaningless signs (*leere Zeichen.*) According to this theory, as Frege understands it, these empty signs themselves are numbers, and they constitute the proper subject matter of arithmetic.[30] That Husserl should concur fully with Frege's total rejection of such a theory of arithmetic should be obvious from the foregoing summary of his views. The *Prolegomena* shows much greater understanding of the significance of formalism, but even there his philosophy of arithmetic is not formalistic. His formal logic is the correlate of formal ontology, and in large parts of the work he is concerned not with a specific formal science but with the form of theory in general.

From the above survey of the Frege-Husserl correspondence of 1891,[31] it becomes clear that Frege did not quite show any recognition of the presence of the *Vorstellung-Sinn* distinction in Husserl's Schröder review. However, as we have already seen, this distinction is there, which suggests that Husserl was already on his way, independently of Frege's 1894 review, toward the objective conception of logic of the *Prolegomena*.

IV

Let us now look at other comments by Frege on the Husserl papers of 1891. We know that in his May 24, 1891, letter to Husserl, Frege writes that Husserl's Schröder review had made him decide to publish his own thoughts on Schröder's book, and that his comments on it may appear in the *Zeitschrift für Philosophie und philosophische Kritik*. However, Frege's "Kritische Beleuchtung einiger Punkte in E. Schröders Vorlesungen über die Algebra der Logik" finally appeared four years afterward in the *Archiv für systematische Philosophie*.[32] In this review, Frege, among other

things, brings out the essential points of difference between Schröder's concept of *'Gebiet'* (domain) and the logical concept of class,
and points out how Schröder unknowingly oscillates between the
two. Insofar as the logical concept of class is concerned, Frege
considers it entirely mistaken to take a class as consisting of individual things, as a collection of individuals—a mistake which according to him, derives from Schröder's attempt to extend his *Ge-
bietakalkül* to the logic of classes.[33] And yet, asks Frege, how else
is a class constituted if one abstracts from common properties?
"Only through the fact that the classes are determined by the
properties which their individuals should have, only through the
fact that one uses expressions such as 'the class of objects which
are b,' is it possible to express general thoughts when one states relations amongst classes; only through this does one come to logic."[34] Thus Frege agrees with Husserl's comments: the extension
of a concept presupposes the intension of the concept. In Frege's
own words: "In reality I hold the view that the concept logically
precedes its extension, and I consider it a mistake to attempt to
found the class, as extension of a concept, not on the concept itself but on the individual things."[35] Despite this agreement with
Husserl's point of view, however, Frege refuses to side with *Inhaltslogik* against the so-called *Umfangslogik,* and adds: "Nevertheless,
I am in many respects possibly closer to the author (i.e. to Schröder) than to those whom one could call, in opposition to him, logicians of content (*Inhalt*)."[36] Obviously he has Husserl in mind. The
question naturally arises: why does Frege reject the conception of
an *Inhaltslogik* even though he does not agree with a purely extensional analysis of classes?

The reasons become partly clear when one considers his remarks
on *Inhaltslogik* in the "Ausführungen über Sinn und Bedeutung"[37]
which possibly belongs to the period 1892–95. Frege writes:

> Even if one has to concede to the *Inhalts*-logicians that the concept itself,
> as contrasted with its extension, is the foundation, nevertheless it should
> for that reason be understood not as the meaning (*Sinn*) of the concept-
> word, but as its reference, and the *Umfangs*-logicians are nearer the truth
> insofar as they locate in the extension (*Umfang*) an essential meaning (*Be-
> deutung*) which, though not itself the concept, is yet very closely con-
> nected with it.[38]

We have already found that the *Inhaltslogik* is a logic of meanings. Although Frege regards the concept as primary and extension
as derivative, he also considers the concept itself to be the *reference* of a concept-word. A logic of concepts, then, would be a

logic not of Sinne but of Bedeutungen (in Frege's senses of those words), hence closer to an extensional logic. The following paragraph further clarifies Frege's argument:

> They [the Umfangs-logicians] are right when, because of their preference for the extension of a concept to its intension, they admit that they regard the reference of words, and not their meaning, to be essential for logic. The Inhalts-logicians remain too happily with the meaning, for what they call "Inhalt," if it is not quite the same as Vorstellung, is certainly the meaning (Sinn). They do not consider the fact that in logic it is not a question of how thoughts come from thoughts without regard to truth-value, but that, more generally speaking, the progress from meanings (Sinne) to reference (Bedeutung) must be made; that the logical laws are first laws in the realm of references and only secondarily mediately relate to meaning (Sinn). [39]

Also, in the same "Ausführungen," Frege makes reference to Husserl's distinction between whether a name has a Sinn and whether an object corresponding to it exists. But he finds this distinction insufficient, for Husserl does not distinguish between proper names and concept-words, and as we saw earlier, Frege differs widely from Husserl on this point. Again there is no reference to Husserl's distinction between Vorstellung and Sinn. The one likely recognition of this is the covert statement that the Inhalt of the Inhalts-logicians, if it is not Vorstellung, must be the Sinn. [40]

V

We may sum up our conclusions insofar as the Frege-Husserl relationship during the years 1891–94 is concerned:

1. The two men arrived at the Vorstellung-Sinn-reference distinction independently of each other.

2. Husserl's overcoming of psychologism and acceptance of a theory of objective pure logic was fundamentally independent of Frege's 1894 review of the Philosophie der Arithmetik. The basic change had occurred in 1891. That this should have occurred in the very year of publication of the Philosophie der Arithmetik is made all the more plausible by the following note by Husserl, belonging to a much later date:

> I have read a great deal in the Philosophy of Arithmetic. How immature, how naïve and almost childish this work appears to me. Even then, with reason, I suffered pangs of conscience in connection with its publication. Actually I was already beyond that stage of my development when I published it. Indeed it derived in essence from the years 1886-87. [41]

3. (a) Frege agrees with Husserl that the concept of a class pre-supposes the concept of concept, that the extension of a concept presupposes the intension. (b) Nevertheless, while Husserl went on to develop the idea of an *Inhaltslogik* and subsequently a logic of meanings (though he did not quite reject *Umfangslogik,* to be sure, but wavered between (i) asserting a bare equivalence between the two logics and (ii) asserting the primacy of the *Inhaltslogik*), Frege sides with *Umfangslogik* and that for two reasons: (α) his belief that logic is concerned not with mere consistency of thoughts but with their truth-value, and (β) his theory that the reference of concept-words is the concept itself (as contrasted with Husserl's view, which may also be said to be the standard view, that the concept is the Sinn of the concept-word.)

We cannot here undertake a discussion of the question whether these two Fregean theses are acceptable. But we know now exactly where the two men stood in relation to each other between the years 1891 and 1894.

RESPONSE BY DAGFINN FØLLESDAL

Husserl's Conversion from Psychologism and the Vorstellung–
Meaning–Reference Distinction: Two Separate Issues

Mohanty, in his article, contests my conjecture in *Husserl und Frege* (1958) that Frege may have been an important factor in Husserl's conversion from the psychologism of *Philosophie der Arithmetik* to the anti-psychologism of *Prolegomena.*

Mohanty supports his contestation with three claims:

(1) Husserl arrived at the *Vorstellung*-meaning-reference distinction independently of Frege.

(2) Husserl's overcoming of psychologism and acceptance of a theory of objective, pure logic was fundamentally independent of Frege's 1894 review of *Philosophie der Arithmetik.* The basic change had occurred in 1891.

(3) Husserl worked out a program for an *Inhaltslogik* and subsequently a logic of meanings in "Der Folgerungskalkul und die Inhaltslogik" (1891).

I will consider these claims one by one:

First, I agree with Mohanty that Husserl did not arrive at the *Vorstellung*-meaning-reference distinction through Frege. In fact, Frege's discussion of this distinction in his letter to Husserl of May 24, 1891, to which Mohanty refers, was prompted by Husserl's use of a similar distinction in his *Philosophie der Arithmetik*. Husserl was conversant with related distinctions in Bolzano and Mill, whom he knew through his studies with Brentano.[1*] I find Bolzano's distinction between objective and subjective Vorstellungen particularly helpful for understanding Husserl's phenomenology, and since 1962, when I first taught a course on phenomenology and its background, I have devoted several lectures in this course to Bolzano. In brief presentations of phenomenology, however, I often refer to Frege for this distinction, since Frege is especially clear and precise and since I can normally presuppose that my audience knows him. Still, when I discuss where Husserl got the distinction, I always mention Bolzano and Mill. See, for example, page 421 of "An Introduction to Phenomenology for Analytic Philosophers":

> Frege's distinction is rather natural, and the same, or similar, distinctions have been clarified by other philosophers. There are indications of such distinctions even in Plato and Aristotle, and the Stoics made use of a distinction very similar to that of Frege. Husserl was aware of a related distinction from John Stuart Mill, and he had found similar ideas in Bolzano.[2]

There is, therefore, no disagreement between Mohanty and myself on this issue. Husserl definitely arrived at the Vorstellung-meaning-reference distinction independently of Frege.

Mohanty's third claim, that Husserl in 1891 worked out a program for an Inhaltslogik and subsequently a logic of meaning is, of course, also one with which I am in full agreement.

Our disagreement begins with Mohanty's second claim, that Husserl's overcoming of psychologism was fundamentally independent of Frege's 1894 review of the *Philosophie der Arithmetik*, having already occurred in 1891. That Husserl in 1891 distinguished between Vorstellung, meaning, and reference does not justify this claim, nor does Husserl's 1891 program for an Inhaltslogik. Both of these themes in Husserl are compatible with his adhering to psychologism. Whether one accepts psychologism depends on how one conceives of meanings, as psychological processes or as "ideal" entities, as Husserl called them later. It also depends on one's epistemological views on logic and mathematics.

In *Husserl und Frege,* which Mohanty discusses, I went through Husserl's writings, including all the ones Mohanty refers to, and found that, up to and including Husserl's 1894 article "Psychologische Studien zur elementaren Logik, I-II," *Philosophische Monatshefte* 30 (1894), pp. 159-191, Husserl seems to stick to his psychologistic conception of logic and mathematics. Then, between 1894 and 1896, there occurs a radical change; Husserl never published the second volume of *Philosophie der Arithmetik* and in 1896 started on what was to become his first phenomenological work, *Logische Untersuchungen.* In *Husserl und Frege* I asked to what extent Frege's criticism of psychologism, in the introduction to *Grundgesetze* and in his review of Husserl's *Philosophie der Arithmetik,* might have influenced Husserl's development. A detailed examination of Frege's arguments against psychologism and the changes in Husserl's views during this period made me conjecture that Frege may have been an important factor in Husserl's conversion.

There is nothing in the articles and passages referred to by Mohanty which indicates that Husserl had a nonpsychologistic conception of meaning in 1891. And Mohanty does not discuss the various arguments I give in *Husserl und Frege* for the conjecture that Frege may have been instrumental for turning Husserl away from psychologism.

Let me end by mentioning additional evidence for my conjecture, which has become available during the last few years:

First, thanks to the painstaking labor of Karl Schumann in his *Husserl-Chronik: Denk- und Lebensweg Edmund Husserls,* we now know that Husserl kept working on the second volume of *Philosophie der Arithmetik* off and on until 1894, the year of Frege's review. As late as November 1894, Husserl wrote in a letter to Meinong that after a long break he was working on that volume and was hoping to finish it the next spring.[3] As mentioned earlier, by 1896 Husserl had clearly given up the attempt to work out a philosophy of logic and mathematics on the psychologistic foundation laid in Volume 1 of *Philosophie der Arithmetik.*

That Husserl rejected *Philosophie der Arithmetik* is clear from the foreword to the *Logische Untersuchungen,* where he says:

> I began work on the prevailing assumption that psychology was the science from which logic in general, and the logic of the deductive sciences, had

to hope for philosophical clarification. For this reason psychological re-
searches occupy a very large place in the first (the only published) volume
of my *Philosophy of Arithmetic.*[4]

The course of my development has led me to drawing apart, as regards
basic logical convictions, from men and writings to whom I owe most of my
philosophical education, and to drawing rather closer to a group of thinkers
whose writings I was not able to estimate rightly, and whom I had consulted
all too little in the course of my labours.[5]

Husserl gives the following account of his breakthrough:

I became more and more disquieted by doubts of principle, as to how to
reconcile the objectivity of mathematics, and of all science in general, with
a psychological foundation for logic. In this manner my whole method,
which I had taken over from the convictions of the reigning logic, that
sought to illuminate the given science through psychological analyses, became shaken, and I felt myself more and more pushed towards general
critical reflections on the essence of logic, and on the relationship, in particular, between the subjectivity of knowing and the objectivity of the
content known. Logic left me in the lurch wherever I hoped it would give
me definite answers to the definite questions I put to it, and I was eventually compelled to lay aside my philosophical-mathematical investigations,
until I had succeeded in reaching a certain clearness on the basic questions
of epistemology and in the critical understanding of logic as a science.[6]

There remains the problem that although Husserl recommends
Frege's criticism of psychologism in *Logische Untersuchungen,*[7]
and also on other occasions praises Frege's *Grundlagen*[8] and *Funk-
tion und Begriff,*[9] there is no explicit acknowledgment in Husserl's
work of his having been influenced by Frege. However, here are
three oral expressions of indebtedness. One was reported to me by
Roman Ingarden. He told me that he once asked Husserl whether
Frege had influenced him, and Husserl answered, "Frege's Bedeutung war entscheidend."[10]* Another is reported in "From Husserl
to Heidegger: Excerpts from a 1928 Freiburg Diary by W.R. Boyce
Gibson." According to Boyce Gibson, "Husserl remarked that
Frege's criticism was the only one he was really grateful for. It
hit the nail on the head."[11] A third is mentioned in Schumann,
Husserl-Chronik:

H. Spiegelberg, *Scrap-Book* (A. Osborn): *Andrew Osborn* visited H. 1935
in Black Forest to ask him about Frege's influence on the abandonment of
the psychological approach of the "Philosophie der Arithmetik." H. con-
curred, but also mentioned his chance discovery of Bolzano's work in a
second-hand book store.[12]

The reference to Bolzano is important. Although Frege may have been "entscheidend" for Husserl's conversion from psychologism to antipsychologism, which in all probability took place during 1894-96, a full study of the emergence of phenomenology must include factors other than Frege. Husserl seems to have been influenced in this period not only by Frege and Bolzano but also by Lotze, Hume, Leibniz, and Natorp. And, above all, there are Husserl's own ideas and insights. Even when there are similarities and contact, there is not always influence.[13]

II

Basic Concepts and Theory

3
Husserl's Theory of the Intentionality of Consciousness

Aron Gurwitsch

Husserl's theory of intentionality may be understood as motivated by two historical problems. The first, which may be traced back to Descartes, concerns the objective and, we may say, objectively cognitive significance of mental states, their reference to extramental facts, events, and items of any kind. Perhaps of still greater importance is the second problem, one which arises most clearly in connection with Hume's theory of Ideas—namely, the problem of the consciousness of any object given as identically the same through a multiplicity of mental states, experiences, acts. Because of its fundamental importance, we shall start by considering the problem of the consciousness of identity, which—we submit—has found a solution in Husserl's theory of intentionality. After that theory has been expounded, at least in its basic outlines, the problem mentioned in the first place will no longer present any considerable difficulties.

The notion of intentionality plays a major role in all Husserl's writings, with the exception of *Philosophie der Arithmetik*. Here we can obviously not enter into a study of the development which that notion has undergone along with that of Husserl's thought in general.[1] In view of Professor Chisholm's contribution we abstain also from presenting Brentano's conception of intentionality and

setting forth its difference from that of Husserl.[2] Since we approach
the theory of intentionality from a specific point of view—namely,
the problem of the consciousness of identity, we shall have to
overemphasize certain aspects of that theory or, more correctly,
to emphasize them more than Husserl did himself. In doing so,
however, we remain faithful to the spirit of Husserl's theory and
its leading intentions. Finally, we shall exclude from our presentation a few doctrines, especially the notion of sense-data and the
egological conception of consciousness, which play a certain role
in Husserl's theory of intentionality. Not endorsing those doctrines,[3] we may abstain from dwelling upon them, because they do
not seem to us to be of crucial importance for what we consider
most essential to the concept of intentionality. The justification
of our departure from Husserl would lead us too far afield to be
attempted here.

a. The Notion of the Object as Meant or Intended (the Noema)

The consciousness of identity cannot be accounted for in terms
of Hume's theory of Ideas, that is to say, on the grounds of the
traditional conception of the mind. Hence a totally new and radically different conception is required in which the consciousness
of identity no longer appears as an *explicandum* but, on the contrary, is made the defining property of the mind, that essential
property without which the mind could not be what it is. For
that reason it is insufficient, though true and valid as a first approximation, to define intentionality as directedness, saying that
in experiencing an act of consciousness we find ourselves directed
to something—for example, in perceiving we are directed to the
thing perceived, in remembering we are directed to the event recalled, in loving or hating we are directed to the person loved or
hated, and the like. Directedness merely denotes a phenomenal
feature of the act, inherent and immanent, a feature that appears
and disappears along with the act to which it pertains. If intentionality is thus defined, the question remains unanswered as to
how we can become aware of the identity of the "something" to
which the multiple acts are directed, considering that each one of
those acts possesses directedness as a phenomenal feature of its
own. Therefore the theory of intentionality must be based upon
the notion of the "something" that we take as identical and whose
identity we may disclose and make explicit by the appropriate
considerations.

As a convenient point of departure we choose a special phenomenon—namely, the understanding of meaningful verbal expressions—a phenomenon whose analysis forms the subject matter of the first investigation of Husserl's *Logische Untersuchungen.*[4] To lay bare what is involved in the understanding of meaningful expressions, let us contrast our experience in hearing a phrase like "the victor of Austerlitz" or "New York is the biggest city in the U.S.A." with the experience we have when we hear a noise in the street, a sound like "abracadabra" or an utterance in a foreign language with which we are not familiar. In the latter cases we have merely an auditory experience. In the former cases we also have an auditory experience, but one that supports a specific act of interpretation or apperception by means of which the auditory experience becomes a vehicle of meaning or a symbol. The same holds in the case of reading, except for the immaterial difference that the visual experience of marks on paper takes the place of the auditory experience. The specific acts that bestow the character of a symbol upon perceptual experiences may be called acts of meaning apprehension. Like all other acts, they, too, are psychological events occurring at certain moments in time. By means of the following line of reasoning, we may establish the distinction between the act of meaning apprehension and the meaning apprehended. We remember that on numerous occasions we uttered or heard the phrases mentioned. Recalling those occasions, we recall them as different from one another because of their different temporal locations. At the same time we become aware of the fact that what we meant and had in view on those occasions and what we mean now is the same: on all these occasions there presents itself to, and stands before, our mind "the one who won the battle of Austerlitz," or Napoleon as the victor of Austerlitz, or New York under the aspect of its number of inhabitants in comparison with other American cities. Furthermore, we take it for granted that all who listen to our utterance, provided they are familiar with the symbolic system used—in this case the English language—apprehend the same meaning. Each person experiences his own act of meaning apprehension which he cannot share with anybody else. Yet through all these multiple acts, distributed among any number of persons, and for each person, varying from one occasion to the other in the course of his life, the same meaning is apprehended. If this were not so, no communication, either in the mode of assent or dissent, would be possible. For a proposition to be accepted or rejected it must first be understood.

The identical entity that we call "meaning" may be defined as a certain person, object, event, state of affairs which presents itself, taken exactly as it presents itself or as it is intended. Consider the two phrases: "the victor of Austerlitz" and "the initiator of the French legal code." Though both meanings refer to the same person, Napoleon, they differ from one another insofar as in the first case Napoleon is intended under the aspect of his victory at Austerlitz and in the second with regard to his role in the establishment of the French legal code. The difference in question has been expressed by Husserl as that between the "object which is intended" and the "object *as* it is intended."[5] It is the latter notion which we identify with that of meaning. For a further illustration we mention another of Husserl's examples.[6] In hearing the name "Greenland," each one of us has a certain thought or representation of that island; that is to say, the island presents itself and is intended in a certain fashion. The same holds for the arctic explorer. Both he and any one of us intend the same object. However, Greenland *as* intended and meant by some of us with our sketchy, highly vague, and indeterminate representation obviously differs from Greenland *as* meant by the arctic explorer, who has been to the island and knows it thoroughly.

Two multiplicities, each related to an identical entity, must be distinguished from one another. On the one hand we have the multiplicity of acts through all of which the same meaning is apprehended; on the other hand there is the multiplicity of meanings, of "objects as intended," all referring to one and the same "object which is intended."

For the sake of simplicity we have confined ourselves to such meanings as refer to real objects, persons, or events. This simplification makes it easy to see that meanings cannot be identified with physical objects and occurrences any more than with psychological events. From the fact that a plurality of meanings can refer to the same object, it follows that none of the meanings coincides with the object. Real events like the battle of Austerlitz take place at a certain moment in time. But it is absurd to assign a temporal place to the meaning of the phrase "the battle of Austerlitz" and to ask whether it precedes, succeeds upon, or is simultaneous with another meaning, though any one of the acts through which the meaning is apprehended occupies a definite place in time. There are no spatial relations between meanings any more than there are causal effects exerted by meanings either upon one another or upon anything else. We are confronted with entities of a special kind—aspatial, atemporal, acausal, hence unreal or ideal—which have a specific nature of their own. Between these entities obtain relations of a particular sort, the like of which is nowhere else encountered. As a simple example we may mention the relations, studied in logic, that obtain between propositions as a special class of meanings.

Our results can easily be generalized. For the sake of brevity we limit ourselves to perceptual experience. When we perceive a thing—for example, a house—we do so from the point of observation at which we happen to be placed, so that the house appears under a certain aspect: from one of its sides, the front or the back, as near or far, and the like. It appears, as Husserl expresses it, by way of a one-sided adumbrational presentation.[7] Maintaining our point of observation, we may alternately open and close our eyes. We then experience a sequence of acts of perception, all differing from each other by the very fact of their succeeding upon one another. Through all of these perceptions not only does the same house appear, but it also appears under the same aspect, in the same orientation—in a word, in the same manner of adumbrational presentation. Again we encounter an identical entity—namely, that which is perceived exactly as it is perceived, the "perceived as such" (das Wahrgenommene als solches). It stands in the same relation to the acts of perception as does the meaning apprehended to the acts of meaning apprehension. One may generalize the term "meaning" so as to use it beyond the domain of symbolic expressions and speak of perceptual meanings. Husserl also denotes the "perceived as such" as "perceptual sense" (Wahrnehmungssinn), because by virture of it a given perception is not only a perception of a certain thing but also a determinate perception of that thing —that is to say, a perception through which the thing presents itself in this rather than another manner of adumbrational appearance.[8] Husserl's most general term here is that of noema,[9] a concept that comprises meanings in the conventional sense as a special class. Noema denotes the object as meant and intended in any mode whatsoever, hence includes the mode of perceptual experience.

Having distinguished the perceptual noema from the act of perception—the noesis—we have further to distinguish it from the thing perceived. The latter may be seen from different points of view—it may appear under a variety of aspects: from the front, the back, one of the lateral sides, and the like—while the perceptual noema denotes the thing perceived as presenting itself under one of those possible aspects. Again we have to apply the distinction between the "object which is intended"—the thing perceived—and the object *as* it is intended"—the perceptual noema, or the thing perceived *as* it is perceived. A multiplicity of perceptual noemata are related to the same thing, just as in the previous example a multiplicity of meanings were seen to refer to the same object.

Let us consider from a different point of view the difference between the perceptual noema and the thing perceived. The house may be torn down, but none of the pertinent noemata is affected thereby.[10] Even after its destruction the house may still be remembered, and it may be remembered as presenting itself under one or the other of the aspects under which it had previously appeared in perceptual experience. To be sure, the noema is no longer a perceptual one; it is rather a noema of memory. The point is that two or even more noemata, their differences notwithstanding, may have a certain stratum in common, a stratum that Husserl denotes as "noematic nucleus."[11] Within the structure of every noema, the distinction must be made between the noematic nucleus and "noematic characters," which, incidentally, belong to several dimensions.[12] By means of this distinction it is possible to account for the verification of a nonperceptual experience by a perceptual one. When in actual perceptual experience a thing proves to be such as it had been assumed, thought, believed, etc., to be, it is that the nucleus of the nonperceptual noema is seen to coincide and even to be identical with that of the perceptual noema, while the noematic characters indicating the mode of givenness or presentation remain different on either side.[13] Both the identity of the noematic nucleus and the difference concerning the characters are required for and essential to the phenomenon of verification.

b. Consciousness Defined as Noetico-Noematic Correlation

In the center of the new conception stands the notion of the noema, of the object meant and intended, taken exactly and only as it is meant and intended. Every act of consciousness is so essentially related to its noema that it is only with reference to the latter that the act is qualified and characterized as that which it is—for example, that particular perceiving of the house as seen from the front, that determinate intending of Napoleon as the victor of Austerlitz and not as the defeated of Waterloo. Traditionally, consciousness has been interpreted as a one-dimensional temporal order, a conception whose most consistent elaboration lies in Hume's theory. To be sure, acts of consciousness are psychological events that take place and endure in time and stand under the laws of temporality, to which Husserl has devoted detailed analyses.[14]

Though temporality undoubtedly denotes a fundamental aspect of consciousness, that aspect is not the only one. The temporal events called "acts of consciousness" have the peculiarity of being actualizations or apprehensions of meanings, the terms "apprehension" and "meaning" being understood in a very general sense beyond the special case of symbolic expressions. It pertains to the essential nature of acts of consciousness to be related and to correspond to noemata. Rather than being conceived of as a one-dimensional sequence of events, *consciousness must be defined as a noetico-noematic correlation,* that is to say, a correlation between items pertaining to two heterogeneous planes: on the one hand the plane of temporal psychological events, and on the other hand that of atemporal, unreal, that is to say, ideal entities that are the noemata, or meanings understood in the broader sense. Furthermore, it is a many-to-one correlation insofar as an indefinite multiplicity of acts can correspond to the same noema. Correlated terms demand and require each other. To establish the identity of the noema we had to contrast it with, hence refer it to, a multiplicity of acts. Conversely, it can be shown (though this is not the place to do it) that no account of the temporality and especially the duration of an act of consciousness is possible without reference to the noema involved.[15] Thus the conception of consciousness as noetico-noematic correlation brings to light the indissoluble connection between consciousness and meaning (Sinn). It shows consciousness to be essentially characterized by an *intrinsic duality,* which is to take the place of the Cartesian dualism.

To evaluate the historical significance of the innovation, let us consider in which respect it constitutes a break with the tradition. In the first place the theory of Ideas is relinquished, especially the principle that the mind is confined to its own mental states, which alone are directly and immediately given to it. Undoubtedly the mind lives exclusively in its mental states, its acts. Each act, however, is correlated to a noema which—as we have stressed—is itself not a mental state, an act of consciousness, a psychological event. Relatedness to essentially nonmental entities is the very nature of mental states. Furthermore, the noema is defined as the "object as it is intended," i.e., as the object in question appearing in a certain manner of presentation (under a certain aspect, from a certain point of view, etc.), an object capable, however—we must now add—of appearing in different manners of presentation. The definition of intentionality as directedness can now be given its legitimate meaning. Experiencing an act of consciousness, we are directed to

Kantian?
phenomenal
ist?!

an object insofar as in the structure of the noema corresponding to the act there are inscribed references to further noemata, to different manners of presentation of that object. Objective reference of mental states is no longer an insoluble problem as with Descartes; nor is it to be explained and accounted for subsequently. On the contrary, it proves to be essential to the acts of consciousness—not as an additional phenomenal feature of the arts, of course, but rather in the sense of the conception of consciousness as a noetico-noematic correlation.

As a consequence, consciousness can no longer be interpreted as a self-sufficient and self-contained domain of interiority. This interpretation follows from the Cartesian dualism, the severance of *res cogitans* from *res extensa* to which Descartes was led in endeavoring to lay the foundations of the incipient new science. It must be stressed that nature in the sense of modern physics is not the same as the world of common, everyday experience. In the latter world things not only present spatial forms, stand in spatial relations to one another, and change those relations in the course of time, but also exhibit specific qualities, the so-called secondary qualities, and are endowed with characters which, like those of instrumentality, utility, and cultural value, refer to human purposes and activities.[16] Quite generally, in the world of common experience the corporeal in the spatiotemporal sense is intertwined and interwoven with the mental and the psychological in all its forms. Nature in the modern scientific sense is the result and product of an artful method applied to the world of common experience. That method consists, among other things,[17] of abstracting spatiotemporal extendedness to the disregard of whatever is mental or psychological, relegating the latter to the purely subjective domain. In this way one arrives at a single coherent and self-contained context encompassing all spatiotemporal things and events. The success of this abstractive procedure suggests its application in the opposite direction—namely, a counterabstraction of what is "subjective" to the disregard of what pertains to the spatiotemporal, hence "objective," domain. However, the attempt at such a counterabstraction fails to yield a self-sufficient and self-contained domain of interiority. Turning to and concentrating upon the life of consciousness, one does not discover occurrences that take place in a closed domain and merely succeed upon one another, as Hume's theory of the mind would have it. Rather one encounters apprehensions *of* meanings; perceptions *of* houses, trees, fellow human beings; memories *of* past and expectancies *of* future events;

and the like. Generally speaking, one encounters dealings in several manners and modes with mundane things and events of the most diverse description as well as with nonmundane entities like numbers and geometrical systems, which are not mental states or psychological occurrences any more than they are mundane existents. The very failure of the counterabstraction discloses the essential reference of acts of consciousness to objective entities of any kind, hence also to mundane—that is, spatiotemporal—objects. This failure marks the breakdown of the Cartesian dualism.

Since phenomenology is based on the theory of intentionality, it must not be identified with or even too closely assimilated to intuitionistic philosophy or introspectionism as advocated by Bergson.[18] For consciousness to be grasped and studied in its authentic and aboriginal state, it must first, according to Bergson, undergo a purification from whatever contamination or admixture has accrued to it by way of contact with the objective external world, which is not only a spatial but also a social world. Obviously, such a methodological principle presupposes the Cartesian dualism. What Bergson considers a denaturalization of consciousness appears in the light of the theory of intentionality as an expression of its genuine nature. Insistence upon that difference, profound as it is, must not, however, preclude the recognition that many of Bergson's analyses have phenomenological significance or, to speak with greater prudence, may by a proper reinterpretation be given phenomenological significance.

Because of the intentionality of consciousness, we are in direct contact with the world. Living our conscious life, we are "at" the world, "at" the things encountered in that world. This should be seen as a consequence of the theory of intentionality rather than being credited as original with subsequent existentialist philosophies. A glance at the phenomenological theory of perception makes that clear. We recall the definition of the perceptual noema as the thing perceived appearing from a certain side, under a certain aspect, in a certain orientation—briefly, in a one-sided manner of adumbrational presentation. The decisive point is that notwithstanding the one-sideness of its appearance, it is the thing itself that presents itself, stands before our mind, and with which we are in contact. Noetically speaking, perceptual consciousness is an original (albeit incomplete because one-sided) experience of the thing perceived appearing in "bodily presence" (in Leibhaftigkeit). Perceptual consciousness must not be interpreted in terms of profoundly different modes of consciousness—as, for example, by means of images, signs, symbols, and the like.[19] Accordingly, the perceptual noema must not be mistaken for an Idea in the Cartesian sense—that is to say, the substitute for, or representative of, a reality only mediately accessible. With the phenomenological theory of perception, we submit, the traditional theory of Ideas is definitively overcome.

c. On the Notion of Objectivity

There remains the task of defining the relationship between the perceptual noema and the thing perceived. While actually appearing in a determinate manner of adumbrational presentation, the thing is capable of appearing in other manners. It actually so appears in the course of the perceptual process when, for example, we walk around the thing and, in general, perceive it under conditions of different sorts. In the course of that process, the thing is perceived as identically the same, presenting itself from different sides, under varying aspects, in a variety of orientations. The thing cannot be perceived except in one or the other manner of adumbrational presentation. It is nothing besides, or in addition to, the multiplicity of those presentations through all of which it appears in its identity.[20] Consequently, the thing perceived proves to be the group, more precisely put, the systematically organized totality of adumbrational presentations. Both the difference and the relationship between the thing perceived and a particular perceptual noema can now be defined in terms of a noematic system as a whole and one member of that system. This is in agreement with the previous formulation that every particular perception, its incompleteness and one-sidedness notwithstanding, is an original experience of the thing perceived appearing in bodily presence. In fact, it is the perceptual apprehension of a noematic system as a whole from the vantage point of one of its members.

Two questions arise. One concerns the organizational form of the noematic system, the other the manner in which its membership in the noematic system is inscribed in the structure of every particular noema. Both questions can only be mentioned here, not discussed.[21] At present we must confine ourselves to stressing that the thing perceived also proves to have noematic status. As a noematic system it is a noema itself, but a noema of higher order, so to speak.

Just as the theory of intentionality involves a new conception of consciousness or subjectivity, so, too, it entails a reinterpretation of the notion of objectivity. Traditionally, the objective has been opposed to the subjective as entirely alien to it, so that for an object to be reached in its genuine and authentic condition, all mental—that is, subjective—activities and their contributions must be disregarded, if not eliminated altogether. In the light of the theory of intentionality, this conception of objectivity, which derives from the Cartesian dualism, can no longer be upheld. The objective reference that is essential to acts of consciouness corresponds to a no less essential relationship of objects to acts of consciousness, especially to their noemata. The disclosure of the thing perceived as a noematic system—that is to say, an intentional correlate[22]—is in perfect conformity with the here propounded general conception of consiousness as a correlation. Furthermore, several levels of objectivity must be distinguished from one another, in consequence of which the notions of subjectivity and objectivity prove to be affected by a certain relativity.

Every particular meaning or noema as an identical entity can be considered as objective in contrast to the multiple subjective acts that are correlated with it, especially if it is remembered that those acts may be distributed among a plurality of persons. A particular perceptual noema, defined as the thing appearing under a certain aspect, is in turn to be characterized as subjective with respect to the perceived thing itself, of which the former is a one-sided perceptual adumbration, with respect to the noematic system of which the particular noema is a member. The things perceived and perceivable form, in their totality, the perceptual world, the world of pure experience, or as Husserl calls it, the life-world (*Lebenswelt*). It is the world such as it is understood, conceived, and interpreted to be by a certain social group which unquestioningly accepts it as reality. The life-world is an essentially social phenomenon.[23] Accordingly, it differs from one social group to the other and also for a given social group in the course of its historical development. At every phase of this development and for every social group, the respective life-world counts as objective reality. Over against this multiplicity of life-worlds, the question arises of a world common to all social groups. This is an objective world in a second, more profound sense. More precisely, the question concerns a set or system of invariant structures, universal insofar as they are by necessity exhibited by every sociohistorical life-world.[24] Of this common world, which perhaps should not be called life-world but rather the world of pure perceptual experience, the diverse life-worlds in the proper sense appear as varieties to be relegated to the status of merely subjective worlds. Finally there is objectivity in the specific sense of modern science: the objectivity of the scientific or scientifically true and valid universe as constructed on the basis of perceptual experience by means of mental operations and procedures into whose analysis we cannot enter here. From the point of view of the universe of science, the world of perceptual experience appears in turn as subjective.

Sketchy and incomplete though these remarks are, they may suffice to illustrate, if not substantiate, the thesis that what is meant by objective must not be conceived as severed from the life of consciousness. Moreover, the ascent to higher levels of objectivity, far from requiring the progressive elimination or, at least, disregard of mental activities and operations, on the contrary involves them in increasing complexity; it involves syntheses of consciousness of ever-widening scope. As an intentional correlate, the object of every kind and level proves to be an accomplishment (*Geleistetes*) whose clarification, especially the clarification concerning its objectivity and existence, requires that it be referred to the accomplishing (*leistende*) mental operations. Accounting in this manner for an object of whatever sort is tantamount to disclosing its "equivalent of consciousness."

Conclusion

Husserl's program of constitutive phenomenology, a generalization and radicalization of the Cartesian program, attempts to account for objects of all possible kinds in terms of subjective, conscious life. A superficial survey of some levels of objectivity may give an idea of the extent of that tremendous task. For the sake of completeness we recall in passing the sense of objectivity which pertains to the ideal orders of being and existence in the Platonic sense or, in Husserl's parlance, to the eidetic realms. In the theory of intentionality we found the theoretical instrument both necessary and sufficient for the realization of that task. Herein appears the historical significance of that theory.

We could as well have started from the theory of intentionality, conceived as a theory of the mind in a merely psychological setting, regardless of philosophical interests. The radical innovation which that theory entails for the conception of the mind and thus for psychological thinking defines its historical significance in a further respect. Consistently developing the theory of intentionality conceived in a psychological orientation, and pursing it to its ultimate consequences, would have led us to the idea of constitutive phenomenology in a way Husserl has followed himself in the Amsterdam lectures and the article in the *Encyclopaedia Britannica*. [25] The theory of intentionality thus serves both as a motivating force, as far as the conception of the idea of constitutive phenomenology is concerned, and as the theoretical instrument for its realization. In other words, provided proper allowance is made for the transcendental reduction, which could here be mentioned only in passing, the full elaboration of the theory of intentionality proves coextensive with and even identical with the philosophy of constitutive phenomenology.

4

Husserl's Notion of Noema

Dagfinn Føllesdal

The general theme of phenomenology, according to Husserl, is intentionality—that is, the peculiarity of consciousness to be consciousness *of* something (*Ideen*, I, p. 204).

This concern with intentionality Husserl had taken over from his teacher, Brentano. According to Brentano,

> Every mental phenomenon is characterized by what the scholastics in the Middle Ages called the intentional (and also mental) inexistence of an object, and what we could call, although in not entirely unambiguous terms, the reference to a content, a direction upon an object. [1]

This may sound commonplace, but it leads to difficulties—for example, when we try to apply the principle to a person who has hallucinations or to a person who thinks of a centaur. Brentano held that, even in these cases, our mental activity, our thinking or our sensing, is directed toward some object. The directedness has nothing to do with the object's being real, Brentano held; the object is itself contained in our mental activity, "intentionally" contained in it.

However, whereas the view that the objects of acts are real leads to difficulties in the case of centaurs and hallucinations, the view that the objects are unreal, whatever that may mean, leads to difficulties in the case of many other acts, e.g., acts of normal perception: it seems that, on this view, what we see when we see a tree is not the real tree in front of us but something else, which we would also have seen if we had been hallucinating.

So we are faced with a dilemma.

Husserl resolved this dilemma by holding that although every act is directed, this does not mean that there always is some object toward which it is directed. According to Husserl, there is associated with each act a noema, in virtue of which the act is directed toward its object, if it has any. When we think of a centaur, our act of thinking has a noema, but it has no object; there exists no object of which we think. Because of its noema, however, even such an act is directed. To be *directed* simply is to have a noema.

Husserl's notion of noema, therefore, is a key notion in his theory of intentionality and, thereby, in his phenomenology. According to Husserl, a proper understanding and grasp of the distinctions connected with the noema "is of the greatest importance for phenomenology, and decisive for giving it a right foundation" (*Ideen,* I, p. 239).

In this paper, I shall present a number of theses concerning the noema and support them by systematic arguments and textual evidence from Husserl's writings. I shall try to make the picture of the noema that thereby emerges as accurate and complete as is permitted by the evidence that is available in Husserl's various published and unpublished works.

My main thesis is the following:

1. The noema is an intensional entity, a generalization of the notion of meaning (Sinn, Bedeutung).

This thesis and its consequences go against the usual interpretations of Husserl, but they accord well with Husserl's own writings. Thus, in the third volume of *Ideen,* p. 89, Husserl says: "The noema is nothing but a generalization of the idea of meaning (Sinn) to the field of all acts."

In many of his other works, Husserl expresses similar views. Thus in *Ideen,* Volume I, he says, "Originally, these words ['Bedeuten' and 'Bedeutung'] related only to the linguistic sphere, that of 'expressing.' It is, however, almost unavoidable and at the same time an important advance to widen the meaning of these words and modify them appropriately, so that they in a certain way are applicable to the whole noetic-noematic sphere: that is to all acts, whether they are intertwined with expressing acts or not" (p. 304).

And in *Ideen,* I, p. 233, Husserl characterizes the full noema as a "'Sinn' (in the widest sense)." Compare p. 219 and p. 223.

One should be aware of an ambiguity in Husserl's use of the word 'Sinn' as applied to the noema. Sometimes he means the full noema, other times just a part of it, a part which may be the same in acts of many different kinds—for example, acts of perceiving, remembering, imagining, etc. Our second thesis is therefore the following:

> 2. A noema has two components: (1) one which is common to all acts that have the same object, with exactly the same properties, oriented in the same way, etc., regardless of the "thetic" character of the act—that is, whether it be perceiving, remembering, imagining, etc., and (2) one which is different in acts with different thetic characters.

The first of these components Husserl calls "noematischer Sinn" (p. 321) and also, alternatively, "der Gegenstand im wie seiner Bestimmtheiten" (p. 312) and "gegenständlicher Sinn" (p. 250). Compare p. 249 and p. 322. The second component he calls the noematic correlate of the "Gegebenheitsweise" of the object (pp. 323, 250) or of the "Weise, wie der Gegenstand bewusst ist." An important part of the "Gegebenheitsweise" is the "thetic character," the "Setzungscharakter" of the act (p. 323).[2] Another part that enters into the "Gegebenheitsweise" is the "filling," the "Anschauungssinn." As we should expect, Husserl says that the second component, like the first, can be regarded as a component of the act's "Sinn" in an extended sense (p. 233). In the *Logical Investigations* (5. Unters., §§20–21), Husserl calls the first component "Materie," the second "Qualität," and the two together "Sinn." In *Ideen,* Husserl normally uses 'Sinn' for the first component, 'Noema' for the two together.

A third thesis is the following:

> 3. The noematic Sinn is that in virtue of which consciousness relates to the object.

This thesis, too, is well supported by the Husserlian text. Thus, in *Ideen,* I, p. 316: "Consciousness relates in and through this Sinn to its object." And "each intentional experience has a noema and in it a Sinn, through which it relates to the object" (p. 329). Compare also pp. 316, 318.

A key point in Husserl's phenomenology is the following:

> 4. The noema of an act is not the object of the act (i.e., the object toward which the act is directed).

This is a crucial difference between Husserl and Brentano: Brentano's dilemma, mentioned at the beginning of this paper, arose because he held that the object that gives the act its directedness is the object toward which the act is directed. Brentano struggled throughout his life to make clear the relation of the act to its object, but he never succeeded in making this salutary distinction.

The object of an act is a function of the act's noematic Sinn in the sense that

> 5. To one and the same Noema, there corresponds only one object.

In fact, Husserl even asserts that: "Sameness of Sinn occurs only where the object, besides being identically the same, is meant in 'the same Sinn', that is, from the same side, with the same properties etc." (NuS p. 4). See also *Logische Untersuchungen*, II (1928), §28, p. 416.

The converse, however, is not the case:

> 6. To one and the same object there may correspond several different noemata.

This is trivially true in view of thesis 2, since two noemata that have the same noematic Sinn and therefore (as just observed) the same object can nevertheless have different thetic characters, hence be different noemata. Thus, for example, acts of perception, memory, etc., can have the same object. However, thesis 6 may be strengthened to:

> 6. To one and the same object there may correspond several different noematic Sinne.

This follows, in fact, from the quotation from Husserl's *Noema und Sinn* that we just gave in order to support our thesis 5. The object being identically the same is not sufficient to guarantee sameness of Sinn; we also have to require that the object be given from the same side, with the same properties etc. Compare also *Ideen*, I, p. 321 and *Logische Untersuchungen*, II, p. 416.

The noemata help to individualize the acts, in that

> 7. Each act has one and only one noema.

Compare, for example, NuS, p. 2: "Each [act has] *its* noema as its individual characteristic."

It should be noted that the converse does not hold: to one and the same noema there may correspond several distinct acts. These acts will be similar; they will be directed toward the same object, with exactly the same properties and oriented in the same way; and they will have the same thetic character. Yet they may be distinct acts; they may, for example, have different temporal coordinates.

As could be expected, the noemata are like linguistic Sinne in most respects. Thus the following important consequence of thesis 1 should be noted:

8. Noemata are abstract entities.

As textual support of thesis 8 we note the following: Husserl says in *Ideen,* I (p. 222): "The tree, the thing in nature, is by no means the perceived tree as such, which belongs inseparably to the perceiving as the perceptual Sinn. The tree can burn, may be dissolved into its chemical elements, etc. The Sinn, however—the Sinn of *this* perception, which belongs by necessity to its essence—cannot burn, it has no chemical elements, no forces, no real properties." In the manuscript *Noema und Sinn,* Husserl says: "Sinne are nonreal objects, they are not objects that exist in time" (NuS p. 109). And further in the same manuscript: "A Sinn does not have reality, it is related to a temporal interval through the act in which it occurs, but it does not itself have reality [Dasein], an individual connection with time and duration" (NuS p. 114).

Here Husserl is talking about the noematic Sinn, but, since the other components of the noema are also "Sinn" components (p. 223), the same presumably applies to them and, thereby, to the whole noema. Husserl says in *Ideen,* p. 314, that all noematic Sinne and complete noemata belong to one and the same species. That the noema is not a spatial object is clear from *Ideen,* I, p. 97, where Husserl observes that spatial objects can be experienced only through perspectives (Abschattungen). Since in principle noemata are not experienced through perspectives, they are not spatial objects.

Closely connected with this is the following point, which is contrary to most currently accepted views on what the noemata are:

9. Noemata are not perceived through our senses.

This view is not clearly expressed in any of Husserl's published writings. However, it is an immediate consequence of thesis 8, and, if it should turn out to be false, thesis 8 and several of our other theses would fall with it. It is therefore important to find and evaluate whatever evidence there is for or against thesis 9 in Husserl's writings. The closest Husserl comes to expressing his view on it in his published writings is on p. 97 in *Ideen,* I, where he observes that all visible objects can be experienced only through perspectives. Since noemata, as just mentioned, are not experienced through perspectives, they are not visible. Presumably, they are not perceived by the other senses either.

In the unpublished manuscript *Noema und Sinn,* however, to which I referred earlier, Husserl is more explicit on this point. He says there, in a long passage which I will quote in full:

> The perception is perception "of" ("von") this Sinn, but not in the way in which the perception is perception of this house. The perception "has" the Sinn, but the Sinn is not perceived. Now I judge with respect to the perception that it has this Sinn, and that it accordingly (according to its Sinn) is characterized as perception of a renaissance building, whose façade has sandstone columns etc. If I close my eyes and have the house correspondingly given to me in memory, then I say again of the memory that is it memory of the same Sinn, in it the same thing is presented through memory which was formerly perceived. And if I am describing a mere fantasy, then I say again that according to its Sinn, it is a fantasy of . . . and there is the possibility that a fantasy has exactly the same Sinn as a perception (NuS p. 4).

Again, Husserl is talking about the noematic Sinn, but as noted above the remark presumably applies to all components of the noema.

One might wonder how, then, one gets to know anything about the noemata. Husserl's answer is

10. Noemata are known through a special reflection, the phenomenological reflection.

Our earlier theses on the noema now help us to see what this reflection is and what it is not. It is a grasping of a Sinn. To quote Husserl: "Toward this Sinn . . . one may always direct a peculiar reflection, and *only* what is grasped in it is the basis of the phenomenological judgment" (p. 222). Also in *Noema und Sinn* Husserl stresses that "the reflecting judgment of phenomenology and logic is directed toward the Sinn, hence not toward that which is the object of the nonreflecting judgment itself" (NuS pp. 99–100). That the whole noema and not just the noematic Sinn is reflected upon, is made clear in several places, for example, in *Ideen,* p. 369.

Phenomenological reflection is, hence, not a special way of looking or using our senses; the objects grasped in phenomenological reflection are, as we have already observed in the preceding two theses, abstract and nonperceivable.

According to Husserl,

11. The phenomenological reflection can be iterated.

That is, to quote *Noema und Sinn,* "The Sinn corresponding to an object is in its turn an object . . . it can be made the object of a judgment. . . . As such it has a Sinn of the second level: the Sinn of a Sinn . . . hence we come to an infinite regress, insofar as the Sinn of the Sinn may in its turn be made an object and then again has a Sinn and so on" (NuS pp. 107–108). As Husserl points out, this again has a consequence that "the Sinn cannot be a real component of the object" (NuS p. 108).

This is one of many striking similarities between Husserl's notion of noema and Frege's notion of Sinn. There are also important differences, however. Thus, for example, whereas Frege held that in contexts like "believes that . . .' terms refer not to their ordinary reference but to their ordinary Sinn, Husserl held, as we have seen (thesis 4), that acts normally are directed toward ordinary objects and not toward Sinne or noemata of such objects. This leads to major differences in their analyses of act contexts.

We might like to know in much greater detail what noemata are. Like Frege, Husserl is not very helpful. One of the few hints Frege gave concerning his Sinne was that they serve to illuminate aspects of the reference.[3] This fits the noemata to some extent, in that acts with a common object but with different noemata can be said to focus on different aspects of their object, to grasp it from different points of view. Also, Husserl, like Frege, held that a physical object has an infinity of noemata and Sinne corresponding to it and can never be exhausted by any of them. Physical objects are "transcendent," to use Husserl's term (*Ideen,* I, pp. 100, 238 ff.; compare Frege, "Über Sinn und Bedeutung," p. 27).

Husserl gives more help. According to thesis 3 above, the noema, or more precisely the noematic Sinn, is that in virtue of which consciousness relates to an object. Take seeing as an example. That seeing is intentional, object-directed, means that the near side of the thing we have in front of us is regarded only as a side of a thing, and that the thing we are seeing has other sides and determinations which are co-intended to the extent that the full thing is regarded as something more than the one side. These determinations are not perceptually filled; they are more or less vaguely represented, and lead us to further perceptual processes which make the invisible visible. (Merleau-Ponty, *Phen. of Perception*).

The noema is a complex system of such determinations (*Ideen,*

I, p. 93) which make a multitude of visual, tactile, and other data be appearances of one object (*op. cit.*, pp. 173–174). To quote Husserl: "The pure perceptual data . . . are not themselves perspectives, but they become perspectives through that which we also call apprehension (Auffassung), just that which gives them the subjective function of being appearances of the objective" (*op. cit.*, p. 163).

It is in this way, through perspectives, that we perceive objects. As long as the further course of our experience fits the more or less vaguely predelineated pattern, we continue to perceive the same object and get an ever more many-sided experience of it, without exhausting the pattern, which develops with our experience of the object to include new, still unexperienced determinations. Sometimes our experiences do not fit into the predelineated pattern. We get an "explosion" of the noema, and a new noema of a new and different object. We are subject to misperception, to illusion or hallucination, as the case may be, and we say that the old act did not have the object that it seemed to have.

12. This pattern of determinations, together with the "Gegebenheitsweise," is the noema.

My twelve theses concerning the noema by no means exhaust the subject; they barely put us in a position to ask questions like: If phenomenology is a study of meaning, in an extended sense, then what light does it throw upon the questions concerning meaning that have played a major role in philosophy since its beginnings and which are a major concern of so many contemporary philosophers? Does phenomenology overcome the difficulties that are besetting so many ancient and recent theories of meaning? A close study of Husserl's work can, I think, give partial answers to these questions. And, even if the answers should be negative, I trust that such a study will help to bring out more clearly what these difficulties consist of.

5

Husserl's Identification of Meaning and Noema

Ronald McIntyre and David Woodruff Smith

The key notion in Husserl's theory of intentionality, and perhaps in his phenomenology, is that of *noema*, Husserl's notion of the content of a mental act. Husserl conceives *noemata* as "meanings." The force of this conception of noemata, we shall argue, is that, for Husserl, *linguistic* meanings—the meanings (*Bedeutungen*) that are expressed in language—and noematic meanings—the meanings (*Sinne*) that attach to acts (strictly the object-determining components)—are one and the same. For, according to Husserl, every linguistic meaning is a noematic Sinn expressed, and every noematic Sinn is in principle expressible and therefore a linguistic meaning.

1. Husserl's Conception of Linguistic Meaning

In the first of his *Logical Investigations*[1] Husserl explicitly discusses linguistic, or semantic, meaning—which he calls Bedeutung. He supports a threefold distinction between subjective mental events; the objective entities, including concrete physical things, to which words customarily refer; and the equally objective, but abstract, entities that words express as their meanings (*LI*, I, § 6, p. 276).

Linguistic meanings are thus not events of consciousness. In contrast with the "real" events that occur as temporal constituents of a stream of consciousness, meanings are "ideal" entities. Husserl uses two different terms that might translate as 'real,' both of which carry implications of temporality. 'Reell,' which he uses to characterize events in the stream of consciousness, seems to mean "occurring in internal, or phenomenological, time." His other term, 'real,' he says, "keeps the notion of thinglike transcendence which the reduction to 'reell' immanence in experience is meant to exclude" (*LI*, V, §16, p. 577, n. 2*): it thus seems to mean "occurring in external, or objective, time." Yet a third term, 'wirklich,' is used (not quite consistently) by Husserl to characterize physical individuals occurring in both external time and external space. To say that meanings are "ideal" is just to say that they are not "real" in *any* of these senses.

Husserl considers different kinds of entities to be ideal: in particular, meanings, "species," and numbers. "Species," so-called in *Logical Investigations,* are a kind of universals; in *Ideas* and his later writings Husserl calls them (along with numbers and perhaps other sorts of abstract entities) "essences." The recognition of meanings as ideal entities thus does not precisely determine their ontological category. In the first edition of *Logical Investigations* (1900/1901), Husserl emphasized the "shared" character of meanings: the acts of consciousness underlying a speaker's utterance and a hearer's understanding seem to involve a *common* entity as meaning. Husserl thus assumed meanings to be a kind of "species," or "universal objects," which are instantiated by such particular acts but which—in keeping with their ideality—exist independently of their instantiations (cf. *LI,* I, §31, p. 330). On this view, meanings are properties shared by speakers' and hearers' acts of intending the same object or the same type of object, properties characterizing them as directed to these entities. Even at this point Husserl was careful to distinguish meanings, taken as universals instantiated by acts, both from the objects of those acts and from related essences or properties of objects. The property of being red, for example, is an essence of all red *objects;* but the meaning "red," on this view, is a property of *acts* directed to red things.

By the time of *Ideas* (1913), when Husserl had developed a more general notion of act-meaning (Sinn), the view that meanings are act-essences, properties literally instantiated by acts, had been abandoned. There he adopted instead the view that meanings are abstract entities correlated with acts and expressible by words but in no sense properties or parts of acts. Apparently he came to think of them as sui generis, perhaps as a special sort of abstract particulars. Such entities are today called "intensional" entities.

2. *Every Linguistic Meaning is a Noematic* Sinn

Linguistic meanings, as intensional entities, are ontologically independent of consciousness. Yet, Husserl maintains, they stand in close relation to consciousness, for language is used to make public what is in our minds. Husserl says:

> All expressions in *communicative* speech function as *indications*. They serve the hearer as signs of the "thoughts" of the speaker, i.e., of his meaning-giving (*sinngebenden*) mental processes (*psychischen Erlebnisse*).
> (*LI*, I, §7, p. 277*)

These "thoughts" or "meaning-giving" acts of the speaker are, Husserl says, "intimated" (*kundgibt*) or—in ordinary language—"expressed" by the speaker's utterance of the expressions (*LI*, I, §7, p. 277). We shall argue that for Husserl the meanings (Bedeutungen) *expressed* by words are the noematic Sinne of the "meaning-giving" acts of consciousness underlying and intimated by the utterings of the words. So, on Husserl's view, *linguistic* meanings are themselves *act*-meanings. [2*]

Linguistic behavior is complicated business. To express a meaning in words is to perform an "action," a bit of bodily behavior related to underlying intentional processes of consciousness. The bodily aspect of a "speech-act" (a term that Husserl does not use) consists of producing an expression—that is, a sound pattern or written inscription (*LI*, V, §19, p. 583). But a *meaningful* utterance of an expression also has its intentional aspect. Husserl says:

> The meaning-animated (*sinnbelebten*) expression breaks up, on the one hand, into the *physical phenomenon* forming the physical side of the expression, and, on the other hand, into the *acts* which give it meaning (*Bedeutung*)....
> (*LI*, I, §9, p. 280*) [3]

Linguistic behavior may be initiated by various volitions, depending on just what the speaker hopes to bring about by means of the behavior. But in any case (except soliloquy), the speaker aims to achieve his end by conveying a certain meaning to the hearer by uttering certain words. In *every* speech act (even soliloquy), Husserl says, the speaker must be acting with the purpose of *expressing a meaning* by uttering the appropriate words. Otherwise, he will merely be making sounds without really *saying* anything.

> The articulated sound-complex (the written sign, etc.) first becomes a spoken word or communicative bit of speech when the speaker produces it with the purpose (*Absicht*) of "expressing himself about something" by its means, in other words when in certain mental acts he lends (*verleiht*) it a meaning (*Sinn*) which he wants to communicate with the hearers.
>
> (*LI*, I, §7, pp. 276-277*)

The passage just cited also tells us what it is for a person purposefully to "express himself about something": certain of his *acts* of consciousness "confer on" or "lend" (*verleiht*) his words their meaning (Sinn). These acts Husserl variously calls *meaning-giving* acts (*sinngebenden Akte; Akte welche Bedeutung geben*) or *meaning-lending* (*sinnverleihenden, bedeutungverleihenden*) acts (cf. *LI*, I §§7, 9). "In virtue of such acts," he says, "the expression is more than a merely sounded word. It *means* (*meint*) something . . ." (*LI*, §9, p. 280).

Husserl's metaphor of "giving meaning" is to be taken quite literally: the meaning "given" the uttered expression in a speech act *is* just the noematic Sinn of the "meaning-giving" act that "underlies" the speech act. In that underlying act—as in acts of consciousness generally—we intend a certain object or state of affairs, and we intend it via the act's noematic Sinn.[4] This intended object is what receives our primary attention in the speech act:

> When we normally execute an expressing as such, we do not *live* in the acts which constitute the expression as a physical object; our "interest" does not belong to this object; rather, we live in the meaning-giving (*sinngebenden*) acts; we are exclusively *turned toward* the objective (*Gegenständlichen*) that appears in them; we *aim* at it, we *mean* (*meinen*; intend) it in the special, *pregnant* sense [i.e., attentively].   (*LI*, V, §19, p. 584*)

If we succeed in communicating with our hearer, we will convey to him a meaning whereby he will come to intend this same object. Indeed, he will intend it through the same noematic Sinn we do (barring, we might caution, adjustments for demonstrative pronouns such as 'this,' 'here,' etc.). For, according to Husserl, *the meaning expressed as the Bedeutung of the words is the meaning, the noematic Sinn, of the underlying act.* This meaning is what is communicated from speaker to hearer. So the underlying act literally "gives" or "lends" its meaning to the expression uttered in the speech act.

In *Logical Investigations* Husserl seems usually to presuppose rather than explicitly to state this key point, that a Bedeutung expressed in language *is* the noematic Sinn of an underlying, meaning-conferring act.[5] But opening his later (1929) *Formal and Transcendental Logic,* he is both explicit and clear. In par. 3, on "Language as an Expression of 'Thinking,'" Husserl says:

> In speaking we are continuously performing an internal act of meaning (act of meaning = *Meinen*), which fuses with the words and, as it were, animates them. The effect of this animation is that the words and the entire locution, as it were, *embody* in themselves a meaning (*Meinung*), and bear it embodied in them as their sense (*Sinn*). [Husserl here footnotes *LI,* I.] [In] this act of meaning (*Meinen*) . . . there is constituted . . . the meaning (*Meinung*)—that is, the *Bedeutung, the Sinn*—expressed in the locution. For example, if we utter a judgment, we have effected, in union with the words of our assertive statement, a unity of judging, of inwardly "thinking" asserting. No matter what other psychic producings may also be effected, . . . we shall pay attention only to what is fused on, namely *the acts of judging that function as meaning-giving (sinngebende) acts,* i.e., that *bear in themselves the judicial meaning* or opinion (*Urteilsmeinung*) *that finds its expression in the assertoric sentence.*[6]

So, Husserl says, the meaning expressed in an assertively uttered sentence *is* the meaning (the noematic Sinn) of the speaker's underlying act of judging; and it is this expressed meaning that the speaker communicates to his hearer. Suppose, for example, that Holmes has just completed a bit of brilliant "deduction," thus coming to believe that the murderer is in this very room. This judgment is an act of consciousness: its object, on Husserl's view, is a state of affairs—the murderer's being in this very room—and its noema includes a Sinn, in virtue of which Holmes's judgment is directed to this state of affairs. Now let us suppose that Holmes wishes to share this bit of information with Watson: he turns to Watson and says, "The murderer is in this very room." It is part of Holmes's purpose in uttering these words to express the noematic Sinn of his act of judgment, so that Watson can also intend the same state of affairs through that same Sinn. Holmes succeeds in *communicating* with Watson, in "sharing" that Sinn, only because the meaning (Bedeutung) expressed by his words *is* the noematic Sinn of his judgment and becomes the noematic Sinn of Watson's intention.

The simple kind of assertion represented by this example is a special case of what Husserl takes as a more general account of the relation of expressed meaning to acts. The acts whose meanings are expressed will be different for different kinds of speech acts. And the acts whose Sinne are expressed in any case need not be actually occurrent: an assertion, for example, may be accompanied not by an occurrent act of judging, but by the disposition so to judge, i.e., by a belief. Husserl's general view is that words used in speech acts, of whatever kind, express as *their* meanings the noematic Sinne of acts of consciousness: the meanings (Bedeutungen) expressed in words are themselves the meanings of acts— that is, noematic Sinne. This view, which pervades *Logical Investigations* (especially the sixth), is explicitly recapitulated in *Formal and Transcendental Logic:*

> What we have learned from the example of the assertive statement holds good universally. . . . *Thinking* includes . . . every mental process (*Erlebnis*) in which the Sinn that is to become expressed becomes constituted in the manner peculiar to consciousness—the Sinn that, if it does become expressed, is called the Bedeutung of the expression, particularly of the locution as used on the particular occasion. The process is called thinking, whether it is a judging, a willing, an asking, or an uncertain presuming. [7]

We need not go further here into a discussion of the phenomenology of language. What is central to our concerns is the connection between linguistic meaning and noematic Sinn. As we see that linguistic meanings are themselves noematic Sinne expressed, we begin to see that Husserl takes the noematic Sinne of acts and the linguistic meanings expressed in language to be the same entities. But the main argument for identifying noematic Sinne with linguistic meanings lies with the thesis that the noematic Sinn of any act is in principle expressible in language. So let us turn now to that thesis.

3. *Every Noematic Sinn is a Linguistic Meaning*

Husserl, we have argued, sees linguistic meanings as the meanings, the noematic Sinne, of acts. Linguistic expressions serve to express in publicly observable behavior the Sinne of intentional acts of consciousness. In this way language serves to make our intendings known to others. In this section we consider Husserl's thesis that *every* noematic Sinn is in principle expressible in language. This thesis is the basis of our claim that noemata and their components are "intensional entities."

In assertion we *express* the noematic Sinn of, say, a judgment. This meaning, in virtue of its being expressed, is called a "linguistic" meaning or Bedeutung. But Husserl believes that acts and their meanings are not intrinsically linguistic. One may judge something without *saying* anything at all. Indeed, *every* act, "publicized" or not, has a meaning, the same meaning it would have if it were put into language. It is this general notion of meaning, expressed or not and pertinent to all acts, that Husserl calls 'Sinn.' He says:

> Originally these words ('Bedeuten' and 'Bedeutung') relate only to the sphere of speech, of "expression." But it is almost inevitable and at the same time an important advance for knowledge to extend and suitably to modify the meaning of these words so that in a certain way they apply to . . . all acts, whether these involve expressive acts or not. . . . We use the word 'Sinn' . . . in its wider application. (*Ideas*, §124, p. 304)

Sinn is thus conceived as an extension of Bedeutung, so that meaning as Sinn is no longer exclusively, intrinsically, or even primarily a linguistic notion. (Strictly speaking, 'Sinn' refers to the component of an act's noema that accounts for the act's directedness to its object. But the *whole* noema, Husserl suggests, may also be thought of as a Sinn in a less specific use of the term: cf. *Ideas* 90:223). Acts such as hoping, remembering, imagining, and perceiving have meanings in the general sense of Sinne. And although there is nothing intrinsically linguistic about these acts and their meanings, their Sinne are intensional entities of a kind with the meanings expressed in language. We might not commonly think of a person "hoping aloud," "imagining aloud," or (especially) "perceiving aloud"; yet the Sinne of all these acts are expressible in language.

Indeed, *any* Sinn, the noematic Sinn of *any* (actual or possible) act whatsoever, is in principle expressible through language. And when the Sinn of an act *is* expressed, as we saw in section 12 above, *it* is the Bedeutung of the words that express it. Whether a Sinn actually is expressed or not, Husserl believes, there is, or in principle could be developed, some linguistic expression whose Bedeutung is that Sinn. This we may call the *expressibility thesis*. Husserl asserts it explicitly in *Ideas:*

Whatever is "meant (*Gemeinte*) as such," every meaning (*Meinung*) in the noematic Sinn . . . of any act whatsoever is expressible through "linguistic meanings" (*durch* "*Bedeutungen*"). . . . "Expression" is a remarkable form, which allows itself to be adapted to all "Sinne" . . . and raises them to the realm of "*Logos.*"   (124:305)

The expressibility of noematic Sinne finally makes good the claim that they are *intensions.* Where we first saw that every Bedeutung is a Sinn expressed, we now see that every Sinn is expressible, hence (at least potentially) a Bedeutung. In short, we have here just *one* class of meaning entities—noematic Sinne—that play a role both in language and in acts of consciousness generally. The *intensional* entities that get expressed in language and the noematic entities that mediate the intentionality of acts are the *very same* entities. With this identification of noematic Sinn and linguistic meaning, Husserl's antipsychologistic view of meaning generalizes from a thesis about logic and semantics to a thesis about phenomenology and theory of intentionality generally: noematic Sinne are nonpsychological intensional entities.

The expressibility thesis is important for understanding Husserl. But let us take care that we not misconstrue the claim it makes. In the first place, the thesis does not claim that every Sinn has actually been expressed. Nor does it claim that actually existing natural languages—or even humanly possible languages—are rich enough to express every Sinn. Husserl says in *Logical Investigations:*

There is . . . no intrinsic connection between the ideal unities which in fact operate as meanings (*Bedeutungen*), and the signs to which they are tied. . . . We cannot therefore say that all ideal unities of this sort are expressed meanings. Wherever a new concept is formed, we see how a meaning becomes realized that was previously unrealized. As numbers—in the ideal sense that arithmetic presupposes—neither spring forth nor vanish with the act of enumeration, . . . so it is with . . . meanings . . . to which being thought or being expressed are alike contingent. There are therefore countless meanings which . . . are merely possible ones, since they are never expressed, and since they can, owing to the limits of man's cognitive powers, never be expressed.   (I, 35:333)

A second point warranting care is that the thesis as formulated applies specifically to the noematic Sinn of any act. But, in addition to its expressible Sinn, the noema of an act includes other components, correlated with what Husserl calls the *Gegeben-*

heitsweise, or "way of givenness" of the act (*Ideas,* §§91, 92, 99, 132, 133). These components relate to the degree of clarity with which the object of an act is intended, the features of the object that are singled out for attention, the "intuitional fullness" (if any) of the act, and the act's "thetic character." Husserl argues that when an act is brought to expression, these further components are *not* part of the Bedeutung expressed.

The reason seems largely to be that the meanings we share when we communicate in language are—and are intended to be—invariant with respect to the more particular aspects of their presence in particular acts. "Talk of sameness of sense, of sameness of understanding of words and sentences," Husserl says in *Logical Investigations,* "points to something which does not vary in the varied acts thus brought to expression" (V, §30, p. 617). And because of the "generality of expression, he says in *Ideas,* "never can all the particularities of the expressed be reflected in the expression" (§126, p. 310). Husserl specifically cites clarity and attentiveness as such particular features of acts, features whose noematic correlates are apparently too idiosyncratic to be expressed.

For roughly the same reason, any "intuitional" element in an act's noema is not expressed when the act is brought to expression. The noema of an intuitive act, such as visually perceiving an object, and the noema of a non-intuitive presentation of the same object (merely thinking of it, for example) may have the very same Sinn (*Ideas,* §91; *LI,* V, §20). But merely to think of an object is far from actually *seeing,* "intuiting" it. In the intuitive act the object is *sensuously* given, experienced with what Husserl calls "intuitional fullness" (cf. *LI,* VI, esp. §§21-29). This "fullness" is reflected in the act's noema, as a noematic correlate distinct from the act's noematic Sinn. But when a perceptual act is brought to expression, Husserl says, the expressed "content" is "the identical meaning (Bedeutung) that the hearer can grasp even if he is not a perceiver" (*LI,* I, §14, p. 209*). Since the noema of a nonperceptual act has no "fullness" component, the Sinn, but not the fullness component, of a perceptual noema is what is expressed as a Bedeutung when expression is founded on an underlying perception.

Another component of an act, also reflected in the act's noema, is what Husserl calls the act's "thetic character," the kind or species of the act, marking it as an act of perception, or memory, or whatever (*Ideas,* §§91, 92, 99). In *Logical Investigations,*

(VI, §2) Husserl effectively maintains that when an act is brought to expression, the noematic component correlated with its thetic character is not part of the meaning expressed. Husserl's point there has nothing to do with "generality." Rather, it is simply that, for instance, in expressing his judgment that the murderer is in this very room, what Holmes expresses is the Bedeutung "The murderer is in this very room"; he does not express the Bedeutung "I judge that the murderer is in this very room." (The latter would be the Sinn of a *different* act, Holmes's act of reflecting on his original judgment and judging that he had so judged.)

So, for Husserl *only the Sinn* of the act underlying an expressive utterance is expressed. Nonetheless, Husserl's discussion of different senses of "expressing" an act in *Logical Investigations* (VI, §§2-3) suggests that further noema components *are* expressible in a more indirect way. When I judge that *p* and I say "*p*," I express the Sinn but not the thetic component of the noema of my judgment. When I say "I judge that *p*," though, I express the Sinn of another judgment *about* my first judgment (cf. *LI*, VI, §2; *Ideas*, §127, p. 313). Now, although Husserl does not explicitly say so, this second Sinn includes both the Sinn *and* the thetic component of the noema of my first judgment. In Husserl's primary sense of "expressing" an act, my first utterance expresses my first judgment: it is this judgment that lends its Sinn to the uttered words. And my second utterance expresses, in that sense, my second judgment. But in Husserl's second sense of "expressing" an act, my *second* utterance "expresses" my *first* judgment: both Sinn and thetic components of my first judgment's noema appear in the Bedeutung of the uttered words, for both are included in my second judgment's more complicated Sinn, the Sinn that serves as that Bedeutung. In this way the thetic component of my first judgment's noema is "expressed" as a Bedeutung in my second utterance. Intuitiveness, and also clarity and attentiveness, probably ought also to be expressible in this indirect way. To generalize, it thus seems that all noematic components are capable of serving as components of *some* Sinn and are in that sense expressible as linguistic Bedeutungen.

This point, though Husserl does not formulate it himself, would ensure that all noematic components are intensional entities. Indeed, there is evidence that Husserl did conceive of the noema and all of its components—and not just of the noematic Sinn—as meanings or intensions. Of the *Gegebenheitsweise* components Husserl says, "As *characters of* the, so to speak, 'ideal' (*'Ideellen'*) they themselves are 'ideal' and not real (*reell*)" (*Ideas,* §99, p. 250). And Husserl sometimes uses the word 'Sinn' to describe the complete noema. When, as is the rule, he reserves 'Sinn' for the object-oriented component of the noema (the "objective Sinn" or "noematic Sinn"), he suggests that the word 'Satz' ('proposition') would appropriately describe the combination of the noema's Sinn component and thetic component (*Ideas,* §133, p. 324). Either terminology reinforces the interpretation of the whole noema and its components as intensions.

The importance of expressibility, we have seen, is that it is what finally identifies noematic Sinn and linguistic meaning. And the importance of that identification is twofold.

That noematic Sinne are expressible, and hence linguistic meanings, shows that noemata as conceived by Husserl are more familiar than we might have thought. Because noemata and specifically Sinne are the heart of Husserl's theory of intentionality (hence, of his phenomenology), Husserl himself spent an extraordinary amount of effort and ink on describing how to become acquainted with noemata and noematic Sinne. The method he called "epoche" or "transcendental-phenomenological reduction." The result he sought is a direct, reflective acquaintance with noemata—or, more generally, with that which is "transcendental," including noemata and also "noeses," "hyletic data," and the "transcendental ego." The difficulty with phenomenological reflection, though, is not so much whether we *can* do it as just *how* to do it. And Husserl's descriptions of how to do it, in terms of "bracketing" or "suspending" any positing of the existence of the object of consciousness, are not terribly helpful. We do, however, already know and understand a good deal of language. If Husserl's view of language is correct, we thus already have a working acquaintance with lots of *linguistic* meanings. And since these meanings are themselves noematic Sinne, that means we already have, by way of our language, a working acquaintance with lots of noematic Sinne. Even in the absence of a clear description of *how* noemata are grasped, the expressibility of Sinne assures us that they *are* familiar and that we *do* grasp them all the time.

Just as Husserl's identification of noematic Sinn and linguistic meaning illuminates his notion of noema, so also it puts the notion of linguistic meaning itself into a broader perspective.

That linguistic meanings are themselves noematic Sinne emphasizes the fact that referring, asserting, and linguistic activities
generally, are founded on underlying *intentional* phenomena.
Independently of whether he is completely correct on the details
of how language and intention mesh, Husserl's valuable insights
into the role of meaning in intentionality generally deserve the
closest attention of philosophers of language.

6

Husserl's Theory of Perception

Dagfinn Føllesdal

In acts of perception our senses play a role, providing certain boundary conditions which the noema has to fit. These boundary conditions are found in all acts of perception, and also in some other acts in which our senses play a role, for example acts of remembering brought about by sensory impressions. According to Husserl, whenever our senses are stimulated, we have certain experiences called *hyle* or hyletic data, from the Greek word for matter (ὕλη). These experiences are not by themselves experiences of an object, but they normally occur as components of more comprehensive experiences, acts, which in addition to the hyle contain experiences of an intentional kind, the noeses. The noesis "informs" the hyle, so that this multitude of visual, tactile, and other data is unified into a set of appearances of one object.

The color of an object, its shape, and various other of its features are objects of our acts, and are experienced in the way we experience physical objects. They are objective entities, experienceable by various subjects from various perspectives. The round shape of a table top, for example, may be experienced as round, elliptical, etc., depending on our point of view. Likewise, its color will appear different depending on light conditions, whether

we wear colored glasses, etc., and a tone will sound different depending on the acoustics of the room, our location in it, etc.
Shapes, colors, sounds, etc. are *perspected variables,* Husserl says,
as opposed to the *perspective variations* through which we are
aware of them. These perspective variations are examples of what
Husserl calls hyletic data. The perspected variable and the perspective variations are interdependent, linked through the complex
system of determinations which we have called the noema. Part of
what the phenomenology of perception sets out to do is to explore these basic principles of perception according to which the
perspective variations are linked together, so as to be perspectives
of one perspected variable.

It is, however, only within the context of the full act, with its
noetic components, that the hyle can be identified with perspective variations. To quote Husserl: "The pure perceptual data ...
are not themselves perspectives, but they become perspectives
through that which we also call apprehension (*Auffassung*), just
that which gives them the subjective function of being appearances
of the objective."[1]

In a full act, all the noetic and hyletic components together
make it an act with some particular object. Within the act there
are certain subunits, certain noeses informing certain hyle into a
perspective of the act's object. It is these various perspectives that
Husserl somewhat misleadingly calls sense data.

In one of the best books on the subject, Aron Gurwitsch
criticizes Husserl for holding that hyletic data "remain really
unchanged with regard to the different noeses operating upon
them." Gurwitsch argues that "data devoid of all articulation,
hyletic data in the strict sense, do not exist at all. What is given
depends on the structural connections within which it appears."[2]

However, Husserl was well aware of this difficulty. In *Ideen*[3]
he characterizes the hyle-noesis schema as provisional, and in a
manuscript dated between 1918 and 1921 he writes:

> We can not place side by side two components in intuition, sense and fil-
> ling. We can only obtain the difference by contrasting the empty and the
> filled sense, that is, through a synthesis of intuition and empty conscious-
> ness. Perhaps we could say: the abstract identical, that we call sense with
> regard to different acts of consciousness, is an essence (sense-essence),
> which particularizes in a special mode, and in two basic modes: in the
> mode of intuition [Anschaulichkeit] (and within the realm of perception

in the mode of primordial intuition [*originäre Anschaulichkeit*]) and in the mode of non-intuition, the empty mode.[4]

Hence, there are no noeses-independent hyletic data that can be re-identified from one act to another. The hyle can perhaps only be characterized as something ego-foreign that enters into our acts and limits what we can experience—that is, limits the stock of noemata that are possible in a given situation. The assortment is never narrowed to just one; it is fundamental to the phenomenological view of perception that the material factors never uniquely determine the noema of an act, nor even its object.

A. Example

By way of illustration of the preceding, consider, for example, the perception of a tree. When we see a tree, we see something with a number of sides and aspects that are not at that moment facing us. The noema of our act has a number of components that are not filled by hyle. By moving around and using our senses, more and more of these components can be filled. While we do this, some of the components that are presently filled will no longer remain filled, but they still remain determined, because of our memory of past filling. During this process the noema is being continuously replaced by a series of more and more rich and refined noemata of the object, and as long as our further experience remains harmonious, we come to have an ever more confirmed belief that there is a tree in front of us, which has the properties we attribute to it. However, if a conflict arises in this process, if we come to have hyle that are incompatible with our noema, an "explosion" of the noema takes place, and the noema is replaced by a noema of a different object. Thus if we go around the tree and find no back side, we say no longer that we see a tree, but perhaps that we see a stage prop or have an hallucination.

B. Hallucinations

When one hallucinates, one has hyle that fit with some components of a noema of some ordinary physical object, but other hyle are missing—corresponding, for example, to other senses. For an hallucination there is no object; we have only some hyle and a noema and noesis, as if there were some object there.

Hallucinations are different from misperceptions in that in the case of the hallucination there is no noema of any object that can replace the original noema and fit harmoniously with all further use of our senses. In hallucination the hyle one has cannot be regarded as brought about by some causal chain in which the object of the act plays a part, there being no object of the act. Instead, the hyle are regarded as due to the influence of illness, drugs, etc. on the organism. Studies concerning the causal origin of the hyle are, of course, part of pyschology, not phenomenology. That is, they take place in the natural attitude, not in the reflective phenomenological attitude.

C. Illusions

Illusions, together with hallucinations, are a source of some of the major philosophical problems of perception and at the same time a touchstone for the adequacy of any theory of perception. Particularly, theories like Husserl's, according to which we are perceiving physical objects and their properties and not sense data, often turn out to be inadequate to handle illusions.

According to Husserl, illusions are transcendent objects[5]; like material objects in general, they can be observed by different observers, and noemata of illusions contain determinations of the various hyle we will have when we move around, put a measuring rod along the object, etc. Illusions differ from ordinary physical objects in that the pattern of determinations in the noema is different from what it normally is.

Consider, for example, the well-known illusions in which two equal lines appear to be of unequal length. Looking at the two lines, I may be aware that I am having an illusion and expect that the two lines will come out the same length when measured by a measuring rod. In this case I am, at least so far, correctly perceiving an object. Or, being unfamiliar with this illusion, I may expect the readings of the measuring rod to be different, in which case there is no object corresponding to my noema. I am misperceiving, because of my being confronted with an object so unlike anything I have experienced to that point.

7

Husserl's Perceptual Noema

Hubert L. Dreyfus

Everyone who has studied Husserl's *Ideas* would agree that the notion of the noema is central to Husserl's theory of consciousness and, in particular, that the notion of the perceptual noema is central to the Husserlian theory of perception. This should be no surprise, since for Husserl intentionality is the defining feature of consciousness, and intentionality is defined in terms of the necessary correlation of noesis and noema. What is surprising is that running through the commentaries on Husserl's theory of consciousness there is a fundamental disagreement as to what Husserl has in mind when he speaks of the perceptual noema. Moreover, this division seems to go completely unnoticed.

The opposition is obscured by the tendency of all interpreters to explain the noema in terms of a set of synonyms proposed by Husserl himself. Thus all would readily agree that the perceptual noema is the intentional correlate of perceptual consciousness: it is neither a (*real*) physical object, nor a (*reell*) momentary state of consciousness, but rather a meaning, an ideal entity correlated with every act of perception, whether the object intended in that act exists or not.

Two interpreters, however, have undertaken the task of translating Husserl's technical vocabulary into other terms and in so doing have unwittingly revealed a systematic ambiguity running through the whole constellation of noema terminology. Crudely put, Dagfinn Føllesdal interprets the perceptual noema as a concept, while Aron Gurwitsch takes it to be a percept. Føllesdal traces the development of the perceptual noema back to Husserl's adoption of Frege's distinction of sense and reference. According to Føllesdal the perceptual noema is an "abstract entity"[1] "in virtue of which an act of perception is directed toward its object."[2] The noema itself is never sensuously given but is "entertained" in a special act of reflection called the phenomenological reduction.

Gurwitsch, on the other hand, while recognizing the Fregean filiation of the concept, has attempted to explicate Husserl's notion of the perceptual noema in terms of the findings of Gestalt theory. Thus for Gurwitsch the perceptual noema is a concrete sensuous appearance, through which the object of perception is presented: "We interpret the perceptual noema ... as a Gestalt-contexture whose constituents are what is given in a direct sense experience."[3] This noema is not, in a strict sense, perceived, since only a physical object can be perceived. It is, however, perceptually given and can be thematized in a special act of attending to the perceptual object—Gurwitsch's version of the phenomenological reduction.

Føllesdal's reading is recent and claims to do nothing more than explicate the Husserlian texts, so it has not given rise to a school of interpretation.[4*] Gurwitsch's version, however, dating from 1929 and proposing to "advance and to develop further rather than merely expound"[5] Husserl's view, has had a broad influence. The Gurwitschian interpretation of the noema is taken for granted in the works of Cairns,[6*] Schutz,[7*] Boehm,[8] Fink,[9] Solomon,[10*] and Tugendhat,[11*] to emerge transformed into a criticism of Husserl in the writings of Merleau-Ponty.

The ambiguity revealed by these interpretations so consistently contaminates the terms Husserl uses to explain his noema that it has so far proven impossible to decide definitively which of these two interpretations is correct.[12*] In any case, that decision is more important for the historian of philosophy than for the phenomenologist. What is important for us is to work out the conception of consciousness and of phenomenology which follows from each view and then to decide which interpretation fits the phenomena.

In keeping with this goal, the first section of this paper, although incidentally marshaling evidence that the Føllesdal interpretation of the noema is more consistent with Husserl's development, is mainly meant to bring out the stark contrast between two possible antecedents of the noema. This contrast then enables us in the following section to understand Gurwitsch's interpretation of the noema as an attempt to fill a fundamental gap in Husserl's system and, incidentally, it enables us also to marshal evidence that this is not what Husserl could or did propose. Then in the final section we will be in a position to see how Gurwitsch's radical and original interpretation of the perceptual noema, if frankly and consistently read back into Husserl's thought, would lead to a total transformation of Husserl's project for doing transcendental phenomenology.

Husserl's Conceptualization of Perception— The Noema as Interpretive Sense

All Husserl interpreters agree that the perceptual noema, introduced by Husserl in *Ideas,* represents a generalization of Husserl's theory of meaning to perception. To understand the noema, then, we must follow this process of generalization.

In the First Logical Investigation, Husserl begins by distinguishing the physical manifestations of linguistic expressions (noises, marks on paper, etc.) from the acts of consciousness which give them meaning. Then, turning to an analysis of the meaning-conferring acts, Husserl notes that such acts are always correlated with a meaning or sense. It is by virtue of this sense that an expression intends or means an object, regardless of whether the object aimed at is actually present in a fulfilling intuition. Since the meaning does not depend on the existence of anything beyond the act itself, Husserl calls the meaning the content of the act. This ideal content, Husserl declares, does not belong to the real world of changing objects or even to our stream of consciousness, since this too belongs to the "temporal sphere." Rather, "meanings constitute . . . a class of concepts in the sense of 'universal objects.'"[13]

Husserl's analysis of linguistic expressions in terms of meaning-giving act, ideal meaning, and fulfilling intuition exactly parallels the distinctions of idea, sense, and reference in Frege's article "On Sense and Reference."[14] This is no coincidence. Husserl's first book, *The Philosophy of Arithmetic,* was criticized by Frege for being too psychologistic—that is, for "a blurring of the distinction between image and concept, between imagination and thought." Images, Frege had argued, are psychic events confined to each man's mind, whereas "it is quite otherwise for thoughts; one and the same thought can be grasped by many men."[15]

Husserl simply accepted and applied Frege's distinctions:

> The essence of meaning is seen by us, not in the meaning-conferring experience, but in its "content," the single, self-identical intentional unity set over against the dispersed multiplicity of actual and possible experiences of speakers and thinkers.[16]

The only change Husserl made in Frege's analysis was terminological. Husserl proposes to use "object" (*Gegenstand*) for "reference" (*Bedeutung*), and "meaning" and "sense" (Bedeutung and *Sinn*) interchangeably for "sense" (Sinn), since this is closer to German usage, and "it is agreeable to have parallel, interchangeable terms in the case of this concept, particularly since the sense of the term 'meaning' is itself to be investigated."[17]* The meaning of "Sinn" (or "Bedeutung") and its function in knowledge and experience becomes henceforth the subject of all of Husserl's work, and our task will be to follow the generalization of meaning in its transfer to the field of perception.

To begin with, Husserl notes with approval Brentano's dictum that: "In perception something is perceived, in imagination, something imagined, in a statement, something stated, in love, something loved . . . etc.,"[18] and he follows his teacher in taking the "intentional relation . . . to be the essential feature of 'psychical phenomena' or 'acts.' . . ."[19] He then appeals to his theory of meaning to argue that every act is at least correlated with a sense. He admits that in our ordinary everyday attitude we have before our mind the referent, not the sense, of our acts; but, he holds, the sense is always present, and we can make it explicit as an object of study if we turn from a straightforward to a reflective attitude.

> Instead of becoming lost in the performance of acts built intricately on one another, and instead of (as it were) naïvely positing the existence of the objects . . . we must rather practise "reflection," i.e., make these acts themselves, and their immanent meaning-content, our objects.[20]

This method of reflection, which turns the intentional correlate of an act into an object, is not a method invented by the phenomenologist. Although it is an unnatural (*wider natürlich*) orientation for the active involved individual, it is perfectly natural for the reflective thinker and has from the beginning been practiced by logicians.

> If we perform the act and live in it, as it were, we naturally refer to its object and not to its meaning. If, e.g., we make a statement, we judge about the thing it concerns, and not about the statement's meaning,

about the judgment in the logical sense. This latter first becomes objective to us in a reflex act of thought, in which we not only look back on the statement just made, but carry out the abstraction (the Ideation) demanded. This logical reflection is not an act that takes place only under exceptional, artificial conditions: it is a normal component of *logical* thinking.[21]

In this logical reflection we become aware of what we do not ordinarily notice, viz., that, when we are thinking of, wishing for, or passing judgment on objects or states of affairs, there is a thought, a wish, or a judgment involved. Between our thinking and the object or referent of our thinking lies the sense, which, as Frege puts it, "is indeed no longer subjective like the idea, but is yet not the object itself."[22] Frege uses a suggestive analogy to show the role of these objective meanings in conception.

> Somebody observes the Moon through a telescope. I compare the Moon itself to the reference; it is the object of the observation, mediated by the real image projected by the object glass in the interior of the telescope, and by the retinal image of the observer. The former I compare to the sense, the latter is like the idea or experience. The optical image in the telescope is indeed one-sided and dependent upon the standpoint of observation; but it is still objective, inasmuch as it can be used by several observers.[23]

The real image in the telescope is not normally what is observed. If it could be observed by the observer changing his position and looking at it through some instrument which itself involved a real image, the situation would be analogous to what the phenomenologist or logician is doing. The phenomenologist can at will, through an act of reflection, change the intentional correlate of his act into an object of a second-order act. He can think of the thought rather than the object he is thinking about, and he then becomes aware that the thought was present all along. He can also reflect on the second-order thought by which his attention was directed to the first-order thought, etc. On reflection we can thus discover something thought in each act of thinking, something wished in each wishing, something judged in each judging, etc., whether the objects of these thoughts, wishes, and judgments exist or not. Even though we are not ordinarily reflectively aware of this fact, it is nonetheless reflected in our grammar, which treats the objects thought of, wished for, judged about, etc., as *indirect* objects, suggesting thereby that the proximate object is the thought, the judgment, the wish. A signifying act can thus be said to have its

own intermediary object, the sense, whether it is confirmed by a
filling act or not—that is, whether it corresponds to any real object
or state of affairs.

Thus the intentionalist thesis that every act has a correlate is
saved, at least for the signifying acts such as thinking, judging, etc.
But what about perception, the filling act par excellence, by
means of which the signifying acts are confirmed? In perception, is
something always perceived?

To save the intentionalist thesis that all acts always have objects,
Husserl must generalize his threefold analysis of signifying acts to
perceptual or, more generally, to filling acts. He must exhibit a
perceptual sense as correlate of the perceptual act, to correspond
to the conceptual sense we have seen to be correlated with each
signifying act. And he must show why we can speak of the sense as
"what is perceived" in every act of perception.

Husserl's defense is not convincing. He begins plausibly by
noting:

> We distinguish, in a perceptual _statement,_ as in every statement, between
> content and _object;_ by the "content" we understand the self-identical
> meaning that the hearer can grasp even if he is not a percipient. [24]

But he then goes on to claim without further argument that when
a sense-fulfilling _act_ has an object, "object" can mean one of two
things: on the one hand, it can mean the referent, or "_more properly,_" it can mean "the object's ideal correlate in the acts of
meaning-fulfillment . . . _the fulfilling sense (erfüllende Sinn)._"[25]
Yet we are not told how we know there is such a fulfilling sense or
why it is properly called the object of the act. Rather, Husserl
seems to expect us to accept this fulfilling sense on the basis of a
parallel with the way linguistic sense-conferring acts are always
correlated with a conferred meaning.

> The ideal conception of the act which _confers meaning_ yields us the Idea
> of the _intending meaning,_ just as the ideal conception of the correlative
> essence of the act which _fulfills meaning_ yields the fulfilling meaning, like-
> wise _qua_ Idea. This is the _identical content_ which, in perception, pertains
> to the totality of possible acts of perception which intended the same ob-
> ject perceptually, and intend it actually as the same object. This content is
> therefore the ideal correlate of this _single_ object, which may, for the rest,
> be completely imaginary. [26]*

But what is this identical content which belongs to all perceptual
acts which intend the same object regardless of whether that object
exists? So far this is by no means clear. Husserl is aware that "the

application of the terms 'meaning' and 'sense' not merely to
the content of the meaning-intention . . . but also to the content
of meaning-fulfillment, engenders a most unwelcome ambiguity. . . ."[27]

Indeed, there is trouble here; for while signifying acts can be
viewed as opaque (to adopt Russell's terminology) and thus always
correlated with a sense, fulfilling acts—by virtue of their function
of presenting the state of affairs itself—can never be construed as
referentially opaque in ordinary discourse.[28*] An example will
help to highlight this difference. Suppose that, unknown to me,
my neighbor, whom I see every day, is the murderer of John.
Suppose further that each day I spend some time thinking about
this neighbor, admiring him, etc. At his trial I could honestly
testify that I had not for a moment thought about the murderer,
admired him, etc. But to say that, up to the moment of his conviction, I had never *seen* the murderer would be outright perjury.
For, seeing my neighbor, I had seen the murderer whether I knew
it or not. A fulfilling act seems to go directly to its object. This
difference in function between signifying and fulfilling acts is so
fundamental that it remains to be shown that there is any fulfilling
sense at all.

Before he can legitimately introduce the fulfilling sense as an
intentional correlate, Husserl must extend his discussion of intentional experience beyond the discussion of signifying acts which is
his focus in the first of the *Logical Investigations*. In the Fifth and
Sixth Investigations Husserl undertakes this generalization. The
Fifth Investigation studies the essential relation of *all* acts to their
ideal content, and the Sixth studies the relation of signifying acts
to fulfilling acts and that of fulfilling acts to their objects.

According to Husserl, when we perform an act of perception,
we are directly aware of a perceptual object. Since the perceptual
act is a fulfilling act, we can be sure that its object must have two
characteristics: it must be recognized as fulfilling a certain signifying intention, and it must be sensuously given, for "a signitive
intention merely points to its object, an intuitive intention gives
it 'presence,' in the pregnant sense of the word. . . ."[29] Thus the
perceptual act, in order to fulfill its function, must coordinate two
components: an act which intends a certain object as having certain characteristics, and an act which presents the object, thereby
fulfilling or failing to fulfill this intention. Perception is veridical
if we can adjust these two acts so that their meanings coincide

and there emerges a unity of coincidence (*Deckung*) between what is taken and what is given.

> In other words, the thing which, from the point of view of our acts is phenomenologically described as fulfillment, will also, from the point of view of the two objects involved in it, the intuited object, on the one hand, and the thought object, on the other, be expressly styled "experience of identity," "consciousness of identity," or "act of identification." A more or less complete *identity* is the *objective datum which corresponds to the act of fulfillment*, which "appears in it." This means that, not only signification and intuition, but also their mutual adequation, their union of fulfillment, can be called an act, since it has its own peculiar intentional correlate, an objective something to which it is "directed."[30]

If the intentionalist thesis is to hold for all acts, we must be able to exhibit the intentional content of each of these acts. We must show that each component act has an ideal correlate which it retains, whether there is a corresponding perceptual object or not.

It is relatively easy to identify the intentional correlate of the signifying component. The signifying act is the act which intends the object as having certain characteristics. Husserl calls its intentional correlate the matter of the act.[31]* "Since the matter . . . fixes the *sense* in which the representative content is interpreted (*aufgefasst*), we may also speak of the interpretive sense (*Auffassungssinn*)."[32] The act of taking, we have seen, like any conceptual act, can be directed toward an object whether or not there is any such object. I can, for example, mistakenly take a dust particle on the lens of my telescope to be a planet, which I take to be the planet Venus. In such cases, even if there is no such object as I take there to be, the act of taking has nonetheless its intentional content, its interpretive sense.

It would seem we could treat the other act component of perception in the same fashion. The intuitive act, too, must have its intentional correlate, which determines that it is an intuition of this object rather than another. If the intuitive act did not have such content, we could never tell whether our anticipations had been fulfilled. The content of the intuitive act must tell us, as completely as possible, the determinations of the object being intuited. Then, in the case of successful perception, the intentional contents of the signifying and the intuitive acts will correspond and can be identified.

If at this point, however, we define the intentional correlate of the intuitive act, on a strict analogy with the intentional content of the signifying act, as an abstractable component of the intuitive act which determines what sort of object is being intuited and which can itself then be either empty or fulfilled, we run into difficulty. The intuitive act will indeed have its own intentional content, which can be entertained independently of whether this content is fulfilled or not, but then an act having this content is not necessarily a fulfilling act. And we will have to seek again for an act which necessarily supplies the filling.

Let us review the steps by which we have arrived at this impasse: first of all, in the First Logical Investigation acts were divided into signifying and fulfilling acts. Then the perceptual act, which one would suppose to be a fulfilling act par excellence, was in turn analyzed into *its* signifying and intuitive components. Now the intuitive component of the perceptual act itself has turned out to have an intentional content or signifying component. Thus a regress develops in which sense coincides with sense indefinitely. At each stage we arrive at a fulfilling meaning for an intending meaning, but at no stage does the fulfilling meaning imply a sensuous filling. How are we to end this regress of meaning superimposed on meaning and account for our knowledge of the world?

If we wish to preserve the notion of fulfilling acts which corresponds to our experience of perceiving objects and thus arrive at the end of this regress, so that knowledge is seen to be possible, we must introduce an incarnate meaning, a meaning which is not abstractable from the intuitive content which it informs. This would mean that, although the signifying act and the intentional correlate of the signifying act are unaffected by the existence or nonexistence of the object of that act, the intentional correlate of the intuitive act would be dependent upon there being something to intuit.

To distinguish this incarnate meaning from the interpretive sense (*Auffassungssinn*), the intentional content of the signifying act which is independent of the existence of the object of the act—that is, which can be entertained whether the object exists or not—we would call the intentional content of the intuitive act the intuitive sense (*Anschauungssinn*). This intuitive sense would be an entirely new sort of sense whose existence would be essentially inseparable from the intuitive content of the object whose sense it was. Perception would then be described as the coincidence of the interpretive sense with the intuitive sense.

This would be a complex and convincing theory of perception. It would call attention to the fact that perception is not a purely passive presentational act in which something is merely given, or a pure act of taking in which nothing is given, but that it involves both an act of interpretation, which can be dealt with on the model of conceptual acts, and an intuitive act, which must be analyzed in a unique way.

This may be the view which Husserl eventually adopts,[33]* but it is not the position he holds in the *Logical Investigations.* In this work there is no mention of the intuitive sense, nor could there be, for Husserl has no way of generalizing his conception of a nonspatial, nontemporal, universal, abstract sense to cover a *concrete* "form" which is *inseparable* from the sensuous content it organizes.[34]*

Lacking an *Anschauungssinn,* Husserl is constrained to make the most of this position while at the same time admitting its limitations, viz., that what is left unclear is precisely the relation of the sense of the fulfilling act to the fulfillment itself. Husserl acknowledges this failure in the following difficult passage:

> In our First Investigation (§14) we opposed "fulfilling sense" to meaning (or fulfilling meaning to intending meaning) by pointing to the fact that, in fulfillment, the object is "given" intuitively in the same way in which the mere meaning means it. We then took the ideally conceived element which thus coincides with the meaning to be the *fulfilling* sense and said that, through this coincidence, the merely significant intention (or expression) achieved relation to the intuitive object (expressed this and just this object).
>
> This conceptual formation is entirely correct and suffices for the purpose of pinning down the entirely general aspects of the situation where a signitive intention achieves relation to its intuitively presented object: it expresses the important insight that the semantic essence of the signitive (or expressive) act reappears *identically* in corresponding intuitive acts, despite phenomenological differences on either side, and that the living unity of identification realizes this coincidence itself, and so realizes the relation of the expression to what it expresses. On the other hand, it is clear, in virtue precisely of this identity, that the "fulfilling sense" carries no implication of fullness, that *it does not accordingly include the total content of the intuitive act, to the extent that this is relevant for the theory of knowledge.*[35]

This difficulty is serious but not surprising. Since Husserl's whole conception of phenomenological reflection is based on the claim that one can isolate the intentional correlate, he must necessarily fail to account for the interpenetration of sense and

sensuous *presentation,* which alone would account for knowledge.

Husserl's commitment to the separation of form and matter and
his consequent inability to deal with incarnate meaning is already
present in his original linguistic model. Husserl speaks only of the
act of giving meaning to meaningless sounds or marks and of the
meaning given. He assumes that the appearance of these objects
is unaffected by the meaning thus superimposed. "While what
constitutes the object's appearing remains unchanged, the intentional character of the experience alters."[36] When sounds become linguistically meaningful, however, they do not remain unaffected. A sentence in an unfamiliar language is heard as an
uninterrupted torrent, whereas the same sounds in a familiar language are grouped into words and silences. Thus one would expect
a *fourfold* distinction: marks or sounds, act of giving meaning,
meaning given, and new perceptual entity, the meaningful expression. In *Ideas,* section 124, Husserl again raises this question.
There he first makes his usual distinction between the marks or
sounds and the meaning given: "Let us start from the familiar
distinction between the sensory, the so to speak bodily aspect of
expression, and its non-sensory 'mental' aspect."[37]* Then, having
assumed the traditional distinctions between body and mind,
sensory and nonsensory, he postpones indefinitely any discussion
of the problem raised by the union of sensory and sense in the
meaningful expression:

> There is no need for us to enter more closely into the discussion of . . . the
> way of uniting the two aspects, though we clearly have title-headings here
> indicated for phenomenological problems that are not unimportant.[38]

Likewise in *Ideas* Husserl touches on the epistemological problem of uniting apprehension and intuition, only to drop it. He
introduces the needed *Anschauungssinn,* "the meaning in its intentional *fullness,*" and he equates this notion with the "very important concept of *appearance.*"[39] He even remarks that "In a
phenomenology of external intuitions . . . concepts such as the
ones here set out stand in the center of scientific inquiry."[40] But
he drops this concept after one paragraph, never to take it up
again, and in the margin of his own copy of *Ideas* he wrote, after
"Meaning in the mode of its filling" (*Der Sinn im Modus seiner
Fülle*): "This concept thus conceived is untenable" (*Dieser Begriff*

so gefasst ist nicht haltbar).[41] It seems that Husserl saw the need in a phenomenology of perception for an *Anschauungssinn,* an intuitive sense; but he also saw that, according to his fundamental assumption that sense can be separated from filling in every act, he could not allow such a notion.

Thus strict adherence to the form/matter, mind/body dichotomy dictates the future development of Husserl's phenomenology away from a phenomenology of perception. For if even in perception one must always separate the act of meaning from the act of intuition which fills that meaning, it follows that one can have an account of the interpretive sense (*Auffassungssinn*) but no account of the corresponding intuitive sense (*Anschauungssinn*). One can have an account of what the mind takes the object to be but no account of our bodily interaction with the object in perceiving it.

To save the generality of his conception of intentionality, Husserl must, therefore, abandon an account of outer intuition. He must treat perception as referentially opaque and confine himself to what we take there to be rather than what is given. He can study the conditions of the *possibility* of evidence, confirmation, etc., but never its *actuality*.

After fourteen years of meditation, Husserl made a virtue of this necessity. Phenomenology is henceforth presented as transcendental phenomenology: a theory of how objects are taken or intended but not how they are given or presented—a study of a field of meanings which are entertained independently of whether empirical objects are given as existing (although, of course, one *takes* them to exist). Thus it is only one consistent step from Husserl's admission in the *Logical Investigations* that his phenomenology does not provide a theory of knowledge to the bracketing of existence in *Ideas.* And it is only one step—albeit a very dubious one—from normal logical reflection directed toward the ideal correlates of referentially opaque *conceptual acts* to a special kind of reflection, the phenomenological reduction, in which Husserl claims to abstract the meanings of the referentially transparent *acts of perception* as well.

Gurwitsch's Incarnation of Perception: The Noema as Intuitive Sense

Aron Gurwitsch seems to have sensed the one-sidedness of Husserl's phenomenology of perception and sought to supplement Husserl's account of what is intended or taken in perception with an account of what is presented or given. He found that the Gestalt psychologists were already at work describing "whatever is given to consciousness just as it presents itself in its phenomenal nature"[42] and set as the goal of his doctoral dissertation "to further certain phenomenological problems with the help of Gestalt-theoretical theses."[43]

According to the Gestalt psychologists and Gurwitsch, what is presented in perception is an incarnate form.

> ... the internal organization of the percept reveals itself as unity by Gestalt-coherence ... : a system of functional significances, interdependent and determining each other ... ; there is no unifying principle in addition to the matters unified.[44]

Gurwitsch introduces this perceptual gestalt, "the sense of what is experienced," as a development of what Husserl means by the *Anschauungssinn*. "The term 'sense' does not refer to the meaning of the 'sign.' 'Sense' is to be understood here as when Husserl (*Ideen*, I, p. 274) speaks of the sense of an intuition (*Anschauungssinn*)."[45] Identifying this intuitive sense with the perceptual noema, Gurwitsch then tells us that:

> On the basis of this interpretation of the perceptual noema, it is possible to account for the phenomenon of fulfillment of a merely signifying act by a corresponding perception. Fulfillment occurs when an object intended in a merely signifying mode, e.g., by means of a meaning in the narrower sense, also appears in the mode of self-presentation.[46]

This introduction of an intuitive sense (*Anschauungssinn*) which could coincide with and fulfill an interpretive sense (*Auffassungssinn*) would indeed, if coherent, complete Husserl's phenomenology of perception. Whether it is coherent and whether it is compatible with the rest of Husserl's system, however, requires further investigation.

An evaluation of Gurwitsch's contribution turns on his interpretation of the perceptual noema. By "noema" Husserl means the intentional correlate of any act. It follows that the *perceptual* noema must be a perceptual sense, the intentional correlate of an act of perception. But this is ambiguous: is the perceptual sense (*Wahrnehmungssinn*) to be understood as the interpretive sense (*Auffassungssinn*) or as the intuitive sense (*Anschauungssinn*)?

Husserl introduces the noema in a way which does little to clear up this ambiguity:

> In all cases the manifold data of the really inherent noetic content ... corresponds to the manifold data in a correlative noematic content,

> or, in short, in the noema—a term which we will constantly use from
> now on.
>
>   Perception, for example, has its Noema—at the most basic level its
> perceptual sense (*Wahrnehmungssinn*), that is, the perceived as such.[47]

Gurwitsch, however, without seeming to notice the ambiguity,
opts for the intuitive sense and takes this occasion to identify Husserl's perceptual noema with his own notion of a percept or perceptual gestalt.

> Following the dismissal of the constancy hypothesis, the percept has to be
> considered as a homogeneous unit, though internally articulated and
> structured. It has to be taken at face value; as that which it presents itself
> to be through the given act of perception and through that act alone; as it
> appears to the perceiving subject's consciousness; as it is meant and in-
> tended (the term "meaning" understood in a properly broadened and
> enlarged sense) in that privileged mode of meaning and intending which is
> perceptual presentation. In other words, the percept as it is conceived after
> the constancy hypothesis has been dismissed proves to be what we called
> the *perceptum qua perceptum*, the *perceptual noema*.[48]

But Husserl never says that the perceptual noema is perceptually
presented. To support his interpretation, Gurwitsch must take an
indirect line. Husserl does say that the phenomenological reduction reveals noemata:

> In this phenomenological orientation we can and must pose the essential
> questions: What is this "perceived as such"? What are the essential mo-
> ments of this perceptual Noema?[49]

And the phenomenological reduction does seem to be a technique
for describing what appears exactly as it appears: "We can obtain
the answer to the above question by pure openness to what is
essentially given; we can describe 'what appears as such' in complete evidence."[50] It seems that Husserl must be advocating an
exact description of appearances. And this is what Gurwitsch takes
him to mean when he writes:

> Understood in this way, the procedure of Gestalt theory, in taking the
> psychic purely descriptively and disregarding all constructions, has the
> same significance and methodical function for psychology as the trans-
> cendental reduction has for phenomenology. Objects in the normal sense
> of the word fall away, and noemata alone are left over; the world *as it
> really is* is bracketed, the world *as it looks* remains.[51]

Or, in the same vein:

> As in the natural attitude, so under the phenomenological reduction,

there still corresponds to an act of perception a perceptual noema or perceptual meaning, namely, the "perceived as such," the perceived object as appearing in a certain manner of presentation.[52]

Gurwitsch takes the "perceived as such" quite naturally as a restriction to what is purely perceived, free from any admixture of what for other reasons we might believe is present. But before we can accept this seemingly self-evident reading, we must determine what Husserl means by the phrase "the perceived as such"—indeed, what he means by the phrase "as such" in general. Husserl does sometimes use "as such" in the restrictive sense, as when, in *Ideas,* he speaks of "the sensuous appearance, i.e., the appearing object as such,"[53] or, in the psychology lectures, when he speaks of restricting our description to "the perceived as such, purely in the subjective mode of being given...."[54] But Husserl also has a special use of "as such" which he uses in connection not just with perception but with any conscious act. In continuing the passage introducing the perceptual noema, he relates "the perceived as such" to other sorts of "as such" entities:

> Perception, for example, has its Noema, at the most basic level, its perceptual sense, that is, the perceived as such. Similarly, recollection has its remembered as such precisely as it is "meant" and "consciously known" in it; again, the judging has the judged as such, the pleasing the pleasant as such, etc. We must everywhere take the noematic correlate, which (in a very extended meaning of the term) is here referred to as "sense" precisely as it lies "immanent" in the experience of perception, of judgment, of liking, and so forth.[55]

This complete quotation is less tractable to the Gurwitschian reading. The judgmental noema, the judged as such, immanent in the experience of judging, would seem to be the intentional correlate of the act of judging. It is *what* is judged—that is, the judgment, as distinguished from the object judged *about* taken exactly as it is judged to be. Correlatively, the perceptual noema, the perceived as such, would seem to be the intentional correlate of the act of perceiving, which directs the act to the object perceived just the way it is *taken,* rather than being the object of perception exactly as it is *given,* as Gurwitsch contends.

Husserl himself points out in *Ideas*[56] that the "matter" of the *Logical Investigations* has its "noematic parallel" in the "noematic nucleus" ("Every noema has a 'content,' namely a 'meaning' through which it relates to 'its' object") and implies that the "intentional essence" of the *Logical Investigations* (the matter plus the quality of the act) has its parallel in the full noema. ("If we recall our earlier analysis, we find the full noesis related to the full noema as its intentional and full What.")

For Husserl, then, the perceptual noema, like the intentional essence of a perceptual act, is a meaning *by virtue of which we refer to perceptual objects*. It is *what is intended* in perception in the same way that the judgment is *what is judged* in making a judgment. Gurwitsch agrees with Husserl that the noema is "what is intended," but his interest in Gestalt theory leads him to conclude that the noema is "the object *as* it is intended"[57] rather than the What of the intending. Thus Gurwitsch collapses the object *as referred to* with the *reference to* the object.

This results in a characteristic confusion in each of Gurwitsch's many definitions of the perceptual noema. Already in his doctoral dissertation we are told: ". . . *the sense of consciousness directed toward the theme* . . . the noema of the theme . . . forms the subject matter of investigation of a noematically oriented phenomenology."[58] Yet, only a few lines later, the theme is defined as "that which is *given* to consciousness, precisely just as and only to the extent to which it is given," and we are told that "a phenomenology of the theme is a noematic analysis."[59] Here Gurwitsch refers first to *the sense of the act of intending the theme* as the noema and then identifies the noema with *the theme as given*. In 1966 we still find the same conflation of the What of the act of referring with what is referred to (exactly *as* it is referred to) when Gurwitsch introduces the noema as "an object as *intended* and *presenting* itself under a certain aspect."[60]

All this confusion arises because Husserl chooses to call the What in our intending, rather than what is intended, "the perceived as such." Why does Husserl use such misleading terminology? Why use "the perceived as such" to denote precisely that element in perception which is not perceptually presented? To understand, if not to pardon, such usage we must remember that Husserl first became concerned with "sense" and "referential opacity" through his analysis of linguistic expressions. The basic phenomenon to be analyzed in this connection is that expressions have meanings and that the meanings may refer to objective states of affairs. In this connection, "the meant" is quite naturally used to refer to the meaning of the expression rather than the objective state of affairs. As Husserl notes:

> The terms "meaning" . . . and all similar terms harbour such powerful equivocations that our intention, even if expressed most carefully, still

can promote misunderstanding. . . . Each expression not merely says something, but says it *of* something: it not only has a meaning, but refers to certain *objects*. . . . And, if we distinguish between "content" and object in respect of such "presentations," one's distinction means the same as the distinction between what is meant or said, on the one hand, and what is spoken of, by means of the expression, on the other. [61]

Moreover, since "relation to an actually given objective correlate, which fulfills the meaning intention, is *not* essential to an expression," [62] it seems plausible to say that what is "really expressed" is the meaning rather than the object meant.

We note that there are two things that can be said to be expressed in the realized relation to the object. We have, on the one hand, the *object itself,* and the object as meant in this or that manner. On the other hand, and _more properly,_ we have the object's ideal correlate in the acts of meaning-fulfillment which constitute it, the *fulfilling sense.* [63*]

So, to clear up the ambiguity of the phrase "what is meant," Husserl quite naturally chooses to call the object "what is meant" and to call the sense of the expression "the meant as such"—that is, what is properly and essentially meant. Likewise, in an act of judging, the judgment can be said to be what is essentially judged, and therefore it can be called "the judged as such" (although here it is no longer quite natural to say that what is judged in an act of judging is the judgment rather than the object judged about).

The use of "as such" to refer to the intentional correlate gets more and more obscure as we move further from Husserl's linguistic home base. Only in some technical sense of "essential" is "what is essentially remembered" the memory rather than the object recalled. Moreover, although the question "What is he seeing (or finding pleasant)?" may allow two possible responses—the *description of the object* and *an indication of* the object itself—the perceiver's way of intending the object could hardly be said to be what is essentially seen, the seen as such, since it is not seen, nor could a description of what I take an enjoyed object to be be called the essentially pleasant, the pleasant as such, since the description is not enjoyed at all.

Yet this counterintuitive use of "as such" is exactly what Husserl has in mind. For it is Husserl's basic point, which first becomes explicit in *Ideas,* that *all* acts can be understood on his linguistic model; that "the noema is nothing but a generalization of the notion of meaning to the total realm of acts." [64] Since even perceptual acts can be understood as ways of making sense of our experience by giving a meaning to meaningless data; for Husserl, judging, remembering, perceiving, and enjoying are all forms of meaning-giving, and all have their correlative meaning whether the object exists or not. Just as in the case of the meaning of a linguistic expression—the judgment, the memory, the perceptual sense, and the sense of the pleasurable are what is essential. Thus for Husserl it is natural, even necessary, to speak of these meanings as the judged as such, the remembered as such, the perceived as such, and the pleasant as such, no matter how forced this may sound.

The difficulty revealed in Husserl's need to construct such bizarre terminology and the difficulty his interpreters find in understanding it are a measure of the difficulty of the phenomenological reduction, which generalizes referential opacity beyond the sphere of its everyday application, extending it to all, even filling, acts.

Presented with the expression "the perceived as such" with no explanation, as in *Ideas,* the reader is in a quandary. Since, in the natural attitude, perception is experienced as going directly to its object, there is no genuine ambiguity, not even a trumped-up ambiguity, in the expression "what is perceived" which the qualifier "as such" could serve to clear up. Consequently, counter to Husserl's intention, the "as such" which focuses our attention on what is *essentially* perceived or enjoyed, far from leading us to reflect on what the object is *taken* to be, seems to focus our attention on the object exactly as it is *given.* [65]*

To make matters worse, Husserl seems to introduce the transcendental reduction as just such a way of concentrating on appearances:

> In this phenomenological orientation we can and must pose the essential questions: What is this "perceived as such"? What are the essential moments of this perceptual Noema? We can obtain the answer to the above questions by pure openness to what is essentially *given;* we can describe "what appears as such" faithfully and in perfect self-evidence. [66]

And in his "Critical Study of Husserl's *Nachwort*" Gurwitsch understood Husserl in just this way: "Under the phenomenological *epochē* we deal with thing-phenomena, with 'things' just as they appear, and within the limits in which they appear."[67]

But such a reading, which would turn phenomenological analysis into a sophisticated analysis of what is sensuously given, ignores the fact that these remarks immediately follow the passage where Husserl introduces the noema as "a meaning (in a very extended sense)" which "lies 'immanent' in experiences of perception, judgment, enjoyment, etc.," and which can be "given in really pure intuition."[68] In line with Husserl's generalization of his linguistic model to all acts, this would suggest that the noema is the interpretive sense, and the givenness in question is the result of a special act of reflection.

Gurwitsch, on the other hand, after identifying the noema with what is given in perception, goes on to identify the perceptual noema with Husserl's notion of perceptual adumbration.

> The noema at large being defined as that which is meant as such, the perceptual noema must, accordingly, be determined as the "perceived as such." It turns out to be the perceived thing, just as it presents itself through a concrete act of perception—namely, as appearing from a certain side, in a certain perspective, orientation, etc. In this sense all *manners of appearance and presentation* which we mentioned above in connection with the adumbrational theory of perception are to be considered as *perceptual noemata.*[69]

And once having identified the noema with a perceptual adumbration, and still guided by the notion that the noema is what is essentially perceived, Gurwitsch sees no problem in also identifying the noema with an appearance. He even finds a shred of textual evidence in the isolated passage where Husserl defines appearance as the meaning in the mode of its filling. Citing this passage, Gurwitsch concludes:

> Discussing perception of material things, Husserl frequently uses the term "appearance" (*Erscheinung*), and even the term "image" (*Bild*) occasionally. Both these terms are taken by Husserl as synonymous with the term perceptual noema.[70]

Husserl, however, never says that "appearance," as meaning plus filling, is synonymous with "noema." In fact, he finds this notion of appearance untenable and never uses the term appearance in this way except in this one passage. He does, however, frequently use the term appearance in its normal sense as synonymous with perceptual adumbration—the way the object presents itself from a particular point of view. But Gurwitsch cannot cite *this* use of appearance in defense of his view, since Husserl never identifies appearance in the sense of adumbration with the noema and never refers to adumbrations as meanings.

Indeed, it is hard to determine what Gurwitsch could have in mind when he says that an appearance is a perceptual *sense.* An appearance, as Gurwitsch uses the term, is not a specific temporal appearing, a sense datum, since Gurwitsch makes it quite clear that what distinguishes the noema or perceptual sense from a noesis or psychological event is that the same noema can occur again and again, but neither is it an ideal, abstractable entity like the interpretive sense, since in a perceptual gestalt "a separation between *hylē* and *morphē* is not even abstractly possible."[71]

Perhaps Gurwitsch's perceptual sense might be best thought of as the look of an object, which is *distinguishable* but not *separable* from the object which has that look or appearance. Gurwitsch uses the example of a melody to argue that "What is immediately given, the phenomenological primal material, is given only as articulated and structured."[72] "It is only at its place within an organized structure [such as a melody] that a sensuous item becomes what it is in a given case."[73] This suggests that, although a melody cannot be entertained independently of some sequence of notes, still the melody is a distinguishable organized structure which can be embodied or actualized in various sequences. Thus it could be thought of as a recurring ideal structure, a meaning in an extended sense, which could be actualized in a series of illustrations.[74*] Gurwitsch, however, does not make this point. In his concern with rejecting Husserl's *hylē/morphē* distinction, he is led to the opposite extreme of *identifying* the distinguishable if not abstractable gestalt with its specific embodiments. He does once suggest that the noema is a distinguishable form in speaking of its "actualization,"[75] but his general tendency, as expressed in his identification of the perceptual noema with a perceptual adumbration, is to think of the noema as a specific illustrative appearance, like a specific performance of a melody.

The noema, then, according to Gurwitsch, turns out to be a very special sort of entity, which is neither an act of experiencing nor a material object.

> Each time that we open our eyes, we experience an act of perception, which, once it is past, can never recur. . . . Meanwhile, we perceive not only the same house *qua* physical thing but are also confronted with the same thing as presenting itself to us under the same aspect; briefly, we are faced with the same house perceived as such. The latter being neither the physical house nor an act of consciousness, we have to recognize the perceived *qua* perceived as a special and specific entity—"perceptual noema" is the technical term which Husserl uses.[76]

Such an entity, which can be repeatedly experienced but which is not physically real, can, perhaps, best be understood as a perspectival view of an object. A view from a mountaintop, for example, is not a physical object, but it is not a temporal experience either, since it can be presented to the same viewer again and again and can also be presented to others.

This seems to be what Gurwitsch has in mind, but such an understanding of the noema is hard to reconcile with Husserl's assertion that the noema is a meaning. Gurwitsch would, however, argue that there are two senses of meaning: one, the linguistic sort, in which the sense can be separated from the referent, and the other—meaning in an extended sense—which still involves reference but only the reference of the sensuous aspects of a gestalt organization to other hidden aspects. In this extended sense the meaning *is* the referring of the aspects and so is inseparable from them. Gurwitsch quotes with approval Merleau-Ponty's observation that "the sense is incorporated and incarnated in the very appearances themselves."[77]

Gurwitsch argues that such an incarnate meaning

> proves to be on a par with noematic correlates of any intentional act. It is an ideal unit with neither spatial nor temporal determinations, uninvolved in any causal relation; it pertains to the realm of meanings in the enlarged sense, a realm within which meanings in the more narrow or proper sense form a special domain.[78]

But a perspectival view (as a perceptual gestalt) is still not what Husserl means by the perceptual noema as a sense. The perspectival view is indeed not in *objective* space and time, and it does not entail the existence of any material object; but as a sensuous perceptual presentation it has apparent extension (it fills a greater or smaller portion of the visual field), and it has its own sort of duration (it comes into existence and it ceases to exist at a specific moment in history). Husserl nowhere attributes these sorts of spatiotemporal indices even to meanings in his extended sense. Husserl's extended use seems rather to be the widening of meaning from the linguistically expressible meanings treated in the *Logical Investigations* to the interpretive senses correlated with all acts.

> Originally [the words *bedeuten* and *Bedeutung*] were exclusively related to the sphere of language and expression. It is, however, unavoidable, and at the same time an important advance in knowledge, to broaden the meanings of these words so that they may be applied to the whole noetico-noematic sphere, therefore to all acts, whether these are interwoven with expressions or not.[79]

Moreover, for Husserl the noema is a special sort of meaning. Every noesis is *correlated* with a noema *through which* it intends its object. Thus the noema is not present (even marginally) to ordinary involved consciousness; rather it is presented only in that special act of reflection which Husserl calls the phenomenological reduction. Gurwitsch, however, since he identifies sense and appearance, is led to the view that "a conscious act is an act of awareness, *presenting* to the subject who experiences it a sense, an ideal atemporal unity."[80] But the passage in *Cartesian Meditations* which Gurwitsch cites to back up this statement—"Each cogito . . . means something or other and bears in itself, in this manner peculiar to the meant, its particular cogitatum"[81]—makes no such claim. Rather, it suggests, as we have seen, that Husserl thinks of the meaning as what is essentially meant by the act and thus *contained* in it rather than *presented to* it.

In following out the logic of his identification of the noema with a percept and thus of his identification of the interpretive sense with the intuitive sense and both with the perceptual adumbration, Gurwitsch is ultimately led to adopt the view that objects literally consist of noemata. This is a view which nowhere appears in Husserl's works and which, indeed, explicitly contradicts the views of the master. Husserl does say that the object is meant as verified by the set of its actual and possible perceptual presentations. But Gurwitsch puts this point too phenomenalistically:

> The thing cannot be perceived except in one or the other manner of adumbrational presentation. It is nothing besides, or in addition to, the multiplicity of those presentations through all of which it appears in its identity. Consequently, the thing perceived proves to be the group, more precisely put, the systematically organized totality of adumbrational presentations.[82]

Moreover, since Husserl never identified adumbrations with the perceptual sense, he would never conclude with Gurwitsch that "the perceptual senses are united into systems which are the real perceptual things."[83] This mixture of faithfulness to Husserl (in continuing to hold that the noema is a meaning) and radical innovation (in holding objects to *be* systems of noemata) poses a fundamental problem in interpreting Gurwitsch's phenomenology of perception. If the noema is interpreted as an atemporal, aspatial, nonsensuous, abstractable, ideal entity in Husserl's sense, there is no way to understand how a system of such entities could ever be said to *be* a perceptual object. But if we take the noema as a specific illustration of such an abstract entity—a sensuous perceptual presentation—from which objects could be made up, there is no way to understand how this percept can be said to be ideal in Husserl's understanding of the term.

These difficulties cast doubt on Gurwitsch's contribution to a phenomenology of perception. They also obscure his otherwise outstanding Husserl interpretation. Still, whether Gurwitsch holds that the noema is the structure of a percept or whether it is the percept itself, and regardless of the merits of his attempt to find support for this new interpretation of Husserl's work, one thing is clear: Gurwitsch has raised the question of how to understand the fulfilling sense and has provided an account of the perceptual noema which makes it incarnate in the sensuous perceptual presentation. By refusing to separate the sense from the filling, he has, almost in spite of himself, recognized the special referential transparency of perception. Such a modification of Husserl's attempt to treat perception as referentially opaque is an important step in faithfulness to the phenomenon, even if, as we shall see, it requires greater and greater unfaithfulness to Husserl.

From Transcendental to Existential Phenomenology

Whether Gurwitsch holds that the perceptual noema is an ideal form, distinguishable from the presentations which illustrate it, or whether, as his words suggest, he holds that the noema is a perceptual presentation itself, one thing is certain: he rejects the view, essential to Husserl's whole project, that the noema is separable from its filling. And once Gurwitsch breaks with Husserl on this point, he is committed to more far-reaching changes in the Husserlian system than he seems prepared to admit.

We have seen that Gurwitsch himself draws the important conclusion from his gestalt analyses that one must reject Husserl's distinction between *morphē* and *hylē*, between meaning and filling. He also recognizes that this change, plus careful attention to the phenomena, leads to a rejection of the Husserlian notion of a disembodied, detached, transcendental ego capable of creating these ideal meanings and imposing them on the sensuous manifold.[84]

But at this point Gurwitsch stops short of drawing the further conclusions that his radical break with Husserl's traditional preconceptions entails. To begin with, if the gestalt analysis of perception is correct, and the intuitive sense is inseparable from its filling, the transcendental reduction, as modified by Gurwitsch, will have to be given up. For, if the phenomenologist describes the perceptual object exactly as it is *given,* he will have to admit that it is given as *"bodily present"* with hidden aspects—in short, as existing. If he tries to bracket that existence and claim that what is given is only a perspectival presentation of an object, which *implies* other possible *appearances* but does not entail the *co-presence* of these other *concealed aspects,* he will not be faithful to the phenomenon.[85]* Thus Gurwitsch, who agrees with Husserl that in the natural attitude the perceptual object is experienced as "bodily present," contradicts himself when he says, in claiming phenomenological validity for his phenomenalism:

> On strictly phenomenological grounds, there is no justification for distinguishing the thing itself from a systematically concatenated group of perceptual noemata, all intrinsically referring to and by virtue of their mutual references, qualifying, one another.[86]

It seems that a faithful description of the given and a bracketing of existence, as Gurwitsch understands bracketing, are incompatible.

Husserl does not have this problem. His version of the reduction abstracts the meaning or intending of the objects and the meanings correlated with these intentional acts without concern for the existence or bodily presence of the objects, except as that too is meant or intended.[87]* Gurwitsch, however, does not have this way out. Having denied the *hylē/morphē* distinction and the transcendental ego in his commitment to the incarnate sense, and having thus redefined the reduction as a way of noticing the way the object is given, exactly as it is given, Gurwitsch has no way of shifting the object of investigation so as to avoid the embarrassing fact that existence or thickness is itself phenomenologically presented. He can only redefine existence, giving a phenomenalist account of perceptual thickness as an infinitely open system of thin appearances. But this is tantamount to admitting that the originally given bodily presence can never be recovered from his supposedly neutral phenomenological analysis.

If, following Gurwitsch, we deny the separation of meaning and sensuous content in perception and thus no longer accept Husserl's account of the interpretive sense as an ideal, abstractable meaning imposed by a transcendental ego, we will need some new account of the object's "thickness." If the hidden sides of the object are given as *co-present,* we will need an account of how the subject can be *present with* the object. Therefore, we will have to return to some account of the role of the subject—a role which Gurwitsch wants to reject.

Gurwitsch gets into difficulty with bodily presence because he is forced to stop halfway in his incarnation of perception. He concludes that, since in perception there is no act of meaning-giving whose meaning is abstractable from its sensuous filling, there is no act of meaning-giving at all. He is thus led to *replace* an analysis of the way objects of experience are *taken* with an analysis of the way they are *given* and to reinterpret the activity of the subject—the noesis—as simply the experiencing of the presented gestalts.

> [F]or intentional analysis the ultimate fact and datum is the sense or meaning itself as a structured whole. This necessitates a redefinition of the conceptions of noesis and intentionality. By the term "noesis" we can no longer denote an organizing and apprehending function. . . .[88]

> The only distinction is between the noeses as temporal psychological events and the noemata as atemporal ideal entities pertaining to the realm of sense and meaning.[89]

Having thus eliminated the subject giving meaning to his experience and the meaning he gives, no way remains for Gurwitsch to complete his phenomenology of perception by giving an account of the incarnation of the interpretive sense which parallels his account of the incarnation of the intuitive sense.

Yet the elements of such an account are already required in Gurwitsch's gestalt analysis. Gurwitsch analyzes the experience of a sequence of notes making up a melody, to point out how the notes have the value they have only within the organized perceptual structure, which itself does not exist apart from the notes. As Gurwitsch sees it, indeed, it follows that the organization of the notes, the melody itself, cannot be entertained apart from some illustrative embodiment and thus cannot be imposed by a transcendental subject on otherwise neutral notes. Still, to have a melodic organization, the notes must be *taken as* a melody: a subject must *give* them this organization by anticipating the subsequent notes as a continuation of an on-going melody. Gurwitsch has no philosophic account of this taking. It would seem appropriate, however, following out the implications of his analysis, to think of the interpretive sense as a bodily set, an actualization of a particular habit or skill acquired in becoming acquainted with this piece of music—a skill which, indeed, I cannot entertain apart from its actualization in a given activity of anticipating this particular sequence of notes.

In perception such a body set would be correlated with the experience of the "thickness" of objects. I not only take it that objects have other sides, I am here and now actually set to explore them. So the other sides are not experienced as *possible* experiences implied by the present *appearance;* they are experienced as *actually present* but concealed aspects of the present *object* soliciting further exploration. As a perceiving subject I am therefore not a monadic transcendental ego with the world in me, but neither am I just a field open to a stream of appearances— a being-at-the-world.[90*] I am a situated subject, set to explore objects, whose concealed aspects are co-present to me because I am co-present to them. Only an embodied subject allows such presence.

Our habits or skills for coping with objects are aspatial and atemporal, like the noema. The same skill can be actualized in many different situations. But unlike Husserl's conceptualized noema, skills are not ideal, abstractable meanings. They cannot be entertained apart from some particular activation. However, when actualized, an incarnate meaning (the interpretive sense) can mesh with a particular presentation of an object (the intuitive sense), thereby producing a successful act of perception. Since these perceptual skills, like noemata, are the means *through which* we refer to and unify the objects of experience, they cannot be treated as another object in the field of experience. Gurwitsch again mistakes the noema (this time the incarnate interpretive sense) for a presentation when he argues against Merleau-Ponty that the body must be just another object of consciousness.[91*] The kinesthetic body may be such an object, but not the skill-ful body as percipient.

Now we can see more fully why neither Husserl's nor Gurwitsch's transcendental reduction can be carried out. For Husserl the reduction was that special and detached reflection which the phenomenologist could undertake as transcendental ego in order to entertain meanings apart from their sensuous filling. Gurwitsch, as we have noted, once he had criticized Husserl's form/matter separation and had identified the noema and the perceptual presentation, could not understand the reduction in this way. He had to reinterpret the transcendental reduction as a way of noticing a special realm of being, viz., consciousness in its transcendental function as "the universal medium of access to, and . . . the fountain and origin of, whatever exists."[92] To do this, he had to reinterpret perceptual objects as a system of appearances so as to understand their existence in terms of their "equivalent of consciousness."[93] But, as we have now seen, there is no such field of pure disembodied appearances. There is only the embodied subject coming to grips with embodied objects.

8

Husserl's Account of Our Temporal Awareness

Izchak Miller

Our experience of time is rarely taken account of in the contemporary literature that is devoted to the analysis of perception. Most accounts of perception revolve around such paradigms as the perception of a tree, a table, and other ordinary *enduring* objects. In the majority of cases, our awareness of the endurance of these objects, which is an integral feature of our perceptual awareness of them, is left out of consideration. Enduring objects, furthermore, are but one kind of the physical entities we perceive. Melodies, uttered sentences, movement of bodies, and other physical *processes* and events are objects of perception as common as trees, tables, and the like. A theory of perception must, in the final analysis, account for our perception of such entities, and an account of our perceiving them cannot continue to ignore questions about our *temporal awareness*.

The problem posed by our perception of processes is formulated by Husserl in the following passage:

Let us take a particular melody or cohesive part of a melody as an example. The matter seems very simple at first; we hear a melody, i.e., we perceive it, for hearing is indeed perception. While the first tone is sounding, the second comes, then the third, and so on. Must we not say that

> when the second tone sounds I hear *it*, but I no longer hear the first, and
> so on? In truth, therefore, I do not hear the melody but only the particu-
> lar tone which is actually present.   (*Time*, p. 43)[1]

This problem soon gives way to a more fundamental one:

> Every tone itself has a temporal extension: With the actual sounding I hear
> it as now. With its continued sounding, however, it has an ever new now,
> and the tone actually preceding is changing into something past. There-
> fore, I hear at any instant only the actual phase of the tone . . .   (ibid.)

In other words, whereas it seems true that I am hearing that tone
throughout a certain interval of time, it seems not to be true that I
am hearing all of it (or a temporally extended part of it) at any
given instant of that interval. Yet my perceptual experience is such
that throughout that interval I continuously experience the *continuity* of that tone, and this requires (contrary to the previous
hypothesis) that I experience at any instant of the duration of my
perception more than a mere instantaneous phase of the tone.
How, then, is an instantaneous perceptual experience of the temporal extendedness of a tone possible?

Answering this and other related questions about our temporal
awareness is of crucial importance to Husserl for reasons which go
beyond the mere desire to provide an adequate account of perception. The subject matter of phenomenology is our conscious experience, and Husserl presupposes our ability to *reflect* on our
experiences and discern their essential features. However, our
experiences, or—as Husserl calls them—our acts of consciousness,
are themselves processes, albeit mental processes. How, then, do
we succeed in being reflectively aware at any given instant of anything more than a mere instantaneous phase of the act reflected
upon? According to Husserl, the structure of our temporal awareness which makes the perceptual experience of a tone possible is
the same structure that makes the reflective awareness of an act
possible. Accounting for the possibility of the first is, thus, accounting for the possibility of the second.

Before we turn to the discussion of Husserl's account of our
temporal awareness, a few words about the strategy to be employed are in order. Most of Husserl's notes on time consciousness
were written, sporadically, during the years 1893–1917, and their
contents reflect the major transitions in his general philosophical
outlook which took place in the course of those years. Husserl
never turned to the task of editing these notes into a single,
consistent, presentation of his position on time awareness. The

purpose of this essay is *not* that of tracing the development of Husserl's views on time consciousness (a worthwhile task in its own right). It is, rather, to dredge out of his notes systematically an account of our temporal awareness consistent with his "transcendental" view of intentionality.[2] Husserl's account of perceiving a process—in particular, his account of perceiving a melody—will be used as a vehicle for introducing his account of temporal awareness.

II

Husserl's account of perceiving a melody cannot be understood except within the context of his general account of the perceptual experience. We begin, therefore, by outlining the latter.

In the perceptual situation, according to Husserl, we are "immediately," or "directly," aware of (ordinary) *physical* entities, and—which is of particular present interest—of their temporal properties and relations. For instance, he says: "The *consciousness of succession* is a primordial direct object (*originär gebendes*) consciousness; it is the 'perception' of this succession." (*Time,* p. 65). It will be useful to start by mentioning what it is that Husserl rejects when he insists that the perceptual experience, or the perceptual act, is "direct" with respect to its (purported) physical object: According to Husserl, our perceptual experience of a physical entity is *not mediated* by an (immediate) awareness of something other than that physical entity, such as ideas, images, sensa, percepts, and the like. Throughout his writing, Husserl repeatedly and emphatically rejects Representative Realism as being phenomenologically indefensible.[3] Instead, he insists: "I perceive the thing, the object of nature, the tree there in the garden; that and nothing else is the real object of the perceiving 'intention'" (*Ideas,* pp. 242-243). This is not a mere truism regarding how we use "to perceive," but a claim that the perceptual intention (the perceptual act) does not contain as a constituent an immediate awareness of something *other* than the (purported) physical object itself. In what sense, then, is the perceptual act "direct" with respect to its (purported) physical object? The answer to this question requires an understanding of Husserl's notion of *noema,* and in particular of his notion of the perceptual noema.

According to Husserl, our perceptual acts are directed toward ordinary physical entities. But to say that an act is "directed" is *not* to say that it necessarily has an object. According to Husserl, the directedness (intentionality) of an act is an intrinsic (nonrelational) feature of the act, and it is accounted for by the noema of the act.[4] The main component of the noema—the one which should concern us here—is the noematic *Sinn*. The noematic Sinn is, in fact, that component of the noema of an act which determines the object of the act, if it has one. Husserl's tripartite distinction between the act, its noema and its object corresponds to the Fregean tripartite distinction between the linguistic expression, its sense (Sinn) and its reference.

I argued elsewhere[5] that according to Husserl the noematic Sinn of a perceptual act is a *singular meaning*. When I see, say, a blooming tree, the noematic Sinn of my perceptual act on that occasion is a singular meaning, an "individual concept" of the tree, which "illuminates" (to borrow a Fregean metaphor) the tree in great detail as from a certain perspective. The perceptual act is not the only act whose noematic Sinn is a singular meaning. When I remember a tree, imagine a tree, etc., I also have acts whose noematic Sinne are singular meanings. I call an act whose noematic Sinn is a singular meaning, a "direct-object act."

Among direct object acts there are those which are uniquely directed, and those which are not. For instance, my act of wanting an apple (any apple will do) is a direct-object act, but one which is not uniquely directed. By contrast, my wanting a particular apple (say, the one I see in your hand) is a direct-object act which *is* uniquely directed. According to Huserl, acts of perception are always uniquely directed. Husserl calls a uniquely directed direct-object act, "intuition" (*Anschauung*).[6]

Intuitions are, in turn, divided by Husserl into two classes: intuitions in which, or through which, (purported) objects are "primordially" experienced, and intuitions in which this is not the case. The cxamples he uses to clarify this distinction are taken from the realm of natural, or empirical, experience. Compare the act of perceiving an object with an act of remembering that object. Both acts, according to Husserl, are uniquely directed direct-object acts (intuitions). But, according to him, there is a difference between the ways in which the object is experienced by us through these acts: in perception we have a "primordial" experience of the object, whereas in memory this is no longer the case.[7] It seems that this difference is twofold. First, in perception, unlike memory, the (purported) object of the act is experienced by us as presently confronting our cointended "organism":

The primitive [primordial] *mode of the giving of something-itself* is *perception*. The being-with is for me, as percipient, consciously my now-being-with: I myself with the perceived itself.   (*FTL*, p. 158)[8]

In another place he says,

if I take the perceiving of this die as the theme for my description, I see in pure reflection that "this" die is given continuously as an objective unity . . . The one identical die appears, now in "near appearances," now in "far appearances": in the changing modes of the Here and There, over against an always co-intended, though perhaps unheeded, absolute Here (in my co-appearing organism).   (*CM*, pp. 39-40)[9]

Second, memory is "parasitic" on perception in the sense that the noema of an act of remembering an object essentially involves a reference to a (past) act of perceiving that object, whereas the converse is not the case:[10*]

Memory in its own essential nature is in fact a "modification of" perception. *Correlatively* that which is characterized [in memory] as past presents itself in itself as "having been present," as a modification therefore of the "present," which in its unmodified form is the "primordial," the "corporeally present" of perception.   (*Ideas*, p. 268)

It is this last fact about memory which enables us to pass back and forth between the acts of remembering an object and remembering having perceived that object, which are two different but intimately related acts.

Consideration of cases of misperception brings out another important feature of our perceptual acts. Phenomenologically, cases of (exposed) misperceptions are cases in which, in the course of our perceptual experience of an object, the object comes to be experienced by us as having properties which are *incompatible* with properties it was previously experienced by us as having. In such cases, Husserl says, the noema of our act "explodes"—it is forced to undergo a (more or less) radical adjustment of content. What is of present significance in Husserl's (meager) discussion of such cases is that he maintained that in some important sense the "identity"of the object survives (*qua* intended) the explosion of the noema (even though in some other sense it does not):

we have to make clear . . . the *cases . . . where there is disagreement or determination otherwise* of that X which we are constantly aware of as one and the same—otherwise, that is, than in harmony with the original bestowal of meaning.   (*Ideas*, p. 356)

There must, then, be an element in the noematic Sinn of a perceptual act which "rigidly" maintains the act's directedness toward
one and the same object through a course of experience along
which the noematic Sinn of the act contains incompatible attributions. That is, there must be an element in the noematic Sinn of a
perceptual act which determines an object for the act (if it has one
at all) *regardless* of whether or not that object satisfies the remaining attributive content of that noematic Sinn.[11] In line with Husserl's frequent use of the demonstrative in phenomenological
description of perceptual acts (cf., for example, his previously
quoted description of the perception of a die) and in accord with
my own beliefs about perception, I will refer to the rigid element
in the noematic Sinn of a perceptual act which the consideration
of misperception has brought into light as the "demonstrative"
element in the perceptual noematic Sinn.[12*]

As the consideration of the possible nonexistence of the object
of the act has led Husserl to seek a nonrelational account of the
directedness of the act, so does now the consideration of misperception and, we should add, perceptual illusion lead us to the
recognition of the demonstrative element in the perceptual act. It
is interesting to note that Husserl himself insists that considering
cases of misperception and illusion is indispensable to a phenomenological account of perception:

> [such cases] must be no less taken into our phenomenological reckon-
> ing . . . the courses of perception, in which partial breaches of agreement
> occur, and the agreement can be maintained only through "corrections,"
> must be systematically described in respect of all its essential constit-
> uents . . . Over against the continuous synthesis of agreement, the synthe-
> ses of conflict . . . must come into their rights, for a phenomenology of
> "true reality" the *phenomenology of "vain illusion"* is wholly indis-
> pensable.   (*Ideas*, p. 388)

Unfortunately, Husserl himself indicates only in broad (and sometimes confusing) terms how these cases are to be phenomenologically described.

It is, in my opinion, both correct and compatible with Husserl's
views to maintain that the perceptual act has a demonstrative element built into it. To be sure, the noematic Sinn of a perceptual
act has additional, attributive, features. However, the object of a
perceptual act is not necessarily the one, if any, which happens to
satisfy these attributive features. It is thanks to the demonstrative
element in his act that when Peter sees a bush as a wolf, it is the

bush and not a wolf which is the object of Peter's perceptual act on that occasion—despite the fact that it fails to satisfy the attribution of being a wolf. Similarly, it is thanks to the demonstrative element in our act that when we see a straight stick that appears to be bent when half immersed in water, it is the straight stick and not a bent one which is the object of our perceptual act on that occasion—despite the fact that it fails to satisfy the attribution of being bent.

Husserl's account of the directedness of the perceptual act (augmented with an account of the demonstrative element) comprises the sense in which the perceptual act is said by him to be "direct" with respect to its (purported) object. It should be noticed that the sense in which a perceptual act is "direct" with respect to its (purported) object does *not* involve a claim that this direct awareness provides us with an epistemologically secure access to its object. Indeed, the noematic Sinn of the perceptual act determines the object of its act, if there is one, but it does not guarantee an object for its act, nor does it guarantee that the object (when there is one) satisfies its attributive content.

One more comment might help bring into fuller relief the sense in which a perceptual act is said by Husserl to be "direct" with respect to its (purported) object. I have been maintaining that according to Husserl the noematic Sinn of a perceptual act is a singular meaning. Husserl distinguishes in this respect the act of perception (as well as other direct object acts) from acts whose noematic Sinne are propositions.[13] The act of judging is used by him as a paradigm for the latter, but there are others (I hope that . . , I regret that . . , etc.). I call an act whose noematic Sinn is a proposition, a "propositional act." Now, one of Husserl's reasons for rejecting Representative Realism is that the latter, in all its versions, contains the claim that in the perceptual situation the agent's relation with the perceived physical object is via a judgment, or an inference. Husserl's insistence that the noematic Sinn of a perceptual act is a singular meaning is, in part, an insistence that the perceptual act does *not* (essentially) involve judging anything about the (purported) object of the act.[14*]

This outline of Husserl's account of our perceptual experience will be further elaborated during the discussion of his account of perceiving a melody, to which we now turn.

III

Suppose that I hear a familiar melody played on the clarinet

by my son. Two distinct processes are taking place in my perceptual situation: there is the physical melody token, which is im-
pinging on my senses as it "unfolds" during a certain time interval.
And there is my perceptual awareness of that melody token,
which also takes place during a certain time interval. Being mindful
of time lags, it is indeed not part of the story that they are one
and the same interval of time. Let T be the time interval throughout which I am perceptually aware of the melody. According to
Husserl, I have during T a continuous perceptual act whose noematic Sinn continuously determines the *whole* physical melody
token itself as the object of my act. However, this does not mean
that the melody is continuously experienced by me, during T, as
sounding "all at once"—so to speak. On the contrary, hearing a
melody essentially involves experiencing its constituent tones in
succession. My act, during T, is a continuous process in the course
of which, although the whole melody token is continuously the object of my act, the constituent tones of that melody are successively experienced by me as sounding now. As a tone, in its turn, is
experienced by me as sounding now, the earlier tones are simul-
taneously experienced by me as having sounded, and the later
tones as yet to sound. That the whole melody token, the one and
the same melody token, rather than successive individual tones, is
continuously the object of my act during T is because throughout that interval of time the noematic Sinn of my act is such that
the tones which I successively experience are experienced by me
as constituents, or as parts, of a *single* process—the melody token.

However, each tone token is itself a process occupying some
positive amount of time. So, before the perceptual awareness of a
tone token is used in an account of the perceptual awareness of a
melody, an account of the former must be provided.

Let, then, S be a sub-interval of T throughout which I have a
perceptual awareness of a certain tone of the melody as currently
sounding. Let us leave aside for the moment what is involved in
my taking that tone to be a constituent of the melody and focus
solely on my perceptual awareness of the tone token by itself.
Husserl's account of our temporal awareness is governed by his
adherence to a principle which he inherits from Brentano. Husserl
informs us of Brentano's view:

> A conception which derives from Herbart, was taken up by Lotze, and
> played a major role in the whole following period, operates as an im-
> pelling motive in Brentano's theory. The conception is this: for the com-

prehension of a sequence of representations . . . it is necessary that they be the absolutely simultaneous Objects of a referential cognition which embraces them completely and indivisibly in a single unifying act . . . Such representations would all be impossible if the act of representation itself were completely merged in temporal succession. On this interpretation, the assumption that the intuition of a temporal interval takes place in a now, in a temporal point, appears to be self-evident and altogether inescapable . . .   (*Time*, pp. 40-41)

The idea seems clear: no succession of awarenesses—no matter how close together in time they come—can, by itself, account for an awareness of succession. It must be the case that an awareness of succession derives from simultaneous features of the structure of that awareness. For instance, an awareness of the succession of, say, two tones must involve simultaneous awareness of both tones. Similarly, the continuity of an awareness cannot, by itself, account for a continuous awareness of continuity. It must be the case that a continuous awareness of the continuity of, say, a tone involves an awareness of a temporally extended part of the tone (or the whole of it) at any given *instant* of that awareness. In general, an awareness of a relation (temporal or otherwise) necessarily involves simultaneous awareness of the relata. I will refer to this principle as *The Principle of Simultaneous Awareness,* or *PSA.*

In line with *PSA,* Husserl maintains:

it pertains to the essence of the intuition of time that in every point of its duration . . . it is consciousness of *what has just been* and not mere consciousness of the now-point of the objective thing appearing as having duration.   (*Time*, pp. 53-54)

Husserl, then, describes the perception of a tone in the following way:

The sound is given—that is, I am conscious of it as now, and I am so conscious of it "as long as" I am conscious of any of its phases as now. But if any temporal phase (corresponding to a temporal point of the duration of the sound) is an actual now (with the exception of the beginning point), then I am conscious of a continuity of phases as "before," and I am conscious of the whole interval of the temporal duration from the beginning-point to the now-point as an expired duration . . . At the end-point, I am conscious of this point itself as a now-point and of the whole duration as expired . . . "During" this whole flux of consciousness, I am conscious of one and the same sound as enduring, as enduring now.   (*Time*, pp. 44-45)

Let us turn to my perceptual awareness of a tone during *S*. At any given instant of *S* I am aware, according to Husserl, of a certain instantaneous tone-phase as sounding *now,* and of a continuity of earlier tone-phases (ending with but not including the now-phase) as stretching into the *past* from that instant. Although Husserl concentrates almost exclusively on this past-oriented aspect of our perceptual experience, he also maintains that, in addition, I am anticipatorily aware at that instant of a continuity of tone-phases as stretching into the *future* from that instant. As my act progresses through *S,* a continuously different tone-phase is experienced by me as sounding now, more and more of the tone is experienced by me as elapsed into the past, and less and less of it as still in the future. According to Husserl, then, it is the *whole* tone token which is continuously the object of my perceptual act during *S,* but my perceptual experience is such that that tone token is experienced by me during that interval as from a continuously changing temporal perspective.

Let *t* be an (noninitial and nonfinal) instant of *S.*[15*] According to Husserl, my act, at *t,* has a substructure which is responsible for the particular temporal perspective I have of the tone token at that instant. This substructure consists of a "primal-impression" (or "sensation"), a continuous manifold of "retentions," and a continuous manifold of "protentions." The primal-impression had by me at *t* is that feature of my act which is responsible for my being aware at that instant of a particular tone-phase as sounding *now.* The manifold of retentions had by me at *t* are those features of my act which are responsible for my being aware at that instant of a continuity of earlier tone-phases as extending into the *past* from that instant. And the manifold of protentions had by me at *t* are those features of my act which are responsible for my being aware at that instant of a continuity of later tone-phases as extending into the *future* from that instant. Husserl alternatively refers to a retention as "primal-memory," and to a protention as "primal-expectation." Explicating the notions of primal-impression, retention, and protention is the main part of Husserl's account of our temporal awareness.

According to Husserl, there is an essential connection between the retentions which I have at *t* and earlier primal-impressions had by me: Every primal-impression "is subject to the law of modification"[16] in accordance with which it is succeeded in time by a continuous sequence of retentions. In such a sequence, each retention is "directed" at the very same tone-phase which is the object of the primal-impression it "modifies." However, whereas the primal-impression attributes to its tone-phase *nowness,* the retentions belonging to its modificational sequence attribute to that very same tone-phase *pastness*. The amount of pastness which each retention in such a sequence attributes to the tone-phase is in direct proportion to its location in the modificational sequence, and it increases the farther removed in time it is from the primal-impression it "modifies." As a result of this law of modification, at any instant of my perceptual awareness of the tone I have, apart from a primal-impression, a continuous manifold of retentions belonging to modificational sequences proceeding from earlier primal-impressions, sequences that are still being "generated" at that instant. Although Husserl is not explicit about it, he must have also held that there are other laws in accordance with which I have the protentions that I do have at that instant. Husserl's discussion of the notion of protention is, unfortunately, very sketchy.

Husserl's conception of the structure of my perceptual awareness at *t* is best illustrated by means of the diagram.[17]

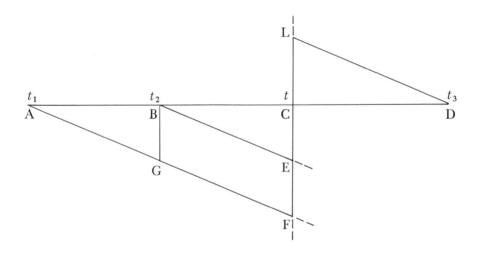

The horizontal line $\overline{AD}$ represents both the time interval *S* and the continuous sequence of primal-impressions which I have during *S*. The points A, B, C, and D represent primal-impressions had by me at t_1, t_2, t, and t_3, respectively. The descending lines $\overline{AF}$ and $\overline{BE}$, not including (respectively) points A and B, represent two continuous sequences of retentions. The sequence of retentions represented by the descending line $\overline{AF}$, not including point A, consists of "retentional modifications" of the primal-impression A had by me at t_1. The sequence of retentions represented by the descending line $\overline{BE}$, not including point B, consists of "retentional modifications" of the primal-impression B had by me at t_2. The magnitude of pastness which any given retention attributes to its tone-phase is represented by the vertical distance of that retention from line $\overline{AD}$. Thus, although G and F (in being "modifications" of the same primal-impression) are retentions of the same tone-phase, F attributes to that tone-phase twice as much pastness as G does. The vertical line $\overline{CF}$, not including point C, represents the continuous manifold of retentions had by me at t. This continuous manifold of retentions corresponds to the continuous sequence of primal-impressions along $\overline{AC}$, not including point C. The vertical line $\overline{CL}$, not including point C, represents the continuous manifold of protentions had by me at t. This continuous manifold of protentions corresponds to the continuous sequence of primal-impressions along $\overline{CD}$, not including point C. The vertical line $\overline{FL}$ represents the substructure of retentions, primal-impression, and protentions had by my act at t.

I have been referring to primal-impressions, retentions, and protentions as "features" of my act, and not as "acts." I have been doing so in keeping with Husserl's view that these are, indeed, "dependent" features of acts, but *not* in and by themselves acts.[18*] It is, nevertheless, a central part of Husserl's account of our temporal awareness that primal-impressions, retentions, and protentions are, like acts, *intentional,* or "directed."[19*] However, according to Husserl they have intentionality, or directedness, *only* as constituents of full-fledged acts. We can explain what Husserl has in mind here by appealing to an early notion of his— *partial intention.* What he means by it is formulated in his *Logical Investigations:*

> All perceiving . . . is, on our view, a web of partial intentions, fused to-gether in the unity of a single total intention. The correlate [object] of this last intention is the thing, while the correlates [objects] of its partial intentions are *the thing's parts and aspects.*   (*LI*, p. 701)[20]

We might, then, say that just as the extratemporal parts and aspects of an object are intended by the act through a "web" of partial intentions, so are its *temporal* parts and aspects intended by the act through a "web" of special partial intentions: primal-impressions, retentions, and protentions. While the "correlate" (intended object) of the act is the whole temporal object, the "correlates" (intended objects) of the primal-impressions, retentions, and protentions are the temporal phases of the "total" object of the act.

As in the case of full-fledged acts, the intentionality, or the directedness, of primal-impressions, retentions, and protentions is an intrinsic (nonrelational) feature of these partial acts. As in the case of an act, the relation of these partial acts (partial intentions) to their object-phases, if there are any, is a relation of reference, a reference that is uniquely determined by their meanings. In virtue of its meaning, a retention is directed not at a present object-phase but at a *past* phase of that object. A primal-impression is directed at a *present* phase of that object, and a protention at a *future* phase of that object. As a consequence of my having those retentions, primal-impression and protentions that I have at *t,* I am aware at that instant of the *whole* temporally extended tone, but as from a certain *temporal perspective.* As my act progresses, more and more of the tone is experienced by me as elapsed, or as past, and less and less as yet to sound, or as future.

According to Husserl, we systematically "constitute" the objects of our perceptual acts as being *concurrent* with our acts of perceiving them.[21] Our primal-impressions intend their (purported) object-phases as occuring *now*—that is, as occurring at the time of their own occurrence. Since the amount of pastness which our retentions attribute to their (purported) object-phases is relativized to the temporal location of the primal-impression they "modify," the elapsed temporal part of the (purported) object is intended as occupying the same time interval as that occupied by the elapsed part of the act of perceiving it. A corresponding statement is also true about protentions.

From the point of view of science this means that our perceptual awareness involves a systematic temporal illusion, since from that standpoint the time of the perception and the time of the perceived always diverge.[22] We do, for instance, see a nova which, science tells us, occurred many years ago as occuring at the time of our seeing it, as we hear a clap of thunder which was produced a few seconds before as being produced while we are hearing it. However, this does not mean that our perceptual acts fail, systematically, to come in "direct contact" with their objects. I argued earlier that our perceptual acts have a demonstrative element. Again, although Husserl himself is not explicit about it, it is thanks to the demonstrative element in my act of perceiving the nova that the nova itself (which happened long before I was born) is, despite its illusive temporal appearance, the immediate, or direct, object of that act. Similarly, it is thanks to the demonstrative element in my act of perceiving the tone that the tone itself (which was produced, say, during the time interval S' whose beginning point is earlier than the beginning point of S) is continuously the immediate object of my act during S.

I mentioned earlier that Husserl's discussion of protentions is sketchy. However, from what he does say it seems that there are, on his view, some significant differences between retentions and protentions, in addition to their being past and future directed respectively. To understand those differences, we must focus now on the fact that our retentions, primal-impressions and protentions intend their respective object-phases not only with respect to their temporal locations but also with regard to their extratemporal qualities. For instance, the retentions, primal-impression, and protentions which I have at t intend their respective tone-phases not only as past, present, and future, but also as *tones* of certain tonal qualities. Keeping this in mind, the following two differences are of interest.

First, according to Husserl, what I retain at any given instant is retained by me as having (at least some) fully determinate extratemporal characteristics; whereas, what I protend at that instant may suffer, and often does, from a uniform extratemporal attributive indeterminacy.[23] However, this, according to Husserl, is only a contingent difference between retentions and protentions: a fully "prophetic" consciousness is, in principle, always possible.[24] Since the extratemporal content of a retention is derived from the primal-impression it "modifies," this difference between retentions and protentions exists to begin with between primal-impressions and protentions.

Second, according to Husserl, in a perceptual act the meanings of my retentions are sensorily "filled"; whereas, in the same act the meanings of my protentions are "unfilled."[25*] Again, the sensory "fullness" of a retention is derived from the primal-impression it "modifies." However, the meaning of my primal-impression is not only "filled," it is said to be "primordially filled." Husserl's notion of filling is a difficult one that requires further study. But we can have *some* idea of what he has in mind by considering what he says about sensory filling in the case of perceiving an ordinary *enduring* object. Let us, then, consider briefly such a case. When we perceive an enduring object, we have a perceptual act the noematic Sinn of which determines that object as from a certain spatial perspective: a certain side of the object is determined as the near side, and others as hidden sides. The noematic Sinn of my act, indeed, contains components that pertain to the hidden aspects of the object, as it contains components that pertain to the near side of that object. Now, the components of the noematic Sinn pertaining to the *near side* of the perceived object are said by Husserl to be "primordially filled":

> The meaning in the perception ... is perceptively filled out, and we become aware of the perceived object with its colors, forms, and so forth (so far as they "fall within perception") [26*] in the mode of the "embodied" ... In the noematic setting we find the character of embodiment (*as the primordial state of being filled out*) blended with pure meaning ...
>
> (*Ideas*, p. 351)

The point which interests us here is this: Regardless of what else it may mean, it seems that, according to Husserl, the difference between the filled and the unfilled components of the noematic Sinn of a perceptual act is correlated with a difference between those features of the perceived object which we experience *evidentially,* and those which we do not. To say of the components of the noematic Sinn of the perceptual act pertaining to the near side of the (purported) object that they are *primordially* filled out is not only to say that the corresponding features of the object are experienced by us *evidentially,* but also that they are evidential to us in the most "original" way that features of the world can be evidentially given—namely, in an "embodied" way, i.e., as presently confronting our co-intended organism. The present tense is significant here:

> ... *perceptions* of things are primordial experiences in relation to all memories ... They are primordial in the sense in which concrete experiences can be that at all. For closer inspection reveals in their concreteness only *one,* but that always a continuously flowing *absolute primordial phase,* that of the living *now.*   (*Ideas*, p. 202)

Clearly, what Husserl means here is not that perception occurs in the "now" and memory does not (which would be absurd) but, rather, that the *object* of perception is experienced by me as presently confronting my co-intended organism, whereas the *object* of memory is not.

Let us now change the story a bit. Suppose that I move around an object while keeping my eyes on it. What is for me the "near side" of that object is now continuously changing. At any given instant of the duration of that perception I have according to Husserl a primal-impression the meaning of which (in a case of perceiving an *enduring* object) determines the *whole* object as the object of my primal-impression, while determining a particular aspect of that object as its *near side* at that instant. The components of the meaning of my primal-impression pertaining to that near side are primordially filled, and in so being they determine that side of the object as confronting my co-intended organism at that instant. In addition to that primal-impression, I have at that instant a manifold of retentions the meanings of which determine the *whole* (one and the same) object as the object of their respective retentions while containing determinations of aspects of that object which have "just" been experienced by me as confronting my co-intended organism, but which are not so experienced by me anymore. According to Husserl, the components of the meanings of my retentions pertaining to these aspects are still "filled," even though not primordially so. That is, these aspects of the object are still experienced by me *evidentially,* even though not in an "original" way.

We now apply these considerations to the case of my perceiving the tone. According to Husserl, the meaning of the primal-impression I have at t is primordially filled, and in being so, it determines a particular tone-phase as confronting my co-intended organism at that instant. In addition, I have at t a manifold of retentions directed at the elapsed part of the tone, a part that was "just" experienced by me as confronting my co-intended organism, but that is not so experienced by me any more. Again, according to Husserl, the meanings of my retentions at that instant are "filled," but not primordially so. That is, the just elapsed part of the tone is still experienced by me *evidentially,* but not any more in an "original" way.

The way I understand Husserl's view, in maintaining that our retentions are "filled" whereas our protentions are not, Husserl maintains that there is an essential *epistemic* asymmetry between our experience of the immediate past and our experience of the immediate future.[27*] This asymmetry is independent of the earlier mentioned contingent asymmetry between the retentional extra-temporal attributive determinacy and the protentional extra-temporal attributive indeterminacy.

I have been discussing our experience of the *immediate* past and the *immediate* future, since according to Husserl our retentonal and protentional spans at a given instant are limited by psychological factors to relatively short durations. However, according to him this is, indeed, only a contingent limitation: as a fully "prophetic" consciousness is, in principle, always possible, so is—according to him—a fully retaining consciousness, in principle always possible. [28]

I turn now to the last part of the exposition of Husserl's account of our temporal awareness. I have been explicating Husserl's conceptions of primal-impression, retention, and protention by appealing to his (early) notion of *partial intention*. Although this appeal may have had an initial explanatory value, it is, nevertheless, *not* a legitimate appeal. To see this we need to take a closer look at Husserl's conception of partial intention.

Husserl characterizes partial intentions as those features of an act which—I am going to say—*individuate* (single out) the parts and aspects of the (purported) object of the act. This notion of individuation applies, to begin with, to the act as a whole. To help clarify what counts as "individuating," consider the following story: suppose that I am hiking in the wilds of India accompanied by a guide. Suddenly my guide stops me with the warning that we are approaching a tiger. Despite my guide's insistence that the tiger is in plain view I fail, at first, to see it, since it blends so well with its surroundings. After a moment of visual search in the direction of my guide's pointed finger, I suddenly see the tiger. I realize that, indeed, if the tiger has not moved, it has been in plain view all along. Now, all other conditions were right for my seeing that tiger, except one: I failed, at first to *individuate* the tiger in my field of vision. In this case, individuating the tiger consists, simply, in my having an act the noematic Sinn of which determines the tiger as the object of that act.

The partial intentions involved in my individuating the tiger are those features of my act which individuate the various parts and aspects of the tiger. This does *not* mean that for *each* part and aspect of the tiger there is a partial intention in my act which individuates it. On the contrary, according to Husserl a "transcendent" object, such as a tiger, always has "more" to it that can be experienced in any one act, or a finite number of acts (i.e., in a finite amount of experience). Nevertheless, those of the tiger's parts and aspects which *are* individuated in my act are so individuated by the presence of appropriate *meaning components* in the noematic Sinn of that act. For each part and aspect of the tiger which is individuated in my act there is a meaning component in the noematic Sinn of my act which determines that part or aspect as a part or an aspect of the tiger.

Among those features of the tiger which are individuated in my act, not all are perceived (primordially experienced) by me in that act. For instance, I individuate a certain side of the tiger as its near side, as I individuate other of its aspects as its (presently) hidden aspects. In seeing the tiger, I do, indeed, see its near side, but I do not see its far side or its other hidden features. However, this way of speaking might be misleading: what I *see* (i.e., the object of my visual act) is determined by no less than the noematic Sinn of my act. In the present case, it is the *whole* tiger, and not merely its near side, which is the object of my visual act. Still, my awareness of the near side of the tiger occupies, in the context of my act of seeing the tiger, a perceptually privileged position over my awareness of its hidden parts and aspects. Husserl attempts to deal with this difference via his notion of primordial filling, always insisting that a near side of an object is experienced by us precisely as such, namely, as a side of a full-fledged object. Another way of characterizing that perceptual privilege is, perhaps, by saying that the near side (or, rather, the near surface), in contrast with the hidden aspects, is so experienced by us in the context of our perceptual acts that by a mere shift of *attention* (everything else remaining precisely the same) it can become in its own right an object of an act of perception.[29*] Be the correct characterization of that difference as it may, the (independent) fact remains that *individuating* an object, or a feature of an object, is a *necessary condition* for perceiving it.

That individuating an entity or a feature of an entity is a necessary condition for perceiving it has some interesting and important consequences. For instance, it does *not* follow from the fact that I, say, see the near surface of an object that I see *all the parts* of that near surface, even if none of them is obscured from my view. In fact, it does not follow from my seeing that near surface that I see *any* of its (proper) parts unless I *individuate* a part, or parts, of that near surface *in addition* to my individuating the near surface as a whole.[30*] More so, it does not follow from the fact that I perceive the near surface of an object that I perceive any, let alone all, of the points on that surface. Clearly, perceptually individuating the near surface of an object does *not* require, nor does it in fact involve, perceptually individuating all the points on that surface.

In fact, there seem to be independent (probably contingent) reasons for which we cannot perceptually individuate very small surfaces (let alone point-surfaces) even if we wanted to. This, however, does not diminish the force of Husserl's claim, namely that perceptually individuating the near surface of an object does not require perceptually individuating any of its proper parts, even if we confine ourselves to perceptible parts.

We now apply these results to the case of our perceiving a tone. Similar considerations to the above make it clear that it does not follow from the fact that I perceive a tone that I perceive *any* of its proper parts, let alone all its instantaneous phases. It is, in general, evident that the perceptual individuation of a *process* does *not* require, nor does it in fact involve, exhaustively individuating its constitutent events. However, according to Husserl's account of our temporal awareness, my perceptual individuation of a tone *requires* that I have retentions, primal-impressions, and protentions which exhaustively "intend" the *instantaneous phases* of that tone. It follows, then, that whatever else they are, retentions, primal-impressions, and protentions *are not partial intentions*.

What, then, are we to make of these features, given that we cannot take them any more to be partial intentions? It is clear that Husserl considered retentions, primal-impressions, and protentions to be *real* (or, rather, in Husserl's terminology, "reell") features of the structure of our temporal awareness, and not mere theoretical fictions. It is equally clear that he conceived of them as *intentional* features of our temporal awareness. However, to deny that they are partial intentions is, it seems, to deny that they have *particular meanings* associated with them. The problem is this: how can Husserl maintain both that retentions, primal-impressions, and protentions are intentional and that they do not have particular meanings associated with them?

Husserl himself does not bring up this question, so no direct answer to it can be found in his writings. However, some of what he does say amounts to an answer to it, or at least it points in the direction in which the full answer should be sought. To recognize this, we must refocus on a feature of our temporal awareness which was introduced from the start without much fanfare, namely that perceiving a process, such as a tone, involves experiencing its *continuous "spread"* throughout a particular interval of time. It was just argued that perceptually individuating a tone does not necessarily involve individuating any of its (proper) temporal parts. On the other hand, perceptually individuating an entity (say, a tone or a near surface of an object) does not consist in intentionally determining merely its temporal and spatial boundaries. Whether it is in the case of individuating a tone or in the case of individuating the near surface of an object, we are not confronted with a mere empty "frame" for an object. Even if no proper part of the tone is further individuated by us, we experience the tone's continuous temporal *extendedness* throughout a particular interval of time, as we experience the near surface's spatial *extendedness* throughout a particular area of space. Whatever we experience of reality, we experience in virtue of there being an appropriate *intentional* feature in our empirical experience. In particular, perceptually individuating a process, such as a tone, involves, as part of "singling it out," a unique intentional structure which is responsible for locating the process, *qua* intended, throughout a particular interval of time. This intentional structure consists of a continuous manifold of (instantaneous) process-phase "intentions" comprising the intentional "beam" which, in the context of an act of perceiving that process, "constitutes" the process in such a way that we experience its *continuous extendedness* throughout a given interval of time.

Husserl's notion of *constitution* does, indeed, come in handy here. Husserl says of the objects of our acts that they are constituted by, or through, our acts. Føllesdal insists, and I concur, that "this does not mean that they are caused by our acts or brought about by our acts, but just that in the act the various components of consciousness are interconnected in such a way that we have an experience as of one full-fledged object."[31] We might, then, say that in perceptually individuating the tone, I *constitute* it phase-by-phase through a continuous manifold of tone-phase "intentions," but I do not thereby individuate it phase-by-phase (and, thus, I do not thereby perceive it phase-by-phase). These tone-phase "intentions" are nothing in themselves apart from the role they play in my perceptually *individuating* that tone; this role being locating the tone, *qua* intended, throughout a particular interval of time. Thanks to this role played by these tone-phase "intentions," I experience the *continuous temporal extendedness* of the tone throughout that interval of time. These tone-phase "intentions" are, indeed, none other than the aforementioned retentions, primal-impressions, and protentions.

We sum up Husserl's account of perceiving a tone as follows: My act of perceiving the tone, during S, is a continuous process throughout which the very same tone token is continuously the object of my act. However, although the very same tone token is continuously the object of my act, it is constituted by me as from a continuously changing *temporal perspective*. As my act progresses, more and more of the tone token is constituted by me as *past,* and less and less as *future.* Just the same, the tone token is *perceived* by me as long as any of its phases is constituted by me as a *now-phase*—that is, as long as any of its phases is an "object" of a *primal-impression* had by me.[32] Now, the very same account applies to the perception of a *melody:*

> In the "perception of a melody," we distinguish the tone *given now,* which we term the "perceived," from those which *have gone by,* which we say are "not perceived." On the other hand, we call the *whole melody* one that is *perceived,* although only the now-point actually is . . . If the purposive intention is directed toward the melody, toward the whole object, we have nothing but perception . . . The whole melody . . . appears as present so long as it still sounds, so long as the notes *belonging to it,* intended in the *one* nexus of apprehensions, still sound. The melody is past only after the last note has gone.   (*Time,* pp. 60–61)

What the object of my perceptual act at *t* is—whether a single tone or a whole melody—depends on the noematic Sinn of my act at that instant, and, given the way I told the story, it is the *whole melody* which is the object of my act at *t,* and not merely one of its tones. What this means is that my perceptual individuation of a tone as currently sounding at *t* is but a *partial intention* in the context of my act at that instant. It is because the "total" intention (the noematic Sinn of my act) has the melody as its object that I experience, at *t,* a *melody* as currently sounding, and not merely a single, unrelated, tone. As in the case of perceiving a single tone, although the very same melody is, continuously, the object of my act during *T,* it is constituted by me as from a continuously changing temporal perspective. As my act progresses, more and more of the tones of the melody are constituted by me as *past,* and less and less as *future.* The *whole* melody, however, is perceived by me as long as any of its tones is individuated by me as currently sounding—that is, as long as any of its tones is such that one of its *phases* is the "object" of a *primal-impression* had by me, or as long as any of the *pauses* between its tones is constituted by me as a pause between tones of that melody.

I cannot conclude without answering a question that might have come to the mind of the reader at some early point, even though at least part of the answer to it must by now be obvious. The question is this: Why does Husserl insist that retentions, primal-impressions, and protentions are *not acts*? Why doesn't he simply refer to them as "memory," "perception," and "anticipation"? For one thing, we know now that this would have committed him to the false view that we perceptually *individuate* processes phase-by-phase, but this is not the only (or even the main) reason. Let us consider briefly the act of remembering. Husserl insists that in an act of remembering a melody the melody is constituted in a way similar to the way it is constituted in an act of perception:

> We remember a melody, let us say, which in our youth we heard during a concert. Then it is obvious that the entire phenomenon of memory has, *mutatis mutandis,* exactly the same constitution as the perception of the melody. Like the perception, it has a favored point; to the now-point of the perception corresponds a now-point of the memory, and so on. We run through a melody . . . we hear "as if" the first note, then the second, etc. At any given time, there is always a sound (or a tonal phase) in the now-point. The preceding sounds, however, are not erased from consciousness . . . Everything thus resembles perception . . .   (*Time,* pp. 57–58)

The main part of the answer to the above question, then, is this: an act of remembering a melody, much like an act of perceiving it, *requires* a structure of retentions, primal-impressions, and protentions, even though in the context of an act of remembering they do not constitute the melody as currently sounding but as having sounded. A corresponding statement is true also about the act of anticipation.

There is more in Husserl's account of our temporal awareness. In particular, there is an account of our (passive) awareness of the continuity (and thereby the unity) of our very awareness, and, as a corollary to it, an account of our experience of the passage of events. But all of this, as the full account of memory and anticipation, must be left for other occasions.

9
Husserl's Theory
of the Pure Ego

Douglas Heinsen

I. Introduction

This essay seeks to clarify Husserl's notion of the pure Ego and the theory surrounding it to the full extent allowed by the texts. It will be shown that this Ego-theory, whether correct or incorrect, at least makes good sense and is entirely consistent with the rest of Husserl's thought.

Now in the *Logical Investigations* Husserl admits an "empirical ego" and a "phenomenological ego," but none further. The empirical ego is simply that of ordinary discourse: it is the human mind ("mental ego") together with its human body ("ego-body"), or in sum the human person (*LI* 541m, 550tm).[1*] This ego is therefore a "thinglike object" (*LI* 541m), and we perceive it "just as we perceive an external thing" (*LI* 551t).

While not "thinglike," the phenomenological ego is also an empirical object, for it is one aspect of the empirical ego: it stands "in the same sort of relation to the mental ego as the side of a perceived external thing . . . stands to the whole thing" (*LI* 550t). Beginning with the empirical ego, Husserl reaches this second ego by means of a "reduction" that is not yet the transcendental reduction of *Ideas*

but merely a process of abstraction that remains fixed in the
natural realm:

> If we cut out the ego-body from the empirical ego, and limit the purely
> mental ego to its [actual] phenomenological content, the latter reduces to
> a unity of consciousness, to a real experiential complex, which we (i.e.
> each man for his own ego) find in part evidently present, and for the rest
> postulate on good grounds. The phenomenologically reduced ego is there-
> fore nothing peculiar, floating above many experiences: it is simply identi-
> cal with their own interconnected unity.   (*LI* 541m, cf. 550tm)

So the phenomenological ego is just the empirical ego's stream of
experience considered in its unity, and accordingly remains a
natural reality.

But the Husserl of *Logical Investigations* is "quite unable to
find" a pure ego, a transcendental subject at work somewhere
'above' or 'behind' the stream of human experience (*LI* 549b).
Nor does he see any need to postulate such an ego. It could only
serve, he thinks, as an ego of pure apperception, a subjective
center of relations which brings all contents of consciousness into
a unity (*LI* 548f). However, no subjective center is required to
unify consciousness, since its

> contents [already] have . . . their own law-bound ways of coming together,
> of losing themselves in [ever] more comprehensive unities, and, in so far
> as they thus become and are one [of their own accord], the phenome-
> nological ego or unity of consciousness is already constituted, without
> need of an additional, peculiar ego-principle which supports all contents
> and unites them all once again. Here as elsewhere it is not clear what such
> a principle would effect.   (*LI* 541–542)

Husserl thus repudiates the pure ego (*LI* 561t): phenomenological
inspection fails to reveal it, and there is, in theory, no work for it
to do.

Beginning with *Ideas* all this is changed. With the advent of the
transcendental reduction and of transcendental idealism, phenomenology ceases to be a descriptive psychology and the empirical and phenomenological egos receive a new status. They are still
realities, but like all realities (*Realitäten*), whether material or
psychological, they are now "merely intentional" objects, "mere
unities of an intentional 'constitution'" (*I* 152). Each such reality
"is, in principle, intuitable and determinable only as the element
[i.e., the meaning] common to the [harmoniously] motivated
appearance-manifolds, but *over and beyond* this, is just nothing
at all" (*I* 139mb, 142m). To imagine that human and worldly

beings are anything more or other than meanings intended by consciousness is "ein widersinniger Gedanke" (*IE* 117b), a counter-
sensical thought.

It is also in *Ideas* that Husserl (now dismissing his earlier skeptical
position in this regard as a mistake: *I* 157n.), first recognizes a pure
ego. Although transcendental, this third ego, henceforth called the
pure Ego (das reines Ich), is still an ego conceived along patently
traditional lines. It "can *in no sense* be reckoned *as a real [reelles]
part or phase* of . . . experiences themselves" (*I* 156b/*IE* 138t). It
is neither an experience nor a process (*I* 156m, *CM* 67m), but
"*the active and affected subject of consciousness* [who] lives in
all processes of consciousness and is related, *through* them, to all
object-poles" (*CM* 66m). Or again, it is "the ultimately constitutive subjectivity," and as such precedes everything worldly,
everything human (*FTL* 238m, 251mb). The Ego "lives" in the
cogito, but "This life does not signify the being of any 'contents'
of any kind in a stream of contents" (*I* 249b). The cogito is to be
understood as an act performed by the Ego; the Ego is an active
being, a being whose act each cogito is (*I* 107m, 109m, 213b,
249m; *CM* 66m). The stream of cogitationes as a whole is the
Ego's "life" (*I* 130f, *CM* 66tm), but the Ego "lives" in the cogito
only in the sense of "bringing it about" (*I* 249m, 294t).

The Ego is accordingly a transcendent entity (*I* 157t). Phenomenology nevertheless knows of the Ego and is able to posit it because
the Ego is "given together with pure consciousness" (*I* 157tb), and
indeed given in such a way that "*The thesis of my pure Ego . . . is
'necessary' and plainly indubitable*" (*I* 131b, 156mb). The Ego is
not literally hidden away inside the cogito. But in consciousness
"each individual event has its essence that can be grasped in its
eidetic purity" (*I* 104t), and "Every '*cogito*' . . . is [essentially]
characterized as act of the Ego, [as] 'proceeding from the Ego'"
(*I* 213b, 214m). The Ego escapes the transcendental reduction and
cannot be suspended because it is essentially entailed by the cogito,
because "no disconnecting can remove the form of the *cogito* and
[thereby] cancel the 'pure' subject of the act" (*I* 214tm; cf. 156f).
"To the *cogito* itself belongs an immanent 'glancing towards' the
object, a directedness which . . . springs forth from the 'Ego,'
which can therefore never be absent" (*I* 109m). Qua Ego, then,
"I . . . *exist for myself with apodictic necessity*" (*FTL* 251b).
"I myself . . . am absolute Reality (Wirklichkeit), given through
a positing that is unconditioned and simply indissoluble" (*I* 131b).

Our problem is to understand the Ego-theory just outlined. Three central questions will guide the discussion.

(1) According to the second edition of the *Logical Investigations,* Husserl reached the pure Ego only after having "learnt not to be led astray from a pure grasp of the given through corrupt forms of ego-metaphysic" (*LI* 549n.). But how does one reach the Ego without recourse to metaphysical speculation? Or variously: how and in what sense is the Ego entailed by the cogito and thereby "given together with pure consciousness"?

(2) If the Ego was originally repudiated at least in part because there appeared, in theory, to be no work for it to do, what function does the Ego serve in Husserl's later writings? Why is the thesis of my pure Ego *necessary*?

(3) On what grounds may the Ego be posited apodictically? These questions can be answered only if we first of all distinguish between the pure and personal Ego and the transcendental ego and monad.

II. The pure (polar) Ego, personal Ego, transcendental ego and monad

The pure Ego per se, the Ego that is *essentially* involved with the cogito, is also called by Husserl the "polar Ego (Ego in the particular sense: mere Ego-pole)" (*CM* 104t, *FTL* 287t, *IZ* 105t). This is the one "identical Ego . . . as the active and affected subject of consciousness" (*CM* 66tm). It is called the polar Ego in part because, while in some sense a "phenomenological datum" (*I* 157t),

> the experiencing Ego is still nothing that might be taken *for itself* and made into an object of inquiry on its *own* account. Apart from its 'ways of being related' [to objects] or 'ways of behaving' [i.e., the cogito acts], it is completely empty of essential components, it has no content that could be unravelled, it is in and for itself indescribable: pure Ego and nothing further.   (*I* 214b)

In another sense, however, "*this centering Ego is not an empty pole of identity,* any more than any *object* is such" (*CM* 66m). For the polar Ego may acquire determinations that are specifically Ego-determinations (*CM* 104t): it may be constituted as having convictions, habitualities, abilities, a personal character, and so forth (*CM* 66f, 77b–8t; *FTL* 246b). But the polar Ego is not identical with its personality and personal determinations (any more than an object is identical with the sum of its properties);

it is, rather, the single identical substrate or bearer of them all, their center or *pole* of unity (*CM* 67mb, cf. *I* 337).

Now if we take the polar Ego together with its abiding personal style and whatever particular determinations it may possess at a given time, we arrive at what Husserl calls the "personal Ego" (*CM* 67b, *I* 151f). (If the body is thrown in as well, there results the human or psycho-physical Ego; with the addition of other such Egos, we reach the social Ego and its Ego-community.) But when so determined, the Ego is no longer essentially entailed by the cogito and ceases to be an object of apodictic knowledge (*I* §§46, 49, 54). Thus the pure polar Ego alone is of concern to us here.

Another entity easily confused with the pure Ego is the transcendental ego. Dorion Cairns notes in his translations of *CM* and *FTL* that Husserl sometimes "uses *Ego* and *Ich* to express different senses. . . . *Ich* has been translated as *Ego* (spelled with a capital) and *Ego* has been translated as *ego* (spelled with a small letter)." (*CM* 3n., *FTL* 19n.) [2*] Yet to my knowledge no one has ever managed to understand exactly what distinguishes *Ich* from *Ego*.

In fact, "das Ich" is always used by Husserl to designate what we have called the pure polar Ego. [3*] We stress again that this Ego is absolutely simple, completely lacking in content and therefore "in and for itself indescribable" (*I* 214b, *IZ* 105t). It is quite otherwise with the ego (das Ego), which *does* have "contents," "components," "internal features" (*CM* 69b, 73b, 75m, 101b). "Any 'Objective' object, *any object whatever . . .* points to *a structure . . . within the transcendental ego*" (*CM* 53b, 71m). These ego-structures are open to a reflective grasp (*CM* 65b, 71m), and indeed it is precisely the transcendental ego and it alone that phenomenology initially seeks to describe and understand (*CM* 30m, 35b–36t, 38t, 72m; *FTL* 274b–275t). This is why phenomenology (at least of the "most fundamental" sort, such as we find in *Ideas*) can be termed a "pure egology" (*CM* 30mb, 38m, 86t; *FTL* 269b), and why the transcendental reduction is at first simply an "explication of the ego" (*CM* 85b, 153b). (This initial or most fundamental stage is left behind only when phenomenology ceases to be a transcendental solipsism: *FTL* 269b–270m.)

What then *is* the ego? By the ego simpliciter Husserl seems to mean merely the Ego's flowing life: the universe of actual and possible subjective processes (*CM* 65b, 73m, 81t). But there is also the "concrete ego" or "monad"; strictly speaking, it is this and not the ego simpliciter which (initially) serves as "the universal theme of [phenomenological] description" (*CM* 38t, 68b); the concrete or monadic ego must therefore embrace everything disclosed or admitted by (fundamental) phenomenology. The ego simpliciter, "the whole of actual and potential conscious life," is thus a constituent part of the monad (*CM* 68tb). The monad is also a "sphere of meanings" and includes all *noemata* and *noematic* unities (*CM* 36t, 38t, 68t, 89b). Hyletic data doubtless belong here as well, along with every *eidos,* for these too are themes of phenomenology. The pure polar Ego (sc. the *active* subject of consciousness) is a final component of the concrete ego (*CM* 68b-69t); this is what allows "both" the Ego and the ego to be counted constitu*ting* as well as constitut*ed* subjects (*CM* 66-67; *FTL* 238m, 251mb) and the transcendental reduction to be described as a *self*-explication of the ego (*CM* 85b, 153b).

Within certain limits and in their own particular ways, the existence and structures of the monadic ego may be established apodictically (*CM* §§9, 46). But our interests are here restricted to the being and apodicticity of the pure polar Ego per se.

III. *The being of the Ego*

Phenomenology is an eidetic and purely intuitive study of the *reell* and the immanent (*I* 191 b). The Ego is not reell but transcendent, not an experience but the subject of experience. If all "deductive theorizing" and metaphysical speculation are excluded from phenomenology (*I* 193t, *CM* 139m), why is the Ego not also excluded? Is it not obviously noumenal in character and therefore inaccessible to transcendental reflection?

THE EGO AS INTENTIONAL OBJECT

In the final analysis there is only one interpretation of the Ego which is fully consistent with Husserl's philosophy as a whole. Consider:

> ... ascending to the broadest, the analytico-formal universalities, one sees that any object (no matter how indeterminately it is thought of, nay, even if it be conceived as void of content) ... is thinkable only as the correlate of an intentional constitution inseparable from it.   (*FTL* 249t)[4*]

> The "object" of consciousness, the object as having identity "with itself" during the flowing subjective process, does not come into the process from outside; on the contrary, it is included as a sense in the subjective process itself—and thus as an *"intentional effect"* *produced by* the synthesis of consciousness.   (*CM* 42m)

Neither a world *nor any other existent of any conceivable sort* comes "from outdoors" into . . . my life of consciousness. Everything outside [i.e., everything transcendent] is what it is in this inside, and gets its *true being* from the givings of it itself, and from the verifications, within this inside—its *true being*, which for that very reason belongs to this inside: [everything transcendent has its true being precisely] as a *pole of unity* in my . . . actual and possible multiplicities . . .

                              (*FTL* 250m, italics added; cf. *FTL* 230b-231, 268b)

Since these passages must evidently apply even to the Ego, our thesis is this. Like the natural world, the spatial thing, the empirical or human ego, *the pure Ego is neither more nor less than an intentional object, a meaning, a noema.* [5*] So long as the transcendental reduction is in force, these entities are held by Husserl to exist solely in his own special sense of "existence" (see *I* §§49-55, 135; *CM* 37mb, 56m, 65b, 95t; *PL* 9b, 23tm). This sense is not arbitrary but in fact a *"sense-explication* achieved *by actual work"* (*CM* 86tm); it is offered as a transcendental *clarification* of our natural (naive) understanding of reality or existence and prevents it from degenerating into absurdity at the hands of science and philosophy (*I* 14-15m, 153; *FTL* 275b). To say that world, thing, and Ego exist in this sense is to say:

(1) that they are meanings actually intended by consciousness, and

(2) that these intendings are harmoniously fulfilled in a fashion appropriate to the meanings in question.

Over and beyond their being intended and fulfilled, however, such objects are "just nothing at all" (*I* 139mb); to suppose that they are anything more would be absurd (*I* 12m, *IE* 117b). If the Ego as intentional object is nevertheless not "merely" intentional but rather an "absolute Reality" (*I* 131b, 139, 152), this only signifies that it is filled in such a way that it may be posited apodictically—that is, in such a way that we may be sure intentions of this meaning will *always* be harmoniously fulfilled (see below, section V).

Whether the Ego exists in this (clarified) sense of existence is a question that clearly falls within the scope of descriptive phenomenology; it asks merely about the nature of experience, hence is both intelligible to and in principle decidable by phenomenology. But whether the Ego exists as a thing-in-itself, a *substantia cogitans* at work (whether posited or not) somewhere 'outside' or 'behind' consciousness is nothing determinable by purely descriptive or intuitive methods; it is a metaphysical issue. Husserl avoids all "metaphysical adventure" on grounds of principle (*CM* 139m) and indeed considers any thought concerning things-in-themselves to be nonsense (*CM* 24mb, 81–86; *I* §55).

THE EGO AS TRANSCENDENT; AS TRANSCENDENTAL

The Ego may of course be posited as a thing-in-itself from the natural standpoint of our everyday and scientific lives, though to be sure it is here intended not as *pure* Ego but as the human or psycho-physical Ego (*CM* 37m, 99f). In this case the Ego is (meant as) "transcendent" in an ordinary metaphysical sense (albeit a sense which upon transcendental explication turns out to be nonsense).

From the transcendental or phenomenological viewpoint, however, the Ego can be nothing other than an intentional object, a meaning, as we have just seen. And yet here again it counts as transcendent. How can an entity still be transcendent which is simply nothing at all apart from its being intended and fulfilled? Although Husserl suggests at one point that there is something "quite peculiar" about the Ego in this regard (*I* 157t), it is elsewhere clear that, qua noema, the Ego is "transcendent" merely in a sense which applies as well to all other noemata: it is an "immanent transcendency" (*I* 157t, *CM* 142b–143t). Every noema is immanent to consciousness in the sense of being absolutely inseparable from it; a noema is "an *'intentional effect' produced by* the synthesis of consciousness" (*CM* 42m), and "Its *esse* consists exclusively in its *'percipi'*" (*I* 265t). On the other hand, every noema is transcendent in that its "being-in-consciousness is a *being-in of a completely unique kind:* not a being-in-consciousness as a really intrinsic component part, but rather a being-in-it 'ideally' as something *intentional,* something appearing" (*CM* 42t). Noemata are therefore *dependent* upon consciousness (*I* 264b), but as ideal rather than real (reell) elements of experience (*I* §§90, 97–99) they nonetheless stand "over against consciousness itself as in principle other, irreal, transcendent" (*I* 263m; cf. *I* 272m, *CM* 26b). The transcendence of the Ego thus in no way belies its intentional status.

The Ego is also termed "transcendental" (*CM* 37m, 72t), which is to say that it is presupposed by the sense and being of the world and therefore "precedes the being of the world" (CM §§10–11; *FTL* 228t, 238m, 251mb). Here again it may seem that the Ego cannot be simply a meaning. However, Ego precedes world "from the standpoint of cognition" (*FTL* 228t), not in order of time. As explicated by phenomenology, "the whole *spatio-temporal world* ... is *according to its own meaning mere intentional Being*" (*I* 139m). As something "intentional," "constituted," the world necessarily presupposes "*a sense-giving consciousness,* which, on its side, is absolute and not dependent in its turn on sense bestowed on it from another source" (*I* 153t); "the whole being of the world consists in a certain 'meaning' which presupposes absolute consciousness as the field from which the meaning is derived" (*I* 153b). Pure consciousness or the ego simpliciter is therefore transcendental in the phenomenological sense (*CM* 26b, *EJ* 49b). But insofar as the Ego is essentially entailed by transcendental consciousness, insofar as consciousness is necessarily the "life" of an Ego, the Ego is also presupposed by the world and is likewise transcendental.

So the precedence of the pure Ego is, as it were, a precedence in retrospect. Though by no means the first thing constituted by consciousness—doubtless world is prior to Ego in this respect— the Ego is intended, fulfilled, and in this sense exists as the constitutive source of all meanings, including its own; conversely, the very significance of the world points back to some such active subjectivity; but if we assert that there "really exists" (in some additional, metaphysical sense) an Ego who has constituted both itself and all other things, and who must therefore have preceded the world in actual order of time, we cease to be phenomenologists and (from the phenomenological point of view) fall into absurdity.

IV. The Givenness of the Ego

Any awareness we may have of the Ego will of necessity be an intentional awareness. As intentional, this awareness is related to its object by virtue of its noema (*I* 345b, *CM* 33tm), which refers to the object via its "content" or meaning, the noematic Sinn (*I* §§128-131). The Sinn is an "abstract form" that "dwells" within the noema (*I* 340t), and is always susceptible to conceptual expression (*I* 336b-337t, 343b). We have already seen how the noematic Sinn of the pure Ego is to be expressed: the Ego is "the active and affected subject of consciousness."

Now every noematic Sinn has as its "necessary centre" a "pure determinable X" (*I* 339tm). This noematic X functions as the substrate or bearer of predicates, as their "central point of unification," but is not itself identical with any of these determinations; taken in and of itself, it is completely devoid of content, an entirely indeterminate something=x (*I* 337, 339m). These descriptions instantly call to mind Husserl's by now familiar view that the Ego, too, is quite without internal features, an "empty pole of identity" or "centering Ego," an "identical substrate of Ego-properties" (*CM* 66f). And now finally we understand what he means: qua intentional object, the polar Ego per se is nothing other than the determinable noematic X of those experiences whereby the Ego is intended (cf. *IZ* 310b–311t).

Shall we say that the Ego *has* a noema, then, or that it *is* a noema? Each is correct in its own way, since "in respect of the noema two generically different concepts of object are to be distinguished": the object is the pure X and *has* a noematic Sinn, or it *is* this Sinn along with the X as its necessary center (*I* 338b). The polar Ego per se is naturally an object of the first sort. It is an empty something=x intended sometimes as the bare subject of consciousness (sc. as pure Ego), and sometimes again as personal Ego, transcendental ego, human ego, etc.

We are concerned with the polar Ego posited as pure Ego, as the active and affected subject of consciousness. There are, of course, certain conditions which must be satisfied if this positing is to be justified. If the Ego is to count as actually existing, its noematic Sinn must somehow be filled with intuitional content. If the Ego is to be posited apodictically, its Sinn must be filled (the Ego must be given to intuition) in some very special way. The givenness of the Ego is thus not that of a fact or premise from which the Ego's existence is then deduced or inferred. Its givenness consists in the intuitional content that may be provided its noema.

Husserl's Ego-theory will remain an enigma until we have said how such filling is secured. So far we are sure only that the Ego is somehow given through or along with the cogito. Husserl elaborates:

> so soon as I glance towards the flowing life . . . and in so doing grasp myself as the pure subject of this life . . . I say forthwith and because I must: *I am*, this life is. . . .
>
> To every stream of experience, and to every Ego as such, there belongs, in principle, the possibility of securing this self-evidence.   (*I* 130m)

> in order to know that the pure Ego exists and what it is, no accumulation of self-experience (however great) can better instruct me than the single experience of a single simple cogito.   (*IZ* 104b, my translation)

Hence the Ego may be filled in reflection upon *any* cogito. How is this possible? It is true that the Ego is for Husserl simply a meaning, a noema, and true again that noemata may be the objects of reflection—but this line of thought carries us nowhere. The Ego-noema is not the noema of *every* cogito upon which we might reflect; and even if it were, Husserl's case would not be advanced in the slightest. Like all noemata, this one is an ideal rather than real (reell) object, and consequently cannot serve as intuitional filling for something meant as actually existing reality. The fact that the Ego is intended is no guarantee it actually exists. While the Ego may indeed be grasped through the immanent perception of any cogito, what is *directly* perceived here is only the cogito itself (which is reell rather than ideal: *I* §97). Yet the Ego is essentially bound up with the cogito, and so is indirectly given along with it.

In order to see exactly how this works we first need to know something about focal and marginal intentionality.

FOCAL AND MARGINAL INTENTIONALITY

Husserl describes the cogito as a "focal act," "wakeful experience" or "explicitly attentive consciousness" (*I* §§ 28, 35, 84). "It is . . . obviously true of all such experiences that the focal is girt about with a 'zone' of the marginal; *the stream of experience can never consist wholly of focal actualities.*" (*I* 107m) Along with the cogito, then, we have a second form of intentionality in our "marginal" or "background" awarenesses.

The cogito is distinctively *my* act, I "live" in it as "bringing it about." Marginal intentions also belong to the Ego as its own, but in another way: taken together, they are the Ego's "background of consciousness" and "field of freedom," the "field of potentiality for the Ego's free acts" (*I* 214m, 249mb). In the case of perception, for example, our marginal intentions subtend a "consciously grasped field of objects" and are themselves "a *potential field of perception* in the sense that a special perceiving (an awareness of the type *cogito*) can be directed towards everything that thus appears" (*I* 223b). If our attention is now focused upon a piece of paper, we are still not cut off from the rest of the world since

certain modifications of [our] experience are possible, which we refer to as a free turning of the "look"—not precisely nor merely of the physical but of the *"mental look"*—from the paper at first *descried* to the objects which had already appeared before, of which we had been "implicitly" aware, and whereof *subsequent* to the directing of one's look thither we are explicitly aware, perceiving them "attentively," or "noticing them nearby."   (*I* 106m)

Such descriptions bring Husserl to characterize the cogito as essentially a "turning towards" or "being directed towards" (*I* 107tm, 224t). This characterization conceals a double point. It indicates that "To the *cogito* itself belongs an immanent 'glancing-towards' the object" (*I* 109m), that a certain "having in one's glance, in one's mental eye ... belongs to the *essence* of the *cogito*" (*I* 109b). But I can direct my attention to an object only if this object is already there for me, already present to me: in the cogito I turn not toward an absolute void, but in each case toward *something* (however indeterminate it may be). The cogito therefore essentially requires

> a *domain of what is pregiven* ... a *passive* pregivenness ... of what is ... already there without any attention [needing to be paid]. All cognitive activity, all turning-toward a particular object in order to grasp it, presupposes this domain of passive pregivenness.   (*EJ* 30t, cf. 72t)

More fully characterized, then, the cogito is a "turning toward something pregiven," and so necessarily involves two factors: a glancing-toward immanent to the cogito, and a passive pregivenness of objects presupposed by it. It is in reflection upon these two factors that the (noematic Sinn of the) pure Ego is fulfilled; with the first of them the Ego is filled as "active" and with the second as "affected subject of consciousness".

But all this must be set out in detail.

THE EGO AS ACTIVE

What happens when I turn toward something already marginally pregiven? My marginal intentions are precisely *intentional,* and as such have their noemata (*I* §§35, 90-91). Is the noema of the object transformed when I pass from a marginal to a focal awareness of it?

Certainly this *may* happen. What is pregiven as "a bush up there on the hill" may reveal itself to more careful inspection as "a man silently watching me," and so on. But the cogito is not *essentially* a reconstitution or retroactive cancellation of the pregiven. In the move from marginal to focal awareness, and conversely, we have "a species of remarkable transformations of consciousness which cut across all other kinds of intentional occurrences" (*I* 246b). According to Husserl, *one and the same noesis* (intentional experience) may at one moment be of the type cogito and at another a merely marginal awareness; in particular, "there belongs ... to every consciousness ... which ... has not from the outset the form of the 'cogito,' the essentially possible modification which transfers it into this form" (*I* 294t; cf. *I* §§35, 92, 115). But such attentional "transformations ... do not of themselves work any change in the noematic effects which belong to this noesis" (*I* 247t).

When Husserl says that our marginal intentions together compose our "field of freedom," he means that consciousness is a field of *potential focal acts,* a field of *already operative* noeses, each with its noema, *through* which our "mental glance" may freely direct itself toward any of a multitude of preconstituted objects. (It is rather as though consciousness were a room dotted with an indefinite number of peepholes: we can at each moment look through any peephole we wish, but the mere fact of our choosing one over the others has no effect upon what is to be seen through them.)

> The glancing ray [of attention] ... passes now through this, now through that [already established] noetic layer.... Within the total given field of ... objects, we glance now at ... the tree which is perceptually present ... then again at a thing standing close by.... Suddenly we direct our glance towards some object of recollection which chances to occur [i.e., has already marginally occured] to us. Our glance, instead of passing through [one of] the noeses of perception, which in a continuous and unitary way ... constitute for us the steadily appearing world of things, goes through a noesis of remembrance into a world of memory, moves about in [the noeses which already subtend] the latter ... and so forth. (*I* 247tm)

But whether my glance does or does not pass through (or, as it were, utilize) a given noesis, sc. whether this noesis does or does not assume the form cogito, it may very well be "that the *noematic* factor of the experience ... remains the same" (*I* 247b).

Or, rather, we should say that the noematic *nucleus* of the experience may remain the same: focal and marginal consciousness may have identically the same object oriented in the same way with just the same more and less determinate features (*I* 247b-248). Still, there *is* a noetic difference here:

> At one time the experience is, so to speak, "*explicitly*" aware of its objective content, at the other implicitly and merely *potentially.* The objective factor ... may already be appearing to us, but *our gaze is not yet* "*directed*" *towards it* ... to say nothing of being "busied" with it in some special way.   (*I* 106-107)

And correlative to this noetic difference there must also be some difference on the noematic side (*I* §98); it lies not in the noematic nucleus, not in the meaning the object holds for attentive versus inattentive consciousness, but in the way the object presents itself (*I* 248-249t). The noematic effect of *purely* attentional transformations

> consists *merely* in this, that in one case of comparison this objective phase has the "preference," and in the other that; or that one and the same [object] is at one time "primarily noted," at another . . . only "just noted" along with something else, if it is not indeed "completely unnoticed," although still continuing to appear. There are indeed different modes [noematic characters] which belong specifically to attention as such.
>
> (*I* 248tm)

Attention or the attending glance is thus comparable to an illuminating beam. "What is attended to . . . subsists in [a] more or less bright cone of light, but can also shelve off into the half shadow and into the full darkness" (*I* 248m). "This alteration of the lighting does not alter that which appears in and through the *meaning* it conveys, but brightness and darkness [do] modify its mode of appearing; they are to be found in . . . the noematic object and there described" (*I* 248m).

Husserl concludes that "The attentional formations, in their modes of actuality [i.e., insofar as they assume the form cogito], possess in a very special sense the *character of subjectivity*" (*I* 249m), or "Ichlichkeit" (*IE* 231m). As something which wanders freely over things that in the meantime remain only what they already were, which highlights them one by one in an arbitrary and always reversible order (an order in no way dictated by the things themselves), attention is just essentially something *active* and *subjective;* since attentional transformations cannot be understood as transformations of their objects or more generally as restructurings of the conscious field, they must be referred to a subjective dimension.[6*] At bottom, Husserl adds nothing to this but merely repeats himself when he describes the cogito as a "glancing towards something pregiven," a "turning" or "focusing of the mental gaze," a "having in one's mental eye," a "taking note of," "being busied with," or "giving the preference to." These phrases are simply meant to express what self-evidently belongs to the cogito, the point everywhere being that attentive consciousness is essentially active and subjective in character.

And "The 'being directed towards,' 'the being busied with'

... [essentially characteristic of the cogito in turn] has this of necessity wrapped in its very essence, that it is just something 'from the Ego'" (*I* 214m, cf. 213b). In other words, Husserl thinks it impossible to describe the cogito adequately or to distinguish it from marginal consciousness without making reference (however hiddenly) to an "active subject," an "Ego" (as he) who turns towards, is busied with, etc. Focal and marginal intentionality are not distinguished by their objects, since these may be identically the same. Although their objects show different noematic characters, this difference (like everything noematic) is an effect produced noetically (*I* 263t, 265t; *CM* 42tm), and is therefore only a symptom of some more fundamental difference on the noetic side. Focal and marginal consciousness are thus separated most fundamentally, along essential noetic lines, only by the "Ichlichkeit" of the cogito, only by the fact that

> To the *cogito* itself belongs an immanent "glancing-towards" the object, a [active subjective] directedness which [cannot be otherwise described than as something that] springs forth from the "Ego."   (*I* 109m)

The Ego, sc. the meaning "active subject of consciousness," might in fine be termed a *descriptive necessity:* it is that significance without which the active subjectivity peculiar to the cogito cannot be comprehended or expressed. The cogito thus *demands* this significance, and it is in this sense that the cogito "gives itself out as radiating from the pure Ego" (*I* 249m), in this sense that the Ego is "given together with pure consciousness" (*I* 157tb). Conversely, this significance (the Ego meant as "active") may be fulfilled in reflection upon any cogito. The filling is the cogito itself, or more precisely its distinctive active and subjective character.

We should add that the Ego meant as "active" may sometimes be filled in a second way. Not every cogito is satisfied merely to contemplate something pregiven. Often our cogito is itself constitutive, it reconstitutes or further determines the pregiven to which it has turned. It may even happen that

> ... on the basis of objects already given ... [we] *constitute new objects originally*. These then present themselves for consciousness *as products*. Thus, in collecting, the collection <is constituted>; in counting, the number; in dividing, the part ... in inferring, the inference; and so forth.
> (*CM* 77b, cf. *I* 315b–316t)

Such manifestly generative subjective processes are naturally open to reflection, and as real (reell) elements of experience may then serve as intuitional filling for the Ego meant not simply as "active" but as the "actively constitutive subject of consciousness".

THE EGO AS AFFECTED

As hinted above, "anything built by [active generation] necessarily presupposes, as the lowest level, a passivity that gives something beforehand" (*CM* 78m). A collection is constituted on the basis of its individual elements, the part is preceded by the whole, etc. And indeed all activity is somehow grounded in passivity: every activity takes its start from something marginally pregiven (*EJ* 30t, 250b). "We can also say that an actual *world* always precedes cognitive activity as its universal ground" (*EJ* 30t). This is true in perception, but equally "in all the other spheres of consciousness" (*EJ* 71mb, 108b).

But let us stick to the case of perception. At least in the first instance the passive pregivenness of objects is here a

> ... *pure affective pregivenness* ... in which there is nothing yet of cognitive achievement ... as, e.g., the barking of a dog which "just breaks in on our ears," without our previously having given our attention to it. ...
>
> (*EJ* 60m)

In other words, perception begins when ". . . the object affects us as entering into the background of our field of consciousness" (*EJ* 29b). Perhaps we then turn to grasp it. We have seen that for Husserl even this contemplative turning-toward is "not a mere suffering of impressions," but already "a cognitive activity of the lowest level," "an *active performance of the Ego*" (*EJ* 59b, 60b, 72t/*EU* 74t).[7]* "As such, it presupposes that something is already pregiven to us, which we can turn toward in perception" (*EJ* 72t). ". . . always preliminary to this [active] grasping is affection, which is not the affecting of an isolated, particular object" (*EJ* 29–30).

> "To affect" means to stand out from the environment, which is always copresent, to attract interest to oneself. . . .   (*EJ* 30t)

> ... it is not mere particular objects, isolated by themselves, which are thus pregiven but always a *field* of pregivenness, from which a particular stands out and, so to speak, "excites us" to perception. . . .   (*EJ* 72t)

Individual items stand out from the environment in perception by *contrasting* with other segments of the field—as, for example, a red patch may contrast with and so stand out against white surroundings (*EJ* 73b, 76b). Every such coming-to-prominence is the work of that manner of passive constitution Husserl calls *association* (*EJ* §§16–17; *CM* §39).

What happens when an object is thus raised to prominence? Its prominence is a sort of insistent obtrusiveness: the object "'strikes' us, and this means that it displays an *affective tendency* toward the Ego" (*EJ* 76m/*EU* 80t).

> This occurs, for example, when ... there is a sound ... or a color which is more or less obtrusive. These lie in the field of perception and stand out from it and, although not yet apprehended, exercise on the Ego a stimulus more or less powerful. ... In the same way, a thought which suddenly emerges can be obtrusive, or a wish, a desire, can get through to us from the background with insistence.   (*EJ* 76b/*EU* 80m)

Such objects "exert a stimulus on the Ego which makes it turn toward, whether it obeys the stimulus or not" (*EJ* 76m/*EU* 80t).

Husserl thus distinguishes three moments in the genesis of any cogito. Preliminary to the cogito is a dual "tendency" which includes (1) "*The obtrusion on the Ego,* the attraction which the given exerts on the Ego" (*EJ* 78t/*EU* 82t), "the mere 'stimulus' which proceeds from an existent in the environing world" (*EJ* 60m), and also (2) "From the side of the Ego, *the tendency to give way,* the being-attracted, the being-affected, of the Ego itself" (*EJ* 78t/*EU* 82t). And in the cogito per se we have (3) a glancing toward the object "*as compliance with*" these preliminary tendencies: "The Ego is now turned toward the object; it has *of itself* a tendency directed toward the object" (*EJ* 78m/*EU* 82m).

This analysis is naturally intended not as theory or hypothesis, but as an eidetic description (*EJ* 49f). The "tendencies" distinguished are present in experience itself, as "we can very easily verify in the conscious field by a retrospective glance—[they] are data which phenomenology is able to exhibit" (*EJ* 77m). When we reflect upon the cogito, we find certain real (reell) factors bound up with it: an affecting (stimulating, exciting, attracting), a reciprocal being-affected (being-attracted, tending to yield), and finally a turning-toward-in-compliance. Moreover, these elements are seen to be *essential* to the cogito as such or to its genesis. Thus Husserl can say of the first two that the cogito *presupposes* them, that they *always* or necessarily precede it (*EJ* 29b–30, 72t; *CM* §§ 38–39). And if to be "awake" is to be conscious in the form of the cogito (*I* 93b, 107b), "To be awakened means [as a matter of essential necessity] to submit to an effective affection" (*EJ* 79t).

The cogito is in sum a turning toward something passively pre-given, a "suffering" or "experiencing something from objects" (*I* 249b) which then "consents to what is coming and [freely] takes it in" (*EJ* 79m). And this for Husserl is the very substance of freedom, life, subjectivity (*I* 249mb). In the end, the being-affected and complying (or resisting) can no more be understood as features of the world than the active turning-toward; they are events, but events that need have no effect upon the structure and significance of what is given to consciousness, and as such they belong to a subjective dimension of experience. In one respect *active*, in another *passive,* the cogito is in all respects essentially *subjective* in nature.

Husserl accordingly says of the being-affected and submitting just what he said of the turning-towards: it "has this *of necessity* wrapped in its very essence, that it is just something 'from the Ego,' or in the reverse direction 'to the Ego'" (*I* 214m). The idea is once again that such phenomena cannot be adequately described without making reference (however hiddenly) to a "conscious subject," in this case a "passive" one, an "Ego" (as he) who is affected, who freely yields to or resists stimulation, etc. The Ego, in this case the meaning "affected subject of consciousness," is that significance which alone renders the subjective passivity peculiar to the cogito accessible to our descriptive grasp; the cogito thus *demands* this significance. Conversely, this significance (the Ego meant as "affected") may be fulfilled in reflection upon any cogito.

We asked at the outset: What function does the pure Ego serve in Husserl's mature phenomenology? We now have our answer. As an intentional object constituted by consciousness, the Ego does not actually *do* or *explain* anything. The meaning "active and affected subject of consciousness" is itself neither active nor affected. Nonetheless, *"The thesis of my pure Ego . . . is 'necessary'"* (*I* 131b); the Ego is *"necessary* in principle" (*I* 156mb). It is a *descriptive necessity,* the primary function of which is to permit an understanding of what essentially belongs to the cogito. And indeed it is hard to see how such phenomena as the yielding to or resisting stimulation—if these *are* genuinely phenomena—could be attributed to the environmental field or accommodated by an entirely egoless conception of consciousness, a conception that speaks only of the world and the experiences constitutive of it.

It is true that our discussion has generally limited itself to what Husserl calls the "original passivity" of association, and that there is also a "secondary passivity" whereby what was once actively constituted (e.g., the physical world) is now just passively given, persisting in the "habitualities" of the "developed" Ego and serving as the basis for such higher level "spiritual activities" as scientific theorizing (*EJ* 108mb, 250b-251t, 279mb; *CM* §§38-39). But the general structures present at the beginnings of perception remain over at these higher levels (*EJ* 71, 108b). Just as when pure association is at work, when our habitualities "become actually operative, the already given objects formed for the central Ego appear, affect him, and motivate activities" (*CM* 79b). Here again activity presupposes passivity; here again reflection discovers an affecting, a being-affected and complying; here again the Ego may be fulfilled as "passive subject."

V. The apodicticity of the Ego

Husserl claims not only that the Ego exists but also that we may have apodictic knowledge of its existence. Apodictic knowledge absolutely "excludes the conceivability that what is [now] evident could subsequently become doubtful" (*CM* 15b). It is grounded in apodictic evidence, evidence that "discloses itself, to a critical reflection, as having the signal peculiarity of . . . excluding in advance every [possible] doubt as 'objectless,' empty" (*CM* 15-16). Now "evidence" is any experience wherein something is intended and fulfilled (*CM* 12t, 15b). Does our fulfilling experience of the Ego prove under critical examination to be authentically apodictic, absolutely incontestable?

This much is clear: if the Ego may indeed be filled in reflection upon any cogito, as Husserl maintains, then surely he is also justified in claiming that the Ego exists—justified at least in that he could not at any given time hope to have better evidence of the Ego than he actually does have. To exist is to be intended and harmoniously fulfilled. Certainly the Ego is (at present) occasionally intended; like any others, our Ego-intentions are open to reflection, and "Every [such] immanent perception necessarily guarantees the existence of its object" (*I* 130t). That these intentions are at present harmoniously filled is again (if true) something established in immanent perception and therefore with apodictic certainty.[8]*

But this much might with equal justice be said, for example, of the natural world, which nevertheless remains a merely "presumptive existence" (*FTL* 251b). "The world is not doubtful in the sense that there are rational grounds which might be pitted against the tremendous force of unanimous experiences [i.e., against the fact that our world-intentions have so far been harmoniously filled], but in the sense that a doubt is *thinkable*" (*I* 132t). And this because

> The existence of a world is the correlate of certain experience-patterns marked out by certain essential formations. But it is *not* at all clear that actual experiences can run their course *only* when they show these patterns: we cannot extract such patterns purely from the essence of perception in general. . . .   (*I* 136b)

The patterns in question being ones which are *not* essential to consciousness and "which can always be continued and . . . therefore never exhausted" (*I* 122m), it is always possible that such "empirical unities" as the natural world or physical thing will fail to develop harmoniously, that all present evidence of them will be gradually outweighed and finally overcome by the future course of our experience, and in short that they will one day be retroactively canceled as in fact never having existed (*I* §§46-49).

Supposing we *now* have good evidence of the Ego and in addition are *sure* we have it, the question of the Ego's apodicticity thus reduces to this: can we be certain our Ego-intentions will *always* be harmoniously fulfilled? So Husserl contends.

Every cogito is intrinsically open to reflection (*I* 111b) and when thus grasped presents itself as essentially involving the Ego. In consequence, the Ego just *cannot* be lacking where the cogito is present (*I* 109m); so long as experiences of this form are to be found in consciousness, the Ego must necessarily be (capable of being) filled.

What is more, if the Ego is filled at all, this will of necessity be a harmonious fulfillment. For the Ego is "a *quite peculiar* transcendence—a non-constituted transcendence" (*I* 157t). Or, rather, it is "in gewissem Sinne nicht konstituierte" (*IE* 138m): in a certain sense non-constituted. Of course it is constituted in the minimal sense of being brought to presence in consciousness. Still, the Ego "has no content that could be unravelled" (*I* 214b); it does not appear onesidedly, as does a thing, always withholding from view something of itself, but is *absolutely simple* and therefore neither susceptible to nor needful of a constitution which pieces it together bit by bit (*IZ* §§24, 28). This is what Husserl means when he says the Ego is an "*absolute* Reality" (*I* §§44, 46).

But if the Ego is not constituted over time as the empirical unity of inexhaustible modes of appearance, there can be no question of its failing to develop harmoniously in the future. There is nothing to develop; as *pure* Ego, it does not have (is not meant as having) any still hidden features, the being of which future experience might then fail to confirm; if it is given at all, then its givenness is already complete—a givenness the future can never amend but only duplicate. Husserl concludes that a retroactive cancellation of the Ego is impossible in principle: the Ego is "plainly indubitable," "given through a positing that is unconditioned and simply indissoluble" (*I* 131b).

10

Was Husserl a Realist or an Idealist?

Harrison Hall

I think the answer which should be given is a simple "No." What makes such an answer appropriate, however, is not so simple a matter.

If we need not be terribly precise,[1]* the realism/idealism issue can be specified in terms of the following question: Is there a world of material objects which exists external to and independent of consciousness? Realism consists in an affirmative, idealism in a negative, answer to this question. At first glance, it appears that every possible answer has already been given on Husserl's behalf. The "common interpretation of Husserl as an idealist,"[2] attributing to him a negative answer to the question, is as alive today as it was when critics such as Ingarden[3] identified its idealism as the fatal defect of the philosphic method introduced in *Ideas* and *Cartesian Meditations*. Küng, for example, thinks it is quite clear that for Husserl "the *noema* (meaning) of the material world has no referent . . ."[4] Both Findlay and Morriston see Husserl as slipping unfortunately into idealism, in spite of his attempts to maintain neutrality on the realism/idealism issue.[5]

The opposite interpretation of Husserl as a realist, attributing to him an affirmative answer to the question of the external and independent existence of the material world, seems at least implicit in defenses of Husserl against the charge of idealism.[6] Ameriks makes this interpretation explicit, finding in Husserl's writings "a good argument for realism . . ."[7]

To complicate matters further, Holmes has argued recently that Husserl's phenomenological method leads to an inability to say whether the answer to the question of the real existence of the world is yes or no, thus forcing Husserl to remain neutral on the metaphysical issue.[8]

From my opening remark it might seem that I mean to endorse some version of Holmes' neutral view against the interpretations of Husserl as either a realist or an idealist. Actually I intend to reject all three of the basic positions sketched above, and for much the same reason in each case. Each of them depends, in varying degrees, on a failure to understand Husserl's phenomenological reflection,[9] the nature and extent of the split between the natural and the transcendental which it produces, and the implications this has for certain parts of the philosophic enterprise. To get right to the bottom lines: (1) Husserl's philosophic position, his "transcendental idealism," is not an idealism at all. (2) The undeniable 'realism' of the natural attitude which Husserl affirms is not a philosophic position; and philosophic realism is an absurd position. (3) Husserl's 'neutrality' is much more radical than any interpreter has suggested. It is not simply that he is unable (or unwilling) to answer the question about the existence of the world and take a stand on the realism/idealism issue. If I am right, his view on the matter should be put much more strongly and is something like this: there is no way to raise such a question and, hence, no legitimate issue here whatsoever.

Intentionality, Meaning, and Phenomenological Reflection

My claim (above) is that misunderstandings of Husserl's position on the realism/idealism issue result from more fundamental misunderstandings of the basic features of his phenomenological method. In this section I will characterize Husserl's technique of phenomenological reflection in sufficient detail to convey his sense of the separation of the natural and transcendental "attitudes." In the section which follows I will show how an understanding of this separation provides interpretations of the passages used to support the idealistic, realistic and neutral readings of Husserl's phenomenology which commit him to none of these positions. In the final section I will comment on the restrictions Husserl seems to place on philosophy and the traditional inclination to ignore them.

It has become almost commonplace to trace Husserl's theory of meaning back to Frege in the following manner.[10] Frege furnished Husserl with the distinctions between subjective mental images, the objective meanings of concepts, and the objects to which the concepts refer in "On Sense and Reference" (1892) and in a review of Husserl's *Philosophy of Arithmetic* (1894). Husserl changed Frege's terminology to bring it into line with ordinary German usage,[11] and then attempted to extend the theory, with varying degrees of success, so that it would be a general theory of consciousness and analogous distinctions could be drawn for every conscious act, perceptual as well as conceptual.[12] What is wrong with this as a historical view is that Husserl was apparently in possession of these distinctions prior to 1892.[13] And it is likely that this way of looking at meaning originates with neither Husserl nor Frege, but can be traced back from either of them at least to Lotze.[14] If we ignore the question of historical accuracy, however, there is a great deal that is right about a view which links Husserl to Frege in this way. The distinctions in Husserl's semantic theory must be essentially identical to Frege's; otherwise the claimed departure from Frege over terminology would be unintelligible.[15] And although Husserl employed these distinctions in some form as early as 1891, it was not until after reading "On Sense and Reference," the preface to the first volume of Frege's *Die Grundgesetze der Arithmetic* (1893), and Frege's review of his *Philosophy of Arithmetic* that Husserl was able to use the distinctions to separate *entirely* questions concerning the origin of concepts within conscious experience from questions concerning the content of those concepts and the relations between such contents which are constitutive of the truths of formal logic and mathematics.[16]

I will break off the historical discussion at this point. Whatever the source of his theory, Husserl's analysis of linguistic meaning in terms of intentional act, ideal meaning, and object of a fulfilling intuition parallels exactly Frege's distinctions between idea or experience, sense, and reference.[17] Linguistic reference is mediated by an abstract entity, namely a meaning or sense. In ordinary experience we "live in" our linguistic acts and their meanings function transparently. Attention is directed toward their objects, not their meanings. However, in "logical thinking" we naturally reflect in such a way that attention is directed toward the meaning rather than the reference of the original act.[18]

The transition to the transcendental phenomenology of *Ideas* can be viewed as the working out of two insights on Husserl's part. The first is that the notion of meaning can be generalized so as to apply not just to linguistic acts, but to all acts. The second is that the *general* move from objects toward which our acts are directed to the meanings through which they are directed, unlike the particular move the logician makes in his restricted sphere of interest, is very *unnatural* and not easily accomplished. I will take these up in turn.

Husserl construes linguistic acts as interpretive. In conscious acts of speaking or writing intelligibly and hearing or reading understandingly, I interpret as meaningful or "give meaning to" the marks or sounds which function as the sensible signs of expressions. And it is in virtue of such meaning that these expressions refer to objects. The description of consciousness in terms of meaning-giving acts stresses the active role that consciousness plays within such experience. What Husserl's generalization of the notion of meaning comes to is the claim that consciousness can and must be understood as active or interpretive in all its functions. Experience is never just the passive registering and subsequent associating of independently meaningful data. It involves the bringing to bear by consciousness of intensional structures or meanings (*noemata*), through which the systematic organization of some less meaningful or *relatively* unstructured material is accomplished. This general claim is most problematic when applied to perceptual acts. It is not at all obvious that there is any interpreting involved in ordinary perceiving; and, as a result, it is unclear whether any distinction analogous to that between meaning and object (or sense and reference) can be intelligibly drawn with respect to acts of perception.

Husserl's firm conviction that there are no insurmountable difficulties here seems to have been supported by the following considerations.

(1) Whatever the differences between the various species of conscious experience, there must be something in general that it is to be conscious. Hence, at least the most general features of linguistic consciousness must be, simply, features of consciousness.

(2) As Brentano had observed, the most general feature of consciousness, the definitive "mark of the mental," is intentionality. That is, consciousness is always *of* or *directed toward* some

objective. If this directedness of consciousness is accounted for in terms of its relation to real objects, the perceptual equivalents of failure of reference (hallucinations, etc.) defy explanation. On the other hand, if this directedness is explained in terms of perceived mental contents (images, percepts, etc.), the distinction between successful and unsuccessful perceptual 'reference' (i.e. veridical and nonveridical perception) disappears. This dilemma is avoided if the intentionality of consciousness can be accounted for in terms of abstract intensional structures (analogs of linguistic meanings) through which consciousness is directed, rather than the real objects, if any, toward which it is directed or the actual mental contents which accompany its directed acts.

(3) In the *Logical Investigations* Husserl held that "The necessity of distinguishing between meaning and object becomes clear when a comparison of examples shows us that several expressions may have the same meaning but different objects, and again that they may have different meanings but the same object."[19] Similar considerations should force an analogous distinction with respect to perception. Different things may be perceived in the same way—for example, the apparently unequal lines in the Müller-Lyer optical illusion and lines which are really of unequal length in a nonillusory setting. And the same physical thing may be perceived in different ways, as in the case of the duck-rabbit drawing and its more sophisticated variations, depending upon the context of the perceptual act and (at least on Husserl's view) the perceptual meanings or noemata which past experience has placed at the disposal of the perceiver. Put another way, this is roughly equivalent to the claim that seeing (perceiving) is always seeing *as* (perceiving *as*). The perceptual meaning or noema is the abstract structure or interpretive schema by means of which perceptual consciousness is directed toward an object under a particular description and with an appropriate set of structured anticipations, past associations, and so on.

So for Husserl the directedness of consciousness toward some objective is always accomplished through the mediation of an abstract interpretive structure, an intensional entity very like a linguistic meaning or sense. The term noema is used to designate this extended notion of meaning. Brentano's thesis that every act has an object is thus transformed by Husserl into the claim that every act has a noema. The noema is neither a real (*real*) material object nor a real (*reell*) subjective mental content. For this reason, Husserl refers to noemata as nonreal (*irreal*) or ideal (*ideal*). To anticipate some of the discussion of the next section, the commitment of (transcendental) phenomenology to (transcendental) idealism follows directly from the observations above. Phenomenology is the science of noemata[20*] (and their correlation with acts of consciousness or *noeses*) and noemata are ideal entities.

Phenomenological reflection is reflection which shifts the focus of attention from the objects of ordinary experience to the noemata which mediate such experience. Its function is to abstract from the (real) existence of the objects to which our conscious acts refer or seem to refer, and thus make available for independent study the (ideal) meanings of those objects or, equivalently, the (ideal) meaning-contents of those acts. But while it may be quite natural for the logician or linguist to attend to the meanings of expressions, judgments, or utterances and ignore the objects or states of affairs to which they might refer, it is very unnatural to make the analogous move in the case of nonlinguistic acts. This is not only due to the fact that the meanings associated with such acts are not part of our ordinary repertoire, not an obvious part of the 'furniture of the world.' It is also due to the nature of the central one of these acts, perception, and its special function within the whole of our experience. Virtually all of our ordinary interests are tied in some way to objects and events in the real world. It is therefore natural for most of our acts to aim at things in this world. But even more important for Husserl is the fact that all of our acts (except acts of phenomenological reflection) take place within the broad context of such interests. As a result there is surrounding each conscious act a natural background of implicit belief in the existence of the real world of facts and things. Husserl refers to this broad context of implicit belief as the *natural standpoint* or *attitude*. It forms the background for all of our nonphilosophical experience, both prescientific and scientific. Since perception is our most direct and fundamental link with the real world, part of its function (and, derivatively, part of the function of other nonlinguistic acts such as memory) is to provide this background or general setting for all of our natural experience. Thus, disconnecting the objective reference from the meaning of the perceptual act is not simply a matter of shifting attention within the natural context of experience, but of transforming or abandoning that context as well. Husserl's thesis that such a general transformation is essential to the practice of philosophy is tantamount to defining philosophy by its unnaturalness. Phenomenological reflection abandons the natural attitude or standpoint by abstracting the (ideal) meaning from the (real) existence both of the objects of natural experience and of the real world background which such experience presupposes. Philosophy is exclusively concerned, according to Husserl, with these abstract meanings rather than concrete existents, the ideal rather than the real; and the primary purpose of phenomenological reflection is to keep the two absolutely separate so that there is no temptation to cross, philosophically, the "unbridgeable gulf between ideal and real."[21]

Transcendental Idealism and Natural Realism

There are a number of things which contribute to misunderstandings of the metaphysical commitment of Husserl's phenomenology as idealistic. Among these are Husserl's own potentially misleading characterizations of his position. He refers to phenomenological reflection as a "reduction," to the experience of the phenomenologist as "reduced experience." At several points in the explication of his method, Husserl attempts to motivate phenomenological reflection (or reduction) by considering the priority and independence of consciousness and its contents as opposed to the merely relative being and possible nonexistence of the real world.[22] And this line of description culminates in the explicit labeling of transcendental phenomenology as "transcendental idealism."[23]

The following passages strongly support a reading of Husserl's method as metaphysically reductive and of its metaphysical product as a variety of traditional idealism.

> Reality and world, here used, are just the titles for certain valid *unities of meaning* ... the whole being of the world consists in a certain "meaning" which presupposes absolute consciousness as the field from which the meaning is derived ...[24]

> The world is a meaning, an accepted sense. When we go back to the ego, we can explicate the founding and founded strata with which that sense is built up ...[25]

> Consequently I, the transcendental phenomenologist, have objects ... *solely as the intentional correlates of modes of consciousness of them.*[26]

> Every imaginable sense, every imaginable being ... falls within the domain of transcendental subjectivity, as the subjectivity that constitutes sense and being. ... If transcendental subjectivity is the universe of possible sense, then an outside is precisely—nonsense.[27]

... every sense that any existent whatever has or can have for me—in respect of its "what" and its "it exists and actually is"—is a sense *in* and *arising from* my intentional life ...[28]

... every sort of existent itself, real or ideal, becomes understandable as a "product" of transcendental subjectivity ...[29]

Only an uncovering of the horizon of experience ultimately clarifies the "actuality" and the "transcendency" of the world, at the same time showing the world to be inseparable from transcendental subjectivity, which constitutes actuality of being and sense.[30]

Some of these passages already contain sufficient clues to prevent misreadings. Others require an indication of the contexts in which they appear in order to counter their idealistic implications. What I am concerned to convey at this point, however, in addition to plausible nonidealistic readings of these remarks, is a sense of why Husserl *could not* have been denying the actual existence of the real world and committing himself to idealism. These passages occur in each of the texts after Husserl has introduced the technique of phenomenological reflection and must be understood within the context produced by such reflection. That context is one in which attention is directed exclusively toward the meanings or noemata which function in our experience and away from the real referents of that experience. The situation is perfectly analogous to that created by shifting our attention from linguistic referent to linguistic meaning—for example, when we note the difference in intension between "the morning star" and "the evening star" and simply ignore the extension of the two expressions. No one would suppose that this restriction of attention is meant to reduce the number of real objects in the universe. Nor would the general claim that a theory of linguistic meaning should be concerned *only* with intensions be taken as equivalent to denying the existence of the real world of which we speak via such intensions. Husserl's theory of meaning (in his extended sense of the term) and his general claim that philosophy is concerned *only* with meaning are just as far from a commitment to idealism. Within the context of phenomenological reflection, the only way one could possibly 'discover' that something did not really exist would be to find that its meaning was somehow incoherent or inconsistent—as one might 'discover' that round squares do not exist simply by an analysis of their meaning. But Husserl nowhere suggests that "material object" or "real world" are self-contradictory notions. In fact, his analysis is just the opposite. The meant "existence" of objects and "reality" of the world have their foundation in the coherence and consistency of the meaning-contents of our experience. This being the case, Husserl fails to deny the actual existence of the real world not just in fact but on grounds of principle. The total separation of the meaning from the object of experience which Husserl adopts as a methodological imperative makes it impossible for the study of the former (i.e., philosophy) to have that kind of implication in the sphere of the latter (i.e., the natural world).

We need to explain, then, just what Husserl is trying to say in the passages quoted or referred to above. Phenomenological reflection is not labeled a reduction because it awards one class of entities (phenomena) the status of reality at the expense of another class (the objects of ordinary experience). Husserl's reduction has nothing whatsoever to do with reductive metaphysical positions. He calls his method a reduction because one of the elements of ordinary experience drops out of the "reduced" experience of the phenomenologist. But this "dropping out" is solely a function of the direction of attention or point of view which the philosopher adopts. The transformation which occurs is on the side of the subject. Nothing happens to the real world of which we are ordinarily aware, except that we purposely shift our attention away from it and, as a result, cease to have it as the object of our experience. The reduction is a reduction in the constituents of our experience, not in the contents of reality. Where natural experience involves both a mediating interpretive structure or meaning and a transcendent object in the real world, the "transcendentally reduced" experience of the phenomenologist involves only interpretive structures or meanings. He reflects in such a way that the meanings which functioned transparently in ordinary experience become the explicit objects of his reflective awareness. Of course, since all experience is directed toward its objective via such abstract interpretive structures, even this reflective experience is mediated by meanings, and phenomenological reflection can therefore be iterated. But in the case of iterated phenomenological reflection, the mediating structure and the object of experience coincide exactly, so that no real transformation is brought about, nothing added to or subtracted from the contents of experience thereby. Only the initial reflective move effects the crucial transition in our experience from the natural world of facts and things to the world of meanings which is the proper domain of philosophy.

This transition from the natural to the philosophical explains Husserl's claims that the world is a meaning or sense and that the phenomenologist encounters objects only as "intentional correlates" (i.e., noemata) of consciousness. Husserl does not mean that what the ordinary man thinks is a real external world of material objects turns out under philosophic scrutiny to be nothing but a collection of immaterial meanings. What he is saying is that once the philosopher restricts his attention, as he must, to the meanings or noemata which mediate ordinary exprience, those meanings are all that he encounters and become the sole subject matter of his investigations and theories. And since the directedness of consciousness toward everything of which we are aware is mediated by noemata, there are noemata or meanings for both the individual objects and real world background of ordinary experience. The phenomenologist studies the meanings through which consciousness is naturally directed toward the world and objects in it.

From this we can also understand Husserl's remarks to the effect that transcendental subjectivity—the total system of experiencable meanings and possible reflective consciousness of them—is closed and complete. To say that every being is in the domain of transcendental subjectivity is to say only that every *thing* which enters into our experience must have its noema or meaning-equivalent within the system of meanings to which we gain reflective access via phenomenological reduction. And this system as a whole is completely separate, different in kind, or, as Husserl puts it, "within a *new dimension*,"[31] from the real world of which it is the meaning. As a result, causal interaction between the realm of meanings and the natural world is inconceivable. The only relation between the two is that effected by the intentional activity of the natural subject whose experience is *of* the natural world *by means of* the noemata or meanings of transcendental subjectivity. And this relation is simply a generalization of the relation between the intension and extension of an expression effected by ordinary acts of linguistic reference.

The preceding explains the independence of the realm of meanings, transcendental subjectivity, from the real world and accounts for Husserl's suggestion that everything (*as meant*) is 'contained' within the former. We have yet to make sense of the priority or absoluteness of transcendental subjectivity and Husserl's claim that everything can be understood as its 'product.' This, of course, will require at least a brief analysis of Husserl's concept of "constitution." Since this concept applies only to transcendental subjectivity, the subjectivity revealed by phenomenological reflection, there can be no question of consciousness literally producing things.[32*] The relation must be between consciousness and the meaning or sense of things within our experience. For Husserl there are at least two ways in which transcendental subjectivity is to be understood as constitutive of the meaning or intelligible structure of experience. The first of these is straightforward, given Husserl's model of conscious activity. The most basic structure of conscious acts is their directedness toward an objective, their intentionality. Without this minimal structure and its more detailed elaborations, there would be no meaningful or intelligible experience of anything. Since it is solely in virtue of the noemata of transcendental subjectivity that consciousness is intentional or directed in general, and of or directed toward specific objects under specific descriptions in particular, transcendental subjectivity may be said to be responsible for or constitutive of whatever meaningful structure our experience has. This accounts for Husserl's labeling of the reduction and the subjectivity it reveals as "transcendental." What is at issue are the conditions for the possibility of our experience referring to or being of objects, both in general and with respect to particular modes of consciousness of them.

The explanation of the second way in which transcendental subjectivity, according to Husserl, is constitutive of the meaning of things in our experience is more difficult. It requires that we take very seriously the close analogy between meaning in the narrow sense, the meaning of expressions or concepts, and meaning in Husserl's broad or extended sense, the noemata of all acts of consciousness. Just as complex concepts may be analyzed or broken down into their simpler components, so can noemata be traced back to the more basic meaning-structures of which they are composed. By "more basic meaning-structures" I do not mean the various components of each noema which correspond roughly to the predicates which must be true of the object if our experience is actually to count as the experience of that object under that aspect—for example, the horizonal components of the perceptual noema of a house which correspond to what I would see were I to walk around it. Every noema has components of this sort which contribute to the meaning of our experience by directing consciousness toward a particular object from a certain point of view and under a specific description. These components are constitutive of the meaning of things in our experience in the manner already discussed—that is, constitutive of the possible reference of our experience to objects and the world. But each noema is also the result of a very different sort of composition, and Husserl uses the term "constitution" to describe this 'process.' The 'components' involved are the logically prior meanings 'contained in' a given meaning, the simpler meanings out of which a more complex meaning can be understood to develop. The developmental stages are revealed by a special investigation within phenomenological reflection which Husserl calls "genetic analysis."[33] The development itself he calls "genetic constitution." The 'genesis' here is clearly logical rather than temporal. Its analysis reveals the logically prior meanings and meaning-compositions or syntheses without which the particular noema under investigation would be unintelligible and, hence, not at the disposal of consciousness. Husserl's theory is that the logical composition of noemata follows certain fixed general laws. Genetic analysis reveals both the pattern of composition of particular meanings and those general laws or universal principles of synthesis according to which every meaning is composed. These principles are treated as features of transcendental subjectivity and function as a set of constraints on meaning in general. Husserl saw these as parallel or analogous on the philosophical or transcendental level (i.e., the sphere of meaning in total abstraction from the world of objects 'meant') to Hume's psychological or empirical "laws of association."[34] Consciousness in its transcendental (or meaning-giving) function may be viewed as synthetic, bringing experience under progressively more detailed unifying structures. The general laws according to which this function is performed and the material[35]* available for synthesis at each level of organization jointly determine the multi-level system of meanings which make up transcendental subjectivity. The clearest and most extended account of how this works is provided by Husserl's "Fifth (Cartesian) Meditation." Here he demonstrates that these general laws of meaning composition together with the constituents of the field of consciousness as they would be if the meaning "other subject" were not at the disposal of consciousness are sufficient to determine the development of that meaning and make possible the reference to an intersubjective or fully objective reality.[36] The levels of meaning disclosed by genetic analysis are arranged in a logical hierarchy to which Husserl applies the metaphor of "foundation"—meanings at each level being "founded upon" those of the previous less structured level and "founding" those of the subsequent level of complexity.[37]*

To say that consciousness in its transcendental function enjoys a (logical) priority over the real world, then, is to make two claims, neither of which entails a commitment to idealism in anything other than Husserl's technical sense of that term.[38] The first of these claims is that transcendental subjectivity as a developed system of meanings or noemata is a necessary (though not sufficient) condition for the reference of experience to the real world. The second claim is that transcendental subjectivity as a set of principles governing the formation or development of meaning in general is a necessary (though, again, not sufficient) condition for the existence of the system of meanings without which objective reference of any sort would be impossible.

Finally, Husserl's remarks about the "absoluteness" of transcendental consciousness and the possible nonbeing of the real world are not intended to confirm the existence of the former and put in serious doubt the existence of the latter. Within the context of phenomenological reflection, the claims involved here (which might have been better left unmade given subsequent misunderstandings) are these. The existence of transcendental subjectivity—that is, of the conditions which make reference possible—does not require the successful objective reference of any of our experience. However the successful objective reference of any of our experience does require the existence of transcendental subjectivity. And the real point of these claims is to motivate the absolute split between meaning and actual existence (as opposed to the meaning or sense of such existence) which Husserl takes to be philosophically necessary. The implications to be drawn are that it makes sense to study the meaning of experience totally abstracted from the reference of that experience; and that it makes no sense at all to drag the question whether the reference of experience to the real world is successful into that study of meaning—that is, into philosophy. This captures entirely the sense of Husserl's commitment to "transcendental idealism." Philosophy's only concern is the meaning of experience; and such meaning consists not of real existents (material or mental) available to extro- or introspection, but of ideal entities (abstract and repeatable) grasped by a reflective act which is essentially conceptual rather than perceptual.

Although the temptation to misread Husserl as a metaphysical realist is not as strong as the opposite temptation, there is ample material from which to construct a case for this interpretation.

Had we wanted simply to oppose one mistake with another, we could have countered the passages cited in support of Husserl's idealism[39] with the following passages which seem to point the other way.[40]

> In advance there is the world, ever pregiven and undoubted in ontic certainty and self-verification.[41]

> All doubting and rejecting of the data of the natural world leaves standing the general thesis of the natural standpoint. "The" world is as fact-world always there, at the most it is at odd points "other" than I supposed . . . but the "it" remains ever, in the sense of the general thesis, a world that has its being out there.[42]

> It (the reduction) is not a transformation of the thesis into its antithesis, of positive into negative; it is also not a transformation into presumption, suggestion, indecision, doubt (in one or another sense of the word); *such shifting indeed is not at our free pleasure.*[43]

> . . . the psyche and the whole Objective world do not lose their existence and existential sense when considered transcendentally . . .[44]

> Particularly in the case of the Objective world of realities . . . phenomenological explication does nothing but *explicate the sense this world has for us all, prior to any philosophizing . . . a sense which philosophy can uncover but never alter . . .*[45]

> There can be no stronger realism than this (Husserl's view), if by this word nothing more is meant than: "I am certain of being a human being who lives in this world, etc., and I doubt it not in the least."[46]

> No ordinary 'realist' has ever been as realistic and as concrete as I, the phenomenological 'idealist' (a word which by the way I no longer use).[47]

Reading these passages as indicative of a philosophical commitment to realism involves the same mistake we encountered earlier in connection with idealism. The split between the natural and the philosophical enforced by phenomenological reflection makes it equally impossible either to affirm or to deny *philosophically* the existence of the real world referents of our experience. For Husserl, either one occupies the object-directed standpoint of natural (empirical) experience from which the existence of the real world is undeniable; or else one occupies the meaning-directed standpoint of philosophical (transcendental) experience from which the existence of the real world is simply not an issue. There is nothing in between these standpoints but serious philosophical confusion.

And Husserl locates most of the philosophic tradition on this confused middle ground. His assumption is that all legitimate philosophical questions are really questions of meaning, not of fact. The principal source of illegitimate—that is, mixed natural-philosophical—questions and answers is the inability to break free of the natural attitude. The result is a confusion of meaning and fact which can take several forms. If we remain firmly within the natural attitude with its focus on facts and things and treat such facts as relevant to questions of meaning, philosophical questions, we are guilty of one or another version of naturalism—an error which Husserl fought especially strongly, having fallen prey to it in the form of psychologism at the beginning of his career. On the other hand, if we *almost* succeed in leaving the natural standpoint, we may get some insight into the nature of transcendental subjectivity and the meaning-contents of experience; but we will not know what it is we have discovered and will, as a result, misunderstand the relation of these discoveries about meaning to the natural world of facts and things meant. Although the mistakes involved here are major ones, Husserl is sympathetic to those who have gone furthest in this direction, viewing them as closest to finding the proper role and method of philosophy—that is, phenomenology, the "science of meaning." Descartes is viewed as stumbling upon transcendental subjectivity, but not fully appreciating its separation from the natural world and, hence, treating it as a thing related causally to other things. He thus becomes the father of philosophical (i.e. transcendental) realism, "an absurd position."[48] What makes *philosophical* realism absurd, given Husserl's understanding of the philosophical (transcendental), is that it makes the relation between meaning (sense) and object (reference) one of causal interaction, which amounts to missing entirely the important distinction between meaning and object which is constitutive of philosophy. Hume gained some insight into the principles which are constitutive of meaning, as well as a sense of the tension between the natural and the philosophical if both are taken to have the same subject matter, namely, the real world. Failing to see that his findings belonged properly to the sphere of meaning rather than the world of fact, the relation between the philosophical and the natural remained mysterious, and Hume's skepticism was the natural result. Subjective idealism, which Husserl clearly rejected,[49] represents an unsatisfactory response to the problem of the relation between the natural and the philosophical, reducing both natural reality and philosophical (transcendental) ideality to the contents of psychological (empirical or nonphilosophical) subjectivity.

The point is that philosophically Husserl is neither an idealist nor a realist—the former position being clearly mistaken and the latter quite absurd on his view. At the beginning of this section we examined Husserl's 'idealism'—finding it not to be an idealism at all. His commitment to "transcendental idealism" turned out to be simply a potentially misleading expression of the fact that the objects of philosophic attention and concern—meanings or noemata— are not part of the real world to which natural experience refers. They are ideal entities in the sense in which linguistic concepts are. That is, they are abstract and repeatable, 'in' consciousness not as real contents but as the "objective sense" of its acts.[50] However, Husserl's realism, to which the passages quoted above seem to attest,[51] cannot be explained away in a similar manner. His realism is very real. The catch is that it is not at all philosophical. The realism Husserl endorses must be located squarely within the natural attitude. The intent of his remarks is to make explicit the implicit background belief in the existence of the real world which defines the natural standpoint. This belief is unqestionable from this standpoint because it forms the broadest and most basic context of natural experience. There is no ground from which one could accept this 'thesis' naturally as a belief among others to be examined on its merits. It is in fact presupposed in every natural examination of our beliefs. That is why Husserl refers to this fundamental belief as the "general thesis" of the natural standpoint. Any serious questioning of it involves a total shift of context toward the unnatural—that is, the philosophical. Descartes' methodological doubt thus becomes, from Husserl's perspective, a confused or partial phenomenological reduction—a departure from the natural world without any understanding of the new 'world' of meanings which such a departure opens up to us.

For Husserl, then, a kind of natural realism is unavoidable. And this realism *is* available for philosophic scrutiny once we abandon the natural standpoint through phenomenological reflection. It is part of the *meaning* of natural experience. But studied as meaning, not as fact, the actual existence of the real world cannot be affirmed philosophically. Philosophy is at pains to understand what it *means* for something to count in our experience as an actually existing reality, what meaning components make it possible for our experience to have as part of its *meaning* a successful reference to the real world. This reference is part of the *sense* of natural experience which, according to Husserl, philosophy can only explicate or uncover.[52] The question that cannot be raised philosophically is a question of fact—namely, is that reference which is built into the meaning of our experience *in fact* successful? This brings us to the interpretation of Husserl as neutral on the idealism/realism issue.

At the beginning of this paper we said that the realism/idealism issue could be specified, imprecisely, in terms of the following question: "Is there a world of material objects which exists external to and independent of consciousness?" It is time to be more precise. There is, first, a *natural* question about the existence of the real world. It asks whether there are, in fact, material objects as well as natural consciousness(es) or mind(s) among the constituents of the real world. There is nothing problematic about this question. It would be answered in the affirmative by anyone from the man in the street to the man of science—that is, by anyone from within the natural attitude.[53]* It is, of course, difficult to imagine circumstances in which there would be any point in asking and answering such a question. But neither what is meant by it, nor the correct response to it, is affected by that fact.[54] There is also a *philosophical* question concerning the existence of the real world. It asks for the meaning-contents of our natural acts which are aimed at this world and for a retracing of the logical development of such contents. Its aim is a clearer understanding of the *meaning* of the reality and existence of the world. As is the case with phenomenological analysis in general, the investigation to which the philosophical question gives rise "(does) not aim at being and (is) not at liberty to be anything but explication of the sense . . ."[55] of our conscious acts.

Philosophy is not in a position either to prove or disprove the existence of the real world which is the most basic assumption of natural experience. But for Husserl this signifies no failure of philosophy to get to the truth of the matter. There is no truth of the matter because there is no question to be answered, and no issue to be resolved, by such proof or disproof, even if they could be provided. Neither the natural nor the philosophical question about the existence of the real world call for that. Nor does either question require that we refrain from answering it. The only constraint is that we answer each on its own terms, staying carefully within the standpoint or context from which alone the respective question can be asked and answered intelligibly. And just as there is no legitimate standpoint in between the natural and the philosophical, so there is no legitimate question that can be squeezed between the two we have discussed. Husserl's answers to the legitimate questions fail to commit him either to idealism or to realism as philosophical positions. His realism is prephilosophical; his 'idealism' nonmetaphysical. And his radical neutrality consists not of the philosophical refusal or inability to answer a metaphysical question, but is, rather, the dismissal of any question that could call for the metaphysical response of the traditional realist or idealist as illegitimate. The philosophic tradition, insofar as it embodies the development of such illegitimate questions and confused responses to them, is, for Husserl, a history of metaphysical naïveté. Viewed positively, however, this history represents the progressive attempt to break free of the natural (philosophically naïve) attitude so that the legitimate metaphysical/ontological questions, questions of the *meaning* of each category of object experienceable, can finally be brought to philosophic attention.

The Limits of Philosophical Inquiry

It should be clear from the preceding that Husserl places severe restrictions on the scope of the philosophic enterprise. Only questions which ask for explications of the meaning of . . . are properly philosophical. Excluded from the philosophic domain are all questions of the form, "Does . . . exist?" They are to be regarded either as out of place or as confused attempts to ask proper philosophic questions of the form, "What is it within our experience for . . . to be meant as actual or existent?"[56]* If, as Husserl believes, this restriction is necessary, then a great deal of past philosophic effort has been wasted. However, I shall not pursue that further here. What I shall do is take one more look at the philosophical limits Husserl prescribes by examining briefly some points at which he seems to be on the verge of going beyond them himself.

I have said that for Husserl the only legitimate question of fact about the existence of the real world of material objects is the natural question; and that this question is unproblematic because of the background beliefs of the only context in which it can occur. It raises the kind of issue which can be settled once and for all by Moore's 'proof'—that is, it calls for no more than a simple pointing out of the ordinary objects we see around us.[57] This is certainly not the question that philosophers have tried to ask, and not the sort of answer that would traditionally have been taken to put an end to the matter. The traditional question goes something like this: "Of course there seems to be a real world of material objects, but are things *really* the way they seem?" And this usually gives rise to an examination of the evidence we have for the existence of such a world, and so on. It is at this point that Husserl seems to enter a discussion in which he should not take part. He engages in careful analyses of the kind of evidence we have for the existence of material objects, gives an account of the distinction between veridical and nonveridical perception—in short, he does what is typically done in response to the 'unnatural' and illegitimate question of fact about the existence of the real world. And, in the process, he gives further grounds for each of the metaphysical misreadings I dismissed in the preceding section. [58*]

I cannot, of course, attempt to give an adequate account of Husserl's theory of perception and perceptual evidence here. [59] A few pieces of that theory will be sufficient for the present purpose. The first of these has to do with the incompleteness ("inadequacy" in Husserl's terminology) of perceptual evidence. In every perceptual situation we experience objects perspectivally. Certain aspects of the object are presented to us; other aspects are intended as also there ("co-present") but are not, strictly speaking, presented to us. (Husserl refers to them as "appresented.") Since Husserl ties the notion of evidential adequacy to the strictly presented, and since every object has an indefinite number of aspects which have not been presented to us, it is the case with any particular object and even more clearly with the real world as a whole that the evidence we have for its existence is incomplete. No matter how extensive our experience, the evidence for perceptual judgments is never all in. [60] Our reasons for accepting them cannot be absolutely conclusive. And the "But are there *really* . . ?" question apparently requires conclusiveness or certainty, not being settled by what we ordinarily think (what "seems") to be the case. This has been taken to imply that the question itself is perfectly in order for Husserl, but that, philosophically, the jury is still out and will be so indefinitely, so that no verdict can be expected. Husserl is forced, therefore, to remain metaphysically neutral.

However, if we look at another feature of Husserl's account of perception, we seem to be pushed toward a different conclusion. What it is for our perceptual experience to provide us with evidence

for the existence of material objects and the real world is for it
to cohere or fit together in a certain way. And even though all
possible experience is never in, the test of that coherence is never
total, it is still the case according to Husserl that there is sufficient
evidence to *compel* us to ascribe real existence to the world and to
numerous material objects in it.[61] This would seem to put Husserl
in a position to confirm, on philosophical grounds, the naïve belief
in the existence of the world. He is thus committed to realism.

Finally, if we think of it along the following lines, Husserl's
treatment of perception reads much like the account that an idealist might give. Everything Husserl has to say about perception and
our evidence for the existence of the real world is, after all, said
in terms of the contents of consciousness. The test for the truth of
perceptual judgments is coherence with our experience, not correspondence with an external reality. The transcendence of things,
their being outside consciousness, turns out upon analysis to be a
"transcendence in immanence"—things are more than the content
of any single conscious experience, but are nothing over and
above the contents of an indefinite system of actual and possible
experiences.

We should suspect that something has gone wrong when interpretations of Husserl seem to point in every metaphysical direction. Something *has* gone wrong, of course, and it is the same error
we have already examined at length. Husserl is, here as elsewhere,
working strictly at the level of meaning. He could undoubtedly
have been clearer about this. He tends to give his readers credit,
once he has introduced and explained the move from the natural
to the philosophical, for being able to keep considerations of
fact and considerations of meaning separate from that point on.
So he does not remind us constantly that his theory is concerned
solely with the meaning of our experience. Husserl expects us to
remember initial warnings like the following.

> What is *essential* for us here is the distinction between the two types of
> investigation (natural and philosophical), each regarded as a universal
> investigation.[62]

Let me suggest very briefly how heeding this warning makes it
possible to sort out the pieces of Husserl's theory of perception in
a way that brings them into line with his general views on the
limits of philosophical inquiry. Husserl's theory is throughout a
theory of perceptual *meaning,* of the *meaning* of our perceptual
acts. This does not, for Husserl, represent an actual restriction of

its scope. There is, on his view, nothing else that a *philosophical* theory of perception *could* be. Husserl's discussion of perceptual evidence is concerned with features of perceptual meaning, not with matters of perceptual fact. Each perceptual noema has both "filled" and "unfillled" meaning components which correspond respectively to the presented and "appresented" aspects of the object meant. The *meaning of* the real existence of objects is the coincidence of "filled" and "unfilled" components in successive members of the open system of noemata which corresponds to the system of possible perspectival orientations of the object relative to a perceiver.[63]* The *meaning of* the existence of the world as a whole is a looser but analogous harmony or coherence among all of the perceptual noemata in our experience.

The "inadequacy" of perceptual evidence does not force a neutral response to the question of fact about the existence of the world. It has no bearing whatsoever on that question. Husserl simply points out by this means an essential feature of each perceptual meaning—namely, its having ("horizonal") components which are not "filled" components of the meanings of any finite set of perceptual experiences. This is meant as an explanation, not a negative evaluation, of the kind of evidence appropriate to perception. Similarly, the compulsion to ascribe existence to objects and the world is not equivalent to a philosophical judgment that these things do in fact exist. What Husserl claims is that, given the meaning of their real existence and the progressive "filling" of the components of that meaning within our ordinary experience, we cannot, as natural subjects, help taking them to exist. This provides a philosophical understanding, not a verification, of our natural beliefs. And, lastly, the suggestion that Husserl's account of perception commits him to idealism depends entirely on confusing the abstract meanings which mediate conscious experience with the real contents of natural consciousness. Husserl seeks to confine philosophical attention to the sphere of meaning. He does not try to limit the objects of natural experience to our subjective mental contents.

In short, Husserl's theories of perception and perceptual evidence do not violate the restrictions he imposes on legitimate philosophical inquiry. The only factual claims about the existence of the real world of material objects are natural (nonphilosophical) ones. And the only evidence for them is our natural perceptual experience. Philosophy is not in a position to check or add to that evidence, and has no business certifying, rejecting, or even

weighing the truth of those claims. Husserl's investigation of perceptual experience aims only at the meaning or sense of those
claims and of that evidence. Its findings do not, and could not,
address or legitimate the traditional metaphysical questions
about the existence of the world.

All this would seem to leave both the difficulty in recognizing
the proper boundaries of philosophic thought and the strong
temptation to exceed them in need of some sort of explanation.
We are, of course, human beings as well as philosophers, and spend
much more time involved in the activities of ordinary life than we
do in philosophical reflection. And it may be that the appropriate
explanation is a psychological one in terms of the effort required
to set aside our habitual interest in the natural world of facts and
things. On the other hand, the difficulty in achieving or maintaining the total "disinterest" Husserl describes may signify much
more than a lack of effort or practice. It may be, as I think both
Heidegger and Merleau-Ponty have suggested, that the absolute
separation of meaning from factual existence in every "region" of
experience is in fact impossible. If this should be the case, the
question whether Husserl has identified the proper philosophic
domain and method could lead to the question whether philosophy
itself is possible.

III

Contemporary Relevance

11

Husserl on Demonstrative Reference and Perception

David Woodruff Smith

At the turn of the century, Husserl offered a penetrating theory of demonstrative reference. It consumed but a few pages of his monumental *Logical Investigations*,[1] yet I think it deserves our closest attention. The theory is important as an extension of a Frege-like theory of meaning and reference to demonstrative pronouns and as a study in the relation between language and thought, especially between demonstratives and perception; it also has import for the phenomenology of perception. Husserl's theory starts with essentially the same insights as David Kaplan's theory of demonstratives in the 1970's.[2] Kaplan provides a powerful and precise development of such a theory in terms of modern logic; Husserl, on the other hand, provides a detailed account of the phenomenological and ontological foundations of such a theory.

Expressions such as 'I,' 'this,' 'here,' and 'now' Husserl called *essentially occasional* expressions.[3] These are expressions whose *referent* depends on the occasion of utterance—on who is uttering the expression, or what the speaker is pointing at before him, or where or when the utterance occurs. But Husserl also held that the *meaning* of such an expression depends on the occasion of utterance. Indeed, he defined an essentially occasional expression as one whose "actual meaning" is determined by "the occasion, the speaker, and the situation" (*LI,* I, §26, p. 315). An essentially occasional expression, Husserl held, gets its meaning from the speaker's "direct" awareness, or "intuition," of the referent. Consequently, the reference is "direct," rather than "attributive." The meaning of 'this,' in particular, is determined by the speaker's direct perceptual awareness of the referent. As we shall see, Husserl also recognized for each occasional expression a second type of meaning that does not depend on the occasion of utterance.

Before sifting Husserl's theory from Husserl's texts, we shall construct a fairly concise formulation and exposition of the theory, starting with a summary of Husserl's general semantical framework. The lion's share of Husserl's attention goes to the demonstrative pronoun 'this' and its relation to perception. Our attention follows suit, but we shall comment briefly at the end on Husserl's generalized view. We shall also comment briefly on the similarities between Husserl's and Kaplan's theories of demonstrative reference and on some implications for the phenomenology of perception.

I

Husserl distinguished the meaning (*Bedeutung*) expressed by an expression from the object (*Gegenstand*) referred to by the expression. And he held that meaning determines reference: the object referred to by an expression is determined by the meaning expressed by the expression. Thus Husserl's basic semantics is very like Frege's.[4] But where Frege developed the systematic details of such a semantics, Husserl developed the details of its relation to the theory of mind.

As is well known, Husserl held that each act of consciousness is *intentional,* or "directed" toward something, a consciousness "of" or sometimes "about" something. He sometimes called a consciousness of an object an *intention* of the object, which terminology will be frequent in quotations and discussion below. Husserl carefully distinguished the *content* of an act from the *object* of the act: the object is that of (or about) which the subject is conscious in the act, whereas the content is an abstract entity that embodies the phenomenological structure of the act, the "way" the object is "given" in the act. For Husserl, the object of an act is determined by the content of the act: the content prescribes an object (in a particular "way"), and the object prescribed is the object of the act. Thus, on Husserl's analysis, an intention consists in a three-place relation among a person, a content, and an object. The content of an act Husserl called the *sense* (*Sinn*) of the act.[5]

For Husserl, the relation of reference is structurally analogous to the relation of intention. As reference is the relation of an expression or utterance to an object via a meaning, so intention is the relation of a person or a mental act to an object via a sense, or content. Moreover, for Husserl, reference is founded on intention. For the referent of an expression uttered on a given occasion is the object of an underlying intention on the part of the speaker, and the meaning of the expression is the sense of the underlying intention. Specifically, the meaning of a declarative sentence uttered assertively on a particular occasion is the sense, or content, of an underlying judgment on the part of the speaker. It is in this sense, for Husserl, that language expresses thought.[6]

The preceding interpretation of Husserl on intention, meaning, and reference has been developed elsewhere.[7] My task here is to lay out Husserl's account of demonstrative reference, framed within the preceding theory of meaning and intention held by Husserl.

Husserl focused on one principal and paradigmatic use of 'this': its use to refer to an object one sees before one, aiding one's hearer perhaps by pointing at the object. His analysis of demonstrative reference, for that central case, comprises the following ten theses:

1. The referent of 'this' depends on the occasion of utterance.

This thesis is, of course, basic to any theory of demonstrative reference. The problem is to say how the referent depends on the occasion of utterance. Husserl's account begins with an important negative thesis:

2. Demonstrative reference is "direct" in that the object referred to by 'this' on a particular occasion of utterance is not determined attributively, i.e., by appeal solely to properties of the object.

The obvious contrast here is with definite descriptions (for example, 'the discoverer of America'), as the referent of a definite description is whatever object uniquely has certain properties (for example, having discovered America).

One might want to say the referent of 'this' is simply the object before the speaker, and demonstrative reference is "direct" in that nothing more is involved. But Husserl sees more. For Husserl, demonstrative reference is founded on the speaker's perception of the referent. It is direct in that it is founded on the speaker's "direct" intention of—his having "directly" in mind—the object he perceives. "Directness" is, for Husserl, a certain phenomenological character of intention. Perception, as a species of "intuition," is itself "direct." (Note: 'direct' does not mean unmediated by sense, as we shall see.) Thus the next two theses:

3. A person's uttering 'this' presupposes his perceiving a certain object and his wanting to speak about it.

4. The referent of 'this' on a particular occasion of utterance is the object of the speaker's underlying perception.

Here and hereafter the presupposed act of perception we call the underlying perception. Thesis 1 is a consequence of Thesis 4, and Thesis 2 is a consequence of Thesis 4 together with Husserl's phenomenological analysis of perception.

One might also want to hold that demonstrative reference is "direct" in that 'this' does not refer by way of a meaning.[8] This view would follow from Thesis 2 if the only kind of meanings prescribing individuals (those sometimes called individual concepts) were the meanings of definite descriptions, those that determine an object solely by appeal to its properties. But Husserl holds that 'this' does refer by way of a meaning, and it is a non-descriptive meaning. The introduction of meanings for essentially occasional expressions, however, complicates the basic picture of meaning and reference. On the one hand, if the referent of 'this' depends on and so may vary with the occasion of utterance, then it seems the meaning of 'this' must depend on and so may vary with the occasion of utterance; for the referent on a given occasion is determined by, is a function of, the meaning on that occasion, as the general theory of meaning and reference would require. But on the other hand, it seems the meaning of 'this' is fixed and well understood independently of the occasion of utterance. Husserl meets both of these intuitive demands, by recognizing two types of meaning for 'this':

5. 'This' has two types of meaning: a generic meaning that does not depend on or vary with the occasion of utterance, and a particular meaning that depends on and so may vary with the occasion of utterance.

For Husserl, both types of meaning for 'this' stem from the speaker's underlying perception. On a given occasion of utterance, the speaker has "directly" in mind the object he sees. This direct intention presupposes the given perception, and the two types of meaning expressed by saying 'this' are components of the sense, or content, of that direct intention. (A simpler view would say the direct intention just is the speaker's perception, but as we shall see, Husserl argues for this slightly more complicated view.) The generic meaning of 'this' may then be characterized as follows:

6. The generic meaning of 'this' is the sense that embodies the general phenomenological character of having directly in mind an object one sees.

This sense is present on any occasion of demonstrative reference in the speaker's underlying direct intention of the referent.

To characterize the particular meaning of 'this,' we need to call on Husserl's account of the sense of a perception. Husserl finds two fundamental components in the sense of an act of seeing an object. One, which he calls an "X," presents the perceived object "itself," or "simpliciter" and "in abstraction from all predicates"; the other presents the properties the object is given as having.[9] The X reflects the object's direct presentation in perceptual intuition. Now, when a person utters 'this,' he has in mind and so refers to the object he sees before him. He has that same object in mind because the X in the sense of his perception recurs in—we might say is "borrowed" by—the sense of his direct intention. And that X is the particular meaning expressed by his utterance of 'this':

7. The particular meaning of 'this' on a given occasion of utterance is that constituent of the sense of the speaker's underlying perception which presents the object perceived "itself"—the "X" in the sense of the perception.

Since the object presented in a perception depends on what is perceived as before the subject, the X in the sense of a perception depends on the occasion of perception—that is, as given in the perception. So the particular meaning of 'this' on a given occasion of utterance will depend on the occasion as given in the speaker's underlying perception.

Whereas the two types of meaning for 'this' are both embodied in the speaker's consciousness on the occasion of utterance, the hearer is in a different plight. The hearer is familiar with the generic character of perception and of having in mind what one sees; so he knows the generic meaning of 'this.' But he must interpolate the speaker's particular meaning by surveying the circumstance of utterance, by looking for the object the speaker is looking at (and perhaps pointing at). The X in the sense of the speaker's perception of that object is then the particular meaning of 'this' on the present occasion. In this way, the generic meaning of 'this' together with the visible circumstances of utterance "indicate" the particular meaning of 'this' to the hearer. (Cf. *LI,* I, §§ 2, 26; VI, § 5). Thus:

> 8. The particular meaning of 'this' on a particular occasion of utterance is "indicated" to the hearer by the generic meaning together with the circumstance of utterance, specifically, what the speaker is looking at (and perhaps pointing at).

Of course, 'this' is used in complete sentences, and that complicates matters slightly. Suppose, seeing a coin on the sidewalk before him, a person says, 'This is a Swiss franc.' His utterance of this sentence expresses a propositional meaning that is the sense of his underlying judgment that "this," the object he sees, is a Swiss franc. That judgment presupposes his perception of the coin at his feet, because it is about the object he sees. And the subject component of the sense of the judgment is, it would seem, the X component of the sense of the perception, being the particular meaning expressed by 'this.' So:

> 9. When a person utters a sentence 'This is ϕ' on a given occasion, the particular meaning of 'this' on that occasion—the X in the sense of the speaker's underlying perception—serves as subject component of the sense of the speaker's underlying judgment.

One further principle Husserl would have held for demonstratives is this:

> 10. The object referred to by 'this' on a particular occasion of utterance need not exist.

This thesis precludes for Husserl a "causal" theory of demonstrative reference holding that 'this' refers to what causally affects the speaker's senses in the appropriate way; it also precludes the simple view that 'this' refers to the object appropriately situated with respect to the perceiver (and perhaps his pointing finger). Thesis 10 makes room for Macbeth's hallucinating an object before him and referring to it, saying 'This is a dagger.' Of course, such cases are unusual and may try a hearer's patience, but Husserl would have allowed them. Thesis 10 is a consequence of Thesis 4 together with Husserl's fundamental position that one can be conscious "of" an object—in particular, in perception—even if no such object exists. Generally, with reference founded on intention,

Husserl did not restrict reference to successful reference.[10]* We cite 10 last, though, because the problems it raises are not special to demonstrative reference for Husserl, and so we should be able conveniently to by-pass Thesis 10.

Here in Theses 1–10 we have a reconstruction of Husserl's analysis of demonstrative reference for 'this' used vis-à-vis perception. We shall now proceed to extract the analysis from Husserl's texts, dealing with some complications of interpretation as they arise and noting parenthetically Theses 1–9 as they emerge (10, we said, does not come from Husserl's specific discussion of demonstratives).

II

Husserl's theory of demonstrative reference is found in his *Logical Investigations* (1900-01), primarily in Investigation I, §26, and Investigation VI, §5. In I, §26, he introduces the topic of essentially occasional expressions, offering a definition (which we cited in our opening remarks), discussing somewhat briefly the words 'I,' 'this,' and 'here,' and observing two types of meanings for essentially occasional expressions. But it is in VI, §5, that we really see how his theory works. There he addresses 'this' used in the "expression" of a perception, or a judgment founded on perception (cf. §§4–5). We shall begin with the latter discussion of 'this.'

So far as I know, Husserl did not pursue essentially occasional expressions elsewhere. He did, however, pursue the sense of perception in later works. We shall draw on his sharpened account of the sense of perception in *Ideas* (1913), §131, where the notion of an "X" component in the sense of a perception is articulated. This notion plays a recognizable role in the *Investigations* analysis of demonstrative reference; making it explicit brings the analysis into somewhat sharper focus.

In one prominent and paradigmatic use of 'this' (Husserl acknowledges others), the referent of 'this' on a particular occasion of utterance is precisely the object the speaker then sees (hears, etc.). Often, of course, the speaker physically points at the object. But on Husserl's view, the perception itself is the basic determinant of reference. Evidently the pointing is but a dramatic aid to help the hearer determine more precisely what the speaker is talking about. Suppose, Husserl says, "I have just looked out into the garden and now give expression to my perception in the words: 'A black bird flies up'" (VI, §4, p. 680; with translation changes). Or I say, "'This . . . is a black bird; this black bird flies up'" (p. 680; with translation changes).

> If perception never constitutes the full meaning of a statement grounded on perception, it seems nonetheless to make a contribution to this meaning, and to do so in cases of the sort just dealt with. . . . 'This' is an essentially occasional expression which only becomes fully meaningful when we have regard to the circumstances of utterance, in this case to an actually performed perception. The perceived object, as it is given in perception, is what the word 'this' means (*ist mit dem 'dies' gemeint*).
> (VI, §5, p. 682; with translation changes)

(It is clear from this passage that Husserl holds Theses 3 and 4 and of course 1, though he jumps right into a discussion of meaning, taking for granted the issue of reference.)

It is important that, unlike some philosophers, Husserl assumes that "essentially occasional" expressions such as 'this' *express meanings*. But he distinguishes two types of meaning for them:

> Essentially occasional expressions have no doubt a meaning (*Bedeutung*) which varies from case to case, but in all the changes a common element is left over, which distinguishes such ambiguity from that of casual equivocation. The addition of intuition (i.e., perception) has as effect that this common element of meaning, indeterminate in its abstraction, can determine itself. Intuition, in fact, gives it determinateness of objective reference (*Richtung*).   (VI, §5, p. 683; with translation changes)

The meaning element common to any use of 'this' (vis-à-vis perception) Husserl calls its "indicating" (*anzeigende*) meaning (p. 686). This is the meaning that would be characterized in a dictionary, perhaps somewhat roughly by "the object visually before the speaker." (We offer a more accurate characterization later.) This meaning concerns only the "universal *semantic function*" of the expression (cf. I, §26, p. 315, concerning 'I'). It alone does not determine the object referred to on a particular occasion of utterance of 'this'; the addition of perception fills in the indicating meaning somehow so that a definite object of reference is determined. In contrast, the meaning of 'this' which varies from one occasion of utterance to the next, Husserl calls its "indicated" (*angezeigte*) meaning (VI, §5, p. 686). This meaning presents the particular object referred to on that occasion and is determined by the speaker's perception of the object on that occasion. (We seek a fuller characterization shortly below.)

Husserl homes in on the indicating and indicated meanings of 'this' by contrasting the hearer's with the speaker's plight:

For the hearer, in whose momentary field of vision the thing to be pointed out (*das Aufzuweisende*) is perhaps not present, only this indeterminately general thought is aroused: Something is being pointed to (*hingeweisen*). Only when a[n intuitive, or perceptual,] presentation (*Vorstellung*) is added . . . is there constituted for him determinateness of pointing (*Hinweisung*), and so a full and authentic meaning (*Bedeutung*) for the demonstrative pronoun. For the speaker there is no such sequence: he has no need of the indeterminately pointing *idea* (*unbestimmt hinweisenden Vorstellung*) which functions as "indicator" (*Anzeige*) for the hearer. Not the idea of the pointing (Hinweisung) but the pointing itself is given in his case, and it is *eo ipso* determinately directed thingward: from the first the speaker has the "indicated" meaning, and has it in a presentative intention immediately oriented toward intuition . . .

If I say 'this' . . . the true aim of my talk lies not in [the] general element, but in the direct intending of the object in question. Toward it and its fullness of content (i.e., intuitive, or perceptual, fullness) I am directed. . . . In this sense a direct intention is the primary and indicated meaning.

(VI, §5, pp. 686-687; with translation changes)

So the indicated meaning is—or, Husserl would better say, inheres in—a "direct intention." Other passages, on which we shall comment below, amplify Husserl's conception of indicating and indicated meaning. (The preceding passages articulate Thesis 5, suggest 6, and implicitly contain 8.)

According to Husserl, demonstrative reference is "direct." This view deserves attention in its own right, and it is fundamental to Husserl's characterization of indicating and indicated meanings. Husserl says:

Essentially occasional expressions are . . . much like proper names, insofar as the latter function with their authentic meaning. For a proper name also names an object 'directly.' It refers to (*meint*) it, not in the attributive way as the bearer of these or those properties, but without such 'conceptual' mediation, as that which it 'itself' is, just as perception might set it before the eyes. (*LI*, VI, §5, p. 684; with translation changes)

(Here note Thesis 2.) This passage implies that neither names nor demonstratives express the sort of meanings expressed by definite descriptions. Thus Husserl's view of names and demonstratives is like that of the 1970's, found in the work of Keith Donnellan and Saul Kripke on names and David Kaplan on demonstratives. (Note that Husserl uses '*meinen*' sometimes for the relation of referring and sometimes for the relation of expressing or meaning (*bedeuten*). This is analogous, when discussing reference, to his use of '*meinen*', when discussing intention, sometimes for the relation of subject to object of consciousness and sometimes for the relation of subject to content, or sense.)

Now let us ask precisely what sort of meaning is the indicated meaning of 'this' on a given occasion of utterance. My understanding is that it would seem to be what Husserl later—in *Ideas*, §131—called an "X," a sense that simply presents a certain object "itself," "in abstraction from all predicates"—a mere intensional token of the object. For what the speaker wishes to convey is primarily just a sense of a particular individual, the one before him, without calling on any specific properties of that individual. Indeed, the proposal that the indicated meaning is an X fits well with Husserl's discussion in *Logical Investigations*, even though Husserl did not explicitly describe such components of sense as X's in the *Investigations*. Husserl often describes the sense of an act as "the object as given" (cf. *Ideas*, §§90-91). Earlier we quoted Husserl as saying, "The perceived object, as it is given in perception, is what the word 'this' means (*gemeint*)" (p. 682). In the quotation about "directness," he says that a proper name refers to an object "as that which it 'itself' is, just as perception might set it before the eyes": that is, as it "itself." These remarks come very close to saying that the indicated meaning of 'this' is an X.

We know the indicated meaning is *determined* by the speaker's perception (see pp. 686-687, quoted above), and in *Ideas* (§131) Husserl says that the sense of a perception consists of an X together with a content of predicate senses. It would seem that the X expressed as the indicated meaning of 'this' is the X in the sense of the speaker's perception. When a person says 'This is a black bird,' he expresses the sense of an underlying judgment grounded on his current perception (cf. *LI*, VI, §3); specifically, the judgment is *about* the object presented in the perception. Thus it would seem that for Husserl the X in the perception is borrowed by the judgment, serving as the subject component of the judgment's sense, and so is the indicated meaning expressed by 'this.' (Here note Thesis 8.)

The proposal that the indicated meaning is specifically the X in the speaker's perception (being Thesis 7) finds some support in Husserl's discussion in *Logical Investigations*. In the considered passages of the sixth Investigation and their environs (§§3-5), Husserl is discussing the "expression" of a perception, which the demonstrative 'this' serves—that is, the "expression" of a judgment founded on perception. Much earlier in the *Investigations*

(I, §14), he says that where one expresses the content of a perception, this content is the meaning expressed (p. 290). And of this meaning he says:

> This is the *identical content* which, in perception, pertains to the totality of possible acts of perception which intended the same object perceptually, and intend it actually as the same object. This content is therefore the ideal correlate of this *single* object, which may, for the rest, be completely imaginary. (p. 291)

The meaning that Husserl is discussing is evidently what he subsequently calls the indicated meaning of 'this' as used in expressing the content of a perception (in *LI*, I, §26, and VI, §5). What he here conceives as "ideal correlate," or sense, he conceives in *Ideas* as "noematic correlate," or again sense; a sense is a "correlate" of an object in that it stands for the object. Now, the notion of an X is just that of a constituent of sense that stands for a definite, or "single," object and recurs in the senses of different perceptions intending the same object. So it seems that, for Husserl, the indicated meaning of 'this' would be the X in the sense of the speaker's perception.

It seems clear that for Husserl the indicated meaning of 'this' on a particular occasion of utterance is an X, and an X that presents the object of the speaker's underlying perception. To be sure, this interpretation resolves the meaning of passages in the *Investigations* into the sharper views in *Ideas*, but the resolution is little more than fine-tuning. However, the *Investigations* offers some important resistance to the further proposal that the relevant X is for Husserl the X *in* the sense of the underlying perception. I think the resistance arises, though, from a mistake Husserl would not have made with the sharper view of *Ideas*.

The resistance lies in Husserl's insistence that the indicated meaning of 'this' is *determined* by but is not a *part* of the content of the speaker's perception:

> Perception . . . *realizes the possibility* of an unfolding of my act of this-intention (*Dies-Meinens*) with its definite relation to the object, e.g., to this paper before my eyes. But it does not, on our view, itself constitute the meaning (*Bedeutung*), not even a part of it.
>
> Insofar as the act-character of pointing (*Hinweisung*) is oriented to intuition, it achieves a definiteness of intention (*Intention*) which fulfills itself in intuition . . . For a pointing intention (*Meinen*) remains the same, whichever out of a manifold of mutually belonging perceptions may underlie it, in all of which the same, and *recognizably* the same, object

appears. The meaning (*Bedeutung*) of 'this' is again the same when, instead of a perception, some act from the manifold of imaginative presentations is substituted for it, an act presenting the same object through a picture in a recognizably identical manner. . . .

We hold, therefore, that *perception is an act that determines but does not contain meaning* (*Bedeutung*). This is confirmed by the fact that essentially occasional expressions like 'this' can often be used and understood without an appropriate foundation of intuition. Once the intention (*Intention*) to an object has been formed on a suitable basis, it can be revived and exactly reproduced *without* the help of a suitable act of perception or imagination.   (*LI*, VI, §5, p. 684; with translation changes)

We can put Husserl's argument in this passage as follows. The reference of 'this' on a given occasion is founded on an underlying intention of a particular object: the referent of 'this' is the object of that intention, and the indicated meaning of 'this' is the content, or sense, of that intention. (Cf. the surrounding passages, pp. 682–84, 685–86). The underlying intention is a "direct," or "pointing," intention. And it is determined by the speaker's intuition, or perception, of the object: it is a direct intention of the same object that is presented in the perception, and it is "fulfilled" in the perception, finding sensuous support therein. But, Husserl claims, for reasons we shall recite in a moment, the "this"-intention is not a part of, but is founded on, the speaker's perception of the object. So, Husserl concludes, the meaning of 'this' is not a part of the sense of the perception. This conclusion rules out the possibility that the indicated meaning is the X *in* the sense of the perception.

Now, it seems to me Husserl has erred in inferring that the indicated meaning cannot be a part of the sense of the speaker's perception. Let us grant for the moment that the this-intention underlying the utterance of 'this' is not a part of the underlying perception. Nevertheless, the same sense may be shared by the this-intention and the perception. The sense of a direct, or pointing, intention would, in the terms of *Ideas*, be an X; an X is just the sort of sense that would capture the phenomenological structure of a direct intention. But it is a main feature of X's that the same X recurs in the senses of many possible perceptions of the same object (cf. *Ideas*, §131). It is only natural to assume, then, that the same X would be present in the sense of a perception of a certain object and in the sense of another, direct intention of that same object. So it seems clear that with the notion of X from *Ideas*, Husserl should have held the same X to serve as the sense of the this-intention and as the X component of the sense of the underlying perception. Thus, with the sharpened view of *Ideas,* he should not—and perhaps would not—have concluded that the indicated meaning of 'this' is not a part of the sense of the speaker's underlying perception.

There remains a further problem with Husserl's reasoning. Even if Husserl had agreed that the sense of the this-intention is the X in the sense of the underlying perception, he could still hold, as he did, that the this-intention is not a part of the perception. Is this latter view defensible? Perhaps, but the reasons Husserl offered (in the argument of the quotation above) are uncompelling and of uneven merit. The "pointing" this-intention is separate from the perception that determines it, Husserl argues, because (i) that pointing intention would be the same if it were determined by any other perception of (recognizably) the same object, (ii) the intention would be the same if it were determined instead by an act of imagining the same object, and (iii) it would be the same if it occurred—if it were "revived"—after the given perception. Now, reason (iii) is a bad one: uttering 'this' in reference to an object seen at an earlier moment is a different use of 'this' than the use under analysis; it is not a reference to something directly presented in one's current perception, but a reference "back" to something previously presented (albeit then in a direct way)—it is not a properly demonstrative use of 'this' but a kind of *anaphoric* use of 'this.' Reason (ii) is a dubious one: it is not clear that one can imagine a definite object, the same as is given in a certain perception, unless one has already had that perception and on its basis imagines its object; but I am not sure that using 'this' to refer to an object one previously saw and one now imagines is a properly demonstrative use—it may again be an anaphoric use. The first reason, (i), is the most plausible. It is natural to hold that when a person says 'this' referring to an object he sees, his utterance serves to convey only his direct intention of that object; the reference abstracts away from the object's presentation in that particular perception, from the specific way the object is given in that perception, from everything about the object as presented save its identity. Thus we *might* want to separate the direct intention underlying the utterance from the perception determining that intention, as Husserl does. Still, this move is not forced. We might hold that the direct intention *is* a constituent part of the speaker's current perception. The speaker does not convey anything else in the perception. And *were* he currently experiencing instead another perception of the same object, his perception might include this very same direct intention of the object; his current direct intention of the object might have been fleshed out into a distinct perceptual act. So Husserl's first reason for divorcing the this-intention from the perception determining it is not compelling. There is one further piece of reasoning Husserl might offer: 'this' is used in sentences, and underlying a person's utterance of a sentence 'This is . . ' is a judgment about the object he sees; since different statements and so different judgments can be founded on the same perception (cf. *LI,* VI, §4, p. 681), the speaker's underlying judgment should be distinguished from its founding perception; so, Husserl might conclude, the this-intention which is a constituent part of the judgment is not a constituent part of the perception. (Note here Thesis 9.) This reasoning, too, is inconclusive: why can't the same direct intention occur in the perception and also occur as the subject component of the judgment, since the judgment is about the object being currently perceived?

Husserl would have had a simpler theory of demonstrative reference if he had allowed the direct intention underlying an utterance of 'this' to be a proper constituent of the perception that determines it, that central part of the perception whose structure is captured by the X expressed as the indicated meaning of 'this.' The source of his resistance to the simpler view seems to have been his emerging difficulty concerning the sense of perception as intuition.[11] The sixth of the *Investigations* is a study of intuitive acts. It is launched by the discussion of the expression of perceptual acts by use of demonstratives, wherein Husserl urges that perception determines but does not embody meaning (§5). Husserl proceeds (in §§6ff., especially §§8 and 14) to distinguish "empty" acts of "signification"—for example, merely thinking of an object—and "fulfilling" acts of intuition—for example, seeing an object, which presents an object "itself" (§14, p. 712) and which fulfills in virtue of its sensuous character (§14, p. 713). An act of ordinary perception is then a complex experience, a synthesis of a conceptual, "interpretive" intention and a sensuous, "intuitive" intention come into "coincidence" (*Deckung*) (§14, pp. 713–714). And it would seem, then, that the content of such a complex act is a synthesis of an "interpretive" sense (cf. §26, p. 741) and a "fulfilling," or purely intuitive, sense (cf. §28, p. 743, and also *LI,* I, §14) brought into coincidence. Only interpretive sense, Husserl thinks, is properly expressible as linguistic meaning, and only signifying acts—not fulfilling acts—

yield their sense as linguistic meaning. (That is the point of *LI*, I, §14, and VI, §5). When Husserl separates the direct intention underlying an utterance of 'this' and contributing its content as indicated meaning from the perception that determines the intention, he is apparently taking the perception as a *pure* sensuous intuition and not a complex act comprising both intuitive and interpretive intentions. If the X were imported from *Ideas,* it would presumably be located in the intuitive sense of a perception (in *LI*, I, §14, the "identical meaning" we said would be an X is a fulfilling sense). But the X should also be located in the interpretive sense of the perception; for the intuitive and interpretive intentions in the perception are brought into coincidence by a synthesis of "identification" (cf. *LI*, VI, §8), and it is by virtue of sharing the same X that the two intentions have the same object.

By the time of *Ideas* Husserl's view of perception had simplified somewhat (cf. §§85, 97). An act of perception, in *Ideas,* consists of a sensory phase and an interpretive phase that "gives" it sense. But these are phases of one act rather than separate intentions that form a synthetic act. The act of perception does not, then, include an act of intuition as a constituent part; rather, it is itself an act of intuition (cf. §1 of *Ideas*). Accordingly, an act of perception does not involve two senses, one intuitive and the other interpretive; rather, it has one sense that is interpretive but is also intuitive insofar as it "informs" the sensory phase of the intuitive act. The simpler view of perception in *Ideas* might have allowed Husserl to go with the simpler view of demonstrative reference, but he did not in *Ideas* return to the topic of demonstrative reference.

I think we should give Husserl's discussion of demonstrative reference in *Logical Investigations* the benefit of his discussion of the sense of perception in *Ideas;* yet there are elements of the *Ideas* view of perception that we cannot impress on the *Investigations* without altering its view of perception and demonstrative reference. Accordingly, we can interpret the indicated meaning of 'this' as an X, and with only slight modification we can take it to be the X in the sense of the speaker's underlying perception. But we cannot without significant alteration take the speaker's this-intention to be part of his underlying perception.

(The preceding discussion is the rationale for our formulation of Theses 6 and 7.)

We now inquire more precisely what Husserl takes the indicating meaning of 'this' to be.

Husserl develops the notion of essentially occasional expressions in terms of the hearer's understanding of such words (*LI*, I, §26). Words like 'table' and 'red' are understood independently of the circumstances of utterance. But occasional expressions like 'this' and 'I' are understood only by attending to the "intuitive circumstances" of utterance (*LI*, I, §26, p. 315). In order to understand an utterance of 'this,' the hearer must in general have perceptual access to the speaker's perceived circumstances. The hearer knows the general semantic function of 'this,' determined by its indicating meaning; by also seeing what is before the speaker, he can ascertain the "actual meaning" of 'this' on that occasion. Husserl says:

> 'This' read in isolation . . . lacks its proper meaning, and is understood only to the extent that it arouses the concept of its pointing (*hinweisenden*) function (which we call its indicating meaning). In each case of normal use, its full and actual meaning can only grow out of the prominent presentation of the thing that it makes its object.
>
> (*LI*, I, §26, p. 317; with translation changes)

Thus the indicating meaning together with the occasion of utterance "indicate" the indicated meaning of 'this' to the hearer: knowing the generic meaning of 'this' and what the speaker is looking at in saying 'this,' the hearer can inductively infer the "actual meaning" of 'this' on that occasion. (Cf. *LI*, I, §2 on "indication" and §§1-14 on language as conveying thought.)

Having laid out the distinction between the indicating and indicated meaning of 'this' and the role of 'this' in "expressing" perception (*LI*, I, §26, and VI, §§1-5), however, Husserl observes that the distinction can be taken in two ways. (Cf. *LI*, VI, §5, Addendum, pp. 686-687). On one interpretation, or theory, the distinction is between

> the two mutually resolving thoughts which characterize the hearer's successive understanding: *first* the indefinite idea of something or other meant (*Gemeinten*) by 'this,' *then* the act of definitely directed pointing (*Hinweisung*) into which a completing presentation transforms it. In the latter act we have the indicated, in the former the indicating meaning.
>
> (pp. 686-687)

By "pointing," Husserl means "direct intention"—mental pointing, so to speak (see the end of the paragraph from which the quotation is drawn). On the second theory:

> If we confine ourselves to the complete, definitely directed pointing which the speaker has from the beginning, we can again see something double about it: the general character of pointing as such, and that which determines it, which narrows it down to a pointing to 'this.' The former can again be called an indicating meaning, or rather the indicating element in the indissoluble unity of meaning, insofar as it is what the hearer can immediately grasp by virtue of its expressive generality, and can use to indicate what is meant (*Gemeinten*). (p. 687)

Husserl then says (p. 687) that the second distinction is the one intended in the first Investigation (§26). So his considered view is the second theory.

The initial exposition of indicating meaning (*LI*, 1, §26, pp. 316-317, concerning 'I' and 'this') is indeed quite ambiguous. It might suggest as many as three candidates for the indicating meaning of 'this': (i) a second-order meaning that is a part of the content of the hearer's consciousness and designates the indicated meaning, which is a part of the content of the speaker's consciousness—perhaps the sense of "the sense (the X) of the speaker's direct intention of the object he perceives"; (ii) a metalinguistic meaning that is akin to (i) but calls on the "semantic" or "pointing" function of the word 'this' (cf. pp. 315, 317), to refer to what the speaker sees before him—perhaps the sense of "the sense (the X) of the direct intention underlying the speaker's utterance of 'this' to refer to the object he perceives"; (iii) a meaning that is a part of the content of the speaker's underlying direct intention of the object he perceives, and that embodies the generic "way" in which the object is presented in that intention—perhaps the sense of "object before me" or, as most naturally and accurately expressed if Husserl is right, "this (the object perceptually before me)". Of these candidates for indicating meaning, Husserl rejects the first, would presumably reject the second, and endorses the third.

Thus both indicating and indicated meaning reside in the speaker's consciousness, in his "direct intention" of the referent (p. 687). The indicated meaning is, on our construction, an X that presents that particular object and so depends on the occasion of utterance. And the indicating meaning, we now see, is a sense that embodies the generic mode of presentation in such a direct intention; on any occasion of utterance, this component of sense is present in the speaker's consciousness, so it does not vary with the occasion. The indicating meaning "indicates" the indicated meaning to the hearer because the hearer is familiar with the generic mode of presentation that constitutes the indicating meaning. Note that the "general character of pointing" that constitutes indicating meaning (p. 687) is not the "quality" or "thetic character" of direct intention (as Husserl calls that character of an act—say, an act of imagination—that distinguishes it from other species of acts: cf. *LI*, V, §20, *Ideas*, §129); it is rather the general character of an object's being presented as before one (or, more precisely, as being a certain object which by presupposition is the object seen as before one). For the indicating meaning is a meaning that concerns the object as given, a meaning "indeterminate in its abstraction" that is given "determinateness of objective reference" by "the addition of intuition" (p. 683, quoted earlier).

(In the preceding, observe the case for Theses 6 and 8.)

III

Part I offered a formulation and exposition of the theory of demonstrative reference I take to be Husserl's (with a touch of help). Part II offered the textual analysis on which the interpretation is based. We close with some observations offering perspective on the theory.

Husserl's analysis of demonstratives is put forth as a species of a general analysis of essentially occasional expressions. Generally, "essentially occasional" reference—referring by uttering 'this,' 'I,' 'here,' 'now'—is founded on the speaker's "intuition" of the referent, which Husserl conceived as "direct" or "pointing" intention and which we might call "acquaintance" with the referent. The hearer knows the general character of the type of intention on which the uttered word is customarily founded; this is embodied in the generic, "indicating" meaning of the word. On the basis of his own "intuitive" awareness of the circumstances of utterance, then, the hearer is able to ascertain the referent and the particular, "indicated" meaning of the word on that occasion of utterance—an X.

Of the personal pronoun 'I' Husserl says:

> In solitary speech the meaning of 'I' is essentially realized in the immediate presentation of one's own personality (*Persönlichkeit*), and thus therein also lies the meaning of the word in communicative speech. Each man has his own I-presentation (and with it his individual concept of I) and this is why the word's meaning differs from person to person. But since each person, in speaking of himself, says 'I', the word has the character of a universally operative indication of this fact. Through this *indicator* (*Anzeige*) the hearer achieves understanding of the meaning, he takes the

person who confronts him intuitively, not merely as the speaker, but also as the immediate object of this speaker's speech. The word 'I' has not itself directly the power to arouse the specific I-presentation; this becomes fixed in the actual piece of talk. It does not work like the word 'lion,' which can arouse the idea of a lion in and by itself. In its case, rather, an indicative function mediates, crying as it were, to the hearer 'Your vis-à-vis means (*meint*) himself.'   (*LI*, I, §26, p. 316)

The next paragraph introduces the distinction between indicated and indicating meaning for 'I.' Notice that the above passage seems to put forth the alternative notion of indicating meaning that Husserl rejected in the sixth Investigation, where he referred to this introduction of the concept. Also notice that it is not at all clear what one's immediate self-presentation consists of, but surely the hearer's intuitive awareness of the speaker and so of the speaker's referent for 'I' is perceptual.

Husserl then proceeds to apply the general theory to 'this' and 'here' as further examples (pp. 316-318). Each occasional term presents different details of analysis to be worked out, but it is clear that a general type of analysis is in the offing.

Husserl's analysis of demonstrative reference seems a careful and plausible piece of descriptive analysis. Indeed, a very similar analysis is found in David Kaplan's recent work on the logic of demonstratives,[12] which tends to confirm the analysis.

Kaplan too holds that demonstrative reference is "direct." This requires, at least for Kaplan, that it is not mediated *à la* Frege by a descriptive meaning. And Kaplan, too, holds that there are two types of meanings, or intensions, associated with 'this,' or 'that.' The *content* of 'this,' were it uttered on a given occasion, is an intension that simply determines the referent on that occasion. The *character* of 'this' is an intension that determines for a given occasion of utterance what would be the content of 'this' were it uttered on that occasion. Thus content depends on the occasion of utterance, and character does not.

Husserl's selection for indicated and indicating meanings of 'this' can be seen as an ontological specification of what precisely Kaplan's content and character are for 'this.' For, strictly, Kaplan defines character as the function that assigns to each context of utterance the content 'this' would have if uttered in that context; and he defines the content as the function that assigns to each possible world a fixed individual, the individual appropriately "demonstrated" on that occasion. But these functions are not meanings in the sense of Frege or Husserl; rather, they represent meanings, or what meanings do. Different proposals as to what exactly the represented meanings are, are compatible with Kaplan's definition of content and character. One proposal is that found in Husserl. Its motivation lies in Husserl's view that demonstrative reference is founded on the speaker's direct intention of the referent.

Kaplan himself has tended toward a different ontological specification of content and character. The function defined as content might be viewed as a mere technical construction along the lines of the customary possible-worlds analysis of intensions. The "content" of 'this' on a given occasion of utterance is, for Kaplan as I have understood him, really just the object referred to, the object appropriately before and demonstrated by the speaker (and, if you will, causally affecting his senses). Thus demonstrative reference is "direct" in that there really is no meaning involved that mediates the reference in a Frege-like way. The function that assigns the given object to any possible world—and which might be called "content"—does not determine the object of reference but is rather itself determined by the object. This specification yields a theory of demonstrative reference quite different from Husserl's; in particular, it treats "directness" in a quite different way. "Character," too, might be specified differently.[13]*

A more detailed comparison of Husserl's and Kaplan's views must await another occasion of utterances on 'this.' The importance of the structural similarity of their theories is twofold. If Husserl's views are correct, they provide a phenomenological foundation for Kaplan's logic of demonstratives. And if Kaplan's logic accurately represents the functioning of demonstratives, it provides a modern, technical development for Husserl's views.

Parallel to Husserl's theory of demonstrative reference is a partial analysis of the intentionality of perception. Perception has a "demonstrative" character, it may be held.[14] For, like demonstrative reference or its underlying direct intention, perception is oriented to the circumstances in which the act of perception occurs. It is natural to propose, then, that the content, or sense, of a perception includes two components: a generic sense that is present in the content of any perception of an individual, and a particular sense that presents the particular object seen on the occasion of the given act of perception. The generic sense embodies a general phenomenological character of perception, the generic way in which an object is presented in perception. It is, we might say, the sense "object before me." And the particular sense would include the X that presents the particular object given in the specified act of perception. Here, then, we have a partial account of the content through which an object is intended in perception.

This account of the sense of perception is compatible with Husserl's account of perception, especially in *Ideas,* but it is not articulated by Husserl per se.

All we have so far is a parallel between this account of perception and Husserl's account of demonstrative reference. But I think there is also a conceptual connection. Suppose in *phenomenological description* of an act of perception that I am enjoying, I say 'I see this coin' or 'I see this as a coin.' In that case, it seems, my utterance of 'this' is founded on a direct intention that is not merely determined by but coincides with my perceptual intention of, my perceptual acquaintance with, the object I refer to. Husserl argued that in general the underlying intention should be distinguished from the perception on which it is based. But however that view may fare, in at least the case of phenomenological description the function of 'this' is not merely to refer to the particular object given in the perception but also to refer to it in the "way" it is given. So in this case it seems 'this' expresses the sense of my direct perceptual intention of the object I see. And that sense includes a generic sense and an X as described above.

The preceding analysis of the demonstrative structure of perception is importantly incomplete. For the generic sense in a perception is too general to pick out the object of perception on the given occasion, and the X is too impoverished. The generic sense must be fleshed out with the details of sensuous presentation in order to present a particular object before one, the result being a structure of sense that "introduces" the X. Very basic problems in the phenomenology of perception are there at issue. A full account of how demonstrative reference is achieved will ultimately depend on such issues concerning how the intentionality of perception is fundamentally achieved.

12
Intending and Referring

Ronald McIntyre

The key notion in Husserl's theory of intentionality is his notion of "noema," or "noematic *Sinn.*"[1] According to Husserl, it is the noema of an act of consciousness that accounts for the act's being directed toward a certain object in a particular way; in that sense, Husserl sees intentionality as a relation to an object via an intermediate entity, the act's noema. Føllesdal, stressing Husserl's conception of the noema as a generalization of essentially the same notion of meaning that is found in Frege's semantic theory, has illuminated this theory of intentionality by comparing it with Frege's theory of linguistic sense and reference.[2] For Frege, it is via a meaning (a linguistic meaning, or Sinn) that a linguistic expression is related to its referent; and for Husserl, it is via a meaning (an "act-meaning," or noematic Sinn) that an act is related to the object it intends. And so Husserl's account of intending is strikingly similar to Frege's account of referring: intending, like referring, is a relation mediated and determined by meaning.

Understanding noemata as meanings—that is, as abstract intensional entities of the sort that are expressed in language— thus yields a "semantic" model of intentionality. This model is illuminating, not because the notions of linguistic meaning and reference are intrinsically clearer than Husserl's notions of noema and intention, but simply because most philosophers are more familiar with the concept of meaning as a semantic notion and with the role it is supposed to play in a Fregean theory of reference. In semantics, however, familiarity with meanings has bred contempt: philosophers of language generally seem to agree that, at the very least, Fregean meanings do not, by themselves, provide an adequate general account of how expressions are related to their referents. In this paper I want to examine some of these negative conclusions about the role of meanings in semantic theory to see what consequences they have for Husserl's theory of intentionality. First I shall note some salient features of Husserl's conception of intentionality as a phenomenological notion and the methodological restrictions they impose on the kind of theory he can offer. Then, drawing especially on work by Donnellan, Kripke, and Putnam, I shall argue that insofar as Frege's theory of reference *is* a model for Husserl's theory of intentionality, Husserl's theory fails to provide an account of intentionality that is adequate to his conception of it. I shall also discuss some non-Fregean elements that seem to be present in Husserl's accounts of both reference and intention, but I shall argue that his appeal to them is not consistent with the methodological restrictions that his phenomenological conception of intentionality imposes.

1. Husserl's Conception of Intentionality and its Methodological Consequences

To understand the kind of theory of intentionality Husserl gives and the role that noemata play in it, it is important first to understand how he conceives intentionality itself. Husserl sometimes describes it as a sort of *relation* holding between an act (or the subject of an act) and an intended object. Intentional experiences, he says, are always a "consciousness *of* something," and "insofar as they are a consciousness of something, they are said to be 'intentionally related' to this something."[3] But, Husserl believes, "intentional relations" are not ordinary, empirical relations. And, as Husserl understands these "relations," a theory that would explain them must not appeal to empirical facts about the object intended in an act or to any empirical relations that obtain between this object and the conscious subject of the act.

Husserl rejects the view that the objects of intentional relations are entities of some extraordinary kind (what are sometimes called "intentional objects"). He insists, to the contrary, that the things we desire, perceive, judge about, or otherwise intend are usually quite ordinary sorts of entities. Indeed, in typical cases the object intended in an act is an objectively real, "transcendent" entity, paradigmatically a physical object (see, for example *Ideen*, §§41-43; §90, p. 224; *LI*, V, §11). When someone sees a tree, for example, the object of his perception is not a sense datum or any other sort of unusual object but an actual tree, a physical object that others can also see and that exists independently of its being perceived. Nonetheless, Husserl holds, the intentionality of an act is not essentially dependent on the ontological status of the object toward which the act is directed or on any empirical facts about that object. An act of hallucinating a monster or phantasizing a centaur, for instance, is just as intentional as an act of seeing a tree, although in neither of the former cases does the appropriate object exist at all (cf. *LI*, V, §11, pp. 558-559; *Ideen*, §23, pp. 50-51; §46, p. 108). Hence, that an act is "intentionally related" to a particular object does not entail that such an object exists. Furthermore, Husserl notes, acts may be directed toward the same object and nevertheless differ in their intentionality and so be different acts (see *LI*, V, §20, pp. 588-589; *Ideen*, §131, p. 321). For example, if the man who makes annoying phone calls to my wife is in fact my next-door neighbor, an act of detesting my neighbor would be directed toward the very same object as my act of detesting the man who makes the calls, but it would be a quite different act with different intentionality. Consequently, that I detest the caller does not entail that I detest my neighbor, even though the caller and my neighbor are the same person. Intentional relations, then, as Husserl conceives them, are not to be thought of as relations of the usual sort. In logician's terminology, they are "intensional"—that is, non-extensional—relations: as our examples show, they fail to satisfy the logical principles of extensionality, especially the principles of existential generalization and substitutivity of identity.

Now, these "non-extensional" features of intentional relations lead Husserl to a crucial conclusion with important methodological consequences. The intentionality of an act, he believes, is determined by the act's own intrinsic character—by what he sometimes calls the "phenomenological content" of the act—and does not depend on the nature of the intended object in itself or even its existence. "It is inherent in the essence of each experience itself not only that, but also of what, it is a consciousness," he says in

Ideen (§36, p. 80). And in *Logical Investigations:* "That . . . a presentation relates to a certain object in a certain way is not due . . . to anything external to the presentation but to its own inner peculiarity alone" (V, §25, p. 603). The focus of Husserl's theory of intentionality, accordingly, is not on the object intended in an act or on any empirical facts about it, but on the act's "phenomenological content." It is this "content" that gives the act, as part of its own internal structure, the character of being "a consciousness of" something. Consequently, Husserl believes, a proper analysis of what it is for an act to be "intentionally related" to an object, even in those cases in which the object does, in fact, exist, cannot be an analysis that presupposes or implies the *de facto* existence of the intended object, nor can it draw on any extra-phenomenological facts about the object or its contingent, empirical relations to the subject (cf. *LI,* V, §20, p. 587; §25, p. 603; *Ideen,* §90, p. 225).

Husserl's focus on the inner structure of intentional experiences characterizes his resulting theory as *phenomenological,* in a very basic sense of that term. The purpose of such a theory is to explicate the various aspects of an act's intentionality purely in terms of the act's content. Husserl himself lays out a quite complex account of an act's content,[4*] but what is most important for our concerns is the element of content which he characterizes as a "meaning" or "sense" (a Sinn). In *Logical Investigations* Husserl calls this element of content the "matter" of an act: "The matter," he says, "is that peculiar side of an act's phenomenological content that not only determines *that* it grasps the object but also *as what* it grasps it, the properties, relations, categorial forms, that it itself attributes to it," and he there characterizes an act's matter as its "interpretive sense" (its *Auffassungssinn*) (V, §20, p. 589). It is this meaning-component of an act's content that Husserl in *Ideen* and subsequent writings calls the "noema" or, more specifically, the "noematic Sinn" of an act.[5*] Husserl emphasizes in *Ideen* that an act's noematic Sinn is not literally a part of the act in the way the act's temporal components are; rather, it is an atemporal, "ideal" (or abstract) meaning-entity instantiated, so to speak, in the act so that through this entity the object of the act is intended (see §§88–90, 97, 128).[6] It is, then, the meaning-content, the noematic Sinn, of an act that gives the act its directedness toward something; and to explicate an act's intentionality in terms of the act's phenomenological structure is primarily to explicate the role of this entity in intentionality. And so we now see an important part of what Husserl's theory of intentionality via meaning must do: it must explain how an act's noematic Sinn itself, without empirical help, can establish a special, non-extensional sort of relation between the act and its object.

2. Husserl's Emphasis on the "Definiteness" of Intentional Relations

Before we critically examine the details of Husserl's theory, another important feature of his conception of intentionality must be noted: Husserl thinks of intentionality as, paradigmatically, a relation of an act to some *one specific* object, whose identity is determined by the act's noematic Sinn. Intentionality, he says, is "definite" or "determinate" (*bestimmt*), inasmuch as an act's directedness consists in the act's "being related to a *certain* (*gewisse*) object and not another" (*LI*, V, §20, p. 587; with translational changes). For Husserl, an act's phenomenological content does not merely determine that the act is directed toward some object or other but it determines precisely *which* object the act is directed toward. He says: "The act's matter [i.e., its noematic *Sinn*] . . . makes its object count as this object and no other . . ." (*LI*, V, §20, p. 589). "The matter tells us, as it were, what object is meant in the act, and in what sense (Sinne) it is there meant" (*LI*, V, §44, p. 652). The noematic Sinn of an act, Husserl seems to believe, gives it an "intentional relation" to an object only because the Sinn itself determines *which* object is intended in the act or (add if you wish) which object would be intended if such an object existed. In that sense, then, an act's noematic Sinn prescribes the identity of the intended object, whether the object so intended exists or not (see also *Ideen*, §135, pp. 331–332).

Now, surely Husserl ought to have recognized cases in which an act is not "definitely" directed toward a specific entity. These cases include such "indefinite," or "*de dicto*," intentions, if I may call them that, as my desiring a new car, when I have not yet selected the one I want; or my believing that someone is at the door, but not knowing who it is; or a shopkeeper's expecting her next customer, having no idea who that person will be. There are many such cases in which an act's phenomenological content is too non-specific, apparently, to determine which object is intended in the act, but amazingly Husserl almost totally ignores them. In one of perhaps only two mentions of such acts in *Logical Investigations* he cannot even decide whether they deserve to be called "intentional." He says:

> Desire does not always seem to require a conscious relation to what is desired . . . we are often moved by obscure drives or pressures towards unrepresented goals. . . . One may say: This is a case of mere . . . "desire-sensations" . . . i.e., of experiences really lacking an intentional relation, and so also remote in kind from the essential character of intentional desire. Alternatively one may say: Here we are dealing with intentional experiences, but with such as are characterized by indeterminately (*un-bestimmt*) directed intention. . . . The idea we have when "something" stirs, when "it" rustles, when "somebody" rings, etc. . . . is "indeterminately" directed; and this "indeterminateness" belongs to the intention's essence, wherein it is determined as presenting an indeterminate "something." (V, §15, p. 575; with translational changes; cf. VI, §10, p. 700; A possible third mention is in V, §20, p. 589, n.1)

If we were to choose the alternative of speaking of these "indefinite" or "indeterminate" experiences as "intentional," there would be instances of intentionality in which the noematic Sinn does not prescribe the identity of the object intended in an act. But for that very reason Husserl seems to consider these experiences to be, at best, defective in their intentionality.

Husserl's virtually ignoring acts that in this way leave undetermined the identity of their objects is certainly a serious omission. Nonetheless, it is clear that his own paradigms do exclude them and that his emphasis is on acts that are definite in intention, such as my believing that *my mother* is at the door, or expecting *Bert Dreyfus* to enter the shop, or seeing *this object* as an apple tree. Much of our subsequent discussion will focus on these *"de re"* intentions, as they are sometimes called, and our concern will be to understand how the noematic Sinn of such an act can give it an intentional relation to "a *certain* object and not another."

3. The "Identifying-Description" Model of Intention and Its Difficulties

As Husserl conceives it, then, intentionality is a special, non-extensional sort of relation to a specific object—a relation that is determined by the act's phenomenological content, especially its noematic Sinn, in a way that is independent of the existence of the object and the empirical facts about it. Now, as we have already noted, there is a close relationship between this conception of intentionality via noematic Sinn and the Fregean conception of reference via meaning. Indeed, Husserl's own views about the

nature and role of noematic Sinne in intentionality developed
from his generally Fregean views about linguistic meaning and the
relation of language to intentional activity.[7] According to Husserl, the meanings that we express publicly in language are just the
same entities that, as noematic contents of consciousness, give
structure and significance to our thoughts, judgments, and intentions in general. Referring by means of language, Husserl held, is
then but the "public" side of intending, and reference, like intention, is defined in terms of sense, or meaning. "Reference to an
object is constituted in the meaning," he says. "To use an expression meaningfully (mit Sinn), and to refer expressively to an
object . . . are thus one and the same. It makes no difference
whether the object exists . . ." (LI, I, §15, p. 293; with translational changes). Given Husserl's view, then, a plausible account
of how the sense of a linguistic expression can be said to determine a specific referent, independent of the de facto existence of
that referent, should put us well on the way to understanding how
the noematic Sinn of an act can give it an "intentional relation"
to a specific object. By the same token, however, to whatever
extent sense *cannot* determine the object of reference in the linguistic case, it seems that it will not be able to do so in the more
general case of intentionality either.

How is it, then, that sense is supposed to determine reference?
The classical view that has developed from Frege takes the sense
of a singular term to be *descriptive* of the object referred to: the
sense prescribes properties possessed by at most one entity and
thereby determines that entity (if there is one) as the referent of
the term. On this view, singular reference in general is construed
on the model of definite description. Thus, names are held to be
synonymous with definite descriptions (or clusters of definite
descriptions), so that a name refers to whatever individual uniquely
satisfies the appropriate description. This "identifying-description"
theory of reference (which I shall call the "ID theory" for short)
maintains that (a) each name or other singular term has a "descriptive" sense prescribing properties that characterize at most one
entity, and (b) a singular term *refers* to a certain entity if and only
if that entity is the one and only one having (all or a sufficiently
important subset of) the properties prescribed by the sense of the
term.[8]

Much of what Husserl says about noematic Sinne and their role
in intentional relations to individuals suggests a theory of intentionality that works, in these cases, like the "ID theory" of

reference. (Intendings of more complex "objects" will require a
somewhat different sort of analysis. For example, propositional
acts or attitudes, according to Husserl, are directed toward states
of affairs and their noematic Sinne are propositional in structure.)
In *Ideen,* §130, Husserl tells us that the noematic Sinn of an
individual-directed act has a "content" consisting of "predicate-
senses" prescribing the properties the object of the act is intended
as having.[9] The senses making up this "content" are "descriptive"
of the object, then, just as the ID theory would have it. And in
§129 he says that it is "by means of" its content that a noematic
Sinn "is related to an object" (p. 318). A "semantic" rendition
of how a noematic Sinn determines an intentional relation between act and object, modeled on the Fregean ID theory of
reference, thus suggests itself: (a) the "content" of a noematic
Sinn is a complex descriptive sense, of the sort that would be
expressed linguistically by use of a definite description, and (b)
an act is *intentionally related* to a certain object if and only if
that object is the one and only entity having (all or a sufficiently
important subset of) the properties prescribed by the content
of the act's Sinn.

This "Fregean" way of conceiving noematic Sinne and the intentional relations they determine does shed some light on two of
the features of intentionality which we noted earlier. For example,
on the ID theory of intention an act may have a noematic Sinn
whose content prescribes properties that *no* object in fact possesses. In that case, the act will be intentional even though it is
not directed toward any existent object, just as an expression may
have meaning even though there is in fact no entity to which it
refers. And the ID theory allows that the Sinne of different acts
may have contents prescribing different properties that are in
fact possessed by the very same object. In that case, different
acts with different noematic Sinne will intend the same object,
just as different expressions with different meanings may refer
to the same referent.

Recently, though, the "identifying-description" theory of
reference has come under heavy attack from philosophers of
language.[10] In particular, it has been convincingly argued that
however well the ID theory may work for definite descriptions, it
fails to explain the relation of *names* to their referents. I shall
draw out of these arguments three criticisms of the ID theory
that raise especially serious problems for a theory of intentionality that would take this theory as its model. The first two

are rather straightforward; the third will require a bit more discussion.

First, names are often used, and used successfully, to refer to an individual of whom the speaker (and perhaps the hearer as well) knows *no* definite or identifying description. Many people who use the name 'Socrates,' for example, would be hard-pressed to say more about Socrates than that he was "a famous Greek philosopher." But this description is not definite, for it does not distinguish Socrates from, say, Plato or Aristotle. Yet it seems implausible to suppose that all these people, when they use the name 'Socrates,' are referring "indefinitely" to Socrates, Plato, Aristotle, and everyone else who meets this description. Indeed, it seems that the name *rather than* the description is used not just for brevity but to ensure that it is Socrates himself, and no one else, who is being referred to. And if this is so, a name does not always refer to its bearer by virtue of some descriptive sense prescribing properties that only the bearer possesses. The same considerations apply to the ID theory of intentionality. If someone knows of Socrates only that he was a famous Greek philosopher, the predicative content of his act's noematic Sinn will surely be too meager to pick out Socrates uniquely; and yet an act of intending Socrates should be a paradigm "definite" intention. In this sort of case, then, it seems that an act's directedness toward a specific individual is not determined by the descriptive content of the act's Sinn, or at least not by that content alone.

A second problem is that the ID theory often yields the wrong referent for a name or the wrong object for an act. The definite description most commonly associated with the name 'Columbus,' to use one of Kripke's examples, is 'the discoverer of America.' But the sense of that description would relate 'Columbus' to the person who in fact did discover America, and whoever that was, it probably was not Columbus. So the ID theory would yield the false conclusion that most people who use the name 'Columbus' are not referring to Columbus but to Lief Erikson, perhaps, or maybe even to someone whose name and deeds are still unknown. As for intending, consider a modified version of Donnellan's famous example.[11] Suppose at a wine-tasting party I am introduced to Jones, who immediately impresses me as the only person I've seen there who is drinking from a martini glass. Thereafter, every time I remember Jones I fix on the description 'the man who was drinking a martini at the wine-tasting party,' so that the content of my noematic Sinn is essentially just the sense of this description. But now suppose further that Jones was actually not drinking a martini at the party (his glass contained water, say), though some other fellow, who spent the entire evening out of sight on the patio, in fact was. In that case, if the ID theory were correct, each time I thought myself to be remembering or otherwise intending Jones I would actually be intending this other fellow, whose presence at the party is completely unknown to me. In general, the ID theory seems to force the absurd conclusion that if most (or perhaps only one) of one's beliefs about an individual are false then one cannot be intending *that* individual and, in fact, may quite unsuspectingly be intending some *other* individual whom one has never seen or even heard of. Contrary to the account provided by the ID theory, though, what seems really to happen in these cases is that the directedness of the act somehow "by-passes" the descriptive content of the act's Sinn, so that the act intends the appropriate object, not *via* this content, but *despite* it.

The third problem with the ID theory stems from the fact that, on this theory, reference and intention are heavily dependent on what is merely contingently true in the actual world. Consider, for example, the definite description 'the husband of Xanthippe.' This description happens to be true of Socrates, but it is easy to imagine circumstances in which Xanthippe would have married someone else. Under those circumstances—or, as modal semanticists say, in "possible worlds" in which those circumstances are realized—'the husband of Xanthippe' refers not to Socrates but to some other smooth-talking Athenian. Indeed, definite descriptions in general (barring essentialism) have this feature of referring to different individuals given appropriately different circumstances, or in appropriately different possible worlds. Now, Kripke and Putnam, especially, have argued that names, unlike definite descriptions, are used as "rigid designators," referring to the *same* entity in different possible worlds. Consequently, they hold, the relation between name and referent is not adequately accounted for by the ID theory of reference—even if a description associated with a name happens to be uniquely satisfied, in the actual world, by the appropriate individual. Fortunately, for our purposes it is not necessary to go into these further arguments. The important point for us is that, in general, it is possible for different individuals to satisfy the same definite description. This feature of definite descriptions, I want to argue, makes the ID model inadequate to Husserl's conception of intentionality, independently of the two

problems we have already uncovered. For if an act's directedness is
determined by the identifying descriptive content of the act's
Sinn, then the Sinn will relate the act to *different* objects under
appropriatedly different circumstances. And if this is so, the Sinn
of an act cannot establish an intentional relation that is *both* non-
extensional and definite, as Husserl's conception of intentionality
requires. Let's see why.

On a non-extensional account of intention, the noematic Sinn of
an act is supposed to give the act an intentional relation toward
some object, even if the object intended fails to exist; and if the
intention is definite, the Sinn is supposed to determine exactly
one such object. But which object would this be, if the ID theory
is correct? Under different possible circumstances, any number of
different entities can have the properties that the content of an
act's Sinn prescribes; and if no *actual* object has these properties,
then no one of these different entities has any greater claim to
being the object of the act than any other. Consider, for example,
an act of intending Sherlock Holmes, and suppose the Sinn-content
of this act is the sense of the description 'the detective who lived
at 221B Baker Street.' No actual person meets this description,
and so the object of this act (if it has one) is not to be found in
the actual world. However, we can conceive of "possible worlds"
in which someone living at 221B Baker Street was a famous detective. The problem, though, is that in some such possible worlds
one particular person meets the appropriate description while in
other possible worlds some quite *different* person (still called
'Sherlock Holmes') does so. Since the descriptive content of the
Sinn does not discriminate among these different individuals who
could satisfy that content, it is impossible to say—appealing to the
Sinn-content alone—just *which* object is intended in the act. Where
the object of an act does *not* exist, then, the act's noematic Sinn
will not, on the ID theory, single out a unique object as that
toward which the act is directed, and so the act will not be definite
in intention.

Now, we might choose to say (following Føllesdal) that when
no *actual* object satisfies the content of an act's Sinn, the act
simply has no object at all. But the ID theory is really no better
off in cases in which an act intends an existing object. For even if
there *is* an actual entity that satisfies the descriptive content of the
Sinn, there seems to be no *phenomenological* basis for singling out
that entity as the intended object, rather than one of the myriad
other entities that, in their respective possible worlds, also satisfy

that content. Indeed, I can think of no way to do so that would not give preference to the empirical fact that that entity *does* happen to be an existing individual. But such an appeal to what is only contingently true of the actual world is not consistent with Husserl's view that intentional relations are independent of the existence of their objects and are determined purely by the "phenomenological content" of an act. Whether an act is directed toward an existing object or not, then, the ID theory fails to explain how the relation between act and object is both non-extensional and definite.[12*]

In sum, there are at least two main reasons for rejecting the Fregean, or identifying-description, theory of reference as a model for a theory of intentionality, especially for a theory that would be adequate to Husserl's conception of intentionality. First, an ID theory of intending fails to account for cases, such as the two we first considered, in which an act's directedness toward its object is largely independent of the particular descriptive content in the act's noematic Sinn. And, second, the ID theory is not capable of preserving Husserl's view that an act's intentionality is determined by the phenomenological content of the act alone, without empirical help, while at the same time accounting for the "definiteness" of intention that Husserl himself emphasizes. Indeed, in light of this second failure, an ID theory of intentionality seems much better suited to "indefinite," or *de dicto,* intentions than to definite ones. For an indefinite intention, such as the shopkeeper's act of expecting her next customer, is indefinite precisely *because* its noematic Sinn does not identify any one specific entity as object, just as the ID theory would have it. And so, ironically, the theory of intentionality that Husserl seems most strongly to have suggested better fits the indefinite acts he chose to ignore than the definite acts he sought to explain.

4. *"Direct" Reference and Intention: Further Difficulties for Husserl*

Although our discussion has so far contained no hint of it, there is some evidence that Husserl did not wholeheartedly embrace an identifying-description theory of either reference or intentionality and that he did not think of a noematic Sinn as just a complex descriptive sense of the Fregean sort. In *Logical Investigations* Husserl offers a theory of meaning and reference for proper names and demonstratives that differs markedly from the ID theory. And in *Ideen* he distinguishes from the descriptive "content" of a noematic Sinn another Sinn-component, which he calls the "determinable X" in the Sinn. Husserl's description of this second component suggests that the relation between the object intended in an act and the particular characteristics it is intended as having is much less intimate than the ID theory would have it. In this section I shall try to see whether Husserl's theory of intentionality can be made less problematic by incorporating these further considerations.

Husserl describes the structure of a noematic Sinn (paradigmatically, the Sinn of a perception) in *Ideen*, §§129–131. There he distinguishes two components in the Sinn: its "content" and its "determinable X." According to Husserl, the content of a noematic Sinn consists of senses of predicates that attribute *properties* the object is intended as having (§130). But a Sinn's X-component is a sense of a different sort: it correlates with the *object* itself, the object that is intended as "bearing" these properties (§131, p. 320). Whereas the whole noematic Sinn (content + X) relates to the object under a particular description (viz., the description prescribed by the Sinn's content), Husserl says that the X relates to the object "simpliciter," "in abstraction from all predicates" (p. 321).[13*] Accordingly, Husserl emphasizes that different noematic Sinne can have the same X and relate to the same object, even though their predicative contents are not the same (pp. 320–321). Hence, the X-component, unlike the content, is not tied to any particular description of the object. And the X plays a key role in relating different Sinne with different contents to the *same* object: "Different Sinne relate to the same object," Husserl says "just insofar as they can be organized into unities of Sinn, in which the determinable X's of the united Sinne come into congruence (*Deckung*) with one another . . ." (p. 322). The X thus seems to be a "non-descriptive" component of sense in the noematic Sinn, a sense that presents an act's object directly, without prescribing properties of the object, and in a way that is largely independent of the particular descriptive content of the Sinn.

Husserl does not tell us more about what kind of sense an X is or how its relation to an object is achieved, but he does discuss a kind of *linguistic* sense that he takes to be similarly nondescriptive. According to Husserl, the senses expressed by demonstrative expressions and proper names relate these expressions to their referents "directly": "not attributively, as the bearer of these or those properties, but without such 'conceptual' mediation, as what [the object] *itself* is, just as perception might set it before our eyes"

(*LI*, VI, §5, p. 684). This view suggests that we might take the X in a noematic Sinn to be a sense of the kind expressed by demonstratives or proper names, rather than of the kind expressed by definite descriptions, and let the X, rather than the content, in a Sinn be the major determinant of *which* object is intended in an act. The relation of an act to its object would then be—at least in part—like the relation of a demonstrative or proper name to its referent and not, as the ID theory would have it, like the relation of a definite description to the object that satisfies it.[14]

Such an interpretation of intentional relations, modeled on the "direct" reference of proper names and demonstratives, would enable Husserl's theory to avoid the problems engendered by the ID theory of reference and intention. For an act's intentional relation to its object would then also be achieved "directly," without the "'conceptual' mediation" invoked by the ID theory. But such a notion of "direct" intention would seriously modify our original Fregean understanding of how meanings determine intentional relations, and it is not at all clear that these modifications are compatible with Husserl's own attempt to understand intentional relations phenomenologically and nonempirically. For, on Husserl's account, the meanings expressed by demonstratives and proper names seem to determine reference "non-conceptually" only by calling in contingent factors concerning the object of reference and its de facto relation to the user of the expression.

Specifically, Husserl says, the reference of names and demonstratives is "direct" because a speaker uses these expressions to refer to an object with which he is immediately presented in an act of "intuition" (*Anschauung:* paradigmatically, a perception of the object), and it is this immediate, intuitional, relation to the object—rather than the speaker's conception (*Auffassung*) of the object or the descriptions of it he is prepared to give—that determines which object is being referred to.

> The meaning of both types of directly naming expressions originates in intuition (*Anschauung*), by which the direction of the naming intentions is first oriented toward an individual object. . . . A person unacquainted with the city Madrid "itself" [lacks] the meaning peculiar to the word 'Madrid.' Instead of the direct reference (*Meinens*), which only an intuition of the city could arouse, he must make do with an indirect indication of this reference, mediated by ideas of characteristic properties and the concept of being called such and such.
>
> (*LI*, VI, §5, p. 685; with translational changes)

So an object directly referred to is simply that object the speaker is now seeing (or otherwise intuiting), irrespective of any conception he may have of it. The reference of a proper name or demonstrative is still determined by a meaning, Husserl believes. But unlike the Fregean meanings appealed to by the ID theory of reference, the meaning that determines a direct relation to an object does not embody a description that determines which object is being referred to. And because it does not, Husserl says that "the meaning could not acquire its *determinate* relation to the object meant without the aid of intuition" (*LI,* VI, §5, p. 683; with translational changes). Now, however Husserl's notion of intuition is to be explicated, there is a pressing problem for Husserl here: the problem of whether an appeal to intuition independent of conception can be incorporated in an account of intention that remains compatible with his views on phenomenological method and the nonempirical nature of intentional relations.[15] For now it seems that the object of intention (or reference) will be determined not solely by the phenomenological content of an act—by a meaning, or noematic Sinn, that belongs to the "internal" character of the act itself—but also by the "external" and contingent fact that a certain object rather than another happens to be present in the subject's immediate environment.

The contingent, empirical nature of "direct" reference and intention is especially apparent in Husserl's account of the reference of demonstrative expressions, such as 'this.'[16] Husserl notes that these expressions are "essentially occasional," having different referents on different occasions of use (*LI,* I, §26; VI, §5). The referent on each occasion *is* determined by a meaning, Husserl holds; but since this meaning depends on an intuitive presentation of an object, he says that the meaning itself varies with, and so depends on, "the occasion, the speaker, and the situation" (*LI,* I, §26, p. 315). That a demonstrative term refers to one object rather than another thus seems to depend partly on the empirical situation in which the term is used and, apparently, on the contingent fact that that object happens to be appropriately related to the speaker in that situation: the referent of 'this' depends on which object is actually situated before the speaker; the referent of 'I,' on who is actually speaking; and so on (cf. *LI,* I, §26), pp. 315-318). A theory of intentionality modeled on the reference of demonstratives would accordingly not be a purely phenomenological theory appealing to the meaning-content of an act alone. Rather, it would also bring into the theory, as essential to an act's intentionality, factors that philosophers of language classify as "pragmatic" rather than "semantic"—contextual factors concerning the subject of the act, the particular occasion on which the act takes place, and the empirical situation in which it occurs. But it is precisely factors of this sort which Husserl's phenomenological conception of intentionality and his method of phenomenological reduction are designed to remove from consideration.

Concluding Remarks

Husserl's theory of intentionality now appears to be in serious difficulty. The fundamental tenet in the theory is his view that an act's intentional relation to its object is determined solely by the act's phenomenological content and is independent of any contingent, empirical relations that may obtain between the act and existing entities. But how does an act's content determine this relation? If, for further explanation, we appeal to Husserl's account of the descriptive "content" of the noematic Sinn, we find that the theory faces the same problems encountered by the "identifying-description" theory of reference. And given these problems, I have argued, Husserl's theory cannot explain some very ordinary cases of intentionality, nor can it account for the "definiteness" that Husserl himself emphasizes. On the other hand, if we attempt to circumvent these problems by treating the Sinn's "X"-component as a demonstrative element of sense—so that intentional relations are like demonstrative reference—we find Husserl's theory incompatible with his own fundamental commitment to a purely phenomenological account of intentionality.

These difficulties are of central importance to Husserl's entire phenomenological enterprise. For the basic theory discussed here— that the intentionality of an act is determined by the act's phenomenological content, primarily its noematic Sinn—is the theoretical framework underlying all his more detailed analyses of specific kinds of intentionality. In fairness to Husserl, though, it should be noted that these more detailed analyses embellish the basic theory as I have discussed it, with my exclusive emphasis on the Sinn of an act, in various ways. Particularly evident in Husserl's later writings is an increasing willingness to broaden the notion of "phenomenological content," so that the content relevant to determining an act's intentional relation to its object finally expands to comprise not only the noematic Sinn of that act but also the Sinne of various of the subject's "background" experiences and beliefs. The relevant beliefs may include not only a priori beliefs but also general empirical beliefs about the kind of object intended and perhaps even specific beliefs based on past experience with the object itself.[17] With this expansion, ultimately an act's intentionality is determined not just by some specific Sinn or meaning-pattern that prescribes the act's object, but by a subject's whole belief-system, which provides a sort of phenomenological context in which the act, with its specific Sinn, occurs.

This movement toward an holistic approach to intentionality and meaning should surely be welcomed, but I think it does not get to the heart of the basic problem underlying the difficulties we have been discussing. For the basic problem, as *existential* phenomenologists have long urged, concerns Husserl's conception of intentionality itself and the methodological restrictions it imposes: the problem is how a theory of intentionality that confines itself to the phenomenological content of consciousness—no matter how much this content includes—can ever explain the actual involvement of consciousness with the existing reality in which it, in fact, lives.

13
Intentionality and Possible Worlds: Husserl and Hintikka

J. N. Mohanty

Hintikka would agree with Husserl that an intentional act has its sense or noema. But instead of interpreting intentionality as directedness toward objects (in which the sense or noema serves as the medium of such directedness), Hintikka would rather understand it in terms of possible-worlds semantics. In the case of perception, Hintikka agrees with Husserl that perception is intentional, but he argues that the intentional character of acts of perception should be construed in terms not of their being directed but of their being informational. The thesis that perception is informational means to him that perception refers to many different possible worlds, "for the notion of (semantical) information is closely tied to that of a possible world: to specify an information is to specify a set of possible worlds."[1] This leads him to the position that "to specify what *a* perceives is to specify the set of all possible worlds compatible with his perceptions."[2]

With this we have arrived at the main contrast that runs through Hintikka's writings on intentionality: the contrast between understanding intentionality as directedness (Brentano and Husserl) and understanding it in terms of possible-worlds semantics. It is with this contrast that I shall be primarily concerned in this paper.

I

Intentionality, on the first view, is the property of being directed toward an object. On Hintikka's view, "a concept is intentional if and only if it involves (i.e. if its semantical explication, not overt features of its use, involves) the simultaneous (in a logical, not temporal sense) consideration of several possible states of affairs or courses of events."[3] On the directedness thesis, as held by Husserl, the direction of an act is established by the meaning or noema of the act. The meaning determines what the object of an act is. Hintikka appears to have two main criticisms of this formulation. In the first place, this locution is "partly metaphorical" and stops short of saying *how* the noema determines the object. Secondly, the thesis tends to make the noema, the meaning, into "a single entity, however abstract."[4] In spite of Frege's distinction between concepts and objects, the Fregean *Sinn* and the Husserlian *noema* alike become objects, completed entities, individuals in the logician's sense.

I will first comment on these two points. It is not so much the charge of being "partly metaphorical"—the complaint that the Frege-Husserl thesis does not say *how* the noema (or the Sinn) of an act determines its object—which deserves to be taken seriously. After all, the locution 'possible worlds' is no less partly metaphorical. And Hintikka may not altogether avoid reification of meanings, for they become set theoretic entities (viz. functions) according to his view. In both cases, then, we need to go behind the metaphors and salvage whatever is of logical and phenomenological value in them. What is it that we expect of a theory of meaning (of the Frege-Husserl type) when we want it to answer the question "*How* does the Sinn determine its object?"? What the Frege-Husserl theory does not give, and what the Hintikka theory appears to be giving, is a recipe for finding out what the reference of a given sense is. This ties up with Hintikka's claim that whereas the Frege-Husserl Sinn is an abstract entity, a complete object (contrary to Frege's own concept of 'concept'), on his own theory the Sinn is, rather, a function (in accordance with Frege's original intuition) whose arguments are possible worlds and whose values are the individual objects of reference in those worlds. It appears as if such a concept of Sinn does indeed provide a recipe for determining what the object of reference is. If we have a given noema N, it is to be construed as a function $N: \{W_i\} / \{O_i\}$, from a set of possible worlds $\{W_i\}$ to a set of objects $\{O_{ij}\}$. This concept of meaning does indeed seem able to provide what the Frege-Husserl concept cannot—namely, an account of *how* the meaning determines its reference.

However, this is only a seeming advantage. In order for this advantage to be real, one may be required to know W_i independently of knowing O_i. In other words, one would be expected to know the arguments—that is, the possible worlds—prior to "picking out" the objects of reference in those worlds. Only if this were so, would it make sense to say that the meaning is a function from possible worlds to references. This, however, is not the case. We have to begin with, let us say, the putative O_n (Socrates as he is in the actual world), and then conceive of an alternative to it, O_{n-1} (Socrates without snub nose).

The former characterizes the actual world W_n, the latter a possible world W_{n-1}. What, then, I know of a possible world is what I know of some of its members. To say, then, that the meaning function serves to assign to a possible world a value—that is, an individual—is not saying anything informative. What Hintikka is asserting is *not* that one has a prior knowledge of possible worlds, but that to have a concept is to have in one's conceptual system certain possible worlds. I do not want to dispute that in an important sense this is true. To know the meaning of a term—say, 'red'—is to know what it is to be red, which includes the ability to recognize a thing as red under various different circumstances. That the concept of 'meaning' has something to do with that of 'possibility' (and both with that of 'essence') cannot be denied. It is quite another thing to accept the explication of this relationship in terms of a semantics (or, ontology) of possible worlds. Hintikka himself appears to sense this when he writes: "It would be more natural to speak of different possibilities concerning our 'actual' world than to speak of several possible worlds. For the purpose of logical and semantical analysis, the second locution is much more appropriate than the first, however, although I admit that it sounds somewhat weird and perhaps also suggests that we are dealing with something much more unfamiliar and unrealistic than we are actually doing."[5]

One may want to answer my point by saying either that (i) we can tell, in various counterfactual situations, which object was picked out by N, or (ii) that given descriptions of various counterfactual situations we can say which object N would pick out. What is important is that one who has mastered the meaning of a term would be able to pick out the term's extension in various counterfactual situations. If these counterfactual situations are the possible worlds, then understanding the sense is knowing which individual, in each case, is being referred to. While this is unexceptionable, all that it means is that to know the use of a concept is to be able to determine its extension under many different circumstances—that is, to be able to identify a, b, and c as cases of N, even if they otherwise differ a great deal among themselves. To hypostatize those possible differences as constituting possible worlds, and to regard the individuals identified as images of N under those worlds is obfuscating—for the purpose of providing a semantics to a formal system—what is a much simpler situation—namely, that concepts provide rules for recognizing identities amid differences.

The fact is that on Hintikka's account the meaning function in question is one given in extension—that is, simply as a set of ordered pairs $\{<W_1, O_1>, \ldots <W_i, O_i> \ldots\}$ All it gives is a *list* of what is "picked out" in each world by N. We have no account of why O_i is the image *under* N *of* W_i—that is, why O_i is picked out; we have nothing in virtue of which O_i is the relevant object in W_i. As long as our interest is simply providing semantics for various sorts of intensional logics, the lack of a genuine concept of sense does not matter. But for purposes of a phenomenology which is to provide descriptive structures of acts of consciousness, including the so-called propositional attitudes, the extensional function is far too inadequate.

In effect, I do not want to suggest that a possible-worlds interpretation of intentionality is totally mistaken, or that it does not capture something of our intuitions about intentional acts. What I am questioning is the descriptive-clarificatory value of that interpretation, and therefore its relation to phenomenology. There is certainly an awkward sense in which some intentional acts are about possible worlds, a less awkward and more straightforward sense in which they are about possibilities and possible variations of the actual world; but their being about such possibilities is precisely what needs explication. In other words, the idea of intentional directedness is thereby being pushed one step backward, not eliminated. It won't do to say that *this* being about is not directedness. Husserl at least does not want to restrict intentional directedness to a relation to an actual qua actual.

Hintikka does indeed recognize acts. But deprived of intentionality in the sense of directedness or even in the sense of intending a sense, the sole burden of their acthood falls on what they are about—namely, possible worlds. In *this* respect, he seems closer to giving a sort of "improved reconstruction" of Frege than of Husserl. The Fregean Sinne are grasped by mental acts; they are the senses of signs, not of acts. The Fregean acts are not intentional in the full-blown Husserlian sense. If the Fregean Sinne can be "reconstructed" in the manner suggested by Hintikka, that does not assure the value of that reconstruction as an explication of Husserl. Husserlian noemata are intentional correlates of acts. There are no noemata save in relation to acts. The act and its noema build one concrete structure, of which the act and the noema are distinguishable but inseparable aspects. The Husserlian noemata are not self-complete entities, not reified individuals—however true these characterizations may be of the Fregean Sinne. They are *abstract* entities in two different senses: first, in the sense that they are not concrete, sensible, spatiotemporally individuated particulars, but, secondly, also in the sense that they cannot be by themselves, but are always correlates of acts, and inseparable parts—moments, not pieces—of an act-noema structure.

If directedness is a descriptive feature of acts, the further question, *how* such directedness is possible, is from one point of view pointless. What is needed other than recognizing, on the basis of descriptive evidence, that, as Brentano put it, "In the representation something is represented, in the judgment something is acknowledged or rejected, in desiring it is desired, etc.,"[6] which could possibly answer that *how* question? As already pointed out, giving the function in extension as a set of ordered pairs is not an answer to such a question.

In a sense, Husserl also was *not* satisfied with the *mere* acceptance of that descriptive feature. He saw in it further room for careful analysis-cum-description. He, in fact, was also seeking to answer a *how*-question when he replaces the simple

$$\text{act} \longrightarrow \text{object}$$

structure by the

$$\text{act} \longrightarrow \text{sense (or noema)} \longrightarrow \text{object}$$

structure. But even this structure, he felt, is inadequate. To make it intelligible, he undertook a careful delineation of the structure of the noema.[7] The matter is further complicated by the fact that the act has a temporal duration, while the object referred to may be re-identified in time. This leads Husserl to ask how the identity of an object is constituted in time and, also, how identification and reidentification are possible in the stream of time-consciousness.[9] If, then, to show *how* directedness is possible is to replace the simple act-object structure by a more detailed structural description of the situation that obtains, the Husserlian theory has it.

II

Hintikka's account of intentionality is developed in the context of a theory of propositional attitudes in general and of perception in particular. Since his comments on Husserl bear heavily on Husserl's theory of perception, his reformulation of the Husserlian concept of intentionality in terms of possible-worlds semantics has a strong basis in his understanding of perception. It will serve my present purpose to give only a bare statement of his relevant theses on perception, to which reference has already been made. From the point of view of phenomenology, it is quite unproblematic to say that "to specify what someone, say *a,* perceives is to describe what the world is like according to his perceptions (whether they be veridical or not)." From this Hintikka proceeds in a direction apparently very different from the phenomenologist. These perceptions, he says, do not fix the world uniquely; therefore the description of what the world is like according to *a*'s perception is "logically speaking not unlike a disjunction of several different alternatives concerning the world."[9] From which it follows that to specify what *a* perceives is to give the set of all possible worlds compatible with his perceptions. Perception, then, is intentional in the sense that its logical explication involves reference to several possible worlds. Hintikka is thereby led to reinterpret two major Husserlian theses. The 'transcendence' of objects means nothing but the inexhaustible multiplicity of the possible worlds that are compatible with our beliefs about such objects and as members of which these objects can occur.[10] Secondly, the Husserlian notion of the constitution of an object is the same as the idea of identification of an object across many different possible worlds.[11]

Now, one may begin by asking, in what sense does my perception of the thing here before me involve reference to many possible worlds, and, furthermore, how does this reference to many possible worlds tie up with the phenomenology of perception? I find two distinct though related senses in which Hintikka's thesis could be understood, and there is textual support for both. One is that all perceptual sentences are to be construed as having propositional objects (by reducing direct object constructions to 'perceives that' constructions), and propositions are to be construed as sets of all those possible worlds in which they are true.[12] Another way of understanding the thesis in that, all perception being perspectival, no particular perception of an object completely exhausts all aspects of it, so that there are many, possibly infinitely many, descriptions under which one and the same object could be perceived. Thus there is a whole set of mutually compatible descriptions under which perceptual identification of one and the same object would be valid. Each such description may then be construed as a partial possible world. It follows that specification of what I perceive now requires reference to all these possible descriptions, each true of the object I perceive, and so compatible with my perceiving what I do perceive.

With regard to the first-mentioned way of understanding Hintikka's thesis, I will not question for the present the validity of the proposed reduction of direct-object constructions, in the case of perceptual sentences, to propositional constructions. Assuming that '*a* perceives that p' is fundamental, and granting, as we should, that p is true in many possible worlds—that is, is compatible with many different states of affairs not all of which are actual—it does *not* seem to follow that '*a* perceives that p' is equivalent to '*a* perceives that p is true in many possible worlds,' where the latter sentence may be reformulated as 'There are possible states of affairs s′, s″, . . . such that they are compatible with p, and *a* perceives that this compatibility holds good.'

To suppose that this equivalence should hold good on the Hintikka thesis may be regarded as based on too strong an interpretation of that thesis. Perhaps a weaker interpretation would capture better what is meant. According to this weaker interpretation, it is not that when *a* perceives that p he in fact perceives or thinks that p is true in many possible worlds or that there are many possible states of affairs compatible with p. What is claimed, rather, is that a logical explication of what *a* perceives requires locating p as a member of those other compatible possible worlds. It is not clear, however, why logical explication, whether of *what* *a* perceives to be the case or of *a*'s perceiving whatever he perceives, requires this—unless these possible states of affairs, or partial possible worlds, are also *only* those possible descriptions which are compatible with p *and* under which the same object could be perceived. (This restriction is necessary, for the possible states of affairs compatible with p may be anything whatsoever, so that if reference to such irrelevant states of affairs be required for semantical explication of what *a* perceives, the consequence would certainly be counterintuitive, if not absurd.)

For Hintikka, what is at issue is the claim that a specification of the contents of any one perception in effect involves several possible worlds. In a private communication to me, he points out that perception, on a first approximate account, involves two different "worlds": the actual and the world as it appears to me. The expression "the world as it appears to me" again does not denote one unique world, or even a part of one unique world. What we in fact have are, rather, a great variety of perceptions: disjunctive ("The man over there is either John or Morris"), and negative ("The man in the corner is not Jakko Hintikka"), for example. If these are quite appropriate accounts of what one sees, and if each of these leaves many different possibilities open as to *who* he is or what it is that one is seeing, then in order to explicate what one sees, one needs to specify which possibilities (possible states of affairs) are compatible with what one sees and which ones are incompatible with it. The same is true also of cases where the perceptual judgment is neither disjunctive nor negative, but rather singular, categorial ("This is red"). For even in the latter sorts of cases, if one can describe one's temporary sense impressions, one can come up with *all* those states of affairs which are compatible with one's perceptions at the time. In effect, what Hintikka is saying is that any of our perceptions (beliefs, desires, etc.) divides the worlds into those which are compatible with it and those which are incompatible with it, so that a full semantical explication of what we perceive should include reference to all those worlds which are compatible with it.[13] It should be noted that even momentary sense impressions or descriptions of them are, for Hintikka, such small-scale possible worlds.[14]

Again, we need to keep the semantical-ontological interest apart from the phenomenological-descriptive. The following theses, all of which Hintikka asserts, are no doubt true:

T1   To understand what a sentence says is to know what to expect of
      the world in case the sentence is true.

T2   Every perceptual determination is incomplete, and specifying what one perceives does involve reference to possibilities of further determining the content of one's perception.

T3   Once I have a description of what I perceive ('p') then all possible states of affairs may be divided into two groups: those that are compatible with p and those that are not. (If what I am perceiving is *b*, sentences "about" things quite unrelated to *b* will be true in some, but not all, of the worlds compatible with what I perceive. It is to exclude these, that I suggested earlier the relevancy requirement.)

While agreeing with these theses, I want to question how best, from a *phenomenological* point of view, to understand and appropriate them. Corresponding to T1 and T2 we have, in phenomenology, the following theses:

*T1   To grasp the meaning intention of an act is to know what sort of experience would fulfill that intention.

*T2   All perception is perspectival, such that each act of perceiving as well as its noema carries with it a horizon of pre-delineated potentialities for further determinations.

As may easily be discerned, neither *T1 nor *T2 suggests the theme of possible worlds, although such semantic talk may very well be superadded to them without either adding to their intelligibility or increasing their descriptive content. It is true that a phenomenology of perception cannot accept a completely deterministic theory of perception. It has to recognize that every perception leaves open a horizon for further determinations: *this is true as much of the disjunctive and negative perceptual judgments as of the singular affirmative categorial ones.* The horizon includes both possible acts and also possible further determinations of the act's object. There are infinitely many possible perceptual acts which may be directed toward one and the same object. Many different noemata may relate to one and the same object, just as numerically many different acts may have an identical noema. The questions that need to be asked are: which of the two, the many possible *acts* of perceiving or the many possible noemata, are to be regarded as corresponding to Hintikka's possible worlds? The two alternatives do not coincide. For, many numerically distinct acts may have an identical noema, and many different noemata may refer to one and the same object. The identical noema is the Sinn, the meaning function. What then are the possible worlds which are the arguments of the function? Are they the many possible acts? That is most unlikely. Are they the many descriptions under which one and the same object may be perceived? But a description is the

Sinn, so a function, not its argument. Furthermore, since many different noemata or Sinne may refer to one and the same object, if we construe two different Sinne as two different possible worlds, the meaning function would be one which yields the same value for two or many different arguments. I suppose what Hintikka has in mind is that in this case the values—that is, the objects, are different, although we still have to raise the question of transworld identification. I think that is too great a price to pay for the proposed construction of intentionality. The fact is that the meaning determines the reference; it is of no use to introduce possible worlds as intervening entities.

It is really T_3 which is both true and forms the main support of Hintikka's appeal to 'possible worlds.' I have nothing against T_3; my only point is that T_3 does not describe perceptual experience but concerns what must be the case if a perceptual statement is true. T_3, therefore, cannot belong to phenomenology.

Hintikka's mode of speaking suggests that we have a whole set of perceptual descriptions laid out before the logician, each defining a (partial) possible world. But for the perceiver, this is not the case. In most cases, as one perceptual act passes on to the others directed to the same object, the sense of identity is carried along with it. As Aron Gurwitsch put it: "To be aware of an object means that, in the present experience, one is aware of the object as being the same as that which one was aware of in the past experience, as the same as that which, generally speaking, one may be aware of in an indefinite number of presentative acts."[15]

III

To return now from Hintikka to Husserl. Husserl also had an *ontology,* and it would be useful for our purpose to take a look at it. Let us pose a question, currently being asked in ontology, and look for Husserl's answer to it: Does an individual belong to just one world or may the same individual exist in more than one possible world? Did Husserl subscribe to the theory of Worldbound Individuals (as Plantinga calls the former alternative)[16] or did he hold something like the latter view, thereby being required to have a theory of transworld identification? Initially it appears as though the theory of worldbound individuals is in no need of specifying those properties of the individual under consideration which are to be regarded as essential to it, while the other theory, which holds that one and the same individual may be in many possible worlds, is thereby committed to precisely such an essentialism. As

Plantinga rightly points out, however, the theory of worldbound individuals does have an answer to the question which of Socrates' properties are essential to him. This answer is that *all* of his properties are essential to him. Although Husserl's views on this issue are indeed difficult to ascertain, there is no doubt that he was very close in his thoughts to this *problem,* and I suspect that he moved away gradually from an essentialism that allows an individual to be in many possible worlds to one that does not. Husserl asserted that an individual has its *own* essence, and also that an essence, which is the complete essence of an individual capable of being by itself, is a *concretum.*[17] Now this, by itself, does not amount to the strong thesis that all the properties of an individual down to the lowest differentiations are essential to an individual. It depends upon how strongly one wants to understand the idea of 'concretum.' To me it appears that if the concretum is to be an independent essence, it cannot but include *all* properties of the individual under consideration, including its spatiotemporal location and duration. In that case the individual simply cannot, while remaining the same individual—that is, with the same *concretum*—be in many possible worlds.

When Husserl comes explicitly to deal with these issues, he appears to be committed to this view. In *Experience and Judgment* he writes, "*individuation* and *identity of the individual,* as well as the identification founded on it, *is possible only within the world of actual experience, on the basis of absolute temporal position.*" Consequently, "the experience of imagination in general provides no individual objects in the true sense but only *quasi-individual* objects and a *quasi-identity* . . ."[18] Husserl's reason for holding this view is that an individual must be thoroughly determined with regard to its properties. "In the actual world, nothing remains open; it is what it is."[19]* But the imagined object, the possible object, has only those determinations which are imagined and, thereby, stipulated, so that "a complex of imaginings never comes to an end that does not leave open the possibility of a free development in the sense of a new determination."[20] Not being thoroughly determined, an imagined object cannot be an individual in the strict sense. The actual Socrates is either snub-nosed or not, one of these properties belongs to him to be sure. Of the imagined Socrates as belonging to a possible world other than the actual, the principle of excluded middle does not hold good. As long as it is not imagined or stipulated to be either, it is neither: not only nothing is said or known about him in this regard, but there is, in fact, in the structure of the imagined individual a zone of indeterminacy. It "becomes" snub-nosed, when imagination fills in this gap, *adds* this determination, removes the indeterminacy. Since some such indeterminacy will always be there, and we cannot stipulate all determinations down to the *hic et nunc,* the imagined object qua imagined will lack complete individuation.

Likewise, an imagined world is a quasi-world. Husserl writes: "The universe of free possibilities in general is a realm of disconnectedness: it lacks a unity of context."[21] Different positings (or quasi-positings) of possible objects do not *necessarily* belong to one unified framework (although it is *possible* for different acts of imagining to cointend one and the same object).

If individuation, strictly speaking, is intraworldly and requires one spatiotemporal framework, and if imagined worlds are quasi-worlds as much as imagined individuals are quasi-individuals, for Husserl, it makes no sense to ask whether an individual of the actual world is the same as or different than an individual in a world that is merely possible. It is also equally pointless to ask whether an individual in one possible world is the same as an individual in another possible world.

> How are the singularizations of temporal points, temporal durations, etc., related to one another within different imaginary worlds? We can speak here of the likeness and similarity of the components of such worlds but never of *their identity,* which *would have absolutely no sense;* hence, no connections of incompatibility can occur, for these would indeed presuppose such identity. *It makes no sense, e.g., to ask whether the Gretel of one fairy tale and the Gretel of another are the same Gretel,* whether what is imagined for the one and predicated of her agrees or does not agree with what is imagined for the other, or, again, whether they are related to each other, etc. *I can stipulate this*—and to accept it is already to stipulate it—but then both fairy tales refer to the same world. Within the same tale I can certainly ask such questions, since, from the beginning, we have a single imaginary world; but the question ceases to make sense where the imagination ceases, where it does not supply more precise determinations; and it is reserved to the development of imagination, in the sense of the pursuance of the unity of a complex of imaginings, to seize upon determinations arbitrarily (or, in the case of instinctively continuing again, to leave open the possibility of such determinations).[22]

It seems from the foregoing exposition that Husserl holds a theory of worldbound individuals. An objection may be raised against this as an exposition of Husserl's own views, and as to the relevance of it for discussions of the contemporary concern with possible worlds.

One may want to point out that the foregoing discussion of imaginary worlds is highly interesting but virtually irrelevant to the issues.[23] But the point about the discussion is missed if it is taken to concern only the ordinary contrast between the actual and the imaginary or fictional. The fact that the actual itself is the most interesting possible world does not obliterate the distinction between the sense in which the actual is *also* possible and the sense in which the non-actuals are *merely* possible. Although the actual world as well as the merely possible worlds are all *possible* in the sense of being logically possible (howsoever one may want to define 'logical possibility'), there nevertheless is a distinction between the logically possible that is "realized" or is also actual and the "merely" logically possible. The merely logically possible world, or state of affairs, "story" or "novel," is, according to Husserl's thesis, *constituted* by intentional acts which share with the acts of imagining the character of being *quasi*-positional. We have therewith moved from ontology to constitutive phenomenology. Husserl's primary concern is with the *constitution* of the various sorts of possibility, as also of the various senses of 'actuality.' Thought of merely possible worlds—that is, of possible worlds other than the actual—I believe, on Husserl's theory, is a sort of thinking which requires a "modification" of the original doxic modalities. The resulting belief is not a serious belief, the supposition not a serious supposition, the act of positing the possible not a serious positing act.[24] Even if all sorts of possibility are not constituted in fictional imagining, certainly 'possible worlds' and 'possible individuals' in the most pregnant sense are constituted in acts that are quasi-positional modifications of originally positing acts.[25]*

We have found Husserl denying that an actual individual and a possible (quasi-) individual could be the same. However, this does *not* mean that there is *no sense at all* in which we are justified in saying: "'The same' object which I just now imagine could also be given in experience: this same merely possible object (and thus *every* possible object) could also be an actual object." Conversely, one can say of every actual object that it need not be actual; it would then be a "mere possibility."[26] This locution, perfectly justified, does *not* mean: the same individual can be in many possible worlds. "The same object" is not the object pure and simple, for, Husserl writes, "when we simply speak of an object, we posit it as actual, we intend the actual object." What is meant by "the same object" is rather the "complete sense," that is, the full noema minus the thetic quality. It is this sense which may have sometimes the character "actual" and sometimes may be posited with the character "possible." If this is "the individual essence" of the particular object, then, of course, one can say the actual and the merely possible may be "the same." But *this identical noematic content* is *not itself the identical individual* through many possible worlds.

IV. Intentionality, *de dicto and de re*

One of Hintikka's major objections against the Brentano-Husserl understanding of intentionality as directedness is that it cannot account for *de dicto* acts, which "do not seem to be directed to a particular object in any natural sense of the word."[27] I will not raise the question whether the account of this distinction in terms of possible-worlds semantics is a satisfactory *philosophical* account, for that question, loaded no doubt, would lead to deeper issues concerning what is to be considered, after all, as a philosophical account, and there is no way of coming to terms with that in this paper. So the best I can do is to suggest the more likely Husserlian response to the challenge. Let us note the following theses, all of which, I think, are Husserl's:

T4 All intentional acts refer, that is, are directed toward, or are about, something.

T5 For an object to be the object toward which an act is directed, it is not necessary that the object exist.

T6 In the case of a propositional act (that is, an act expressible in a propositional form), we have to distinguish between the object-about-which and the intentional correlate of the act. The latter is always, in the case of a propositional act, a fact; the former may or may not be a fact. If the propositional act be the belief that the next Prime Minister of India will be a socialist, the object-about-which is the next Prime Minister of India, while the intentional correlate of the act is the fact that the next Prime Minister of India will be a socialist. This distinction obtains whether the act is *de re* or *de dicto*.

T7 Different intentional acts may intend one and the same object under different descriptions. While doing so, they may also intend the object *as being the same* as intended in some other acts under different descriptions, or they may not.

T8 An intentional act may intend its object emptily or with evidence. If the evidence presents the object intuitively, precisely as it is described or meant, then the act is "filled." Paradigmatic of the latter are acts in which an object is seen *as* such and such.

Keeping these theses T4–T8 in mind, let us now ask: Where does the *de re–de dicto* distinction fit in? The initial temptation to rely on T5 is misleading. Hintikka certainly is clear on this point. He writes, in reply to comments by Findlay, "Nor is the possible non-existence of individuals the crucial issue in the so-called *de re–de dicto* distinction." He admits that on his formal reconstruction a *de re* reading does presuppose real existence, but insists that that is surely due only to "unfortunate limitations of the current notation of modal and epistemic logic."[28] The crucial question, as he points out, is uniqueness or well-definedness, not non-existence. Husserl's problem, let us recall, is not about *de re* acts. In fact, one gets the *mistaken* impression that for Husserl all intentionality is *de re*. The idea of intentionality as directedness, the requirement that there be an object-about-which, does not make the act *de re*. But what, on Husserl's theory, is the object toward which an act *de dicto* is directed? Surely, it is not a fact, if that fact itself is not the object-about-which.

Shall we look for an answer in T8, and hold that an act is *de dicto* if and only if it is unfulfilled, empty, merely signitive, and an act is *de re* if and only if it is fulfilled, backed by intuitive evidence? Fulfilled acts, according to Husserl, put one in touch with the object-itself. Unfulfilled, empty, and signitive acts do not do so. They are, therefore, *de dicto*. They nevertheless have their objects-about-which, but in a manner that does not permit exportation.

However, not all is right with this. It is not obvious that all intentional acts that are *de re* are fulfilled. If I believe, emptily—without evidence, based possibly on my hunch—that Indira Gandhi will be the next Prime Minister of India, the belief is still *de re*, for it is a belief about Indira Gandhi, and one can say that there is a definite individual about whom I believe that she will be the next Prime Minister of India. Thus I have an *ex-hypothesis* empty belief, which is *de re*. Likewise, there is a sense in which my belief that the next Prime Minister of India will be a socialist may not be a mere guess but may well be founded on as much first-hand evidence as is available at this time about the political forces operating in that country. This belief, then, is, in a sense, supported by evidence, and may in fact be true; yet I may not be believing in particular of any *given* individual that he or she will be the next Prime Minister of India and will be a socialist.

We are then led to give up the hope that the empty–filled distinction is going to help us in accounting for the *de dicto–de re* distinction. But there is no doubt that the two distinctions have something to do with each other, inasmuch as both the pairs have something to do with the description-acquaintance distinction of Russell and the opaque-transparent distinction of Quine. One other aspect of the *de dicto–de re* distinction is, as is well known, that in the *de re* case the mode of specification of the object is not relevant, while in the *de dicto* case it is relevant. Keeping these in mind, could we start afresh?

One difference between the belief that the next Prime Minister of India will be a socialist and the belief that Indira Gandhi will be the next Prime Minister of India is that the linguistic expression of the latter belief contains a singular term, in this case a proper name, which denotes the *x* of which we can conclude that this is what the belief is *about* or directed toward; whereas the linguistic expression of the former belief does not contain any such singular term or name. "The next Prime Minister of India" does not uniquely denote an *x,* it does not provide an identifying description either. The crucial issue is whether the person possessing the belief has in mind a particular person, whether he knows *who* it is that he believes will be the next Prime Minister of India, for which it would suffice to have at his disposal a proper name which "rigidly" designates him or her or, failing a name, a "vivid" representation (*à la* Kaplan), of the person. Now the beginning point may be to ask whether the distinction between name and description as it has come to obtain in contemporary modal logic—that is, between rigid and nonrigid designators—is acceptable in Husserlian phenomenology. It seems to me that Husserl believed in a theory of names according to which names, even proper names, have sense, as distinguished from mere reference.[29] Consequently, the presupposition underlying the *de dicto–de re* distinction as formulated by Hintikka—that proper names or rigid designators somehow put the intentional act in (direct) relation to a *res* as it is in itself, whereas nonrigid designators or descriptions do not, and so do not relate the act to any *res* whatsoever—may have to be called in question. This would be tantamount to calling into question also the associated concept-intuition, proposition-thing, and fact—object distinctions. It is not that at any level of discourse these distinctions do not matter, but that the distinctions are relative to a given discourse. There are, in fact, different types of objects, a hierarchy of them, of which only those of the lowest type may be regarded as pure individuals and objects of pure perception in any strict sense. Objects of all different sorts may be intentionally referred to, and under all different descriptions ranging from the most generic to the most specific. If the object-about-which is not a well specified object, it may still be an object determined by a generic description. An act may intend its object in the specificity of *what* it is, or it may still be about it in the generality of one of its predicates. When the former is the case, exportation is permitted; when the latter is the case, exportation is not. But that is not to be construed as suggesting that the *de dicto* belief is not *about* an object; it is *not* surely about an object *regarded as* a well specified unique individual. It nevertheless has its object-about-which. The belief "The next Prime Minister of India will be a socialist," construed *de dicto*, is about the next Prime Minister of India. Its object-about-which is the next Prime Minister of India. (Note that the fact that it refers to a future, as yet undetermined, contingency is misleading and irrelevant. The relevant point is that the person having the belief believes something about an object which, *in that belief,* is given only one explicit determination—that is, that the person be the next Prime Minister of India. There are obviously other implicit determinations—for example, that he be human, a politician, and an Indian.) *Only if it be the case that* for an act to be directed toward an object it must also be directed toward it in its uniqueness—that is, under descriptions that uniquely identify it or under a name that rigidly designates it, would it be imperative for us to admit that *de dicto* acts are not directed toward whatever they are about. But there is no reason why we should accept this requirement.

What makes us resist the inclination to recognize that a *de dicto* belief that the next Prime Minister of India will be a socialist is *about* the next Prime Minister of India is (i) that exportation does not go through and (ii) that, in the world, there is no unique individual designated by "the next Prime Minister of India." Neither of these is an adequate reason for withholding recognition. Both have to do with *ontology,* with what may or may not be said to belong to the world in the natural sense. A phenomenological theory of intentionality cannot make use of that ontology, but has to provide an account of it by specifying what sort of intentional acts are those in which an individual, in that naive ontological sense, comes to acquire its specifications and so its alleged individuality. One such act, for example, is that of naming.

For the purpose of this paper, a more radical conclusion, consistent with Husserlian thinking, need not be drawn. Once the basic presuppositions—such as the distinctions between name and description, intuition and concept, individual and proposition, are relativized—it may be possible to lay down a range of variations in the context of which fully *de re* and totally *de dicto* constructions would be two extreme limits, enchanting to logicians for the simple structures they exhibit, but precisely for that reason not illustrated in the actual intentional acts performed in actual living contexts.

V. Primacy of the Actual?

In view of this *Auseinandersetzung* of phenomenology with possible-worlds semantics, can it be said that phenomenology is committed to a primacy of the actual? Contrary to the impression this paper may have created in the minds of some readers, I must say 'no.' That no experience, no act, and no object is given without its horizon of possibilities is one of the well established theses of phenomenology. The interpenetration of the actual and the possible is a thesis common to both Husserlian and Heideggerean phenomenologies. Husserlian constitution analysis refers back, inevitably and constantly, to the possibilities of performing intentional acts of appropriate sorts, to the 'I can' of consciousness. In view of these rather well known theses, it would be a mistake to ascribe to Husserlian phenomenology the thesis of the primacy of the actual.

For the limited purposes of this paper, however, we can state the sense in which it is true that everything actual involves possibilities, and the sense in which possibilities refer back to the actual. Everything actual involves possibilities, which are intentionally predelineated in its horizon; these are what Husserl calls *motivated* possibilities. Here anticipations are motivated by what is presented, anticipations that may be either fulfilled or frustrated. These may also be called *presumptive* and *open* possibilities. When, however, one speaks of 'pure possibilities,' these are not motivated by any actual perception but, rather, are freely postulated (and constituted) by an 'as-if' transformation. Every actual consciousness and every actual object can be "transformed" into an as-if consciousness and an as-if object. This transformed 'phantasy-consciousness' constitutes the pure possibilities.

There are a series of forms of consciousness in which different forms of possibilities come to be intended. By virtue of the fact that consciousness can always objectify any of its achievements, "It is possible that . . ." may be objectified, reified into "the possibility of . . . ," whereby an objectivity of a higher order is constituted out of the modalized forms of consciousness and their intentional objects. But, as said above, no object is constituted without the 'I can' consciousness; it belongs to the sense of any *object,* of any type whatsoever, that it can be identified, reidentified, referred to again. Thus at the heart of the *constituting* consciousness—what Husserl often grandiosely calls transcendental subjectivity—there is a possibility consciousness. This 'I can' is very far from being a *modal* concept.

Our argument with Hintikka is at every step, just as at every step, I think, phenomenology cannot take just that step, which would lead to possible-worlds semantics. It cannot take that step in order to remain phenomenology and not fall into the naïveté of an ontological discourse.

RESPONSE BY JAAKKO HINTIKKA

Phenomenology vs. Possible-Worlds Semantics: Apparent and Real Differences

Professor Mohanty's fascinating paper[1] not only discusses the surprising difficulties of finding any deep differences between Husserlian phenomenology and my alternative reconstruction of the concept of intentionality within a version of possible-worlds semantics;[2] it also instantiates these difficulties. Looked upon from my vantage point, Mohanty apparently concedes all that I need for my own theory of "intentionality as intensionality."[3*] These crucial concessions can be seen, for example, in the following theses of Mohanty:

"What is important is that one who has mastered the meaning of a term would be able to pick out the term's extension in various counterfactual situations. If these counterfactual situations are possible worlds, then understanding the sense is knowing which individual, in each case, is being referred to."

"Once I have a description of what I perceive ('p'), then all possible states of affairs may be divided into two groups: those that are compatible with 'p' and those that are not."

To these we may add the result of Mohanty's observation (in section III of his paper), that for Husserl the identity of individuals from one possible state of affairs to another one is not trivially given but has to be constituted.

These theses seem to give me essentially all that I need to reconstruct my own theory of intentionality as intensionality from materials supplied to me by phenomenologists.

Generalizing from the second quote, I can say that each propositional attitude (or other intentional concept), attributed to a person b, effects a division of all possible worlds into two: those that are compatible with b's attitude and those that are not. The semantics of intentional concepts thus essentially involves a multiplicity of possible worlds. From the first quote, we can see that to have a concept is to be able to pick out its referents in a class of possible worlds, which is just what the meaning functions of possible-worlds semanticists do. From the last thesis, it follows that the identity of individuals between different possible worlds is not fixed by logic or by the actual world, but has to be constituted by (as it were) drawing "world lines" connecting the manifestations of the same individual in different worlds. These are the major ingredients of my theory. There thus seems to be very little substantial difference between my theory and Husserl's, as the latter is ably interpreted by Mohanty. Whether one prefers the slogan "intentionality as directedness" to that of "intentionality as intensionality" or prefers to speak of noemata rather than of meaning functions apparently does not matter very much. The important point is the agreement in our substantial views concerning the meaning of acts.

One can even suggest that my explication of the intentionality of a concept as involving a multiplicity of *possibilia* is merely a way of spelling out one of the most interesting and possibly deepest aspects of Husserl's views—namely, the idea that our acts inevitably involve much more than what is "filled" in them. For instance, in an act of perception many things are included in the noema of the act that are not given by the immediate sense-experience itself.[4*] In this sense, Husserlian phenomenology relies on *possibilia* (no matter whether or not we use the misleading term "possible worlds"). Once again, Mohanty agrees:

"That no experience, no act and no object, is given without its horizon of possibilities is one of the well established theses of phenomenology. The interpenetration of the actual and the possible is a thesis that is common to both Husserlian and Heideggerian phenomenologies."

So what is it that really distinguishes phenomenological theories of intentionality from possible-worlds theories? Mohanty suggests several differences, which from my perspective can be divided into three groups.

(1) The first group of alleged differences amounts to pointing out shortcomings of certain versions of the possible-worlds analysis. In virtually all cases, these putative flaws belong to other variants of possible-worlds theory than mine, and in most cases I have forcefully criticized the very same shortcomings independently of Mohanty. (His criticisms will nevertheless tell against other versions of possible-worlds views.)

For instance, it is perfectly true that meaning functions do not spell out how it is that the object of an act (or the reference of a linguistic expression) is determined in different possible circumstances. However, I have (quite independently of Mohanty) stressed the need for developing possible-worlds semantics further so that it deals with suitable operationalizations ("recipes" or "algorithms") of meaning functions rather than these functions as set-theoretical entities (classes of pairs of argument values and function values).[5] Contrary to what Mohanty alleges, I have never claimed that meaning functions *qua* functions automatically give such an operationalization, nor do I believe that they do.

Again, my claim that the realm of all possible worlds does not form a well-developed totality[6] is eminently in line with Husserl's claim, quoted by Mohanty, that "the universe of free possibilities in general is a realm of disconnectedness: it lacks a unity of context." Rather, we must restrict the range of possible worlds to suitably "motivated" possibilities, I believe, again in agreement with Husserl.

Like Mohanty (and Husserl according to Mohanty), I have emphasized the importance of a spatiotemporal framework for the individuation of individuals.[7]

Mohanty accuses me of "reifying" possible worlds, but in virtually every issue where the cash value of such reification might be expected to show up, I am on the same side as Mohanty. For instance, I have emphasized that we cannot even hope to operate actually with any possible world as a completed whole. The best we can hope to do is to deal with parts or partial specifications of possible worlds.[8] This point is clearly an anti-reificationist one, and one with which Mohanty apparently agrees.

(2) Some arguments of Mohanty's purporting to highlight differences between Husserl and Hintikka are just beside the point. For instance, the fact that noemata exist only in relation to acts does not show that they are not individuals according to Husserl.[9*] The telling argument here is the following. If noemata were not individuals, how could they serve as objects of certain acts, viz. of those acts of phenomenological reflection which are so crucial to all phenomenology? Isn't such reflection itself intentional—that is, object-directed?

Again, Mohanty misses my point when he speculates whether it is parallel acts or their noemata that correspond to the alternative possible situations in my account. The answer is, of course, neither. Possible situations ("possible worlds") compatible with what one perceives are what this term says they are: situations compatible with the information one's perception gives one.[10*]

(3) It seems to me that the real differences between phenomenology and my version of the possible-worlds analysis of intentional concepts emerge only indirectly from Mohanty's paper. At several points he complains that my possible-worlds theory of intentionality, even when he finds no real fault with it, lacks "descriptive-clarificatory value" or does not "tie up with the phenomenology of perception," or that it has "semantical-ontological interest" but not "phenomenological-descriptive interest," or that it "cannot belong to phenomenology." Even though Mohanty does not spell out fully what these charges amount to, I think that we can see what is involved. Even though phenomenological meaning analysis recognizes how much more can be present in an act over and above what is filled in it, nevertheless this analysis is bound to be constrained by what *is* present (and hence accessible to phenomenological reflection) in an act. In contrast, a possible-worlds analysis of the meaning of an act is not restricted to ingredients of meaning which can somehow be recaptured by a reflecting consciousness. On the contrary, it is a remarkable feature of much of our conscious experience that all traces of the realm of possibilities against the backdrop of which this experience is enacted are "integrated out."[11] At least, that is what I want to argue. Certainly, it is a remarkable fact about the pos-

sible worlds of a possible-worlds semanticist that they are never present to one's mind individually, one by one, but always come to us in bunches, which we may perhaps subdivide further, but which might even lack ur-elements altogether.[12*] Hence I suspect that, given his phenomenological premises, Mohanty is quite right in being suspicious of my possible worlds and of analyses based on them.[13]

For instance, we cannot intend one particular individual rather than any other without being able to pick it out under a variety of circumstances, for we cannot intend it without individuating it. However, of these counterfactual recognitions, there need not be any explicit awareness in our consciousness. This throws some light back on the contrast of intentionality as intensionality (Hintikka) versus intentionality as directedness (Husserl).

One can also think of various "unconscious inferences" which, according to psychologists of perception, are accomplished by our central nervous system without our being aware of them. Their nature can nevertheless be described by reference to the possible-worlds framework.

These observations do not decide whose approach is the most fruitful one, however. Such questions can be answered only on the basis of further investigations. In this respect the results of my most recent work in this direction are most relevant.[14] They show, it seems to me, that we can reach valuable insights concerning intentionality—its criteria, varieties, and degrees as well as the relative intentionality or non-intentionality of several particular concepts—by means of the possible-worlds framework in spite of the admitted fact that this framework cannot be reached in some of its most fundamental features by phenomenological reflection.

It may even be that similar things must be said of Frege's concept of sense and of the meaning analyses that are based on it. Even though the question needs a much closer scrutiny than can be devoted to it here, it seems to me that a Fregean *Sinn* need not be accessible to phenomenological reflection either.[15*] If so, we have discovered an important limitation of the Frege-Husserl parallelism which in so many other respects has proved to be most illuminating.

All told, it thus seems to me that Mohanty's paper is a most valuable one. He has succeeded, albeit indirectly, in calling attention to certain very important similarities and differences between Husserlian phenomenology and my possible-worlds analysis of intentionality, and perhaps more generally to differences between phenomenological and analytical meaning analysis.

IV

Recent Parallels

Mind 88 (1979)

14

What Is
an Intentional State?

John Searle

I

Many of our mental states are in some sense directed at objects and states of affairs in the world. If, for example, I have a belief, it must be a belief that such-and-such is the case. If I have a wish or a want, it must be a wish or a want to do something, or that something should happen or should be the case. If I have an intention, it must be an intention to do something. If I have a fear, it must be a fear of something or that something will occur. And so on, through a large number of other cases. It is this feature of directedness of our mental states that many philosophers have labeled 'Intentionality'.[1*] Now clearly, not all of our mental states are in this way directed or Intentional. For example, if I have a pain, ache, tickle, or itch, such conscious states are not in that sense directed at anything; they are not 'about' anything, in the way that our beliefs, fears, etc. must in some sense be about something. Furthermore, not all of our Intentional states are even conscious states. I have, for example, many beliefs that I am not thinking about at present and indeed may never have thought about.

Now, the problem that I want to pose here is this: what exactly is the relationship between Intentional states and the objects and states of affairs that they are in some sense directed at or about? Notice that if we try to construe Intentionality on the model of ordinary relations like being on top of or sitting to the left of, then on the face of it, it appears to be a very puzzling relation because for a large number of Intentional states I can have the state without the object or state of affairs that the Intentional state is directed at even existing at all: I can believe that the King of France is bald even if, unknown to me, there is no King of France; and I can hope that it will rain even if it doesn't rain.

In broad outline, the answer that I propose to the question is quite simple. Intentional states represent objects and states of affairs in exactly the same sense that speech acts represent objects and states of affairs. I will develop this answer by making explicit several connections and similarities between Intentional states and speech acts; but it is important at the beginning to avoid creating one fairly obvious sort of misunderstanding. By explaining Intentionality in terms of linguistic acts, I do not mean to suggest that Intentionality is somehow essentially linguistic. The analogy between speech acts and Intentional states is drawn as an expository device, as a heuristic for explaining Intentionality. Once I have tried to make the nature of Intentionality clear, I will argue that the direction of dependence is precisely the reverse. Language is derived from Intentionality, and not conversely. The direction of *pedagogy* is to explain Intentionality in terms of language. The direction of *analysis* is to explain language in terms of Intentionality.

That there is a close connection between speech acts and Intentional states is at least strongly suggested by the parallel syntactical forms of speech-acts verbs and the corresponding Intentional verbs, which name the sincerity conditions of these speech acts. For example, in English, both the verb 'state' and the verb 'believe' take 'that' clauses as sentential complements. Both 'I state that it will rain' and 'I believe that it will rain' are permissible, but neither verb will take the sorts of infinitives that occur with the pairs 'order,' 'want' and 'promise,' 'intend.' I can't say 'I state you to go' or 'I believe you to go.' Nor can I say 'I state to come' or 'I believe to come.' The other two pairs take parallel infinitive forms. Thus 'I order you to go,' 'I want you to go,' 'I promise to come' and 'I intend to come' are all permissible. I will not pursue these syntactical analogies here except to point out that the obvious parallelism between the verb that names the illocutionary act and the verb that names its sincerity condition suggests that something deeper is going on. Leaving aside the syntax, there are at least the following four points of similarity and connection between intentional states and speech acts.

1. The distinction between propositional content and illocutionary force, a distinction familiar within the theory of speech acts, carries over to Intentional states. Just as I can order you to leave the room, predict that you will leave the room, and suggest that you will leave the room, so I can believe that you will leave the room, fear that you will leave the room, want you to leave the room, and hope that you will leave the room. In the first class of cases, the speech act cases, there is an obvious distinction between the propositional content *that you will leave the room* and the illocutionary force with which that propositional content is presented in the speech act. But equally in the second class of cases, the Intentional states, there is a distinction between the representative content *that you will leave the room,* and the psychological mode, whether belief or fear or hope or whatever, in which one has that representative content. It is customary within the theory of speech acts to present this distinction in the form 'F(p)' where the 'F' marks the illocutionary force and the 'p' the propositional content. Within the theory of intentional states we will similarly need to distinguish between the representative content and the psychological mode or manner in which one has that representative content. We will symbolize this as 'S(r)', where the 'S' marks the psychological mode, and the 'r' the representative content.

2. The distinctions between different directions of fit, also familiar from the theory of speech acts,[2] will carry over to Intentional states. The members of the Assertive class of speech acts—statements, descriptions, assertions, etc.,—are supposed in some way to match an independently existing world; and to the extent that they do or fail to do that we say that they are true or false. But the members of the Directive class of speech acts—orders, commands, requests, etc.,—and the members of the Commissive class—promises, vows, pledges, etc.,—are not supposed to match an independently existing reality but rather are supposed to bring about changes in the world so that the world matches the speech act; and to the extent that they do or fail to do that, we do not say they are true or false but rather such things as that they are obeyed or disobeyed, fulfilled, complied with, kept or broken. I mark this distinction by saying that the Assertive class has the word-to-world direction of fit and the Commissive and Directive

classes have the world-to-word direction of fit. If the statement is
not true, it is the statement which is at fault, not the world; if
the order is disobeyed or the promise broken, it is not the order
or promise which is at fault, but the world in the person of the
disobeyer of the order or the breaker of the promise. Furthermore there are also null cases in which there is no direction of fit.
If I apologize for insulting you or congratulate you on winning
the prize, then though I do indeed presuppose the truth of the
expressed proposition, that I insulted you, that you won the prize,
the point of the speech act is not to commit me to either direction
of fit; the point is to express my sorrow or my pleasure about the
state of affairs specified in the propositional content, the truth of
which I presuppose. Now, interestingly, something very much like
these distinctions carries over to Intentional states. If my beliefs
turn out to be wrong, it is my beliefs and not the world which is
at fault, as is shown by the fact that I can correct the situation
simply by changing my beliefs. It is the responsibility of the belief, so to speak, to match the world, and where the match fails I
repair the situation by changing the belief. But if I fail to carry
out my intentions or if my desires are unfulfilled, I cannot in that
way correct the situation by simply changing the intention or
desire. In these cases it is, so to speak, the fault of the world if it
fails to match the intention or the desire, and I cannot fix things
up by saying it was a mistaken intention or desire in a way that I
can fix things up by saying it was a mistaken belief. Beliefs like
statements can be true or false, and we might say they have the
'mind-to-world' direction of fit, whereas desires and intentions
cannot be true or false, but can be complied with or fulfilled.
We might say that they have the 'world-to-mind' direction of
fit. Furthermore, there are also Intentional states that have the
null direction of fit. If I am sorry that I insulted you or glad that
you won the prize, then though my sorrow contains a belief that
I insulted you and my being pleased contains a belief that you
won the prize, my sorrow and pleasure can't be true or false in the
way that my beliefs can. My sorrows and pleasures may be appropriate or inappropriate depending on whether the mind-to-world
direction of fit of the belief is really satisfied, but my sorrows
and pleasures don't in that way have any direction of fit.

Notice that the parallelism between illocutionary acts and their
expressed Intentional sincerity conditions is remarkably close: the
direction of fit of the illocutionary act and that of the sincerity
condition is the same, and in those cases where the illocutionary

act has no direction of fit the truth of the propositional content is presupposed, and the corresponding Intentional state contains a belief.

3. A third connection that underlies the two similarities previously cited is the fact that in general[3*] in the preformance of each illocutionary act with a propositional content, we express a certain Intentional state with that propositional content, and that Intentional state is the sincerity condition of that type of speech act. Thus, for example, if I make the statement that p, I express a belief that p. If I make a promise to do A, I express an intention to do A. If I give an order to you to do A, I express a wish or a desire that you should do A. If I apologize for doing something, I express sorrow for doing that thing. If I congratulate you on something, I express pleasure or satisfaction about that something. All of these connections, between illocutionary acts and expressed Intentional sincerity conditions of the speech acts are internal; that is, the expressed intentional state is not just an accompaniment of the performance of the speech act. The performance of the speech act is necessarily an expression of the corresponding intentional state, as is shown by Moore's paradox. You can't say, 'It's snowing but I don't believe it's snowing,' 'I order you to stop smoking but I don't want you to stop smoking,' 'I apologize for insulting you, but I am not sorry that I insulted you,' 'Congratulations on winning the prize, but I am not glad that you won the prize,' and so on. All of these sound odd for the same reason. The performance of the speech act is *eo ipso* an expression of the corresponding intentional state; and consequently, it is logically odd, though not self-contradictory, to perform the speech act and deny the presence of the corresponding intentional state.[4*]

Now, to say that the intentional state which constitutes the sincerity condition is expressed in the performance of the speech act is not to say that one always has to have the intentional state that one expresses. It is always possible to lie, or otherwise perform an insincere speech act. But a lie or other insincere speech act consists in performing a speech act, and thereby expressing an intentional state, where one does not have the intentional state that one expresses.

4. The notion of conditions of satisfaction applies quite generally across both speech acts and intentional states in cases where there is a direction of fit. We say, for example, that a statement is true or false, that an order is obeyed or disobeyed, that a promise is kept or broken. In each of these we ascribe success or

failure of the illocutionary act to match reality in the particular direction of fit provided by the illocutionary point. To have a term, we might label all of these conditions 'conditions of satisfaction' or 'conditions of success.' So we will say that a statement is satisfied if and only if it is true, an order is satisfied if and only if it is obeyed, a promise is satisfied if and only if it is kept, and so on. Now, this notion of satisfaction clearly applies to intentional states as well. My belief will be satisfied if and only if things are as I believe them to be, my desires will be satisfied if and only if they are fulfilled, my intentions will be satisfied if and only if they are carried out. The notion of satisfaction seems to be intuitively natural to both speech acts and Intentional states and to apply quite generally, wherever there is a direction of fit.[5*]

What is crucially important to see is that in general the speech act will be satisfied if and only if the expressed psychological state is satisfied. Thus my statement will be true if and only if the expressed belief is correct, my order will be obeyed if and only if the expressed wish or desire is fulfilled, my promise will be kept if and only if my expressed intention is carried out. The conditions of satisfaction of the speech act and the conditions of satisfaction of the expressed intentional state are in general identical. The only exceptions to this are cases where the intentional state comes to be satisfied by way of something which is independent of the achievement of the illocutionary point of the speech act. Thus, for example, if you do the thing I order you to do, but do not do it by way of obeying my order or because I gave the order, but for some independent reason, we are less confident about saying that the order was really obeyed than we are about saying that my wish that you should do it was in the end satisfied. But with these few exceptions about the world-to-word direction of fit, we can say in general that an illocutionary act is satisfied if and only if the expressed Intentional state is satisfied. Furthermore, notice that just as the conditions of satisfaction are internal to the speech act, so the conditions of satisfaction of the Intentional state are internal to the Intentional state. Part of what makes my statement that snow is white the statement it is, is that it has those truth conditions and not others. Similarly part of what makes my wish that it were raining the wish it is, is that certain things will satisfy it and certain other things will not.

All of these four connections between intentional states and speech acts naturally suggest a certain picture of Intentionality: every Intentional state consists of a representative content in a certain psychological mode. Intentional states represent objects and states of affairs in exactly the same sense that speech acts represent objects and states of affairs. Just as my statement that it is raining is a representation of a certain state of affairs, so my belief that it is raining is a representation of the same state of affairs. Just as my order to Sam to leave the room is about Sam and represents a certain action on his part, so my desire that Sam should leave the room is about Sam and represents a certain action on his part. The notion of representation is conveniently vague. As applied to language, we can use it to cover not only reference, but predication and other truth conditions or conditions of satisfaction generally. Exploiting this vagueness, we can say that Intentional states represent their various conditions of satisfaction in the same sense that speech acts represent their conditions of satisfaction.

A taxonomy of speech acts is already a taxonomy of Intentional states. Those intentional states that have whole propositions as representative contents, the so called propositional attitudes, can be conveniently divided into those that have the mind-to-world direction of fit, those that have the world-to-mind direction of fit, and those that have no direction of fit. Not all intentional states have entire propositions as representative contents, some just contain representations of objects. If John loves Sally, admires Carter, worships God, and hates Bill, he has four Intentional states each with a representation of some entity, person, or deity.

II

I believe this approach to Intentionality will enable us to see the way to a solution of several traditional outstanding problems about mental states.

1. The question that forms the title of this article—'What is an Intentional state?'—is not, or at least need not be construed as, an ontological question, for what makes a mental state an Intentional state is not its ontological category but rather its logical properties. The traditional ontological problems about mental states are for the most part simply irrelevant to their Intentional features. How are intentional states realized? Are they neural configurations in the brain, modifications of a Cartesian ego, Humean ideas and images floating around in the mind, words occurring to us in thought, or causal dispositions to behave? Such questions are simply irrelevant to the logical properties of Intentional states. It doesn't matter how an Intentional state is realized, as long as the

realization is a realization of its Intentionality. How the representative content and the psychological mode of an Intentional state
is realized in one's psyche is no more a crucial question for us to
answer than it is crucial for us to answer the analogous questions
about how a certain linguistic act is realized. A linguistic act can
be realized in speaking or in writing, in French or in German, on
a teletype or a loudspeaker or a movie screen or a newspaper. But
such forms of realization do not matter to their logical properties.
We would, with justification, regard someone who was obsessed
by the question whether speech acts were identical with such
physical phenomena as sound waves as having missed the point.
The form of realization of an Intentional state is just as irrelevant
to its logical properties as the form in which a speech act is realized is irrelevant to its logical properties. The logical properties
of Intentional states arise from their being representations, and
the point is that they can, like linguistic entities, have logical
properties in a way that stones and trees cannot have logical properties (though statements about stones and trees can have logical
properties) because Intentional states, like linguistic entities and
unlike stones and trees, are representations.

Wittgenstein's famous problem about intention—When I raise
my arm what is left if I subtract the fact that my arm goes up?—
resists solution only as long as we insist on an ontological answer.
Given the non-ontological approach to Intentionality suggested
here, the answer is quite simple. What is left is a representative
content—that I raise my arm; in a certain psychological mode—the
intentional mode. To the extent that we find ourselves dissatisfied
with this answer, I believe that our dissatisfaction reveals that we
have a mistaken model of Intentionality; we are still searching for
a thing to correspond to the word 'intention.' But the only thing
that could correspond is an intention, and to know what an intention is, or what any other Intentional state with a direction of fit
is, we do not need to know the material or psychological properties of its realization, but rather we need to know, first, what are
its conditions of satisfaction; second, under what aspect(s) are
those conditions represented by the representative content; and
third, what is the psychological mode—belief, desire, intention,
etc.—of the state in question. To know the second of these is
already to know the first, since the representative content gives us
the conditions of satisfaction, under certain aspects, namely those
under which they are represented. And a knowledge of the third is

sufficient to give us a knowledge of the direction of fit between the representative content and the conditions of satisfaction.

2. If the approach to Intentionality urged in this paper is correct, then the traditional ontological problems about the status of Intentional objects now have a very simple answer. An Intentional object is just an object like any other; it has no peculiar ontological status. To call something an Intentional object is just to say that it is what some intentional state is about. Thus, for example, if Bill admires President Carter, then the object of his admiration is President Carter, the actual man and not some shadowy intermediate entity between Bill and the man. In both the case of speech acts and the case of intentional states, if there is no object that satisfies the propositional or the representative content, then the speech act and the intentional state cannot be satisfied. In such cases, just as there is no 'referred-to object' of the speech act, so there is no 'Intentional object' of the Intentional state: if nothing satisfies the referential portion of the representative content, then the Intentional state does not have an Intentional object. Thus, for example, the statement that the King of France is bald cannot be true, because there is no King of France, and similarly the belief that the King of France is bald cannot be true, because there is no King of France. The order to the King of France to be bald and the wish that the King of France were bald both necessarily fail of satisfaction and both for the same reason: there is no King of France. The fact that our statements may fail to be true because of reference failure no longer inclines us to suppose that we must erect a Meinongian entity for such statements to be about. We realize that they have a propositional content which nothing satisfies, and in that sense they are not 'about' anything. But in exactly the same way I am suggesting the fact that our Intentional states may fail to be satisfied because there is no object referred to by their content should no longer puzzle us to the point where we feel inclined to erect an intermediate Meinongian entity or Intentional object for them to be about. An Intentional state has a representative content, but it is not about or directed at its representative content.

Of course, some of our Intentional states are exercises in fantasy and imagination, but analogously some of our speech acts are fictional. And just as the possibility of fictional discourse, itself a product of fantasy and imagination, does not force us to erect a class of 'referred to' or 'described' objects different from ordinary objects but supposedly the objects of all discourse, so I am suggesting that the possibility of fantasy and imaginative forms of intentionality does not force us to believe in the existence of a class of 'Intentional objects,' different from ordinary objects but supposedly the objects of all our Intentional states. I am not saying there are no problems about fantasy and imagination; what I am arguing, rather, is that the problems are of the same form as the problems of analyzing fictional discourse.[6]

3. If I am right in thinking that Intentional states consist of representative contents in the various psychological modes, then it is simply a mistake to say that a belief, for example, is a two-term relation between a believer and a proposition. An analogous mistake would be to say that a statement is a two term relation between a speaker and a proposition. One should say, rather, that a proposition is not the *object* of a statement or belief but rather its *content*. The content of the statement or belief that DeGaulle was French is the proposition that DeGaulle was French. But that proposition is not what the statement or belief is about or is directed at. No, the statement or belief is about DeGaulle and it represents him as being French, and it is about DeGaulle and represents him as being French because it has the propositional content and the mode of presentation—illocutionary or psychological—that it has. In a way that 'John hit Bill' describes a relation between John and Bill such that John's hitting is directed at Bill, 'John believes that p' does not describe a relation between John and p such that John's believing is directed at p. It would be more accurate to say in the case of statements that the statement is *identical* with the proposition, construed as stated; and in the case of belief the belief is *identical* with the proposition, construed as believed. There is, indeed, a relation ascribed when one ascribes an Intentional state to a person, but it is not a relation between a person and a proposition; rather, it is a relation of representation between the Intentional state and the things represented by it; only remember that, as with representations in general, it is possible for an Intentional state to exist without anything that satisfies it.

4. This account of Intentionality suggests a very simple account of the relationship between Intentionality-with-a-t and Intensionality-with-an-s. Intensionality-with-an-s is a property of a certain class of sentences, statements, and other linguistic entities. A sentence is said to be Intensional-with-an-s if it fails to satisfy certain tests for extensionality, tests such as substitutability of identicals

and existential generalization. A sentence such as 'John believes that King Arthur slew Sir Lancelot' is usually said to be Intensional-with-an-s because it has at least one interpretation where it can be used to make a statement which does not permit existential generalization over the referring expressions following 'believes,' and does not permit substitutability of expressions with the same reference, *salva veritate*. Traditionally, the puzzles about such sentences have concerned how it can be the case that their use to make a statement does not permit the standard logical operations if, as seems to be the case, the words contained in the sentences have the meanings they normally have and if the logical properties of a sentence are a function of its meaning, and its meaning in turn is a function of the meaning of its component words. The answer suggested by the foregoing account, an answer which I will not develop here, is simply that since the sentence 'John believes that King Arthur slew Sir Lancelot' is used to make a statement about an intentional state, namely John's belief, and since an intentional state is a representation, then the statement is a representation of a representation; and, therefore, the truth conditions of the statement will depend on the features of the representation being represented, in this case the features of John's belief, and not on the features of the objects or state of affairs represented by John's belief. That is, since the statement is a representation of a representation, its truth conditions do not include the truth conditions of the representation being represented. John's belief can only be true if there were such a person as King Arthur and such a person as Sir Lancelot, and if the former slew the latter; but my statement that John believes that King Arthur slew Sir Lancelot has an interpretation according to which it can be true if none of these truth conditions holds. Its truth requires only that John have a belief and that the words following 'believes' in the sentence accurately repeat the representative content of his belief. In that sense, my statement about his belief is not so much a *representation* of a representation, as a *presentation* of a representation, since I present the content of his belief, without committing myself to the truth conditions of his belief.

One of the most pervasive confusions in contemporary philosophy is the mistaken belief that there is some close connection, perhaps even an identity, between Intensionality-with-an-s and Intentionality-with-a-t. Nothing could be further from the truth. They are not even remotely similar. Intentionality-with-a-t is that property of the mind by which it is able to represent other things; ~~Intentionality-with-a-t are Intensional-with-an-s. More about this~~ ments, etc. to satisfy certain logical tests for extensionality. The only connection between them is that some sentences about Intentionality-with-a-t are Intensional-with-an-s. More about this later.

5. It is sometimes alleged that an Intentional state such as desire or wanting cannot be a cause of an action because desires and wants to do something are logically related to the doing of that thing and hence, so the story goes, they cannot also be causally related. But on the account of Intentionality that I am here presenting, a desire to perform an action is precisely a representation of the action to be performed. The way in which the desire to perform the action is logically related to the action is the way that any representation is logically related to the thing it represents. It is internally related to it in the sense that it couldn't be that representation if it didn't represent that thing. But this form of logical connection is no obstacle whatever to the connection also being a causal connection. Indeed, the way in which a desire to do something is causally connected to the doing of that thing is not only not inconsistent with there being the logical connection of representation, but it precisely requires that logical connection. It is not *in spite of* the fact that my desires are logically connected to my actions that my desires can cause actions; on the contrary, it's *only because* my desires are logically related to actions by way of representing them that they can be the sorts of causes of actions that they are. If I want to raise my arm and then, acting on that desire, I raise my arm, the want can only cause me to raise my arm, in the way that wants explain actions, if, in fact, the want was a desire to raise my arm. If the want was a desire to do something else, as a result of having which want my arm went up, then though the want might be a cause of my arm going up, the want will not explain my action of raising my arm precisely because it fails to have the requisite logical connection. Wants motivate, but they motivate the things they are wants to do precisely because they are representations of those things; hence the causal connection requires a logical connection.

I believe this point is quite obvious, but since it runs counter to a certain tradition of discussing these problems, it may be worthwhile to present it as an analogy. The blueprints of a house characteristically figure in the causal story of how the house was constructed. The builders and the contractor characteristically work from the architect's blueprints. Now suppose somebody argues that the blueprints couldn't be causally related to the construction of the house on the grounds that since the blueprints are a representation of that house they were logically related to that house and that for some mysterious reason this precluded them from being causally related to the house. But in answer to this, it is obviously, at least in this case, a piece of sheer mythology to suppose that there is any conflict between the blueprints being logically related by way of representation to the house and their also being causally related to it by way of figuring in its construction; but furthermore, it seems to me equally obvious that it is a condition of the blueprints being causally related to the house, in a way that blueprints characteristically are causally related to the construction of houses, that they should be logically related to the house. They are representations of the house being constructed. Some people who are aware that there is no logical obstacle to two things being both causally related and logically related believe that the way to remove the apparent paradox is to say that the terms of the logical relation have some more intrinsic characterization under which they can be characterized as in the causal relation. Thus they believe that wants can figure as causes of actions because wants can be described in terms of their neurophysiology or some such. I argue on the other hand that the way to remove the paradox is to see that there is no paradox in the first place. No one, I suppose, would argue that blueprints figure causally in the construction of houses only because blueprints have some intrinsic characterization in terms of the cellulose fibers of the paper or the chemical composition of the dye which is printed on the paper. Rather, the causal relation exists only by virtue of the fact that there is a logical relation—that is to say, the blueprint is a representation of a house being constructed, and in exactly the same sense, I wish to argue, the desire to do an action is a representation of the action to be performed.

Once we see that often when it comes to voluntary human actions part of the causal account of the action is that it is done in accord with certain representations, then other examples are easy to hand. For example, giving an order can figure in the causal explanation of an action of carrying out the order because the order is a representation of the action that the addressee is ordered to perform. A man's obeying the order is causally related to the order, but then it is also logically related, because the order is an

order to do precisely that action. What causation requires is that
the cause and the effect should be separate phenomena or at least
separate aspects of the same phenomenon. But they do not require that the one should not be a representation of the other.
On the contrary, many causal relations, particularly where human
action is concerned, require that the one be a representation of the
other.

6. We originally introduced the notion of Intentionality-with-
a-t in such a way that it applied to mental states and the notion of
Intensionality-with-an-s in such a way that it applied to sentences
and other linguistic entities. But it is now easy to see, given our
characterization of Intentionality-with-a-t and its relation to Intensionality-with-an-s, how to extend each notion to cover both
mental and linguistic entities.

(a) The Intensionality-with-an-s of statements about Intentional-with-a-t states derives from the fact that such statements are
representations of representations. But since Intentional-with-a-t
states are representations, there is nothing to prevent there being
Intentional-with-a-t states that are also representations of representations, and thus such states would share the feature of Intensionality-with-an-s that is possessed by the corresponding sentence
and statements. For example, just as my statement that John
believes that King Arthur slew Sir Lancelot is Intensional-with-
an-s because the statement is a representation of John's belief;
so my belief that John believes that King Arthur slew Sir Lancelot
is an Intensional-with-an-s mental state because it is an Intentional
state which is a representation of John's belief, and thus the conditions for its satisfaction depend on features of the representation
being represented and not on the things represented by the original
representation. But of course from the fact that my belief about
John's belief is an intensional-with-an-s belief it does not follow
that John's belief is an intensional-with-an-s belief. If his belief
is that King Arthur slew Sir Lancelot, that belief is completely
extensional. That belief will be satisfied if and only if there is
a unique x such that x is King Arthur and a unique y such that y
is Sir Lancelot and x slew y. It is often said, for reasons that are
totally obscure, that all Intentional entities such as propositions
and mental states are somehow Intensional-with-an-s. But this is
simply confused. Some such states are indeed intensional-with-
an-s, as the previous examples show, but there is nothing inher-
ently intensional-with-an-s about intentionality-with-a-t.

(b) In this article I have explained the Intentionality of mental states by appealing to our understanding of speech acts. But of course the feature of speech acts that I have been appealing to is precisely their representative properties—that is to say, their Intentionality-with-a-t. So the notion of Intentionality-with-a-t applies equally well both to mental states and to linguistic entities such as speech acts and sentences, not to mention maps, diagrams, laundry lists, pictures, and a host of other things. Now, the next question we have to consider is the question how is this possible? Or, rather, what is the relationship between the Intentionality of our mental states, where the mental state seems somehow to be intrinsically Intentional, and the intentionality of certain material phenomena in the world such as utterances, pictures, etc.

There is one obvious disanalogy between Intentional states and speech acts, which is suggested by the very terminology we have been employing. Mental states are states, and speech acts are acts, that is, intentional performances. And this difference has an important consequence for the way that the speech act is related to its physical realization. The actual performance in which the speech act is made will involve the production (or use or presentation) of some physical entity, such as noises made through the mouth or marks on paper. Beliefs, fears, hopes, and desires, on the other hand, are intrinsically Intentional. To characterize them as beliefs, fears, hopes, and desires is already to ascribe intentionality to them. But speech acts have a physical level of realization, *qua* speech acts, that is not intrinsically Intentional. There is nothing intrinsically Intentional about the utterance act, that is, the noises that come out of my mouth or the marks that I make on paper. Now the problem of meaning in its most general form is the problem of how we get from the physics to the semantics—that is to say, how we get, for example, from the sounds that come out of my mouth to the illocutionary act. And the discussion so far in this paper gives us, I believe, a new way of seeing the question. From the point of view of this discussion, the problem of meaning can be stated as follows: How does the mind impose intentionality on entities that are not intrinsically intentional, on entities like sounds and marks that are, construed in one way, just physical phenomena in the world like any other?

There is a double level of intentionality in the performance of the speech act. There is, first of all, the Intentional state expressed, but then, secondly, there is the intention, in the ordinary and not technical sense of that word, with which the utterance is made.

Now it is this second Intentional state—that is, the intention with
which the act is performed—which bestows the Intentionality on
the physical phenomena. Well, how does it work? Anything like an
adequate answer to that question is beyond the scope of this
paper, but in most broad outline the answer is this: The mind imposes Intentionality on entities that are not intrinsically Intentional by intentionally transferring the conditions of satisfaction
of the expressed psychological state to the external physical
entity. The double level of Intentionality in the speech act can be
described by saying that by intentionally uttering something with
a certain set of conditions of success, those specified by the
essential condition for that speech act, I have made the utterance
Intentional and thus necessarily expressed the corresponding psychological state. I couldn't make a statement without expressing a
belief or make a promise without expressing an intention because
the essential condition on the speech act has as conditions of satisfaction the same conditions of satisfaction as the expressed Intentional state. So I impose Intentionality on my utterances by
transferring to them certain conditions of success which are the
conditions of success of certain psychological states. That also
explains the internal connection between the essential condition
and the sincerity condition on the speech act.

As usual, the syntactical and semantic features of the corresponding verbs provide us useful hints about what is going on. If
I say 'John believes that p,' the sentence can stand on its own.
But if I say 'John means that p,' that sentence seems to require
or at least invite completion in the form 'by uttering such-and-
such' or 'by saying such-and-such John means that p.' John
couldn't mean that p unless he was saying or doing something *by
way of which* he meant that p, whereas John can simply believe
that p without doing anything. Meaning that p isn't an intentional
state that can stand on its own in the way that believing that p is.
In order to mean that p, there must be some overt action. When
we come to 'John stated that p,' the overt action is made explicit.
Stating is an act, unlike believing and meaning, which are not acts.
Stating is an illocutionary act that, at another level of description,
is an utterance act. It is the performance of the utterance act with
a certain set of intentions that converts the utterance act into an
illocutionary act and thus imposes Intentionality on the utterance.

III

Because I have made some fairly strong claims in this article, it is perhaps well to conclude by making clear several of the things I am not claiming.

1. I have not analyzed, nor attempted to analyze, the concept of Intentionality. If the characterization of Intentionality in terms of representation were intended to be an analysis, in the classic philosophical sense of giving necessary and sufficient conditions in terms of simpler notions, then it would be hopelessly circular. The notion of representation is as much an Intentional notion as any of the others I have used. A clue to this is the fact that sentences of the form 'x represents y' have both extensional and Intensional readings. Indeed, in the classical sense of philosophical analysis, where one attempts to give logically necessary and sufficient conditions for a concept in terms of simpler notions, I do not believe it is possible to give an analysis of Intentionality. Any attempt to characterize Intentionality must inevitably use Intentional notions, and thus any such attempt will move within what I have elsewhere called the circle of Intentionality.[7]

I have made fairly heavy use of the notion of representation, but it is not essential to do so; one could make all the same points in terms of conditions of satisfaction or conditions of success of the Intentional states without explicitly using the notion of representation. But again to use these other notions in this way is still to move within the circle of Intentionality. All that I claim for the notion of representation is that what I have said about using it is literally true and it facilitates the exposition of these ideas enormously to state them in terms of representation.

2. I have not said anything about the social character of many of our Intentional states. Many of our Intentional states require forms of social interaction—in particular, language—as a necessary condition of their existence. Language, after all, provides us with a system of representation, and using that system, we are able to have Intentional states that we could not have apart from the system. It is hard to see, for example, how a being that did not have a language could believe the binomial theorem or fear a decline in the gross national product.

3. I have not said anything about the primary form of Intentionality: perception. When, for example, I look at the table in front of me, I have a visual experience of that table. But the visual experience is not a *representation* of the table, it is a *presentation* of the table. The visual perception is a direct perception of the table. There is no question here of anything representing anything else. The mistake of all sense-datum theories, at least all those I

am familiar with, is that they attempt to strip the visual experience of its intrinsic Intentionality. But that this must be a mistake
is shown by the fact that even if I am hallucinating the table—that
is, even if there is no table there and my visual experience is simply a hallucination—nonetheless, my visual experience is precisely
a hallucination of a table. Its conditions of satisfaction require a
table to be there as much as do my beliefs or hopes that there is a
table there. That the visual experience has in this way its internal
conditions of satisfaction shows that it is intrinsically Intentional.
Because it is a presentation rather than a representation, it is important how the presentation is realized, in a way that it is not
important how our representations, such as beliefs and desires,
are realized. To say that I have a visual experience whenever I
perceive the table visually is to make an ontological claim, a claim
about the form of realization of an Intentional state, in a way that
to say that all my beliefs have a representational content is not to
make an ontological claim.

4. I have not said anything about the relationship of Intentionality to consciousness. What I actually believe to be the case,
though I do not know how to demonstrate it, is something like the
following: only beings capable of conscious states are capable of
Intentional states. And though any given Intentional state, such as
a belief or a fear, may never be brought to consciousness, it is always in principle possible for the agent to bring his Intentional
states to consciousness. The agent's consciousness is like a scanning machine that is capable of scanning any of his Intentional
states. Without this proviso—that is, without the assumption that
an Intentional state is capable of being brought to consciousness—
the ascription of Intentionality to beings as part of the explanation of their behavior would lose most of its explanatory force.

The only argument I know in favor of this view is that as a
matter of linguistic usage we only ascribe Intentional states to
beings to whom we also ascribe consciousness. That is, just as a
fact about linguistic usage, about the way we employ these concepts, we do not ascribe Intentionality, for example, to plants,
even though we ascribe all sorts of teleological and functional
notions to plants. But it is hard to see how we could attach any
sense to the notion that plants could have fears and beliefs in addition to their needs and ailments unless they were capable of
conscious states. A plant can literally be said to need water and
to be harmed by the drought, but it cannot be literally said to
desire water or believe that it is not getting enough.

15

Methodological Solipsism Considered as a Research Strategy in Cognitive Psychology

Jerry Fodor

. . . to form the idea of an object and to form an idea simply is the same thing; the reference of the idea to an object being an extraneous denomination, of which in itself it bears no mark or character.[1]

The paper distinguishes two doctrines, both of which inform theory construction in much of modern cognitive psychology: the representational theory of mind (according to which propositional attitudes are relations that organisms bear to mental representations) and the computational theory of mind (according to which mental processes have access only to formal-non-semantic-properties of the mental representations over which they are defined).

It is argued that the acceptance of some such formality condition is warranted, at least for that part of psychology which concerns itself with the mental causation of behavior. The paper closes with a discussion of the prospects for a "naturalistic" psychology: one which defines its generalizations over relations between mental representations and their environmental causes. Two related arguments are proposed, both leading to the conclusion that no such research strategy is likely to prove fruitful.

Your standard contemporary cognitive psychologist—your thoroughly modern mentalist—is disposed to reason as follows. To think (for example) that Marvin is melancholy is to represent Marvin in a certain way; viz. as being melancholy (and not, for example, as being maudlin, morose, moody, or merely moping and dyspeptic). But surely we cannot represent Marvin as being melancholy except as we are in some or other relation to a representation of Marvin; and not just *any* representation of Marvin, but, in particular, to a representation the content of which is *that* Marvin is melancholy; a representation which, as it were, expresses the proposition that Marvin is melancholy. So, a fortiori, at least some mental states/processes are or involve at least some relations to at least some representations. Perhaps, then, this is the *typical* feature of such mental states/processes as cognitive psychology studies; perhaps all such states can be viewed as relations to representations and all such processes as operations defined on representations.

This is, prima facie, an appealing proposal, since it gives the psychologist two degrees of freedom to play with and they seem, intuitively, to be the right two. On the one hand, mental states are distinguished by the *content* of the associated representations, and we therefore can allow for the difference between thinking that Marvin is melancholy and thinking that Sam is (or that Albert isn't, or that it sometimes snows in Cincinnati); and, on the other hand, mental states are distinguished by the *relation* that the subject bears to the associated representation (so we can allow for the difference between thinking, hoping, supposing, doubting, and pretending that Marvin is melancholy). It's hard to believe that a serious psychology could make do with fewer (or less refined) distinctions than these, and it's hard to believe that a psychology that makes these distinctions could avoid taking the notion of mental representation seriously. Moreover, the burden of argument is clearly upon anyone who claims that we need *more* degrees of freedom than just these two: the least hypothesis that is remotely plausible is that a mental state is (type) individuated by specifying a relation and a representation such that the subject bears the one to the other.[2]*

I'll say that any psychology that takes this line is a version of the REPRESENTATIONAL THEORY OF THE MIND. I think that it's reasonable to adopt some such theory as a sort of working hypothesis, if only because there aren't any alternatives which seem to be even *remotely* plausible and because empirical research carried out within this framework has, thus far, proved interesting and fruitful.[3] However, my present concern is neither to attack nor to defend this view, but rather to distinguish it from something other—and stronger—that modern cognitive psychologists *also* hold. I shall put this stronger doctrine as the view that mental states and processes are COMPUTATIONAL. Much of what is characteristic of cognitive psychology is a consequence of adherence to this stronger view. What I want to do in this paper is to say something about what this stronger view is, something about why I think it's plausible, and, most of all, something about the ways in which it shapes the cognitive psychology we have.

I take it that computational processes are both *symbolic* and *formal.* They are symbolic because they are defined over representations, and they are formal because they apply to representations in virtue of (roughly) the *syntax* of the representations. It's the second of these conditions that makes the claim that mental processes are computational stronger than the representational theory of the mind. Most of this paper will be a meditation upon the consequences of assuming that mental processes are formal processes.

I'd better cash the parenthetical 'roughly'. To say that an operation is formal isn't the same as saying that it is syntactic, since we could have formal processes defined over representations which don't, in any obvious sense, *have* a syntax. Rotating an image would be a timely example. What makes syntactic operations a species of formal operations is that being syntactic is a way of *not* being semantic. Formal operations are the ones that are specified without reference to such semantic properties of representations as, for example, truth, reference, and meaning. Since we don't know how to complete this list (since, that is, we don't know what semantic properties there are), I see no responsible way of saying what, in general, formality amounts to. The notion of formality will thus have to remain intuitive and metaphoric, at least for present purposes: formal operations apply in terms of the, as it were, shapes of the objects in their domains.[4*]

To require that mental processes be computational (viz. formal-syntactic) is thus to require something not very clear. Still, the requirement has some clear consequences, and they are striking and tendentious. Consider that we started by assuming that the *content* of representations is a (type) individuating feature of mental states. So far as the *representational* theory of the mind is concerned, it's possibly the *only* thing that distinguishes Peter's thought that Sam is silly from his thought that Sally is depressed. But, now,

if the *computational* theory of the mind is true (and if, as we may
assume, content is a semantic notion par excellence) it follows
that content alone cannot distinguish thoughts. More exactly, the
computational theory of the mind requires that two thoughts can
be distinct in content only if they can be identified with relations
to formally distinct representations. More generally: fix the subject
and the relation, and then mental states can be (type) distinct
only if the representations which constitute their objects are
formally distinct.

Again, consider that accepting a formality condition upon
mental states implies a drastic narrowing of the ordinary ontology
of the mental; all sorts of states which look, prima facie, to be
mental in good standing are going to turn out to be none of the
psychologist's business if the formality condition is endorsed.
This point is one that philosophers have made in a number of
contexts, and usually in a deprecating tone of voice. Take, for
example, knowing that such-and-such, and assume that you can't
know what's not the case. Since, on that assumption, knowledge
is involved with truth, and since truth is a semantic notion, it's
going to follow that there can't be a psychology of *knowledge*
(even if it is consonant with the formality condition to hope for
a psychology of *belief*). Similarly, it's a way of making a point
of Ryle's to say that, strictly speaking, there can't be a psychology
of perception if the formality condition is to be complied with.
Seeing is an achievement; you can't see what's not there. From the
point of view of the representational theory of the mind, this
means that seeing involves relations between mental representations *and their referents;* hence, semantic relations within the
meaning of the act.

I hope that such examples suggest (what, in fact, I think is true)
that even if the formality condition isn't very clear, it is quite
certainly very strong. In fact, I think it's not all *that* anachronistic
to see it as the central issue which divides the two main traditions
in the history of psychology: 'Rational psychology' on the one
hand, and 'Naturalism' on the other. Since this is a mildly eccen-
tric way of cutting the pie, I'm going to permit myself a semi-
historical excursus before returning to the main business of the
paper.

Descartes argued that there is an important sense in which how
the world is makes no difference to one's mental states. Here is a
well known passage from the first *Meditation:*

At this moment it does indeed seem to me that it is with eyes awake that I am looking at this paper; that this head which I move is not asleep, that it is deliberately and of set purpose that I extend my hand and perceive it . . . But in thinking over this I remind myself that on many occasions I have been deceived by similar illusions, and in dwelling on this reflection I see so manifestly that there are no certain indications by which we may clearly distinguish wakefulness from sleep that I am lost in astonishment. And my astonishment is such that it is almost capable of persuading me that I now dream.[5]

At least three sorts of reactions to this kind of argument are distinguishable in the philosophical literature. First, there's a long tradition, including both Rationalists and Empiricists, which takes it as axiomatic that one's experiences (and, a fortiori, one's beliefs) might have been just as they are even if the world had been quite different from the way that it is. See, for example, the passage from Hume which serves as an epigraph to this paper. Second, there's a vaguely Wittgensteinian mood in which one argues that it's just *false* that one's mental states might have been what they are had the world been relevantly different. For example, if there had been a dagger there, Macbeth would have been *seeing,* not just hallucinating. And what could be more different than that? If the Cartesian feels that this reply misses the point, he is at least under an obligation to say precisely which point it misses; in precisely *which* respects the way the world is is irrelevant to the character of one's beliefs, experiences, etc. Finally there's a tradition which argues that—epistemology to one side—it is at best a strategic mistake to attempt to develop a psychology which individuates mental states without reference to their environmental causes and effects (e.g., which counts the state that Macbeth *was* in as type-identical to the state he would have been in had the dagger been supplied.) I have in mind the tradition which includes the American Naturalists (notably Peirce and Dewey), all the learning theorists, and such contemporary representatives as Quine in philosophy and Gibson in psychology. The recurrent theme here is that psychology is a branch of biology, hence that one must view the organism as embedded in a physical environment. The psychologist's job is to trace those organism/environment interactions which constitute its behavior. A passage from William James will serve to give the feel of the thing:

On the whole, few recent formulas have done more service of a rough sort in psychology than the Spencerian one that the essence of mental life and

of bodily life are one, namely, 'the adjustment of inner to outer relations.'
Such a formula is vagueness incarnate; but because it takes into account
the fact that minds inhabit environments which act on them and on which
they in turn react; because, in short, it takes mind in the midst of all its
concrete relations, it is immensely more fertile than the old-fashioned
'rational psychology' which treated the soul as a detached existent, sufficient unto itself, and assumed to consider only its nature and its properties.[6]

A number of adventitious intrusions have served to muddy the
issues in this long-standing dispute. On the one hand, it may well
be that Descartes was relying on a specifically introspectionist
construal of the claim that the individuation of mental states is
independent of their environmental causes. That is, Descartes'
point may have been that (a) mental states are (type) identical if
and only if they are introspectively indistinguishable, and (b) introspection cannot distinguish (for example) perception from hallucination, or knowledge from belief. On the other hand, the
naturalist, in point of historical fact, is often a behaviorist as well.
He wants to argue not only that mental states are individuated by
reference to organism/environment relations, but also that such
relations constitute the mental. In the context of the present discussion, he is arguing for the abandonment not just of the formality
condition, but of the notion of mental representation as well.

If, however, we take the computational theory of the mind as
what's central to the issue, we can reconstruct the debate between
rational psychologists and naturalists in a way that does justice to
both their points; in particular, in a way which frees the discussion
from involvement with introspectionism on the one side and be-
haviorism on the other.

Insofar as we think of mental processes as computational (hence
as formal operations defined on representations), it will be natural
to take the mind to be, *inter alia,* a kind of computer. That is, we
will think of the mind as carrying out whatever symbol manipula-
tions are constitutive of the hypothesized computational processes. To a first approximation, we may thus construe mental
operations as pretty directly analogous to those of a Turing
machine. There is, for example, a working memory (corresponding to a tape) and there are capacities for scanning and altering the
contents of the memory (corresponding to the operations of
reading and writing on the tape). If we want to extend the computational metaphor by providing access to information about the

environment, we can think of the computer as having access to "oracles" which serve, on occasion, to enter information in the memory. On the intended interpretation of this model, these oracles are analogs to the senses. In particular, they are assumed to be transducers, in that what they write on the tape is determined solely by the ambient environmental energies that impinge upon them. [7*]

I'm not endorsing this model, but simply presenting it as a natural extension of the computational picture of the mind. Its present interest is that we can use it to see how the formality condition connects with the Cartesian claim that the character of mental processes is somehow independent of their environmental causes and effects. The point is that, so long as we are thinking of mental processes as purely computational, the bearing of environmental information upon such processes is exhausted by the formal character of whatever oracles write on the tape. In particular, it doesn't matter to such processes whether what the oracles write is *true;* whether, for example, they really are transducers faithfully mirroring the state of the environment, or merely the output end of a typewriter manipulated by a Cartesian demon bent on deceiving the machine. I'm saying, in effect, that the formality condition, viewed in this context, is tantamount to a sort of methodological solipsism. If mental processes are formal, they have access only to the formal properties of such representations of the environment as the senses provide. Hence, they have no access to the *semantic* properties of such representations, including the property of being true, of having referents, or, indeed, the property of being representations *of the environment.*

That some such methodological solipsism really is implicated in much current psychological practice is best seen by examining what researchers actually do. Consider, for example, the well-known work of Professor Terry Winograd. Winograd was primarily interested in the computer simulation of certain processes involved in the handling of verbal information; asking and answering questions, drawing inferences, following instructions, and the like. The form of his theory was a program for a computer which 'lives in' and operates upon a simple world of block-like geometric objects. [8] Many of the capacities that the device exercises vis-à-vis its environment seem impressively intelligent. It can arrange the blocks to order, it can issue 'perceptual' reports of the present state of its environment and 'memory' reports of its past states, it can devise simple plans for achieving desired environment configurations, and it can discuss its undertakings (more or less in English) with whoever is running the program.

The interesting point for our purposes, however, is that the machine environment which is the nominal object of these actions and conversations actually isn't there. What actually happens is that the programmer so arranges the memory states of the machine that the available data are whatever they would be *if* there were objects for the machine to perceive and manipulanda for it to operate upon. In effect, the machine lives in an entirely notional world; all its beliefs are false. Of course, it doesn't matter to the machine that its beliefs are false, since falsity is a semantic property and, qua computer, the device satisfies the formality condition; viz. it has access only to formal (non-semantic) properties of the representations that it manipulates. In effect, the device is in precisely the situation that Descartes dreads; it's a mere computer which dreams that it's a robot.

I hope that this discussion suggests how acceptance of the computational theory of the mind leads to a sort of methodological solipsism as a part of the research strategy of contemporary cognitive psychology. In particular, I hope it's clear how you get that consequence from the formality condition alone, without so much as raising the introspection issue. I stress this point because it seems to me that there has been considerable confusion about it among the psychologists themselves. People who do machine simulation, in particular, very often advertise themselves as working on the question how thought (or language) is related to the world. My present point is that, whatever else they're doing, they certainly aren't doing *that*. The very assumption that defines their field—viz. that they study mental processes *qua* formal operations on symbols—guarantees that their studies won't answer the question how the symbols so manipulated are semantically interpreted. You can, for example, build a machine that answers baseball questions in the sense that (for example) if you type in "Who had the most wins by a National League pitcher since Dizzy Dean?" it will type out "Robin Roberts, who won 28." But you delude yourself if you think that a machine which in this sense answers baseball questions is thereby answering questions *about* baseball (or that the machine has somehow referred to Robin Roberts). If the *programmer* chooses to interpret the machine inscription "Robin Roberts won 28" as a statement about Robin Roberts (for example, as the statement that he won 28), that's all well and good, but it's no business of the machine's. The machine has no access to that interpretation, and its computations are in no way affected by it. The machine doesn't know what it's talking about, and it doesn't care; *about* is a semantic relation. [9]*

This brings us to a point where, having done some sort of justice to the Cartesian's insight, we can also do some sort of justice to the naturalist's. For, after all, mental processes are supposed to be operations on representations, and it is in the nature of representations to represent. We have seen that a psychology which embraces the formality condition is thereby debarred from raising questions about the semantic properties of mental representations; yet surely such questions ought *somewhere* to be raised. The computer which prints out "RR won 28" is not thereby referring to RR. But, surely, when I think *RR won 28*, I *am* thinking about RR, and if not in virtue of having performed some formal operations on some representations, then presumably in virtue of something else. It's perhaps borrowing the least tendentious fragment of causal theories of reference to assume that what fixes the interpretation of my mental representations of RR is something about the way that he and I are embedded in the world; perhaps not a causal chain stretching between us, but anyhow *some* facts about how he and I are causally situated; *Dasein,* as you might say. Only a *naturalistic* psychology will do to specify these facts, because here we are explicitly in the realm of organism/environment transactions.

We are on the verge of a bland and ecumenical conclusion: that there is room both for a computational psychology—viewed as a theory of formal processes defined over mental representations— *and* a naturalistic psychology, viewed as a theory of the (presumably causal) relations between representations and the world which fix their semantic interpretations of the former. I think that, in principle, this is the right way to look at things. In practice, however, I think that it's misleading. So far as I can see, it's overwhelmingly likely that computational psychology is the only one that we are going to get. I want to argue for this conclusion in two steps. First, I'll argue for what I've till now only assumed: that we must *at least* have a psychology which accepts the formality condition. Then I'll argue that there's good reason to suppose that that's the most that we can have; that a naturalistic psychology isn't a practical possibility and isn't likely to become one.

The first move, then, is to give reasons for believing that at least *some* part of psychology should honor the formality condition. Here, too, the argument proceeds in two steps. I'll argue first that it is typically under an *opaque* construal that attributions of propositional attitudes to organisms enter into explanations of their behavior; and second that the formality condition is intimately involved with the explanation of propositional attitudes so construed: roughly, that it's reasonable to believe that we can get such explanations only within computational theories. *Caveat emptor:* the arguments under review are, in large part, non-demonstrative. In particular, they will assume the perfectibility in principle of the kinds of psychological theories now being developed, and it is entirely possible that this is an assumption contrary to fact.

Thesis: when we articulate the generalizations in virtue of which behavior is contingent upon mental states, it is typically an opaque construal of the mental state attributions that does the work; for example, it's a construal under which believing that *a is F* is logically independent from believing that *b is F,* even in the case where a = b. It will be convenient to speak not only of opaque construals of propositional attitude ascriptions, but also of *opaque taxonomies* of mental state types; for example, of taxonomies which, *inter alia,* count the belief that the Morning Star rises in the East as type distinct from the belief that the Evening Star does. (Correspondingly, *transparent* taxonomies are such as, *inter alia,* would count these beliefs as type identical.) So, the claim is that mental states are typically opaquely taxonomized for purposes of psychological theory.[10*]

The point doesn't depend upon the examples, so I'll stick to the most informal sorts of cases. Suppose I know that John wants to meet the girl who lives next door; and suppose I know that this is true when 'wants to' is construed opaquely. Then, given even rough-and-ready generalizations about how people's behaviors are contingent upon their utilities, I can make some reasonable predictions (or guesses) about what John is likely to do: he's likely to say (viz. utter), "I want to meet the girl who lives next door." He's likely to call upon his neighbor. He's likely (at a minimum, and all things being equal) to exhibit next-door-directed behavior. None of this is frightfully exciting, but it's all I need for present purposes, and what more would you expect from folk psychology?

On the other hand, suppose that all I know is that John wants to meet the girl next door where 'wants to' is construed transparently. That is, all I know is that it's true of the girl next door that

John wants to meet her. Then there is little or nothing that I can predict about how John is likely to proceed. And this is *not* just because rough and ready psychological generalizations want *ceteris paribus* clauses to fill them in; it's also for the deeper reason that I can't infer from what I know about John to any relevant description of the mental causes of his behavior. For example, I have no reason to predict that John will say such things as "I want to meet the girl who lives next door" since, let John be as cooperative and as truthful as you like, and let him be utterly a native speaker, still, he *may believe* that the girl he wants to meet languishes in Latvia. In which case, "I want to meet the girl who lives next door" is the last thing it will occur to him to say. (The contestant wants to say 'suspender,' for 'suspender' is the magic word. Consider what we can predict about his probable verbal behavior if we take this (a) opaquely and (b) transparently. And, of course, the same sorts of points apply, *mutatis mutandis,* to the prediction of *non*-verbal behavior).

Ontologically, transparent readings are stronger than opaque ones; for example, the former license existential inferences, which the latter do not. But psychologically, opaque readings are stronger than transparent ones; they tell us more about the character of the mental causes of behavior. The representational theory of mind offers an explanation of this anomaly. Opaque ascriptions are true in virtue of the way that the agent represents the objects of his wants (intentions, beliefs, etc.) *to himself.* And, by assumption, such representations function in the causation of the behaviors that the agent produces. So, for example, to say that it's true *opaquely* that Oedipus did such-and-such because he wanted to marry Jocasta, is to say something like (though not, perhaps, *very* like) [11]: "Oedipus said to himself, 'I want to marry Jocasta,' and his so saying was among the causes of his behavior." Whereas to say (only) that it's true transparently that O. wanted to marry J. is to say no more than that among the causes of his behavior was O's saying to himself, 'I want to marry . . .' where the blank was filled by *some* expression that denotes J. [12*] But now, what O. *does,* how he in the proprietary sense behaves, will depend on which description he (literally) had in mind. [13*] If it's 'Jocasta,' courtship behavior follows *ceteris paribus.* Whereas, if it's 'my Mum,' we have the situation towards the end of the play and Oedipus at Colonus eventually ensues.

I dearly wish that I could leave this topic here, because it would be very convenient to be able to say, without qualification,

what I strongly implied above: the opaque readings of propositional attitude ascriptions tell us how people represent the objects
of their propositional attitudes. What one would like to say, in
particular, is that if two people are identically related to formally
identical mental representations, then they are in opaquely type
identical mental states. This would be convenient because it
yields a succinct and gratifying characterization of what a computational cognitive psychology is about: such a psychology studies
propositional attitudes opaquely taxonomized.

I think, in fact, that this is *roughly* the right thing to say, since
what I think is *exactly* right is that the construal of propositional
attitudes which such a psychology renders is non-transparent. (It's
non-transparency that's crucial in all the examples we have been
considering). The trouble is that non-transparency isn't quite the
same notion as opacity, as we shall now see.

The question before us is: 'What are the relations between the
pre-theoretic notion of type identity of mental states opaquely
construed and the notion of type identity of mental states that
you get from a theory which strictly honors the formality condition?' And the answer is: complicated. For one thing, it's not
clear that we have *a* pretheoretic notion of the opaque reading
of a propositional attitude ascription: I doubt that the two standard tests for opacity (failure of existential generalization and
failure of substitutivity of identicals) so much as pick out the
same class of cases. But what's more important are the following
considerations. While it's notorious that extensionally identical
thoughts may be opaquely type distinct (for example, thoughts
about the Morning Star and thoughts about the Evening Star),
there are nevertheless some semantic conditions on opaque type
identification. In particular:

    (a)   there are some cases of formally distinct but coextensive token
           thoughts which count as tokens of the same (opaque) type (and
           hence as identical in content at least on one way of individuating
           contents); and

    (b)   *non*-coextensive thoughts are *ipso facto* type distinct (and differ in
           content at least on one way of individuating contents.)

Cases of type (a): (1) I think I'm sick and you think I'm sick.
What's running through my head is 'I'm sick;' what's running
through your head is 'he's sick.' But we are both having thoughts
of the same (opaque) type (and hence of the same content.)

(2) You think: 'that one looks edible;' I think: 'this one looks

edible.' Our thoughts are opaquely type identical if we are thinking about the same one.

It connects with the existence of such cases that pronouns and demonstratives are typically (perhaps invariably) construed as referring, even when they occur in what are otherwise opaque constructions. So, for example, it seems to me that I can't report Macbeth's hallucination by saying: "Macbeth thinks that's a dagger" if Macbeth is staring at nothing at all. Which is to say that "that's a dagger" doesn't report Macbeth's mental state even though "that's a dagger" may be precisely what is running through Macbeth's head (precisely the representation his relation to which is constitutive of his belief).

Cases of type (b): (1) Suppose that Sam feels faint and Misha knows he does. Then what's running through Misha's head may be 'he feels faint.' Suppose too that Misha feels faint and Alfred knows he does. Then what's running through Alfred's head, too, may be 'he feels faint.' I have no, or rather no univocal, inclination to say, in this case, that Alfred and Misha are having type identical thoughts even though the principle type of individuation is, by assumption, opaque and even though Alfred and Misha have the same things running through their heads. But if this is right, then formal identity of mental representations cannot be sufficient for type identity of opaquely taxonomized mental states.[14*]

(2) Suppose that there are two Lake Eries (two bodies of water so-called). Consider two tokens of the thought 'Lake Erie is wet,' one of which is, intuitively speaking, about the Lake Erie in North America and one of which is about the other one. Here again, I'm inclined to say that the aboriginal, uncorrupted, pre-theoretical notion of type-wise same thought wants these to be tokens of *different* thoughts and takes these thoughts to differ in content. In this case, though, as in the others, I think there's also a counter-vailing inclination to say that they count as type identical—and as identical in content—for some relevant purposes and in some relevant respects. How like aboriginal, uncorrupted, pre-theoretical intuition!

I think, in short, that the intuitive opaque taxonomy is actually what you might call 'semi-transparent.' On the one hand, certain conditions on co-reference are in force (Misha's belief that he's ill is type distinct from Sam's belief that *he's* ill, and my thought *this is edible* may be type identical to your thought *that is edible*). On the other hand, you don't get free substitution of co-referring expressions (beliefs about the Morning Star are type distinct from beliefs about the Evening Star) and existential generalization doesn't go through for beliefs about Santa Claus.

Apparently, then, the notion of same mental state that we get from a theory which honors the formality condition is related to, but not identical to, the notion of same mental state that unreconstructed intuition provides for opaque construals. And it would certainly be reasonable to ask whether we actually need both. I think the answer is probably: yes, if we want to capture *all* the intuitions. For if we restrict ourselves to either one of the taxonomies, we get consequences that we don't like. On the one hand, if we taxonomize *purely* formally, we get identity of belief compatible with difference of truth value. (Misha's belief that he's ill will be type identical to Sam's belief that *he's* ill, but one may be true while the other is false.) On the other hand, if we taxonomize solely according to the pre-theoretic criteria, we get into trouble with the idea that people act out of their beliefs and desires. We need, in particular, some taxonomy according to which Sam and Misha have the *same* belief in order to explain why it is that they exhibit the same behaviors. It is, after all, *part* of the pre-theoretic notion of belief that difference in belief ought *ceteris paribus* to show up in behavior *somewhere* ('*ceteris paribus*' here means 'given relevant identities among other mental states'), whereas, it's possible to construct cases where differences like the one between Misha's belief and Sam's can't show up in behavior even in principle (see note 14, above). What we have, in short, is a tension between a partially semantic taxonomy and an entirely functional one, and the recommended solution is to use both.

Having said all this, I now propose largely to ignore it and use the term 'opaque taxonomy' for principles of type individuation according to which Misha and Sam are in the same mental state when each believes himself to be ill. When I need to distinguish this sense of opaque taxonomy from the pre-theoretic one, I'll talk about *full* opacity and fully opaque type identification.

My claim has been that, in doing our psychology, we want to attribute mental states fully opaquely because it's the fully opaque reading which tells us what the agent has in mind, and it's what the agent has in mind that causes his behavior. I now need to say something about how, precisely, all this is supposed to constitute an argument for the formality condition.

Point one: it's just as well that it's the fully opaque construal of mental states that we need, since, patently, that's the only one that the formality condition permits us. This is because the formality condition prohibits taxonomizing psychological states by reference to the semantic properties of mental representations and, at bottom, transparency is a semantic (viz. non-formal; viz. non-syntactic) notion. The point is sufficiently obvious: if we count the belief that the Evening Star is F is (type) identical to the belief that the Morning Star is F, that must be because of the co-reference of such expressions as 'The Morning Star' and 'The Evening Star.' But co-reference is a semantic property, and not one which could conceivably have a formal Doppelgänger; it's inconceivable, in particular, that there should be a system of mental representations such that, in the general case, co-referring expressions are formally identical in that system. (This might be true for God's mind, but not, surely, for anybody else's [and not for God's either unless he is an Extensionalist; which I doubt.]) So, if we want transparent taxonomies of mental states, we will have to give up the formality condition. So, it's a good thing for the computational theory of the mind that it's not transparent taxonomies that we want.

What's harder to argue for (but might, nevertheless, be true) is point two: that the formality condition *can* be honored by a theory which taxonomizes mental states according to their content. For, barring caveats previously reviewed, it may be that mental states are distinct in content only if they are relations to formally distinct mental representations; in effect, that aspects of content can be reconstructed as aspects of form, at least insofar as appeals to content figure in accounts of the mental causation of behavior. The main thing to be said in favor of this speculation is that it allows us to explain, within the context of the representational theory of mind, how beliefs of different content *can* have different behavioral effects, even when the beliefs are transparently type identical. The form of explanation goes: it's because different content implies formally distinct internal representations (via the formality condition) and formally distinct internal representations can be functionally different—can differ in their causal role. Whereas, to put it mildly, it's hard to see how internal representations could differ in causal role *unless* they differed in form.

To summarize: transparent taxonomy is patently incompatible

with the formality condition; whereas taxonomy in respect of content *may* be compatible with the formality condition, plus or minus a bit. That taxonomy in respect of content *is* compatible with the formality condition, plus or minus a bit, is perhaps *the* basic idea of modern cognitive theory. The representational theory of mind and the computational theory of mind merge here for, on the one hand, it's claimed that psychological states differ in content only if they are relations to type-distinct mental representations, and, on the other, it's claimed that only formal properties of mental representations contribute to their type individuation for the purposes of theories of mind/body interaction. Or, to put it the other way 'round, it's allowed that mental representations affect behavior in virtue of their content, but it's maintained that mental representations are distinct in content only if they are also distinct in form. The first clause is required to make it plausible that mental states are relations to mental representations and the second is required to make it plausible that mental processes are computations. (Computations just *are* processes in which representations have their causal consequences in virtue of their form.) By thus exploiting the notions of content and computation *together,* a cognitive theory seeks to connect the *intensional* properties of mental states with their *causal* properties vis-à-vis behavior. Which is, of course, exactly what a theory of the mind ought to do.

As must be evident from the preceding, I'm partial to programmatic arguments: ones which seek to infer the probity of a conceptual apparatus from the fact that it plays a role in some prima facie plausible research enterprise. So, in particular, I've argued that a taxonomy of mental states which honors the formality condition seems to be required by theories of the mental causation of behavior, and that that's a reason for taking such taxonomies very seriously.

But there lurks, within the general tradition of representational theories of mind, a deeper intuition: that it is not only *advisable* but actually *mandatory* to assume that mental processes have access only to formal (non-semantic) properties of mental representations, that the contrary view is not only empirically fruitless but also conceptually unsound. I find myself in sympathy with this intuition, though I'm uncertain precisely how the arguments ought to go. What follows is just a sketch.

I'll begin with a version that I *don't* like; an epistemological version.

> Look, it makes no *sense* to suppose that mental operations could apply to mental representations in virtue of (for example) the truth or falsity of the latter. For, consider: truth value is a matter of correspondence to the way the world is. To determine the truth value of a belief would therefore involve what I'll call 'directly comparing' the belief with the world; that is, comparing it with the way the world *is*, not just with the way the world is represented as being. And the representational theory of mind says that we have access to the world only *via* the ways in which we represent it. There is, as it were, nothing that corresponds to looking around (behind? through? what's the right metaphor?) one's beliefs to catch a glimpse of the things they represent. Mental processes can, in short, compare representations, but they can't compare representations with what they're representations of. Hence mental processes can't have access to the truth value of representations or, *mutatis mutandis,* to whether they denote. Hence the formality condition.

This line of argument could certainly be made a good deal more precise. It has been in, for example, some of the recent work of Nelson Goodman.[15] For present purposes, however, I'm content to leave it *im*precise so long as it sounds familiar. For, I suspect that all versions of the argument suffer from a common deficiency: they assume that you can't run a *correspondence* theory of truth together with a *coherence* theory of evidence. Whereas, I see nothing compelling in the inference from 'truth is a matter of the correspondence of a belief with the way the world is' to '*ascertaining* truth is a matter of "directly comparing" a belief with the way the world is.' Perhaps we ascertain the truth of our beliefs by comparing them with one another, appealing to inference to the best explanation whenever we need to do so.

Anyhow, it would be nice to have a *non*-epistemological defense of the formality condition; one which saves the intuition that there's something conceptually wrong with its denial but doesn't acquire skeptical/relativistic commitments with which the traditional epistemic versions of the argument have been encumbered. Here goes:

Suppose, just for convenience, that mental processes are algorithms. So, we have rules for the transformation of mental representations, and we have the mental representations which constitute their ranges and domains. Think of the rules as being like hypothetical imperatives; they have antecedents which specify conditions on mental representation, and they have consequents which specify what is to happen if the antecedents are satisfied. And now consider rules *a* and *b*.

(a) If it's the case that P, do such and such.
(b) If you believe it's the case that P, do such and such.

Notice, to begin with, that the compliance conditions on these injunctions are quite different. In particular, in the case where P is *false but believed true,* compliance with *b* consists in doing such and such, whereas compliance with *a* consists in *not* doing it. But despite this difference in compliance conditions, there's something *very* peculiar (perhaps *pragmatically* peculiar, whatever precisely that may mean) about supposing that an organism might have different ways of going about attempting to comply with *a* and *b*. The peculiarity is patent in *c:*

(c) Do such and such if it's the case that P, *whether or not* you believe that it's the case that P.[16*]

To borrow a joke from Professor Robert Jagger, *c* is a little like the advice: 'buy low, sell high.' One knows just what it would be *like* to comply with either, but somehow knowing that doesn't help much.

The idea is this: when one has done what one can to establish that the belief that P is warranted, one has done what one can to establish that the antecedent of *a* is satisfied. And, conversely, when one has done what one can do to establish that the antecedent of *a* is satisfied, one has done what one can to establish the warrant of the belief that P. Now, I suppose that the following is at least *close* to being true: to have the belief that P is to have the belief that the belief that P is warranted; and conversely, to have the belief that the belief that P is warranted is to have the belief that P. And the upshot of *this* is just the formality condition all over again. Given that mental operations have access to the fact that P is believed (and hence that the belief that P is believed to be warranted, and hence that the belief that the belief that P is warranted is believed to be warranted, . . . etc.) there's nothing further left to do; there is nothing that corresponds to the notion of a mental operation which one undertakes to perform just in case one's belief that P is *true.*

This isn't, by the way, any form of skepticism, as can be seen from the following: there's nothing wrong with Jones having one mental operation which he undertakes to perform if it's the case that P and another *quite different* mental operation which he undertakes to perform if *Smith* ($\neq$ Jones) believes that it's the case that P. (Cf. 'I promise . . . though I don't intend to . . .' vs. 'I promise . . . though Smith doesn't intend to . . .'). There's a first person/third person asymmetry here, but it doesn't impugn the semantic distinction between 'P is true' and 'P is believed true.' The suggestion is that it's the tacit recognition of this pragmatic asymmetry that accounts for the traditional hunch that you can't both identify mental operations with transformations on mental representations and at the same time flout the formality condition; that the representational theory of mind and the computational theory of mind are somehow conjoint options.

So much, then, for the formality condition and the psychological tradition which accepts it. What about Naturalism? The first point is that none of the arguments *for* a rational psychology is, in and of itself, an argument *against* a Naturalistic psychology. As I remarked above, to deny that mental operations have access to the semantic properties of mental representations is *not* to deny that mental representations *have* semantic properties. On the contrary, beliefs are *just* the kinds of things which exhibit truth and denotation, and the Naturalist proposes to make science out of the organism/environment relations which (presumably) fix these properties. Why, indeed, should he not?

This all *seems* very reasonable. Nevertheless, I now wish to argue that a computational psychology is the only one that we are likely to get; that qua research strategy, the attempt to construct a *naturalistic* psychology is very likely to prove fruitless. I think that the basis for such an argument is already to be found in the literature, where it takes the form of a (possibly inadvertent) reductio ad absurdum of the contrary view.

Consider, to begin with, a distinction that Professor Hilary Putnam introduces in "The Meaning of 'Meaning'"[17] between what he calls "psychological states in the wide sense" and "psychological states in the narrow sense." A psychological state in the *narrow* sense is one the ascription of which does not "[presuppose] the existence of any individual other than the subject to whom that state is ascribed" (p. 136). All others are psychological states in the wide sense. So, for example, *x's jealousy of y* is a schema for expressions that denote psychological states in the wide sense, since such expressions presuppose the existence not only of the *x*s who are in the states, but also of the *y*s who are its objects. Putnam remarks that methodological solipsism (the phrase, by the way, is his) can be viewed as the requirement that

only psychological states in the narrow sense are allowed as con-
structs in psychological theories.

But it is perhaps Putnam's main point that there are at least
some scientific purposes (for example, semantics and accounts of
inter-theoretical reference) which demand the wide construal. Here,
rephrased slightly, is the sort of example that Putnam finds
persuasive.

There is a planet (call it 'Yon') where things are very much as
they are here. In particular, by a cosmic accident, some of the
people on Yon speak a dialect indistinguishable from English and
live in an urban conglomerate indistinguishable from the Greater
Boston Area. Still more, for every one of our Greater Bostonians,
there is a Doppelgänger on Yon who has precisely the same neuro-
logical structure down to and including microparticles. We can
assume that so long as we're construing 'psychological state' narrowly, this latter condition guarantees type identity of our psychological states with theirs.

However, Putnam argues, it doesn't guarantee that there is a
corresponding identity of psychological states, hither and Yon,
if we construe 'psychological state' *widely*. Suppose that there is
this difference between Yon and Earth; whereas, over here, the
stuff we call 'water' has the atomic structure H_2O, it turns out
that the stuff that they call 'water' over there has the atomic
structure XYZ ($\neq H_2O$). And now, consider the mental state
thinking about water. The idea is that, so long as we construe that
state widely, it's one that we, but not our Doppelgängers, can
reasonably aspire to. For, construed widely, one is thinking about
water only if it is water that one is thinking about. But it's water
that one's thinking about only if it is H_2O that one's thinking
about; water *is* H_2O. But since, by assumption, they never think
about H_2O over Yon, it follows that there's at least one wide
psychological state that we're often in and they never are, however neurophysiologically like us they are, and however much our
narrow psychological states converge with theirs.

Moreover, if we try to say what they speak about, refer to,
mention, etc.—if, in short, we try to supply a semantics for their
dialect—we will have to mention XYZ, not H_2O. Hence it would
be wrong, at least on Putnam's intuitions, to say that they have a
word for water. A fortiori, the chemists who work in what they
call 'M.I.T.' don't have theories about *water,* even though what
runs through their head when they talk about XYZ may be
identical to what runs through our heads when we talk about

H_2O. The situation is analogous to the one which arises for demonstratives and token reflexives, as Putnam insightfully points out.

Well, what are we to make of this? Is it an argument against methodological solipsism? And, if so, is it a *good* argument against methodological solipsism?

To begin with, Putnam's distinction between psychological states in the narrow and wide sense looks to be very intimately related to the traditional distinction between psychological state ascriptions opaquely and transparently construed. I'm a bit wary about this, since what Putnam *says* about wide ascriptions is only that they "presuppose the existence" of objects other than the ascribee; and, of course, *a believes Fb and b exists* does not entail *b is such that a believes F of him,* or even *∃x (a believes Fx)*. Moreover, the failure of such entailments is notoriously important in discussions of quantifying in. For all that, however, I don't *think* that it's Putnam's intention to exploit the difference between the existential generalization test for transparency and the presupposition of existence test for wideness. On the contrary, the burden of Putnam's argument seems to be precisely that 'John believes (widely) that water is F' is true only if water (viz. H_2O) is such that John believes it's F. It's thus unclear to me why Putnam gives the weaker condition on wideness when it appears to be the stronger one that does the work. [18*]

But whatever the case may be with the wide sense of belief, it's pretty clear that the narrow sense must be (what I've been calling) fully opaque. This is because it is only full opacity which allows type identity of beliefs that have different truth conditions (Sam's belief that he's ill with Misha's belief that *he* is; Yon beliefs about XYZ with hither beliefs about H_2O). I want to emphasize this correspondence between narrowness and full opacity, and not just in aid of terminological parsimony. Putnam sometimes writes as though he takes the methodological commitment to a psychology of narrow mental states to be a sort of vulgar prejudice: "Making this assumption is, of course, adopting a *restrictive program*—a program which deliberately limits the scope and nature of psychology to fit certain mentalistic preconceptions or, in some cases, to fit an idealistic reconstruction of knowledge and the world" (p. 137). But in light of what we've said so far, it should be clear that this is a methodology with malice aforethought. Narrow psychological states are those individuated in light of the formality condition; viz. without reference to such semantic properties as truth and reference. And honoring the formality condition is part and parcel of the attempt to provide a theory which explains (a) how the belief that the Morning Star is F could be different from the belief that the Evening Star is F despite the well-known astronomical facts; and (b) how the behavioral effects of believing that the Morning Star is F could be different from those of believing that the Evening Star is F, astronomy once again apparently to the contrary notwithstanding. Putnam is, of course, dubious about this whole project: "The three centuries of failure of mentalistic psychology is tremendous evidence against this procedure, in my opinion" (p. 137). I suppose this is intended to include everybody from Locke and Kant to Freud and Chomsky. I should have such failures.

So much for background. I now need an argument to show that a naturalistic psychology (a psychology of mental states transparently individuated, hence, presumably, a psychology of mental states in the wide sense) is, for practical purposes, out of the question. So far as I can see, however, Putnam has given that argument. For, consider: a naturalistic psychology is a theory of organism/environment transactions. So, to stick to Putnam's example, a naturalistic psychology would have to find some stuff S and some relation R, such that one's narrow thought that water is wet is a thought about S in virtue of the fact that one bears R to S. Well, which stuff? The natural thing to say would be: 'Water, of course.' Notice, however, that if Putnam is right, it may not even be true that the narrow thought that water is wet is a thought about water; it won't be true of tokens of that thought which occur on Yon. Whether the narrow thought that water is wet is about water depends on whether it's about H_2O; and whether it's about H_2O depends on 'how science turns out'—viz. on what chemistry is true. (Similarly, mutatis mutandis, 'water' refers to water is not, on this view, a truth of any branch of linguistics; it's chemists who tell us what it is that 'water' refers to.) Surely, however, characterizing the objects of thought is methodologically prior to characterizing the causal chains that link thoughts to their objects. But the theory which characterizes the objects of thought is the theory of everything; it's all of science. Hence, the methodological moral of Putnam's analysis seems to be: the naturalistic psychologists will inherit the Earth, but only after everybody else is finished with it. No doubt it's all right to have a research strategy that says 'wait awhile.' But who wants to wait forever?

This sort of argument isn't novel. Indeed, it was anticipated by Bloomfield. Bloomfield argues that, for all practical purposes, you can't do semantics. The reason you can't is that to do semantics you have to be able to say, for example, what 'salt' refers to. But what 'salt' refers to is NaCl, and that's a bit of chemistry, not linguistics:

> The situations which prompt people to utter speech include every object and happening in their universe. In order to give a scientifically accurate definition of meaning for every form of a language, we would have to have a scientifically accurate knowledge of everything in the speaker's world. The actual extent of human knowledge is very small compared to this. We can define the meaning of a speech-form accurately when this meaning has to do with some matter of which we possess scientific knowledge. We can define the names of minerals, as when we say that the ordinary meaning of the English word *salt* is 'sodium chloride (NaCl),' and we can define the names of plants or animals by means of the technical terms of botany or zoology, but we have no precise way of defining words like *love* or *hate*, which concern situations that have not been accurately classified . . . The statement of meanings is therefore the weak point in language-study, and will remain so until knowledge advances very far beyond its present state.[19]

It seems to me as though Putnam ought to endorse all of this *including the moral:* the distinction between wanting a naturalistic semantics (psychology) and not wanting any is real but academic.[20*]

The argument just given depends, however, on accepting Putnam's analysis of his example. But suppose that one's intuitions run the other way. Then one is at liberty to argue like this:

1. They do too have water over Yon; all Putnam's example shows is that there could be two kinds of water, our kind (=H_2O) and their kind (=XYZ).

2. Hence, Yon tokens of the thought that water is wet are thoughts about water after all;

3. Hence, the way chemistry turns out is irrelevant to whether thoughts about water are about water.

4. Hence, the naturalistic psychology of thought need not wait upon the sciences of the objects of thought;

5. Hence, a naturalistic psychology may be in the cards after all.

Since the premises of this sort of reply may be tempting (since, indeed, they may be *true*), it's worth presenting a version of the argument which doesn't depend on intuitions about what XYZ is.

A naturalistic psychology would specify the relations that hold between an organism and an object in its environment when the one is thinking about the other. Now, think how such a theory would have to go. Since it would have to define its generalizations over mental states on the one hand and environmental entities on the other, it will need, in particular, some canonical way of referring to the latter. Well, *which* way? If one assumes that what makes my thought about Robin Roberts a thought *about Robin Roberts* is some causal connection between the two or us, then we'll need a description of RR such that the causal connection obtains in virtue of his satisfying that description. And *that* means, presumably, that we'll need a description under which the relation between him and me instantiates a law.

Generally, then, a naturalistic psychology would attempt to specify environmental objects in a vocabulary such that environment/organism relations are law-instantiating when so described. But here's the depressing consequence again: we have no access to such a vocabulary prior to the elaboration (completion?) of the non-psychological sciences. 'What Granny likes with her herring' isn't, for example, a description under which salt is law-instantiating; nor, presumably, is 'salt.' What we need is something like 'NaCl,' and descriptions like 'NaCl' are available only *after* we've done our chemistry. What this comes down to is that, at a minimum, 'x's being F causally explains . . .' can be true only when 'F' expresses nomologically necessary properties of the xs. Heaven knows it's hard to say what *that* means, but it presumably rules out both 'Salt's being what Granny likes with herring . . .' and 'Salt's being salt . . . ;' the former for want of being necessary, and the latter for want of being nomological. I take it, moreover, that Bloomfield is right when he says (a) that we don't know relevant nomologically necessary properties of most of the things we can refer to (think about) and (b) that it isn't the linguist's (psychologist's) job to find them out.

Here's still another way to put this sort of argument. The way Bloomfield states his case invites the question: "Why *should* a semanticist want a definition of 'salt' that is 'scientifically accurate' in your sense? Why wouldn't a 'nominal' definition do?" There is, I think, some point to such a query. For example, as Hartry Field has pointed out,[21] it wouldn't make much difference to the way that truth-conditional semantics goes if we were to say only "'salt' refers to whatever it refers to." All we need for this sort of semantics is some way or other of referring to the extension of 'salt'; we don't, in particular, need a "scientifically accurate" way. It's therefore pertinent to do what Bloomfield notably does not: distinguish between the goals of *semantics* and those of a naturalistic psychology of language. The latter, by assumption, purports to explicate the organism/environment transactions in virtue of which relations like reference hold. It therefore requires, at a minimum, lawlike generalizations of the (approximate) form: *X's utterance of 'salt' refers to salt if X bears relation R to* Δ. Since this whole thing *is* supposed to be lawlike, what goes in for 'Δ' must be a projectable characterization of the extension of 'salt.' But in general we discover which descriptions are projectable only a posteriori, in light of how the sciences (including the non-psychological sciences) turn out. We are back where we started. Looked at this way, the moral is that we can do (certain kinds of) semantics if we have a way of referring to the extension of 'salt.' But we can't do the naturalistic psychology of reference unless we have some way of saying what salt *is;* which of its properties determine its causal relations.

It's important to emphasize that these sorts of arguments do *not* apply against the research program embodied in 'Rational psychology'—viz. to the program that envisions a psychology that honors the formality condition. The problem we've been facing is: under what description does the object of thought enter into scientific generalizations about the relations between thoughts and their objects? It looks as though the naturalist is going to have to say: under a description that is law instantiating—for example, under physical description. But the rational psychologist has a quite different answer. What *he* wants is *whatever description the organism has in mind* when it thinks about the object of thought, construing 'thinks about' fully opaquely. So for a theory of psychological states narrowly construed, we want such descriptions of Venus as, e.g., 'The Morning Star,' 'The Evening Star,' etc., for it is these sorts of descriptions which we presumably entertain when we think that the Morning Star is *F*. In particular, it is our relation to these sorts of descriptions which determine what psychological state type we're in insofar as the goal in taxonomizing psychological states is explaining how they affect behavior.

Final point under the general head: the hopelessness of naturalistic psychology. Practicing naturalistic psychologists have been at least dimly aware all along of the sort of bind that they're in. So, for example, the 'physical specification of the stimulus' is just about invariably announced as a requirement upon adequate formulations of S-R generalizations. We can now see why. Suppose, wildly contrary to fact, that there exists a human population (for example, English speakers) in which pencils are, in the technical sense of the notion, discriminative stimuli controlling the verbal response 'pencil.' The point is that even if some such generalization were true, it wouldn't be among those enunciated by a naturalistic psychology; the generalizations of naturalistic psychology are presumably supposed to be nomological, and there aren't any *laws* about pencils *qua* pencils. That is, expressions like 'pencil' presumably occur in no true, lawlike sentences. Of course, there presumably is *some* description in virtue of which pencils fall under the organism/environment laws of a naturalistic psychology, and everybody (except, possibly, Gibson) has always assumed that those descriptions are, approximately, physical descriptions. Hence, the naturalist's demand, perfectly warranted by his lights, that the stimulus should be physically specified.

But though their theory has been consistent, their practice has uniformly not. In practice, and barring the elaborately circumscribed cases that psychophysics studies, the requirement that the stimulus be physically specified has been ignored by just about *all* practitioners. And, indeed, they were well advised to ignore it; how else could they get on with their job? If they really had to wait for the physicists to determine the description(s) under which pencils are law-instantiators, how would the psychology of pencils get off the ground?

So far as I can see, there are really only two ways out of this dilemma:

1. We can fudge, the way that learning theorists usually do. That is, we can 'read' the description of the stimulus from the character of the organism's response. In point of historical fact, this has led to a kind of naturalistic psychology which is merely a solemn paraphrase of what everybody's grandmother knows: for example, to saying 'pencils are discriminative stimuli for the utterance of "pencil"' where Granny would have said 'pencil' refers to pencils. I take it that Chomsky's review of *Verbal Behavior* demonstrated, once and for all, the fatuity of this course. What *would* be interesting—what would have surprised Grandmother—is a generalization of the form Δ *is the discriminative stimulus for utterances of 'pencil'* where Δ is a description that picks out pencils in some projectable vocabulary (for example, in the vocabulary of physics). Does anybody suppose that such descriptions are likely to be forthcoming in, say, the *next* three hundred years?

2. The other choice is to try for a computational psychology—which is, of course, the burden of my plaint. On this view, what we can reasonably hope for is a theory of mental states fully opaquely type individuated. We can try to say what the mental representation is, and what the relation to a mental representation is, such that one believes that the Morning Star is F in virtue of bearing the latter to the former. And we can try to say how that representation, or that relation, or both, differ from the representation and the relation constitutive of believing that the Evening Star is F. A naturalistic psychology, by contrast, remains a sort of ideal of pure reason; there must *be* such a psychology, since, presumably, we do sometimes think of Venus and, presumably, we do so in virtue of a causal relation between it and us. But there's no practical hope of making science out of this relation. And, of course, for methodology, practical hope is *everything*.

One final point, and then I'm through. Methodological solipsism isn't, of course solipsism *tout court*. It's not part of the enterprise to assert, or even suggest, that you and I are actually in the situation of Winograd's computer. Heaven only knows what relation between me and Robin Roberts makes it possible for me to think of him (refer to him, etc.), and I've been doubting the practical possibility of a science whose generalizations that relation instantiates. But I *don't* doubt that there *is* such a relation or that I do sometimes think of him. Still more: I have reasons not to doubt it; precisely the sorts of reasons I'd supply if I were asked to justify my knowledge claims about his pitching record. In short: it's true that Roberts won 28 and it's true that I know that he did, and nothing in the preceding tends to impugn these truths. (Or, contrariwise, if he didn't and I'm mistaken, then the reasons for my mistake are philosophically boring; they're biographical, not epistemological or ontological.) My point, then, is *of course* not that solipsism is true; it's just that truth, reference, and the rest of the semantic notions aren't psychological categories. What they are is: they're modes of *Dasein*. I don't know what *Dasein* is, but I'm sure that there's lots of it around, and I'm sure that you and I and Cincinnati have all got it. What more do you want?

Bibliography of Works Cited

HUSSERL'S WRITINGS

Husserl, E., *Analysen zur passiven Synthesis. Aus Vorlesungs- und Forschungsmanuskripten, 1918-1926*, ed. M. Fleischer, *Husserliana*, vol. 11 (The Hague: Nijhoff, 1966).

————, *Aufsätze und Rezensionen (1890-1910)*, *Husserliana*, vol. 22 (The Hague: Nijhoff, 1979).

————, *Briefe an Roman Ingarden* (The Hague: Nijhoff, 1968).

————, *Cartesian Meditations*, trans. D. Cairns (The Hague: Nijhoff, 1960).

————, *Erfahrung und Urteil* (Hamburg: Claassen & Goverts, 1948); English version, *Experience and Judgment*, trans. J. Churchill and K. Ameriks (Evanston: Northwestern Univ. Press, 1973).

————, "Der Folgerungskalkül und die Inhaltslogik," *Vierteljahrsschrift für wissenschaftliche Philosophie*, 15 (1891).

————, *Formal and Transcendental Logic*, trans. D. Cairns (The Hague: Nijhoff, 1969).

————, *The Idea of Phenomenology*, trans. W. Alston and G. Nakhnikian (The Hague: Nijhoff, 1964).

————, *Ideen zu einer reinen Phänomenologie und phänomenologischen Philosophie, I, Husserliana* (The Hague: Nijhoff, 1950); English version, *Ideas: General Introduction to Pure Phenomenology*, trans. W. R. Boyce Gibson (New York: Collier Books, 1972).

Husserl, E., *Ideen, III* (The Hague: Nijhoff, 1952).

————, *Die Krisis der Europäischen Wissenschaften und die transzendentale Phänomenologie, Husserliana*, vol. 6 (The Hague: Nijhoff, 1954); English version, *The Crisis of European Sciences and Transcendental Phenomenology*, trans. D. Carr (Evanston: Northwestern Univ. Press, 1970).

————, *Logische Untersuchungen* (Halle: Niemeyer, 1913); English version, *Logical Investigations*, trans. J. Findlay (New York: Humanities Press, 1970).

————, "Noema und Sinn," unpublished manuscript, Husserl Archives.

————, *The Paris Lectures*, trans. P. Koestenbaum (The Hague: Nijhoff, 1967).

————, "Persönliche Aufzeichnungen," ed. W. Biemel, in *Philosophy and Phenomenological Research*, 16 (1956).

————, *Phänomenologische Psychologie, Husserliana*, vol. 9 (The Hague: Nijhoff, 1962).

————, *The Phenomenology of Internal Time-Consciousness*, trans. J. Churchill (Bloomington: Indiana Univ. Press, 1964).

————, "Rezension von Schröders *Vorlesungen über die Algebra der Logik*," *Göttingische gelehrte Anzeigen*, 1, (1891).

HISTORICAL BACKGROUND

Angelelli, I., *Studies on Gottlob Frege and Traditional Philosophy* (Dordrecht: Reidel, 1967).

Aquila, R., "Husserl and Frege on Meaning," *Journal of the History of Philosophy* (1974).

Arnaud, R., "Brentanist Relations," in K. Lehrer, ed., *Analysis and Metaphysics: Essays in Honor of R. M. Chisholm*, Philosophical Studies Series in Philosophy, vol. 4 (Dordrecht: Reidel, 1975).

Brentano, F., *Psychologie vom empirischen Standpunkt*, in *Philosophische Bibliothek*, vol. II (Hamburg: Meiner, 1874).

————, *The True and the Evident*, ed. O. Kraus (London: Routledge & Kegan Paul, 1966).

Chisholm, R., ed., *Realism and the Background of Phenomenology*. (Glencoe: Free Press, 1960).

Føllesdal, D., *Husserl und Frege* (Oslo: Aschehoug, 1958).

Frege, G., "Der Gedanke," in *Beiträge zur Philosophie des deutschen Idealismus*, vol. I (1918); English version, "The Thought: A Logical Inquiry," in P. Strawson, ed., *Philosophical Logic* (Oxford: Oxford Univ. Press, 1967).

————, *Kleine Schriften*, ed. I. Angelelli (Hildesheim: Olms, 1967).

————, "Kritische Beleuchtung einiger Punkte in E. Schröders *Vorlesungen über die Algebra der Logik, Archiv für systematische Philosophie*, I (1895).

————, *Nachgelassene Schriften* (Hamburg: Meiner, 1969).

————, "Rezension von Dr. E. Husserls *Philosophie der Arithmetik*," in *Zeitschrift für Philosophie und philosophische Kritik*, 103 (1894); English version, "Review of Dr. E. Husserl's *Philosophy of Arithmetic*," trans. E. Kluge, *Mind*, 81 (1972).

————, *Translations from the Philosophical Writings of Gottlob Frege*, ed. P. Geach and M. Black (Oxford: Blackwell, 1960).

————, "Über den Zweck der Begriffsschrift," *Jenaische Zeitschrift für Naturwissenschaft*, 16 (1883).

————, "Über formale Theorien der Arithmetik," in *Sitzungsberichte der Jenaischen Gesellschaft für Medizin und Naturwissenschaft für das Jahr 1885* (Jena: Fischer, 1885/86).

————, "Über Sinn und Bedeutung," *Zeitschrift für Philosophie und philosophische Kritik*, 100 (1892); English version, "On Sense and Reference," in P. Geach and M. Black, eds., *Translations from the Philosophical Writings of Gottlob Frege* (Oxford: Oxford Univ. Press, 1966).

Gurwitsch, A., "William James' Theory of the 'Transitive Parts' of the Stream of Consciousness," *Philosophy and Phenomenological Research*, 3 (1943).

James, W., *Principles of Psychology* (New York: Dover, 1890).

Kern, I., *Husserl und Kant: Eine Untersuchung über Husserls Verhältnis zu Kant und zum Neukantianismus, Phenomenologica*, 16 (The Hague: Nijhoff, 1964).

Mohanty, J., "Frege-Husserl Correspondence," *Southwestern Journal of Philosophy*, 5 (1974).

Perry, J., "Frege on Demonstratives," *Philosophical Review*, 86 (1977).

Schumann, K., *Husserl-Chronik: Denk- und Lebensweg Edmund Husserls, Husserliana*, vol. 1 (The Hague: Nijhoff, 1977).

Sluga, H., "Frege's Alleged Realism," *Inquiry*, 20 (1977).

Solomon, R., "Sense and Essence: Frege and Husserl," *International Philosophical Quarterly*, 10 (1970).

Thiel, C., *Sense and Reference in Frege's Logic* (Dordrecht: Reidel, 1968).

BASIC CONCEPTS AND THEORY

Ameriks, K., "Husserl's Realism," *The Philosophical Review*, 86 (1977).

Cairns, D., "An Approach to Phenomenology," in *Philosophical Essays in Memory of Edmund Husserl*, ed. M. Farber (Cambridge: Harvard Univ. Press, 1968).

Dreyfus, H., *Husserl's Phenomenology of Perception: From Transcendental to Existential Phenomenology*, doctoral dissertation, Harvard University, 1963.

Findlay, J., "Phenomenology and the Meaning of Realism," in E. Pivčević, ed., *Phenomenology and Philosophical Understanding* (Cambridge: Cambridge Univ. Press, 1975).

Føllesdal, D., "An Introduction to Phenomenology for Analytic Philosophers," in R. Olson and A. Paul, eds., *Contemporary Philosophy in Scandinavia* (Baltimore: Johns Hopkins Univ. Press, 1972); a longer Norwegian version is in A. Winsnes and E. Skard, eds., *Vestens Tenkere*, vol. 3 (Oslo: Aschehoug, 1962).

Gurwitsch, A., "The Commonsense World as Social Reality," *Social Research,* 29 (1962).

————, "Contribution to the Phenomenological Theory of Perception," in *Studies in Phenomenology and Psychology* (Evanston: Northwestern Univ. Press, 1966).

————, *The Field of Consciousness* (Pittsburgh: Duquesne Univ. Press, 1964).

————, "The Kantian and Husserlian Conceptions of Consciousness," *Studies in Phenomenology and Psychology* (Evanston: Northwestern Univ. Press, 1966).

————, "A Non-Egological Conception of Consciousness," *Philosophy and Phenomenological Research,* 1 (1941).

————, "On the Conceptual Consciousness," *Studies in Phenomenology and Psychology* (Evanston: Northwestern Univ. Press, 1966).

————, "On the Intentionality of Consciousness," in *Philosophical Essays in Memory of Edmund Husserl,* ed. M. Farber (Cambridge: Harvard Univ. Press, 1968).

————, "Perceptual Coherence as the Foundation of the Judgement of Predication," in *Phenomenology and the Theory of Science* (Evanston: Northwestern University Press, 1974).

————, "Phänomenologie der Thematik und des reinen Ich," *Psychologische Forschung,* 12 (1929); English version, "Phenomenology of Thematics and of the Pure Ego: Studies of the Relation between Gestalt Theory and Phenomenology," in *Studies in Phenomenology and Psychology* (Evanston: Northwestern Univ. Press, 1966).

————, "The Phenomenological and the Psychological Approach to Consciousness," in *Studies in Phenomenology and Psychology* (Evanston: Northwestern Univ. Press, 1966).

————, "The Phenomenology of Perception: Perceptual Implications," in *An Invitation to Phenomenology,* ed. J. Edie (Chicago: Quadrangle, 1965).

————, *Studies in Phenomenology and Psychology* (Evanston: Northwestern Univ. Press, 1966).

————, "Towards a Theory of Intentionality," *Philosophy and Phenomenological Research,* 27 (1970).

Hall, H., "Idealism and Solipsism in Husserl's *Cartesian Meditations," Journal of the British Society for Phenomenology,* 7 (1975).

————, "Intersubjective Phenomenology and Husserl's Cartesianism," *Man and World,* 12 (1979).

Holmes, R., "Is Transcendental Phenomenology Committed to Idealism?", *The Monist*, 59 (1975).

Ingarden, R., *Der Streit um die Existenz der Welt* (Tübingen: Niemeyer, 1965).

———, "Die vier Begriffe der Transcendenz und das Problem des Idealismus in Husserl," in A. Tymieniecka, ed., *Analecta Husserliana*, vol. 1 (Dordrecht: Reidel, 1971).

Küng, G., "Husserl on Pictures and Intentional Objects," *Review of Metaphysics*, 26 (1973).

———, "The World as Noema and as Referent," *Journal of the British Society for Phenomenology*, 3 (1972).

Landgrebe, L., "Husserls Phänomenologie und die Motive zu ihrer Umbildung," *Revue Internationale de Philosophie*, 1 (1939).

Lauer, Q., *Phénoménologie de Husserl* (Paris: 1955); English version, *The Triumph of Subjectivity: An Introduction to Transcendental Phenomenology* (New York: Fordham Univ. Press, 1958).

McIntyre, R., *Husserl and Referentiality: the Role of the Noema as an Intensional Entity*, doctoral dissertation, Stanford University, 1970.

Miller, I., *The Phenomenology of Perception: Husserl's Account of our Temporal Awareness*, doctoral dissertation, U.C.L.A., 1979.

Mohanty, J., *The Concept of Intentionality* (St. Louis: Warren Green, 1972).

———, *Edmund Husserl's Theory of Meaning* (The Hague: Nijhoff, 1969).

———, "Husserl's Theory of Meaning," in *Husserl: Expositions and Appraisals*, ed. F. Elliston and P. McCormick (Notre Dame: Notre Dame Univ. Press, 1977).

Morriston, W., "Intentionality and the Phenomenological Method: A Critique of Husserl's Transcendental Idealism," *Journal of the British Society for Phenomenology*, 7 (1976).

Schütz, A., *Collected Papers*, vol. 1 (The Hague: Nijhoff, 1962).

Smith, D., *Intentionality, Noemata, and Individuation: The Role of Individuation in Husserl's Theory of Intentionality*, doctoral dissertation, Stanford University, 1970.

Smith, D., and R. McIntyre, *Husserl and Intentionality: A Study of Mind, Meaning, and Language* (Dordrecht: Reidel, 1982).

———, "Intentionality via Intensions," *Journal of Philosophy*, 68 (1971).

Solomon, R., "Husserl's Concept of the Noema," in *Husserl: Expositions and Appraisals*, ed. F. Elliston and P. McCormick (Notre Dame: Univ. of Notre Dame Press, 1977).

Spiegelberg, H., ed., "From Husserl to Heidegger: Excerpts from a 1928 Freiburg Diary by W. R. Boyce Gibson," *Journal of the British Society for Phenomenology*, 2 (1971).

———, *The Phenomenological Movement* (The Hague: Nijhoff, 1960).

CONTEMPORARY RELEVANCE

Chisholm, R., *Perceiving* (Ithaca: Cornell Univ. Press, 1957).

Church, A., "Outline of a Revised Formulation of the Logic of Sense and Denotation (Part I)," *Noûs*, 7 (1973).

Clark, R., "Old Foundations for a Logic of Perception," *Synthese*, 33 (1976).

————, "Sensuous Judgments," *Nous*, 7 (1973).

Clarke, T., "The Legacy of Skepticism," *Journal of Philosophy*, 64 (1972).

Derrida, J., "La Form et le vouloir-dire," *Revue internationale de philosophie*, 21 (1967).

Donnellan, K., "Proper Names and Identifying Descriptions," in *Semantics of Natural Language*, ed. D. Davidson and G. Harman (Dordrecht: Reidel, 1972).

————, "Reference and Definite Descriptions," *Philosophical Review*, 75 (1966).

Firth, R., "Sense Data and the Percept Theory," *Mind* (October 1949, and January 1950).

Hintikka, J., "Degrees and Dimensions of Intentionality," in R. Haller, ed., *Proceedings of the Fourth International Wittgenstein Symposium* (Vienna: Hölder-Pichler-Tempsky, 1980).

————, *The Intentions of Intentionality and Other New Models for Modalities* (Dordrecht: Reidel, 1975).

————, "Is Alethic Modal Logic Possible?", *Acta Philosophica Fennica* (forthcoming).

————, *Knowledge and the Known* (Dordrecht: Reidel, 1974).

————, *Logic, Language-Games, and Information: Kantian Themes in the Philosophy of Logic* (Oxford: Oxford Univ. Press, 1973).

————, *Models for Modalities* (Dordrecht: Reidel, 1969).

————, "Objects of Knowledge and Belief: Acquaintances and Public Figures," in *The Intentions of Intentionality and Other New Models for Modalities* (Dordrecht: Reidel, 1975).

————, "On the Logic of Perception," in *Models for Modalities* (Dordrecht: Reidel, 1969).

————, "Semantics for Propositional Attitudes," in Davis, Hockney, and Wilson, eds., *Philosophical Logic* (Dordrecht: Reidel, 1969).

Kaila, E., *Reality and Experience* (Dordrecht: Reidel, 1979).

Kaplan, D., *Demonstratives*, unpublished manuscript, 1977.

————, "The Logic of Demonstratives," unpublished manuscript, 1973.

Kripke, S., "Naming and Necessity," in *Semantics of Natural Language*, ed. D. Davidson and G. Harman (Dordrecht: Reidel, 1972).

Lewis, C., *Mind and the World Order* (New York: Dover, 1929).

McIntyre, R., "Husserl's Phenomenological Conception of Intentionality and its Difficulties," *Philosophia* (forthcoming).

Mohanty, J., "Husserl on the Modalities," *Idea,* Bergmann Institute of Philosophy, University of Jerusalem (forthcoming).

Plantinga, A., "Transworld Identity or Worldbound Individuals," in S. Schwartz, ed., *Naming, Necessity, and Natural Kinds* (Ithaca: Cornell Univ. Press, 1977).

Putnam, H., "Meaning and Reference," *Journal of Philosophy,* 70 (1973).

———, "The Meaning of 'Meaning'," in *Philosophical Papers, II: Mind, Language, and Reality* (Cambridge: Cambridge Univ. Press, 1972).

Smith, D., "The Case of the Exploding Perception," *Synthese,* 41 (1979).

Todes, S., "Comparative Phenomenology of Perception and Imagination," *Journal of Existentialism* (Spring and Fall, 1966).

Tugendhat, E., "Phenomenology and Linguistic Analysis," in *Husserl: Expositions and Appraisals* (Notre Dame: Univ. of Notre Dame Press, 1977).

RECENT PARALLELS

Dreyfus, H., *What Computers Can't Do* (New York: Harper & Row, 1979).

Dreyfus, S., "Formal Models vs. Human Situational Understanding," Operations Research Center Report, ORC 81-3, U.C. Berkeley (February 19, 1981).

Field, H., "Tarski's Theory of Truth," *Journal of Philosophy,* 69 (1972).

Fodor, J., *The Language of Thought* (New York: Thomas Y. Crowell, 1975).

———, "Propositional Attitudes," *Monist,* 61 (1978).

———, "Tom Swift and His Procedural Grandmother," *Cognition,* 6 (1978).

Goodman, N., *Ways of World Making* (Indianapolis: Hackett, 1978).

Heidegger, M., *The Basic Problems of Phenomenology,* trans. A. Hofstadter (Bloomington: Indiana Univ. Press, 1981).

———, *Being and Time,* trans. J. Macquarrie and E. Robinson (New York: Harper & Row, 1962).

———, *On the Way to Language,* trans. P. Hertz and J. Stambaugh (New York: Harper & Row, 1971).

Minsky, M., "A Framework for Representing Knowledge," in *Mind Design,* ed. J. Haugeland (Montgomery, Vermont: Bradford, 1981).

Putnam, H., "Minds and Machines," in *Philosophical Papers, II: Mind, Language, and Reality* (Cambridge: Cambridge Univ. Press, 1972).

Searle, J., *Intentionality, an Essay in the Philosophy of Mind* (Cambridge: Cambridge Univ. Press, forthcoming).

———, "Intentionality and the Use of Language," in A. Margalit, ed., *Meaning and Use* (Dordrecht: Reidel, 1979).

———, "Literal Meaning," in *Expression and Meaning* (Cambridge: Cambridge Univ. Press, 1979).

———, "The Logical Status of Fictional Discourse," *New Literary History* (1975).

————, "Minds, Brains and Machines," in *Mind Design,* ed. J. Haugeland (Montgomery, Vermont: Bradford, 1981).

Searle, J., "A Taxonomy of Illocutionary Acts," in K. Gunderson, ed., *Language, Mind and Knowledge, Minnesota Studies in the Philosophy of Science,* vol. VI (1975).

Winograd, T., "Procedures as a Representation for Data in a Computer Program for Understanding Natural Language," M.I.T. A.I. Lab Tech. Report 84 (1971).

Winston, P., *The Psychology of Computer Vision* (Hightstown, N.J.: McGraw Hill, 1975).

Notes

Notes which contain something more than, or other than, textual citations have been marked with an asterisk throughout the volume.

INTRODUCTION (DREYFUS)

1.* Husserl wrote Aron Gurwitsch concerning his review of "Nachwort zu meinen *Ideen* . . .":

Your review has pleased me very much. As far as I look back, it is about the only review based on real understanding of any one of my writings (since the *Logical Investigations*). Only with regard to some passages I could imagine that you have not ultimately penetrated the complete bearing of the reduction, that is, the total revolution which it purports for the idea and method of philosophy over and against the total tradition. [Reprinted in *Life World and Consciousness*, ed. Lester Embree (Evanston: Northwestern University Press, 1972)]

In 1927, disillusioned about his supposed disciple, Martin Heidegger, Husserl wrote Roman Ingarden:

The new article for the Encyclopedia Britannica has cost me a great deal of effort, chiefly because I again thought through from the ground up my basic direction and took into account the fact that Heidegger . . . has not understood this direction and thus the entire sense of the method of phenomenological reduction. [E. Husserl, *Briefe an Roman Ingarden* (The Hague: Nijhoff, 1968)]

2.* Edmund Husserl, *Logical Investigations* (New York: Humanities Press, 1970). The equation of the current notion of a mental state with what Husserl called an act is helpful as a first approximation but requires careful qualification. First, not all mental states are acts. Acts, for Husserl, are always intentional, while mental states such as pain lack intentionality. For this reason a closer approximation to Husserl's term "mental act" would be Searle's term "intentional state."

3. Richard Aquila, "Husserl and Frege on Meaning," *Journal of the History of Philosophy* (1974), pp. 379–380.

4.* J. N. Mohanty, "Husserl's Theory of Meaning," in *Husserl: Expositions and Appraisals*, ed. F. Elliston and P. McCormick (Notre Dame: Notre Dame Univ. Press, 1977), p. 36. On Searle's account statements containing different modal auxiliaries and those containing the negation symbol contain different propositions, but this subtlety need not concern us here.

5.* John Searle, "What is an Intentional State?", this volume, pp. 259–276. For Searle the representative content of such intentional states is clearly propositional. For Husserl too the *noemata* for these acts and others (including perception) are propositional. In *Ideas* he notes that he chooses to ". . . define the term Meaning (*Sinn*) merely as 'ideal content' (*Materie*), and then to indicate the unit of meaning and thetic character as posited meaning [or proposition] (*Satz*)." [Edmund Husserl, *Ideas: General Introduction to Pure Phenomenology*, trans. W. R. Boyce Gibson (New York: Collier Books, 1972), p. 341.]

6.* Ibid., p. 260. Husserl too realizes that the analogy with linguistic acts together with his choice of terminology may be misleading in a similar way. He writes:

The concept of proposition (*Satz*) is certainly extended thereby in an exceptional way that may alienate sympathy, yet it remains within the limits of an important unity of essence. We must constantly bear in mind that for us the concepts meaning (*Sinn*) and posited meaning [or proposition] (*Satz*) contain nothing of the nature of expression and conceptual meaning . . ." (*Ideas*, p. 341).

7. *L.I.*, pp. 595–596.

8. "What is an Intentional State?", p. 264.

9.* As Husserl puts it:

In great measure, that which has been taken for noetic act-analysis has been obtained when the mental glance was directed towards the "meant as such," and it was really noematic structures which were there described. (*Ideas*, p. 332.)

10. Edmund Husserl, *Cartesian Meditations*, trans. D. Cairns (The Hague: Nijhoff, 1960), p. 27.

11. Ibid., p. 6.

12. "What is an Intentional State?" pp. 265–267.

13.* Ibid., pp. 265–266. Although Searle's theory allows him to remain uncommitted, Searle is far from neutral on this point. In his article, "Minds, Brains and Machines" [reprinted in *Mind Design*, ed. John Haugeland (Montgomery, Vermont: Bradford Books, 1981)], Searle argues that no instantiation of a formal structure, and thus no computer program, can have intrinsic intentionality.

14.* Husserl's special kind of idealism, which is compatible with common sense realism, comes out clearly in the following remark:

The relation of my consciousness to a world is not a matter of fact imposed on me either by a God, who adventitiously decides it thus, or by a world accidentally existing beforehand, and a causal regularity belonging thereto. On the contrary, the subjective Apriori precedes the being of God and world, the being of everything, individually and collectively, for me, the thinking subject. Even God is for me what he is, in consequence of my own productivity of consciousness; here too I must not look aside for fear I commit a supposed blasphemy, rather I must see the problem. Here too, as in the case of the other ego, productivity of consciousness will hardly signify that I invent and make this highest transcendency. [Edmund Husserl, *Formal and Transcendental Logic*, trans. D. Cairns (The Hague: Nijhoff, 1969), p. 251.]

15. Edmund Husserl, *Experience and Judgment* (Evanston: Northwestern Univ. Press, 1973), p. 49. Author's italics unless otherwise stated.

16. Edmund Husserl, *The Paris Lectures* (The Hague: Nijhoff, 1967), p. 24 (emphasis mine).

17. *Cartesian Meditations*, p. 53.

18. Ibid., p. 54.

19. Ibid.

20. Ibid.

21. *Formal and Transcendental Logic*, p. 234.

22. Ibid.

23.* "Naturally *pure hyletics* finds its proper place in subordination to the phenomenology of transcendental consciousness. . . . [I]t wins significance from the fact that it furnishes a woof that can enter into intentional formations." (*Ideas*, p. 233.)

24.* Aron Gurwitsch, "On the Conceptual Consciousness," *Studies in Phenomenology and Psychology* (Evanston: Northwestern Univ. Press, 1966), pp. 395–396 (emphasis mine). Husserl's story on the "uncovering" of predicates goes as follows:

We must . . . distinguish the *first series of judgments,* in which there is predicated of each substrate *its own individual moment*—S' is p', S'' is p''. etc.— and, in contrast to this, *the judgments in which the same* p, *as everywhere* like, is predicated as the *universal,* as the identically one in all, that which emerges in p', p'', and so on. This means that the unity is preconstituted in the passive coincidence of likeness of the moments p', p'', and so on, *as the unity of the species* p: on the strength of this, an act of judgment oriented in a new direction is possible, in which, if we return to S' and re-effect the identification, we no longer determine S' by p' as its individual moment but by *p as identically the same in* S, S', and so on. There result the judgments S' is p, S'' is p, and so on, in which p no longer designates an individual predicative core but a general one, namely, the universal as that which is common to two or more S's successively apprehended. (*Experience and Judgment*, p. 324.)

25. Edmund Husserl, *The Crisis of European Sciences and Transcendental Phenomenology*, trans. D. Carr (Evanston: Northwestern Univ. Press, 1970), pp. 243-244.

26. *Formal and Transcendental Logic*, pp. 253-254.

27. Ibid., p. 254.

28. Ibid., p. 251.

29. *Crisis*, pp. 206-207.

30. John Searle, *Intentionality, an Essay in the Philosophy of Mind* (Cambridge, England: Cambridge Univ. Press, forthcoming).

31. *Cartesian Meditations*, p. 94.

32. Hubert Dreyfus, *What Computers Can't Do* (New York: Harper & Row, 1979), pp. 241-242, 250.

33. *Cartesian Meditations*, p. 53.

34. *Experience and Judgment*, pp. 31-32.

35. *Cartesian Meditations*, p. 45.

36. *Experience and Judgment*, p. 331 (emphasis mine).

37. *Cartesian Meditations*, p. 51.

38. *Experience and Judgment*, p. 125.

39. Marvin Minsky, "A Framework for Representing Knowledge," in *Mind Design*, ed. Haugeland, p. 96.

40. Patrick Winston, *The Psychology of Computer Vision* (Hightstown, N.J.: McGraw Hill, 1975), p. 16.

41. *Cartesian Meditations*, pp. 54-55.

42. *Formal and Transcendental Logic*, p. 244.

43. Ibid., p. 246.

44. *Crisis*, p. 291.

45. "A Framework for Representing Knowledge," p. 124.

46. Ibid., p. 102.

47. Martin Heidegger, *On the Way to Language*, trans. P. Hertz and J. Stambaugh (New York: Harper & Row, 1971), p. 33.

48. Martin Heidegger, *The Basic Problems of Phenomenology* (Bloomington: Indiana Univ. Press, 1981).

49. *Being and Time*, p. 21.

50. John Searle, "Literal Meaning," in *Expression and Meaning* (Cambridge, England: Cambridge Univ. Press, 1979), pp. 125-126.

51. Ibid., p. 130.

52. Ibid.

53. *Crisis*, p. 148.

54. Ibid., p. 149.

55. Ibid.

56. *Formal and Transcendental Logic*, p. 245.

57.* It is well-known, for example, that master chess players who have played thousands of games find that the right move simply pops into their minds. As one might expect, the features and rules they report when insistently asked for their search procedures, do not, when implemented on a computer, lead to the choice of a master move. See Stuart Dreyfus, "Formal Models vs. Human Situational Understanding," Operations Research Center Report, ORC 81-3, U.C. Berkeley, February 19, 1981.

58. *Experience and Judgment*, p. 36.

1. BRENTANO AND HUSSERL (FØLLESDAL)

1. See, for example, Gottlob Frege, "Über Sinn und Bedeutung," *Zeitschrift für Philosophie und philosophische Kritik*, 100 (1892), p. 31, Frege's review of Husserl's *Philosophie der Arithmetik* in *Zeitschrift fur Philosophie und philosophische Kritik*, 103 (1894), pp. 329-331, and his "Der Gedanke" in *Beiträge zur Philosophie des deutschen Idealismus*, vol. I (1918), pp. 67-70.

2.* Letter to Oskar Kraus, 1909, published in Kraus' Introduction to volume I of *Psychologie vom empirischen Standpunkt*, p. xlix. Also quoted in Kraus' notes to *Wahrheit und Evidenz*, p. 174 of the English edition, *The True and the Evident* (London: Routledge & Kegan Paul, 1966). Other important letters and essays where Brentano sets forth his view on this issue are found in Parts 3 and 4 of *The True and the Evident*, especially on pp. 77-85, 94-96, 103-104, and 112-114.

3. *Psychologie vom empirischen Standpunkt*, vol. II, p. 137, of the *Philosophische Bibliothek* (Hamburg: Meiner, 1874).

4. Brentano, op. cit., vol. II, p. 163. The translation is Terrell's, in Roderick M. Chisholm, ed., *Realism and the Background of Phenomenology* (Glencoe: Free Press, 1960), pp. 74-75.

5. Brentano, loc. cit.

6. Richard B. Arnaud, "Brentanist Relations," in Keith Lehrer, ed., *Analysis and Metaphysics: Essays in Honor of R. M. Chisholm*, Philosophical Studies Series in Philosophy, vol. 4 (Dordrecht: Reidel, 1975).

7. See particularly Alonzo Church, "Outline of a Revised Formulation of the Logic of Sense and Denotation (Part I)," *Noûs*, 7 (1973), 24-33.

8. For example, Oskar Kraus, in his "Anmerkungen" to volume I of Brentano's *Psychologie vom empirischen Standpunkt*, p. 267.

2. HUSSERL AND FREGE (MOHANTY)

1. E. Husserl, *Logical Investigations*, trans. J. N. Findlay, vol. I (New York: Humanities Press, 1970), p. 47.

2. D. Føllesdal, *Husserl und Frege* (Oslo: Aschehoug, 1958), p. 23.

3. Ibid., p. 25.

4. R. C. Solomon, "Sense and Essence: Frege and Husserl," *International Philosophical Quarterly*, 10 (1970), p. 380.

5. Published in *Göttingische gelehrte Anzeigen*, 1 (1891), pp. 243-287.

6. Published in *Vierteljahrsschrift für wissenschaftliche Philosophie*, 15 (1891), pp. 168-189, 351-356.

7. *Logical Investigations*, vol. I, p. 322.

8.* Thus writes Frege:

First of all, everything becomes presentation. The references of words are presentations . . . Objects are presentations . . . concepts, too, are presentations.

A little later on: "Everything is shunted off into the subjective." [G. Frege, "Review of Dr. E. Husserl's *Philosophy of Arithmetic*," trans. E.E.W. Kluge, *Mind*, 81 (1972), pp. 321-337; esp. 323-324.]

9.* H. Dreyfus, "Husserl's Perceptual Noema," this volume, pp. 97-123. In note 17 to p. 100, Dreyfus rejects Gurwitsch's claim that Husserl discovered the distinction between real mental states and ideal meanings and refers to "Husserl's explicit attribution of this distinction to Frege" in the *Logical Investigations*, I (Findlay edition), p. 292. This reference, however, is misleading. First, this is not the place where Husserl first introduces the distinction. The distinction is introduced, first, in the 1891 Schröder review, as this paper will argue. Secondly, at this place, Husserl is only referring to Frege's different terminology.

10. *Göttingische gelehrte Anzeigen*, I (1891), p. 250.

11.* Thiel considers the terminology of 'sense' and 'reference' obligatory for all Frege works after 1890. Cf. Christian Thiel, *Sense and Reference in Frege's Logic* (Dordrecht: Reidel, 1968), p. 44. Angelelli finds the distinction already in the *Begriffsschrift* ("only the famous terminology . . . is lacking here") and in the *Grundlagen*, §67. Cf. Ignacio Angelelli, *Studies on Gottlob Frege and Traditional Philosophy* (Dordrecht: Reidel, 1967).

12. *Gött. gel. Anz.*, I (1891), pp. 258-259.

13. Ibid., p. 247.

14. Op. cit., p. 246.

15. *Vierteljahrsschrift f. wiss. Phil.*, 15 (1891), pp. 169, 171.

16. *Gött. gel. Anz.*, I (1891), p. 257.

17. Ibid., p. 262.

18. *Viert. f. wiss. Phil.*, 15 (1891), p. 178.

19. *Gött. gel. Anz.*, I (1891), p. 249.

20. *Logical Investigations*, I, pp. 322-325.

21. Ibid., p. 69.

22. Ibid., p. 69.

23. Ibid., p. 244.

24. Ibid., p. 244.

25. Ibid., p. 245.

26. Ibid., p. 245.

27. G. Frege, "Kritische Beleuchtung einiger Punkte in E. Schröders *Vorlesungen über die Algebra der Logik*," *Archiv für systematische Philosophie*, I (1895), pp. 433-436.

28. In *Jenaische Zeitschrift für Naturwissenschaft* (1883), vol. 16, Supplement, pp. 1-10.

29. In *Sitzungsberichte der Jenaischen Gesellschaft für Medizin und Naturwissenschaft für das Jahr 1885* (Jena: Fischer, 1885/86), pp. 94-104 [now reprinted in Ignacio Angelelli, ed., Frege, *Kleine Schriften* (Hildesheim: Georg Olms, 1967), pp. 103-111].

30. Frege, *Kleine Schriften*, p. 105.

31. I am indebted to Professor F. Kambartel of the University of Konstanz, director of the Frege-Archiv, for making these available to me.

32. See note 27.

33. Frege, *Kleine Schriften*, p. 207.

34. Ibid., p. 208.

35. Ibid., p. 209.

36. Ibid., pp. 209-210.

37. In G. Frege, *Nachgelassene Schriften* (Hamburg: Felix Meiner, 1969), pp. 128-136.

38. Ibid., p. 134.

39. Ibid., p. 133.

40. Ibid., p. 133.

41. E. Husserl, "Persönliche Aufzeichnungen," ed. W. Biemel, in *Philosophy and Phenomenological Research*, 16 (1956), pp. 293-302, esp. p. 294 (emphasis mine).

RESPONSE TO *HUSSERL AND FREGE* (FØLLESDAL)

1.* Husserl heard mainly of Bolzano's *Paradoxien des Unendlichen* through Brentano (and also through Weierstrass). He looked at the *Wissenschaftslehre* then, but it was only somewhat later that he came to appreciate this work.

2. "An Introduction to Phenomenology for Analytic Philosophers," in Raymond E. Olson and Anthony M. Paul, eds., *Contemporary Philosophy in Scandinavia* (Baltimore: Johns Hopkins Univ. Press, 1972), pp. 417-430. This paper was first presented as one of a series of lectures on varieties of contemporary philosophy at Harvard in 1962. A longer Norwegian version of the paper was printed in 1962 in A. H. Winsnes and Eiliv Skard, eds., *Vestens Tenkere* (Oslo: Aschehoug, 1962), vol. 3, pp. 157-177. The passage about Mill and Bolzano appeared on page 163 of that version.

3. Karl Schumann, *Husserl-Chronik: Denk- und Lebensweg Edmund Husserls, Husserliana*, vol. 1 (The Hague: Nijhoff, 1977), p. 43.

4. E. Husserl, *Logische Untersuchungen*, vol. I, p. 6; p. 42 of the Findlay translation, *Logical Investigations*, vol. 1 (New York: Humanities Press, 1970).

5. Husserl, op. cit., vol. 1, pp. vii-viii; p. 43 of Findlay's translation.

6. Husserl, op. cit., vol. 1, p. vii; pp. 42-43 of Findlay's translation.

7. Husserl, op. cit., vol. I, p. 169 n.

8. Husserl, letter to Frege, July 18, 1891.

9. Husserl, "Bericht über deutsche Schriften zur Logik in den Jahren 1895-99," dritter Artikel, *Archiv für systematische Philosophie*, 9 (1903), p. 395. Reprinted in E. Husserl, *Aufsätze und Rezensionen (1890-1910), Husserliana*, 22 (The Hague: Nijhoff, 1979), p. 202.

10.* "Frege's significance was decisive." [ed.].

11. H. Spiegelberg, ed., "From Husserl to Heidegger: Excerpts from a 1928 Freiburg Diary by W. R. Boyce Gibson," *The Journal of the British Society for Phenomenology*, 2 (1971), p. 66.

12. Karl Schumann, op. cit., p. 463.

13. See *Husserl und Frege*, p. 17.

3. THE INTENTIONALITY OF CONSCIOUSNESS (GURWITSCH)

1. Q. Lauer in his book *Phénoménologie de Husserl* (Paris: 1955) has followed up on the genesis of the theory of intentionality through four of Husserl's major works which appeared in his lifetime.

2. L. Landgrebe, "Husserl's Phänomenologie und die Motive zu ihrer Umbildung," I, *Revue Internationale de Philosophie*, I (1939), and H. Spiegelberg, *The Phenomenological Movement* (The Hague: Nijhoff, 1960), I, 7, and III, C 2 c.

3. Cf. A. Gurwitsch, "Phänomenologie der Thematik und des reinen Ich," chap. III, sec. 16, and chap. IV, sec. 4, *Psychologische Forschung*, XII (1929) [*Studies in Phenomenology and Psychology* (Evanston: Northwestern Univ. Press, 1966), 253-258 and 278-286. Hereafter referred to as *Studies*]; "A Non-Egological Conception of Consciousness," *Philosophy and Phenomenological Research*, 1 (1941) [= *Studies* . . . 287-300]; and our book, *The Field of Consciousness* (Pittsburgh: Duquesne, 1964), Part IV, chap. II, 6.

4. Husserl, *Logische Untersuchungen*, 2nd ed. (Halle: Niemeyer, 1913), vol. II; see also the condensed but faithful rendering by M. Farber, *The Foundation of Phenomenology* (Cambridge, Mass.: 1941), chap. VIII.

5. Husserl, *Logische Untersuchungen*, II, i, pp. 415f.

6. Ibid., II, i, 418.

7. Husserl, *Ideen zu einer reinen Phänomenologie und phänomenologischen Philosophie*, I (henceforth referred to as *Ideen*, I), §41 [The page numbers refer to the original edition; the edition in *Husserliana*, vol. III (1950), indicates on the margin the pagination of the original edition]; and *Cartesian Meditations*, trans. D. Cairns (The Hague: 1960), §17.

8. *Ideen*, I, §88.

9. *Ideen*, I, Part III, chap. III.

10. *Ideen*, I, p. 184.

11. *Ideen*, I, §91.

12. *Ideen*, I, §§99 and 102ff.

13. Cf. Husserl, *Logische Untersuchungen*, vol. II, i, chap. I, §14, and vi, chap. I, §§8ff.

14. See Husserl's detailed analysis of that phenomenon in *The Phenomenology of Internal Time-Consciousness*, trans. J. S. Churchill (Bloomington, Ind.: 1964), §§10ff, and *Erfahrung und Urteil* (Hamburg: 1954), §23.

15. See our detailed analysis in "On the Intentionality of Consciousness," Part III, *Philosophical Essays in Memory of Edmund Husserl*, ed. M. Farber (Cambridge, Mass.: 1941) [= *Studies* . . . 134-138], and "William James' Theory of the 'Transitive Parts' of the Stream of Consciousness", Part II, *Philosophy and Phenomenological Research*, III (1943) [= *Studies* . . . 306-313].

16. Cf. Husserl, *Die Krisis der Europäischen Wissenschaften und die transzendentale Phänomenologie* (henceforth referred to as *Krisis*), *Husserliana*,

6 (1954), §§ 66ff; and *Phänomenologische Psychologie, Husserliana,* vol. IX (1962), §§ 16ff.

17. For the sake of simplicity we omit mentioning the problems concerning mathematical idealization, which are extensively treated by Husserl in *Krisis,* §§ 8ff.

18. Bergson, *Essai sur les données immédiates de la conscience* (Paris: 1904).

19. Husserl, *Ideen,* I, § 43.

20. Cf. Husserl, *Phänomenologische Psychologie,* pp. 152f, 178f, 182f, and 430ff.

21. A. Gurwitsch, *The Field of Consciousness* (Pittsburgh: 1964), Part IV.

22. Cf. Husserl, *Phänomenologische Psychologie,* p. 184.

23. The social aspect of the life-world is the persistent central theme in most of A. Schütz's writings; cf. his *Collected Papers,* vol. I (The Hague: 1962). See also our article "The Commonsense World as Social Reality," *Social Research,* XXIX (1962).

24. Compare Husserl, *Krisis,* §§ 36f, and *Phänomenologische Psychologie,* §§ 7ff.

25. *Phänomenologische Psychologie* contains the "Amsterdamer Vorträge" and the definitive German text as well as two preparatory drafts of the article in *Encyclopaedia Britannica.*

4. THE NOTION OF NOEMA (FØLLESDAL)

1. Franz Brentano, *Psychologie vom empirischen Standpunkt,* vol. 1, book 2, chap. 1; here quoted from D. B. Terrell's English translation of this chapter in Roderick M. Chisholm, ed., *Realism and the Background of Phenomenology* (Glencoe, Ill.: Free Press, 1960), p. 50.

2. Cf. the unpublished manuscript *Noema und Sinn* (hereafter referred to as NuS), p. 6.

3. "Über Sinn und Bedeutung," *Zeitschrift für Philosophie und philosophische Kritik,* 100 (1892), p. 27.

5. MEANING AND NOEMA (McINTYRE AND SMITH)

The material in this essay will appear in somewhat different form in Chapter IV of our forthcoming book, *Husserl and Intentionality: A Study of Mind, Meaning, and Language* (Dordrecht: Reidel, 1982).

1. Trans. J. N. Findlay (New York: Humanities Press, 1970) from *Logische Untersuchungen,* 2nd ed. (Tübingen: Max Niemeyer Verlag, 1913). References to *Logical Investigations* (abbreviated '*LI*') will be to Findlay's translation. At some points we have slightly modified the Findlay translation; all such instances are noted by '*' following the page reference.

2.* Husserl's development of this view is perhaps the definitive statement of the classical "idea" idea of language, lately disparaged by W. V. Quine. See, for instance, Quine's *Ontological Relativity and Other Essays* (New York: Columbia University Press, 1969), p. 27; Donald Davidson and Jaakko Hintikka, eds., *Words and Objections* (Dordrecht: Reidel, 1969), p. 304.

3. Cf. also *Ideas*, §124, pp. 303-304. [Edmund Husserl, *Ideen*, I *Husserliana* edition (The Hague: Nijhoff, 1950). Page references to *Ideas* are to this edition, and all translations from *Ideen*, I, are our own. Our references will include section numbers to facilitate use of other editions, such as W. R. Boyce Gibson's English translation, *Ideas* (New York: Humanities Press, 1931).]

4. We know this primarily from *Ideas*, §§88-91, 128-131; see David W. Smith and Ronald McIntyre, "Intentionality via Intensions," *Journal of Philosophy*, 68, No. 18 (Sept. 1971): 541-561. But the essentials are also present in *Logical Investigations*, esp. V, §§20-21, where Husserl speaks of "ideal content" or "matter" rather than of "noematic Sinn" (cf. Husserl's comments on *LI*, V, §21, in *Ideas*, §94, pp. 234-235, and §133, p. 324).

5. Its most explicit statement in LI is in V, §21, p. 590 (where "semantic essence"="matter"="Sinn"). The point is well confirmed by Husserl's conception of expression in LI, VI, §§1-15, as well as in *Formal and Transcendental Logic*, §3, and *Ideas*, §124 (both of which we discuss in this section).

6. Husserl, *Formal and Transcendental Logic*, trans. Dorion Cairns (The Hague: Nijhoff, 1969), pp. 22-23 (emphasis ours). (We have substituted 'meaning-giving' for 'sense-bestowing' in the Cairns translation and at one point have retained the German 'Bedeutung' and 'Sinn' where Cairns has 'signification' and 'sense' respectively.)

7. Ibid., pp. 23-24. (Again we have retained 'Bedeutung' and 'Sinn'.)

6. THE THEORY OF PERCEPTION (FØLLESDAL)

1. E. Husserl, *Phänomenologische Psychologie, Vorlesungen Sommersemester 1925*, ed. Walter Biemel, *Husserliana*, vol. 9 (The Hague: Nijhoff, 1962), p. 163.

2. A. Gurwitsch, *Studies in Phenomenology and Psychology* (Evanston, Ill.: Northwestern Univ. Press, 1966), p. 256.

3. E. Husserl, *Ideen zu einer reinen Phänomenologie und phänomenologischen Philosophie. Erstes Buch: Allgemeine Einführung in die Reine Phänomenologie, Jahrbuch für Philosophie und phänomenologische Forschung*, vol. I (Halle: Niemeyer, 1913), §85.

4. E. Husserl, *Analysen zur passiven Synthesis. Aus Vorlesungs- und Forschungsmanuskripten, 1918-1926*, ed. Margot Fleischer, *Husserliana* XI (The Hague: Nijhoff, 1966), p. 363.

5. *Ideas*, §42.

7. THE PERCEPTUAL NOEMA (DREYFUS)

1. Dagfinn Føllesdal, "Husserl's Notion of Noema," this volume, p. 77.

2. Ibid., p. 74.

3. Aron Gurwitsch, "The Phenomenology of Perception: Perceptual Implications," in *An Invitation to Phenomenology*, ed. James Edie (Chicago: Quadrangle Books, 1965), p. 23.

4.* It is, however, shared by such influential thinkers as Jacques Derrida and Maurice Merleau-Ponty.

5. Aron Gurwitsch, *Studies in Phenomenology and Psychology* (Evanston: Northwestern University Press, 1966), p. xv. (Hereafter cited as *"Studies."*)

6.* See Dorion Cairns, "An Approach to Phenomenology," in *Philosophical Essays in Memory of Edmund Husserl,* ed. Marvin Farber (Cambridge: Harvard University Press, 1968), p. 9: "The 'object per se' (or object simpliciter) and 'intentional object' are names for one and the same object only attended in different ways."

7.* Alfred Schutz, *Collected Papers* (The Hague: Nijhoff, 1962), I, pp. 107–108, first identifies the noema with the intentional object, "the noema itself, the intentional object perceived . . . ," and then identifies the intentional object with the percept: "The intentional object of my perceiving is a specific mixture of colors and shapes in a special perspective."

8. Cf. n. 65, below.

9. Cf. n. 65, below.

10.* See Robert C. Solomon, "Husserl's Concept of the Noema," in *Husserl: Expositions and Appraisals,* ed. F. Elliston and P. McCormack (Notre Dame: University of Notre Dame Press, 1977). [For Solomon, "what one sees—for example, in cases of illusion and hallucination—is not y but (y). It is this (y) that Husserl calls the noematic correlate" (p. 174]. And he adds, in what seems a *reductio ad absurdum* of this view, "it is clear that the noema *must,* if it is what directs us to the object, be itself perceived.")

11.* See Ernst Tugendhat, "Phenomenology and Linguistic Analysis," in *Husserl: Expositions and Appraisals,* p. 328; speaking of Husserl's view in *Ideas,* he writes: "The object, together with its ways of being given, is now characterized as 'noema'."

12.* The most serious attempt to settle the question is Føllesdal's paper, "Husserl's Notion of Noema." Føllesdal's theses 8, 9, 10, and 11 are implicitly directed against Gurwitsch's view. Føllesdal wants to establish that the noema is indeed a conceptual entity, which cannot be perceived. Once these two possible interpretations of "noema" are distinguished, however, the evidence for theses 8, 9, 10 and 11 turns out either to assume dogmatically what Føllesdal is trying to establish or to be infected with the very ambiguity these theses are meant to clear up.

Thesis 8. Noemata are abstract entities. Evidence: Husserl says: "The tree in nature is by no means the perceived tree as such. The real tree can burn . . . ," etc.

But Gurwitsch and all those who believe that the noema is a sort of ostensible object—an appearance, as Gurwitsch calls it—would agree that this entity does not have the properties of a physical object, but rather has the special properties of a view of the object. Moreover, both schools would agree that the noema is not a temporal event, since it can be the object of an indefinite number of temporally indexed acts.

Thesis 9 is more decisive. Here Føllesdal contends that noemata are not perceived through the senses.

If this could be shown, then the ambiguity would be definitely cleared up, for Gurwitsch does clearly contend that the perceptual noema is sensuously given. Unfortunately, Føllesdal's argument that "Thesis 9 is an immediate consequence of Thesis 8," that, since the noema is abstract, it cannot be perceived, begs the question at hand. Nor does it help to base the argument on Husserl's claim that "all visible objects can be experienced only through perspectives" and conclude, as Føllesdal does, that, "since noemata are not experienced through perspectives, they are not visible." For from the above it might equally well follow that they are not perceptual objects, which is just what Gurwitsch contends.

At this point, Føllesdal introduces as evidence a quotation from an unpublished manuscript in which Husserl does indeed say that "the *Sinn* is not perceived"; but, as Føllesdal remarks, here Husserl is talking about the *Sinn* and not directly about the perceptual noema. Gurwitsch would presumably agree that the *Sinn* is indeed not perceived, for Husserl himself calls the *Sinn* an abstract component in the perceptual noema. (It must be abstract, for it is what is held in common by a perceptual noema, a memory noema, an image noema, etc., of the same object, seen from the same perspective, etc.)

Thesis 10, that noemata are known through a special kind of reflection, is also critical, but critically ambiguous. Noemata are indeed known through a special reflection; but whether this is a special reflection on a conceptual entity, or whether it is a special way of regarding a perceptual object so as to describe only what is given in a particular act of perception, is unclear. Each interpretation could cite in its favor Husserl's claim that "the reflecting judgment is directed toward the *Sinn,* and hence not toward that which is the object of the nonreflecting judgment." But for Føllesdal this means that the noema is given only in a special act of abstract reflection turned away from the object presented and toward the sense we give that presentation, whereas for Gurwitsch the noema is the object of perception itself attended to in a special way so as to notice exactly what is presented.

Thesis 11, that phenomenological reflection can be iterated, if established, would be decisive provided it could be shown that by iteration Husserl means that *the same sort* of reflection can be repeated at higher levels. For if the noema were an abstract entity, we could indeed reflect on the higher-order noemata involved in reflecting on the first-order noema without changing our mode of reflection; whereas if the noema were a percept singled out by reflection, the mode of reflection involved could not be iterated. Unfortunately, in the passage quoted by Føllesdal, Husserl says only that the meaning used on one level can always be made an object of reflection on a higher level, not that this higher-level entity has to be the same sort of entity revealed on the first level. This leaves open the possibility, compatible with Gurwitsch's account, that, after noticing the perceptual presentation, the phenomenologist could reflect on the abstract entity by means of which he intended the first-order percept, etc.

13. Edmund Husserl, *Logical Investigations,* trans. J. N. Findlay (New York: Humanities Press, 1970), I, 330. (Hereafter referred to as "*LI*".)

14. Gottlob Frege, *Translations from the Philosophical Writings of Gottlob Frege,* ed. Peter Geach and Max Black (Oxford: Blackwell, 1960), p. 59.

15. Ibid., p. 79.

16. *LI*, I, p. 327.

17.* *LI*, I, p. 292. In the light of Husserl's explicit attribution of this distinction to Frege here, it is misleading of Gurwitsch to claim that "the distinction between *meanings as ideal units* and mental states as real *psychological events* (acts), through which meanings are apprehended and actualized, is one of the most momentous and most consequential achievements for which modern philosophy is indebted to Husserl" [*The Field of Consciousness* (Pittsburgh: Duquesne University Press, 1964), p. 177n.]. The most that can be claimed is that Husserl was the first to realize the import of this distinction—a distinction which, thanks to Mohanty's criticism (p. 44) and Føllesdal's response (p. 53), I now see as antedating both Frege and Husserl.

18. *LI*, p. 554.

19. *LI*, p. 555.

20. *LI*, pp. 254-255.

21. *LI*, p. 332.

22. *Philosophical Works of Gottlob Frege*, p. 60.

23. Ibid.

24. *LI*, I, p. 290 (emphasis mine).

25. Ibid. (emphasis mine).

26.* *LI*, I, p. 291. Note that Husserl says that this ideal entity is a *correlate* of the object, as would be expected of the meaning in the Frege-Føllesdal interpretation, not an *aspect* of the object (a member of a family which makes up the object), as in Gurwitsch's account.

27. Ibid.

28.* This is argued in greater detail in my doctoral dissertation, *Husserl's Phenomenology of Perception: From Transcendental to Existential Phenomenology*, Harvard University, 1963.

Chisholm's argument concerning perception words in his book *Perceiving* (Ithaca: Cornell Univ. Press, 1957), p. 172, might appear to present a counter argument to the claim that fulfilling acts must be construed as transparent. In his chapter on "intentional inexistence," Chisholm gives a definition of intentionality which equates intentionality with Frege's indirect reference or what we have been calling "referential opacity." Chisholm then tries to argue, following Brentano, that all psychic acts are intentional. "When we use perception words propositionally, our sentences display the . . . above marks of intentionality," he claims (p. 172). This propositional use might seem to contradict our conclusion that in ordinary usage the act context of perception words is transparent. Chisholm's argument is simple: "I may see that John is the man in the corner, and John may be someone who is ill; but I do not now see that John is someone who is ill." What this shows is merely that sentences involving "see that" display intentionality as defined by Chisholm. But Chisholm does not claim that "see" in this propositional sense is used perceptually. Rather, it could be replaced by "realize" or "take it to be the case that." If we use "see" in a way that is strictly perceptual, the sentence becomes: "I may see John in the corner, and John may be someone who is ill." In which case I *do* see someone who is ill. The intentionality, in Chisholm's sense of the term, vanishes. This shift is instructive. It shows that if we could construe perceiving as "taking" or "seeing" something to be the case, rather than simply seeing something, the intentionalist thesis could be saved. This seems to be precisely Husserl's move in generalizing his theory of meaning to perception.

29. *LI*, I, p. 728.

30. *LI*, p. 696.

31.* *LI*, p. 589. "The matter must be *that element in an act which first gives it reference to an object, and reference so wholly definite that it not merely fixes the object meant in a general way, but also the precise way in which it is meant.*"

It is the matter through which the act attains its object "exactly as it is intended." Like a meaning, the matter is a "universal object" which conveys as completely as possible what specific determinations we take the object to have. Husserl thus calls the matter an "abstract form" (*abstrakter Form*). It is confusing to the reader that what corresponds to the form of the object should be called its matter, but Husserl presumably uses this term because of the capacity of the matter to take on various "qualities," that is, to be affirmed, denied, doubted, etc. Perhaps it is helpful in fixing in mind the way Husserl is using "matter" to think of it as the "subject matter" of the act. For matter in the more traditional sense, Husserl uses the German *Stoff* or, in *Ideas*, the Greek *hylē*.

32. *LI*, I, p. 741.

33.* As Merleau-Ponty has pointed out, Husserl notes in the *Lectures on Internal Time-Consciousness* that "not every constitution has the *Inhalt-Auffassung* schema" (p. 5), which is tantamount to admitting that not all structures can be understood in terms of the imposition of *separable* meanings. In *Erfahrung und Urteil* (Hamburg: Claassen & Govert, 1948), Husserl expresses the same reservation from the other side by distinguishing a "pure or original passivity" from a "secondary passivity" which is the passivity of habit: "Every active grasping of an object presupposes that it is given beforehand. The objects of receptivity with their associative structure are given beforehand in an original passivity. Grasping these structures is the lowest form of activity, the mere reception of the originally passive preconstituted senses [*Sinne*]" (p. 300). The important thing to note in this passage is that there is a form of constitution which was never active and which is not the imposing of sense on some prior senseless data. This suggests that at its lowest level constitution is not the bringing to bear of a form on a distinct material—that is, not *Sinngebung*—but that from the start the material has a certain form.

34.* Husserl does once refer to a perceptual sense (*Wahrnehmungsinn*) and tells us that "the homogeneous unity of the perceptual sense pervades the total representation" (*Logical Investigations*, p. 807), but he does not elaborate on this notion and never employs it again in *Logical Investigations*.

35. *LI*, pp. 743–744.

36. *LI*, p. 283.

37.* Edmund Husserl, *Ideen zu einer reinen Phänomenologie und phäno-menologischen Philosophie*, I, *Husserliana*, 3 (The Hague: Nijhoff, 1950), pp. 303-304 (my translation). Jacques Derrida cites this passage in his article "La Form et le vouloir-dire" (*Revue internationale de philosophie*, No. 81, p. 284), and follows it with the following interesting footnote: "Ces précautions avaient été prises et longuement justifiées dans les *Recherches*. Bien entendu, ces justifications, pour être démonstratives, ne s'en tenaient pas moins à l'intérieur d'oppositions métaphysiques traditionnelles (âme/corps, psychique/physique, vivant/non-vivant, intentionnalité/non-intentionnalité, forme/matière, signifié/signifiant, intelligible/sensible, idéalité/empiricité, etc.)."

38. Ibid.

39. Ibid., p. 325.

40. Ibid.

41. Ibid., p. 482.

42. "Phenomenology of Thematics and of the Pure Ego: Studies of the Relation between Gestalt Theory and Phenomenology," *Studies*, p. 193.

43. *Studies*, p. 177.

44. *Field*, pp. 277-278.

45. "Gestalt Theory and Phenomenology," *Studies*, p. 191.

46. *Field*, pp. 180-81.

47. *Ideen*, I, p. 219.

48. "The Phenomenological and the Psychological Approach to Consciousness," *Studies*, p. 104.

49. *Ideen*, I, p. 241.

50. Ibid.

51. "Gestalt Theory and Phenomenology," *Studies*, p. 194.

52. *Field*, p. 182.

53. *Ideen*, I, p. 128.

54. Edmund Husserl, *Phänomenologische Psychologie, Husserliana*, 9 (The Hague: Nijhoff, 1962), p. 159.

55. *Ideen*, I, p. 219.

56. Ibid., pp. 316-317.

57. Aron Gurwitsch, "Husserl's Theory of the Intentionality of Consciousness," this volume, p. 62.

58. "Gestalt Theory and Phenomenology," p. 183 (emphasis mine).

59. Ibid. (emphasis mine).

60. Aron Gurwitsch, "Towards a Theory of Intentionality," *Philosophy and Phenomenological Research*, 27 (1970), p. 363.

61. *LI*, I, p. 287.

62. *LI*, I, p. 290.

63.* Ibid. (emphasis mine). Note that Husserl here clearly distinguishes the fulfilling sense from the object as meant. He would therefore not identify the fulfilling sense with the noema, as he seems to do in *Ideas*, if, as Gurwitsch contends, the noema is the object as meant.

64. *Ideen*, III, p. 89.

65.* There does seem to be one passage in all the published writing of Husserl which backs up this interpretation of the perceived as such as the directly perceived—a passage from *The Crisis of European Sciences*, Husserl's last and, in that sense, most authoritative work: "At any given time the thing presents itself to me through a nucleus of 'original presence' (*which denotes the continual subjective character of the actual perceived as such*) as well as through its inner and outer horizon" (*Crisis*, p. 165). If one looks up the textual comments on this passage in the Louvain edition, however, one finds that the parenthetical comment which equates the perceived as such with the sensuous original presence is an interpolation by Eugen Fink, Husserl's assistant.

Rudolf Boehm, the editor of several volumes of Husserl's collected works, also follows the Gurwitschian reading:

Die Sache ist eben die, dass Husserl bemerken musste, dass das Noema, was zunächst ein blosses Abstraktions bzw. Reduktions—produkt der Phänomenologie, ein *phänomenologisch* allein absolut Gegebenes scheinen konnte, sich als eine durchaus *phänomenale* 'Realität' aufweisen liess, am Ende gar als das phänomenal Gegebene in der 'Realität.' 'In Wirklichkeit' tritt, was das Warhnehmungsnoema heisst, als das auf, was Husserl ein 'Phantom' nennt" (personal correspondence, January 27, 1963).

66. *Ideen*, I, p. 221.

67. *Studies*, p. 109.

68. *Ideen*, I, p. 221.

69. "Contribution to the Phenomenological Theory of Perception," *Studies*, p. 341.

70. *Field*, p. 183.

71. "Gestalt Theory and Phenomenology," *Studies*, p. 257.

72. *Studies*, p. 256.

73. Ibid.

74.* I am indebted to Samuel Todes for pointing out this possible interpretation of Gurwitsch's noema, as well as for his phenomenology of the differences between conception and perception ["Comparative Phenomenology of Perception and Imagination," *Journal of Existentialism* (Spring and Fall, 1966)], which influenced the over-all approach of this essay.

75. "Phenomenological Theory of Perception," *Studies*, p. 349.

76. "The Kantian and Husserlian Conceptions of Consciousness," *Studies*, p. 155.

77. *Field*, p. 296.

78. *Field*, p. 181.

79. *Ideen*, I, p. 304.

80. "On the Intentionality of Consciousness," *Studies*, p. 138.

81. Edmund Husserl, *Cartesian Meditations*, trans. Dorion Cairns (The Hague: Nijhoff, 1960), p. 33.

82. "Husserl's Theory of the Intentionality of Consciousness," this volume, p. 68.

83. "On the Intentionality of Consciousness," *Studies*, p. 139.

84. Aron Gurwitsch, "A Non-Egological Conception of Consciousness," *Studies*.

85.* Roderick Firth, who tries to reconcile the results of Gestalt psychology and traditional epistemology in his article, "Sense Data and the Percept Theory" (*Mind*, October 1949, and January 1950) develops a view similar to Gurwitsch's. He also defines the material object as a system of appearances, or ostensible objects, but he remains truer to the phenomenon. He remarks that "the ostensible object is not ostensibly ostensible," and he therefore introduces an epistemological (as opposed to phenomenological) point of view. Only from the epistemological point of view can we say that since the material object may be illusory, we *know* that it has no hidden aspects even though it *presents itself* as having them. This approach has its own difficulties. (Cf. my dissertation *Husserl's Phenomenology of Perception*, Harvard University, 1963).

86. *Field*, p. 301.

87.* This way out has its problems, too. Even if we grant the dubious claim that in the perception of ordinary objects the interpretive sense can be entertained as an abstractable entity, it does not follow—it perhaps does not even make sense to hold—that the meaning of pre-objective experience, on the one hand, and the world, on the other, can be entertained in the same way.

88. "Gestalt Theory and Phenomenology," *Studies*, p. 257.

89. *Studies*, p. xxiii.

90.* In one of his last papers, Gurwitsch writes:

[T]he insight that in our perceptual life we are directly and immediately at the things and at the world, far from being due to the subsequent emergence of existentialist philosophy, must be seen as a consequence following from Husserl's theory of the intentionality of consciousness, especially perceptual consciousness ["Perceptual Coherence as the Foundation of the Judgement of Predication" in *Phenomenology and the Theory of Science* (Evanston: Northwestern University Press, 1974), p. 243].

See also "Husserl's Theory of the Intentionality of Consciousness" (this volume, p. 67). It is doubtful that Husserl, with his conceptualization of perception and his transcendental ego as monad, ever allowed for being-at-the-world. Gurwitsch's account, however, like Sartre's, does, indeed, allow being-*at*-the-world, *but it allows for nothing more*. Such an account does not arrive at the existential phenomenology of being-*in*-the-world, in a situation, together with objects.

91.* "Bodily phenomena may be resorted to only as experienced bodily phenomena, that is, phenomena such as they appear and present themselves through our specific awareness of them" (*Field*, p. 305).

92. *Studies*, p. xxiv.

93. *Field*, p. 288.

8. TEMPORAL AWARENESS (MILLER)

1. Edmund Husserl, *The Phenomenology of Internal Time-Consciousness*,

ed. Martin Heidegger, trans. J. S. Churchill (Bloomington: Indiana Univ. Press, 1964). Henceforth this book will be referred to as *"Time."*

2. For a full account of the development of Husserl's thought, cf. H. Spiegelberg's *The Phenomenological Movement*, vol. I (The Hague: Nijhoff, 1969).

3. Cf., for example, Edmund Husserl, *Ideas: General Introduction to Pure Phenomenology*, trans. W. R. Boyce Gibson (New York: Humanities Press, 1931), pp. 242-243. This book will henceforth be referred to as *"Ideas."*

4. Dagfinn Føllesdal, "Husserl's Notion of Noema," this volume, pp. 73-80.

5. Cf. my doctoral dissertation, *The Phenomenology of Perception: Husserl's Account of Our Temporal Awareness*, UCLA, 1979, chapter II.

6. Cf., for example, *Ideas*, p. 49.

7. Ibid., p. 45.

8. Edmund Husserl, *Formal and Transcendental Logic*, trans. Dorion Cairns (The Hague: Nijhoff, 1969). Henceforth this book will be referred to as *"FTL."*

9. Edmund Husserl, *Cartesian Meditations*, trans. Dorion Cairns, (The Hague: Nijhoff, 1960). Henceforth this book will be referred to as *"CM."*

10.* A similar statement would also apply to the act of *expecting*, or anticipating an object. However, it is worth noticing that, unlike the act of remembering, the act of expecting an object need not be a uniquely directed act.

11. This is argued for independently by David Smith in his essay "Husserl on Demonstrative Reference and Perception" (this volume, pp. 193-213) and in his "The Case of the Exploding Perception" (*Synthese*, 41, 1979 pp. 239-269).

12.* Husserl himself does not explicitly say that a perceptual act has a demonstrative element, perhaps because of the following: perception, according to Husserl, helps in "fixing" the reference for a linguistic act of demonstration, but it is not itself an act of demonstration. Still, he frequently uses the demonstrative (as well as other indexical terms, such as 'there,' 'here,' 'now,' 'I,' etc.) in phenomenological descriptions of perceptual acts.

13. *Ideas*, p. 324.

14.* Perceptual verbs do, indeed, occur also in propositional contexts (I see that . . . , I hear that . . . , etc). The way I understand Husserl's view, this does not mean that there are two "kinds" of perceptual acts: direct object and propositional. Instead, his view seems to be that propositional perceptual constructions are used by us to express *perceptual judgments*. Here, again, his view seems to be that a perceptual judgment is not a special kind of judgment (there is just one kind), but rather a judgment made under special circumstances: a perceptual judgment is a judgment passed about an object *in the face of* perceiving that object. In such a case, *two* acts are involved: the (direct object) act of perceiving the object and the (propositional) act of judging something about it, and the latter is said to be "based" on the former.

15.* The analysis of our perceptual experience at these boundary instants offers special difficulties which, although requiring attention, will only distract us from the main issues at hand.

16. *Time*, p. 50.

17. This diagram is an adaptation of Husserl's own diagrams for illustrating the same points. Cf. *Time*, p. 49 & p. 121.

18.* Husserl says: "Retention itself is not an 'act' . . . " (*Time*, p. 161). He also says: "One may by no means misinterpret . . . primal consciousness (primal-impression) . . . as an apprehending act" (*Time*, p. 163; the parenthetical insertion is mine). I take his view of protention to be the same, although he is not explicit about it.

19.* Husserl devotes a whole section of *Time* to emphasizing his view that retentions are "proper intentionalities" having as "objects" *past* phases of the act's "total" object. Cf. *Time*, pp. 52–54.

20. Edmund Husserl, *Logical Investigations*, trans J. N. Findlay (London: Routledge & Kegan Paul, 1970); to be referred to as *"LI."*

21. *Time*, p. 97.

22. Ibid., p. 146.

23. Ibid., p. 140.

24. Ibid., pp. 79–80.

25.* Husserl says in a number of places that protentions, unlike retentions, intend their object-phases "voidly" (cf., for example, *Time*, p. 76). It seems clear that by "voidly" he means "lacking in intuitive *fullness*."

26.* Contextual considerations make it clear that this means: "insofar as they characterize the *near side* of the (purported) object."

27.* Husserl seems to be committed to some version of a *metaphysical* "open future" view of time. I am, however, of the opinion that his *phenomenological* account of our temporal awareness does not presuppose, nor does it entail, such a view of time.

28. *Time*, pp. 52–53n.

29.* As long as we keep in mind that a near surface is also a *transcendent* object, and it is always experienced by us as having more to it than can be "captured" by any one act or a finite amount of experience.

30.* This does not mean that from my seeing the near surface of an object it does not follow that I see any of its *properties*. On the contrary, according to Husserl perceiving an entity always involves perceiving it *as* having some (nonrelational) physical properties, such as color, shape, and the like, But, of course, it does not follow from my seeing the near surface that I see all its properties.

31. Dagfinn Føllesdal, "Phenomenology," *Handbook for Perception*, vol. 1 (San Francisco: Academic Press, 1974), p. 379. Supporting text for this view is, for example, *Ideas*, p. 230.

32. *Time*, p. 61.

9. THE THEORY OF THE PURE EGO (HEINSEN)

1.* Reference to Husserl's works will be made using the following abbreviations.

LI: Logical Investigations, trans. J. N. Findlay (London: Routledge & Kegan Paul, 1970). *I: Ideas*, trans. W. R. Boyce Gibson (New York: Collier Books, 1967). *IE, IZ: Ideen*, I, II (The Hague: Nijhoff, 1950, 1952). *PL: The Paris Lectures*, trans. Peter Koestenbaum (The Hague: Nijhoff, 1967). *FTL: Formal and Transcendental Logic*, trans. Dorion Cairns (The Hague: Nijhoff, 1969). *CM: Cartesian Meditations*, trans. Dorion Cairns (The Hague: Nijhoff, 1960). *EJ: Experience and Judgment*, ed. Ludwig Landgrebe, trans. James S. Churchill and Karl Ameriks (Evanston: Northwestern Univ. Press, 1973). *C: The Crisis of European Sciences and Transcendental Phenomenology*, trans. David Carr (Evanston: Northwestern Univ. Press, 1970).

The letters *t*, *m*, and *b* indicate the top, middle, and bottom thirds of a page, respectively.

2.* Note, too, that "the Ego" of *Ideas* is always a translation of "das Ich."

3.* Certain exceptions to this rule occur in the early sections of *CM*, but are explained by the footnotes at *CM* 28, 66: *Ego* and *Ich* are not distinguished until §31—Husserl worries that this may be too late—and prior to that point are employed loosely, even interchangeably.

4.* And a "correlate" is, of course, a noema or noematic meaning (*I*, 191b, 244b; *CM*, 37m, 386, 95m; *C*, 242m).

5.* And the same will naturally hold good for the Ego's habitualities, abilities, etc. But a cautionary note is perhaps in order here. World, thing, human ego and personal Ego are indeed intentional objects, meanings; but none of them is, simply and without further ado, reducible to a *single* noema. As objects of which no adequate experience (evidence) is possible, each is rather an infinite family of interrelated noemata, both actual and possible. Or, better yet, each is an "objective sense" or "cogitatum qua cogitatum": a total significance of which all our *actual* noemata are more or less incomplete versions but which is implicit in all of them, the noematic sense we *would* achieve were all the horizons of our experience to become fully explicit and determinate (see *C*, 234b; *CM*, 41t, 45, 46mb). But these complexities may be ignored in the present case and we will continue to speak of the Ego as a noema; the pure Ego, if given at all, is of necessity given adequately (see §V), so that here noema and objective sense are simply one.

6.* Husserl's theory of attention is certainly the weakest point in his argument, and it is primarily this which A. Gurwitsch attacks in developing his non-egological conception of consciousness [*Studies in Phenomenology and Psychology*, (Evanston: Northwestern University Press, 1966), pp. 175–311]. According to Gurwitsch, attention *does* materially alter its object, *is* a reconstitution of the pregiven, and may therefore be understood not ". . . in terms of distribution of illumination, but rather in terms of organization of the field of consciousness—that is to say, in terms of *that which is given*." (Ibid., p. 215t) And doubtless Gurwitsch is at least generally correct; whether this circumstance absolutely precludes the existence (the fulfilled positing) of the Ego, merely renders it optional, or leaves it basically intact is much too complicated an issue to be decided here, however.

7.* *EU: Husserl's Erfahrung Und Urteil*, ed. Ludwig Landgrebe (Hamburg:

Felix Meiner Verlag, 1972), of which *EJ* is a translation. The translators of *EU* have chosen to render "Ich" as "ego" (spelled with a small letter). To avoid confusion, I will replace their "ego" with Cairns' "Ego," as has been done here, in each case citing the corresponding passage in EU.

8.* Strictly speaking, since the harmony we have in mind is a harmony over time, some recourse to memory will also be required to establish this point; but our recollection of the past need be no less apodictic than our reflective grasp of the present (*CM*, §§9, 12, 46).

10. WAS HUSSERL REALIST OR IDEALIST? (HALL)

1.* Precision would only be misplaced at this point, since everything turns on whether or not the finer distinctions one might draw are the ones which should be drawn given the details of Husserl's theory.

2. The phrase is K. Ameriks', "Husserl's Realism," *The Philosophical Review*, 86, No. 4 (October 1977), p. 498.

3. R. Ingarden, *Der Streit um die Existenz der Welt*, vol. 2 (Tübingen: Niemeyer, 1965); and "Die vier Begriffe der Transcendenz und das Problem des Idealismus in Husserl" in A.-T. Tymieniecka, ed., *Analecta Husserliana*, vol. 1 (Dordrecht: Reidel, 1971), pp. 37-74.

4. G. Küng, "Husserl on Pictures and Intentional Objects," *Review of Metaphysics*, 26 (1973), p. 679; see also "The World as Noema and as Referent," *Journal of the British Society for Phenomenology*, 3 (1972), p. 21.

5. J. Findlay, "Phenomenology and the Meaning of Realism," in E. Pivčević, ed., *Phenomenology and Philosophical Understanding* (Cambridge: Cambridge Univ. Press, 1975), pp. 155-158; and W. Morriston, "Intentionality and the Phenomenological Method: A Critique of Husserl's Transcendental Idealism," *Journal of the British Society for Phenomenology*, 7 (1976), pp. 36-43.

6. See, for example, D. Smith and R. McIntyre, "Intentionality via Intensions," *Journal of Philosophy*, 68, No. 18 (1971), pp. 559-561.

7. "Husserl's Realism," pp. 498-519.

8. R. Holmes, "Is Transcendental Phenomenology Committed to Idealism?" *The Monist*, 59 (1975), pp. 98-114.

9. The *epoché* or transcendental-phenomenological reduction.

10. See, for example, D. Smith and R. McIntyre, "Intentionality via Intensions"; and H. Dreyfus, "Husserl's Perceptual Noema," this volume, pp. 99-100.

11. See E. Husserl, *Logical Investigations* (New York: Humanities Press, 1970), vol. I, p. 292.

12. See *Logical Investigations*, vol. II, Studies V and VI; *Ideas* (New York: Collier Books, 1962), pp. 153n, 238, 319; and *Ideen, III* (The Hague: Nijhoff, 1952), p. 89.

13. See J. Mohanty, "Husserl's Theory of Meaning" in F. Elliston and P. McCormick, eds., *Husserl: Expositions and Appraisals* (Notre Dame: Univ. of Notre Dame Press, 1977), pp. 20-21; and "Husserl and Frege: A New Look at Their Relationship," this volume, pp. 44-45.

14. See H. Sluga, "Frege's Alleged Realism," *Inquiry*, 20 (1977), pp. 230-233.

15. *Logical Investigations*, vol. I, p. 292.

16. See ibid., pp. 42-43, and p. 179n.

17. P. Geach and M. Black, eds., *Translations from the Philosophical Writings of Gottlob Frege* (Oxford: Blackwell, 1960), pp. 59-60.

18. *Logical Investigations*, vol. I, p. 332.

19. Ibid., vol. I, p. 287.

20.* As Husserl says repeatedly, it is a science of meaning, not of fact.

21. *Logical Investigations*, vol. I, p. 217.

22. See, especially, *Ideas*, pp. 102, 131-133, 139, 142; and *Cartesian Meditations*, p. 21.

23. E. Husserl, *Cartesian Meditations* (The Hague: Nijhoff, 1960), pp. 83-86.

24. *Ideas*, p. 153.

25. *Cartesian Meditations*, p. 52n.

26. Ibid, p. 37; see also p. 21.

27. Ibid., p. 84.

28. Ibid., p. 91.

29. Ibid., p. 85.

30. Ibid., p. 62.

31. E. Husserl, *The Idea of Phenomenology* (The Hague: Martinus Nijhoff, 1964), p. 21.

32.* This is why Husserl puts "product" in quotation marks in the passage quoted above; see n.29 above.

33. *Cartesian Meditations*, pp. 69ff.

34. See ibid., p. 80.

35.* Husserl's notion of matter or *hylē* in this connection is usually a relative notion. What would be formed or structured at a lower level of complexity serves as the matter for a higher level act of structuring or constitution. At the bottom limit Husserl would seem to be stuck with either some unstructured material or stuff which enters into the most basic synthetic act(s), or else a minimally structured level whose structure is not the product of conscious activity. Both alternatives would be extremely problematic. On Husserl's view, unstructured or uninterpreted data should be impossible to experience, and a meaningful structure which did not result from the interpretive activity of consciousness should be completely unintelligible. But there is no need to pursue this problem further here.

36. For more complete discussions see my "Idealism and Solipsism in Husserl's *Cartesian Meditations*," *Journal of the British Society for Phenomenology*, (January, 1976); and "Intersubjective Phenomenology and Husserl's Cartesianism," *Man and World*, 12, No. 1 (1979).

37.* This orders all of the members within each of the general categories of meanings which Husserl refers to as "regions" or "regional ontologies." See *Ideas*, pp. 57-62, 158-160, and 185-186; and *Cartesian Meditations*, pp. 62-64.

38. See pp. 176–177.

39. See pp. 175–176.

40. In addition to the passages below, see *Ideas*, pp. 123, 153; *Cartesian Meditations*, p. 92; and E. Husserl, *The Crisis of European Sciences and Transcendental Phenomenology* (Evanston: Northwestern Univ. Press, 1970), p. 163.

41. *Crisis*, pp. 186–187.

42. *Ideas*, p. 96.

43. Ibid., pp. 97–98 (emphasis mine, first parenthetical material added).

44. *Cartesian Meditations*, p. 147.

45. Ibid., p. 151.

46. *Crisis*, p. 187 (parenthetical material added).

47. Letter from Husserl to Abbé Baudin in 1934, quoted in I. Kern, *Husserl und Kant: Eine Untersuchung über Husserls Verhältnis zu Kant und zum Neukantianismus (Phenomenologica 16)*, (The Hague: Nijhoff, 1964), p. 276n.

48. See *Ideas*, p. 139, and *Cartesian Meditations*, pp. 24ff, for Husserl's comments on the absurdity of philosophical realism.

49. See, for example, *Ideas*, pp. 153–154.

50. See *Cartesian Meditations*, p. 42.

51. See p. 182.

52. See the passage quoted above on p. 182, n. 45.

53.* Provided they are not suffering from severe mental aberration.

54. On this point, see T. Clarke, "The Legacy of Skepticism," *Journal of Philosophy, 64* (1972), pp. 754–757.

55. *Cartesian Meditations*, p. 148.

56.* In Husserl's terminology, this calls for the meaning-component which corresponds to the "existence-sense" or "existence-status" of the thing in question.

57. See G. E. Moore, "Proof of an External World" in *Philosophical Papers* (London: Allen & Unwin, 1959), pp. 126–148.

58.* Both Ameriks ("Husserl's Realism") and Holmes ("Is Transcendental Phenomenology Committed to Idealism?") seem to have been misled by just these considerations.

59. For more extended treatments see D. Føllesdal, "Husserl's Theory of Perception," and H. Dreyfus, "Husserl's Perceptual Noema," both in this volume.

60. See, for example, *Ideas*, pp. 354–361; and *Cartesian Meditations*, pp. 39–42, 57–64.

61. See, for example, *Ideas*, pp. 122–124; and *Cartesian Meditations*, p. 79. In connection with the embodied existence of others, see *Cartesian Meditations*, pp. 128, 137, 148.

62. *Crisis*, p. 145 (emphasis mine and parenthetical material added).

63.* I am not trying to say that Husserl's notion of perceptual "filling" is unproblematic. It may well present an insuperable difficulty for him. All I am saying is that Husserl does not view his theory of evidence as taking him beyond the sphere of meaning.

11. DEMONSTRATIVE REFERENCE AND PERCEPTION (SMITH)

1. Edmund Husserl, *Logical Investigations*, vols. I and II, trans. J. N. Findlay (London: Routledge & Kegan Paul, 1970). German original, *Logische Untersuchungen*, first published in 1900-01. Cited as *LI*.

2. David Kaplan, *Demonstratives* (typescript, xeroxed, UCLA, March 1977; revised version to be published). Also cf. his "The Logic of Demonstratives" (xeroxed, summer, 1971; expanded, 1973).

3. Such expressions have come to be called "indexical" expressions, following C. S. Peirce. Some important discussions in addition to Husserl's and Kaplan's are: Gottlob Frege, "The Thought: A Logical Inquiry," reprinted in P. F. Strawson, *Philosophical Logic* (Oxford: Oxford Univ. Press, 1967); Hans Reichenbach, *Elements of Symbolic Logic* (New York, 1947), §50, "Token-reflexive words"; A. W. Burks, "Icon, Index, and Symbol," *Philosophy and Phenomenological Research*, IX (1949), dealing with Peirce's account of indexicals; Y. Bar-Hillel, "Indexical Expressions," *Mind*, 63 (1954); and John Perry, "Frege on Demonstratives," *Philosophical Review*, 86 (October 1977).

4. Cf. Gottlob Frege, "On Sense and Reference," reprinted in P. Geach and M. Black, *Translations from the Philosophical Writings of Gottlob Frege* (Oxford: Oxford Univ. Press, 1966). Husserl's semantics is found in the first of the *Investigations*.

5. Re the term '*Sinn*' see *LI*, I, especially §§14, 30-35; V, §§20ff; VI, §§11ff; and Husserl's *Ideas: General Introduction to Phenomenology*, trans. W. R. Boyce Gibson (New York: Collier Books, 1972), §§88-90, 128-135. The latter work will be cited as *Ideas*. For an exposition of Husserl's theory of intentionality, see D. W. Smith and R. McIntyre, "Intentionality via Intensions," *Journal of Philosophy*, 68, No. 18 (Sept. 16, 1971). Husserl's theory of intentionality can be drawn from *LI*, I, §14, V, chapters 2 and 3, especially §§10, 12, 20-22; or from *Ideas*, §§84-90, 128-135.

6. The relation of language to thought, reference to intention, is detailed in *LI*, I, and VI, chapter 1. For an exposition, see R. McIntyre and D. W. Smith, "Husserl's Identification of Meaning and Noema," this volume.

7. See, especially, the following: Dagfinn Føllesdal, "Husserl's Notion of Noema," this volume; Dagfinn Føllesdal, "An Introduction to Phenomenology for Analytic Philosophers," in *Contemporary Philosophy in Scandinavia*, ed. R. E. Olson and A. N. Paul (Baltimore: Johns Hopkins Univ. Press, 1972); Hubert Dreyfus, *Husserl's Phenomenology of Perception* (doctoral dissertation, Harvard University, 1963); Ronald McIntyre, *Husserl and Referentiality: The Role of the Noema as an Intensional Entity* (doctoral dissertation, Stanford University, 1970); David Woodruff Smith, *Intentionality, Noemata, and Individuation: The Role of Individuation in Husserl's Theory of Intentionality* (doctoral dissertation, Stanford University, 1970); Ronald McIntyre and David Woodruff Smith, "Husserl's Identification of Meaning and Noema." The interpretation of Husserl's theory of intentionality as analogous to a Fregean theory of reference, stressing *Sinn* as the central notion of Husserl's phenomenology, originates primarily with Føllesdal; the preceding

works are indebted to Føllesdal's lectures on phenomenology during the 1960's. The analogy between intention and reference, and the founding of reference on intention, can be seen emerging in Husserl through *LI*, I, V, and VI. On the relation of Husserl to Frege, see J. N. Mohanty, "Husserl and Frege: a New Look at their Relationship," this volume; J. N. Mohanty, "Frege-Husserl Correspondence," trans. with notes, *Southwestern Journal of Philosophy*, 5 (1974); and J. N. Mohanty, "On Husserl's Theory of Meaning," *Southwestern Journal of Philosophy*, 5 (1974).

8. Kaplan has urged a similar view in lecture, though his formal representation (in *Demonstratives*, cited in n. 2) could also fit a more Husserlian view. See my brief comparison of Husserl and Kaplan at the end of this paper.

9. Cf. *Ideas*, §131. For an exposition of this structure of the sense of a perception, see Smith and McIntyre, "Intentionality via Intensions" (cited in n. 5).

10.* Husserl explicitly says reference does not require the existence of the object referred to: "In meaning (*Bedeutung*), a reference (*Beziehung*) to an object is constituted. To use an expression meaningfully (*mit Sinn*) and to refer expressively to an object (to form a presentation of an object) are one and the same. It makes no difference whether the object exists or is fictitious or even impossible" (*LI*, I, §15, p. 293; with translation changes).

11. For an incisive discussion of Husserl's troubles over intuitive sense, and the issues involved therewith, see Hubert Dreyfus, "Husserl's Perceptual Noema," this volume.

12. See n. 2.

13.* Reflecting on Kaplan's theory, John Perry has proposed a notion of sense to play the role of Kaplan's "character," taking the "sense" of a demonstrative or indexical term to be its "role"; for example, the role of 'I' is to refer to the person uttering it. Cf. Perry, "Frege on Demonstratives" (cited in note 3 above). This notion of role is similar to the second notion of indicating meaning suggested by Husserl's discussion, which we noted above, that stressing the general "semantic function" of the term.

14. Such a view is evident in Romane Clark, "Sensuous Judgments," *Noûs*, 7, No. 1 (March 1973), and Clark, "Old Foundations for a Logic of Perception," *Synthese*, 33 (1976). It can be drawn from Jaakko Hintikka, "On the Logic of Perception," in his *Models for Modalities* (Dordrecht: Reidel, 1969) together with his "Objects of Knowledge and Belief: Acquaintances and Public Figures," in his *The Intentions of Intentionality and Other New Models for Modalities* (Dordrecht: Reidel, 1975). A version of the view is developed in David Woodruff Smith, "The Case of the Exploding Perception," *Synthese*, vol. 41 (1979), pp. 239-269.

12. INTENDING AND REFERRING (McINTYRE)

1. Earlier versions of some of the ideas in this paper were presented at the Western Division meetings of the American Philosophical Association in April 1975, as part of a symposium on "Husserl's Theory of Intentionality in Contemporary Perspective," and at U.C.L.A. in March, 1976, in a talk

entitled "Some New Perspectives on Husserl's Theory of Intentionality." A related paper, "Husserl's Phenomenological Conception of Intentionality and its Difficulties," based in part on the same talks, is appearing in *Philosophia*.

2. See Dagfinn Føllesdal, "Husserl's Notion of Noema," this volume, pp. 73-80; and "An Introduction to Phenomenology for Analytic Philosophers," in *Contemporary Philosophy in Scandinavia*, ed. Raymond E. Olson and Anthony M. Paul (Baltimore: The Johns Hopkins University Press, 1972), pp. 417-429.

3. Edmund Husserl, *Ideen zu einer reinen Phänomenologie und phänomenologischen Philosophie*, I (The Hague: Nijhoff, 1950), §36, p. 80; cf. §84, p. 204. Also see Husserl, *Logical Investigations*, trans. J. N. Findlay (New York: Humanities Press, 1970), V, §§10-13. Hereafter, these works will be cited as '*Ideen*' and '*LI*,' respectively. All translations from *Ideen* are my own, with page references to the German edition; the reader may compare with the English edition, *Ideas*, trans. W. R. Boyce Gibson (New York: Humanities Press, 1931).

4.* Husserl distinguishes an act's "psychological" content from its "phenomenological" content. A study of the former would be an empirical study, relevant to a scientific theory about the actual psychological and/or neurophysiological make-up of human beings. A study of the latter, Husserl believes, is a "transcendental" study of what is necessary for any consciousness to produce the act in question, irrespective of what the true empirical account of human consciousness might be. (See *Ideen*, §§53-54.) Husserl also distinguishes two notions of phenomenological content: "real" (*reell*) content, which is an event occurring at a particular time within a particular stream of consciousness; and "ideal" (*ideal*) content, which may be thought of as the abstract type of which the temporal content is the token (see *LI*, V, §§16, 20, 21, 45). Hence, "ideal" content can be "shared" by different acts of consciousness and by different subjects, while "real" content cannot. In *Ideen* Husserl calls an act's real phenomenological content its "noesis" and its ideal content its "noema" (see §§85, 88, 97). Acts of perception also have a sensory, or "hyletic," content (see *LI*, VI, §14(b); *Ideen*, §§85, 97), but this will not concern us here. These different notions of content are discussed further in David W. Smith and Ronald McIntyre, *Husserl and Intentionality: A Study of Mind, Meaning, and Language* (Dordrecht: Reidel, 1982), chapter 3.

5.* Husserl takes the noema of an act to be a complex meaning-entity, having two main components. The component specifically responsible for the act's intentional relation to its object he calls the "noematic *Sinn*" or "objective *Sinn*" in the noema. The other component relates most prominently to the kind, or species, of the act (for example, its being an act of perceiving rather than remembering). The distinction as made in *Ideen* (§§91-92, 99) corresponds to the distinction between "matter" and "quality" respectively, made in *LI* (V, §20), as Husserl himself notes in *Ideen*, §133.

6. See Føllesdal, "Husserl's Notion of Noema," this volume.

7. See Ronald McIntyre and David W. Smith, "Husserl's Identification of Meaning and Noema," this volume, pp. 81-92 above.

8. For a detailed statement of this, and another closely related theory, see Saul Kripke, "Naming and Necessity," in *Semantics of Natural Language,* ed. Donald Davidson and Gilbert Harman (Dordrecht: Reidel, 1972), pp. 255-260, 277-303.

9. For more details, see David W. Smith and Ronald McIntyre, "Intentionality via Intensions," *Journal of Philosophy,* 68 (1971), pp. 550-553.

10. See the following, for example: Kripke (n. 8 above), pp. 253-303; Keith Donnellan, "Proper Names and Identifying Descriptions," in Davidson and Harman (n. 8 above), pp. 356-379; Hilary Putnam, "Meaning and Reference," *Journal of Philosophy,* 70 (1973), 699-711; and Putnam, "The Meaning of 'Meaning'," in his *Philosophical Papers, II: Mind, Language, and Reality* (Cambridge: Cambridge Univ. Press, 1972), pp. 215-271.

11. In "Reference and Definite Descriptions," *Philosophical Review,* 75 (1966), pp. 281-304.

12.* I trace some further consequences of this third difficulty with the ID model of intending in my *Philosophia* paper (n. 1 above). I argue there that Husserl's account of the "transcendence" of physical objects, developed in terms of his notion of "horizon," in effect commits him to the view that an explanation of an act's intentionality requires a consideration of various possible worlds. I also argue that, in view of this commitment, his notion of definiteness requires that the noematic *Sinn* of an act determine what Jaakko Hintikka and other possible-worlds semanticists call the "transworld identity" of the object intended in an act. These arguments provide further grounds for rejecting the ID theory of intentionality.

13.* See Smith and McIntyre (n. 9 above), pp. 553-557. In §131 Husserl says that the whole noematic *Sinn is* "the 'object as it is determined' (*'Gegenstand im Wie seiner Bestimmtheiten'*)" and that the determinable X of the noema *is* the "noematic 'object simpliciter' (*'Gegenstand schlechthin'*)" (p. 321). I take Husserl's use of quotation marks here to be of crucial importance. In *Ideen,* §89, Husserl introduces a convention whereby an expression enclosed in quotation marks is to be taken as referring to its meaning, and so to a component of a noema, rather than to its ordinary referent. Hence, 'tree'—without quotation marks—refers to a natural object, whereas '"tree"'—in quotation marks—refers to the meaning-component of a noema via which an object is intended as being a tree. Similarly, I take it, '"object simpliciter"'—in quotation marks—refers to a noematic component (the determinable X) whereby an act is related to its object, and so *not* to that object itself.

14. This "demonstrative" interpretation was first suggested to me by Izchak Miller. It is developed by Smith in "Husserl on Demonstrative Reference and Perception," this volume, pp. 193-213 above.

15. Relevant here is Dreyfus' discussion of the intuitional element in perception and the difficulties it poses for Husserl's theory of intentionality: see Hubert Dreyfus, "Husserl's Perceptual Noema," this volume, pp. 97-123 above.

16. See Smith (n. 14 above) for more details than I can offer here.

17.* The role of these "background" beliefs and their relevance to Husserl's theory of intentionality and his notion of horizon are discussed in detail in Smith and McIntyre (n. 4 above), especially in Chapter V, Part 3. The view is scattered in Husserl, but see *Ideen*, §§47, 140, 142, 149, 150; *Cartesian Meditations*, trans. Dorion Cairns (The Hague: Nijhoff, 1960), §§19, 21, 22, 38, 39; and *Experience and Judgment*, trans. James S. Churchill and Karl Ameriks (Evanston: Northwestern Univ. Press, 1973), §§21c, 24-26, 67a, 82-86, 90-93.

13. HUSSERL AND HINTIKKA (MOHANTY)

This is a revised draft of a paper I read at the American Philosophical Association, Eastern Division, meetings in Washington, D.C., 1978. In writing this paper, I have benefited from comments by Chris Swoyer, John Biro, Rick Tieszen, Richard Aquila, and Jaakko Hintikka on earlier drafts.

1. J. Hintikka, *The Intentions of Intentionality and Other New Models for Modalities* (Dordrecht: Reidel, 1975), p. 62.

2. Ibid., p. 61.

3. Ibid., p. 195.

4. Ibid., p. 206.

5. J. Hintikka, "Semantics for Propositional Attitudes" in Davis, Hockney, and Wilson, eds., *Philosophical Logic* (Dordrecht: Reidel, 1969), pp. 21-45, esp. p. 24.

6. Quoted in H. Spiegelberg, *The Phenomenological Movement* (New York: Humanities Press, 1969), I, p. 39-40.

7. For an analysis of the structure of the noema, see my *The Concept of Intentionality* (St. Louis: Warren Green, 1972).

8. Husserl, *The Phenomenology of Internal Time Consciousness*, trans. James S. Churchill (Bloomington: Indiana Univ. Press, 1964).

9. *The Intentions of Intentionality*, p. 61.

10. Ibid., p. 218.

11. Ibid., p. 217.

12. See, for example, Hintikka, *Models of Modalities* (Dordrecht: Reidel, 1969), p. 154.

13. Cf. *Models for Modalities*, p. 91.

14. Ibid., p. 155.

15. A. Gurwitsch, *Studies in Phenomenology and Psychology* (Evanston: Northwestern Univ. Press, 1966), p. 125.

16. A. Plantinga, "Transworld Identity or Worldbound Individuals," in Stephen P. Schwartz, ed., *Naming, Necessity, and Natural Kinds* (Ithaca: Cornell University Press, 1977).

17. Husserl, *Ideen*, I, §15 b-c.

18. E. Husserl, *Experience and Judgment*, trans. James S. Churchill and Karl Ameriks (Evanston: Northwestern Univ. Press, 1973), pp. 173-174.

19.* Ibid., p. 173. This is not incompatible with Husserl's more well known thesis that experience of an individual object always leaves open horizons for further determination. This determinable horizon itself is predelineated, and so is necessarily contained in the structure of the experience of the object.

The sort of lack of determinacy and consequent possibility of determination that this entails is *radically* different from the sort of lack of determinacy and possibility of determination that characterize objects of imagination *qua* imagined objects.

20. Ibid., p. 173.

21. Ibid., p. 356.

22. Ibid., p. 173.

23. Hintikka's private communication to me.

24. Cf. *Ideen*, I, p. 109.

25.* For the constitution of other sorts of possibility, such as presumptive and open, see Husserl, *Experience and Judgment,* §21 b-c, and my "Husserl on the Modalities" (forthcoming in *Idea,* Bergman Institute of Philosophy, University of Jerusalem). Husserl did hold the view that possibilities are given in prepredicative perception. This has been recognized above. What I have sought to deny is the construal of these possibilities in the language of possible worlds.

26. *Experience and Judgment,* Appendix I, p. 381.

27. Cf. J. Manninen and R. Tuomela, eds., *Essays on Explanation and Understanding* (Dordrecht: Reidel, 1976), p. 99.

28. Ibid., p. 117.

29. For Husserl's theory of names, see *Logical Investigations,* and Mohanty, *Edmund Husserl's Theory of Meaning* (The Hague: Nijhoff, 1969).

RESPONSE TO *HUSSERL AND HINTIKKA* (HINTIKKA)

1. J. N. Mohanty, "Intentionality and 'Possible Worlds': Husserl and Hintikka," this volume, pp. 233-251.

2. See Jaakko Hintikka, *The Intentions of Intentionality* (Dordrecht: Reidel, 1975), the title essay.

3.* Roughly, intentionality interpreted as involving essentially a reference to several possible courses of events or states of affairs. This interpretation is significantly modified and put into a wider context in my forthcoming paper, "Degrees and Dimensions of Intentionality," in R. Haller, ed., *Proceedings of the Fourth International Wittgenstein Symposium* (Vienna: Hölder-Pichler-Tempsky, 1980), pp. 239-252.

4.* Føllesdal aptly compares the noema of an object (say, an object of perception) with the sum total of our expectations concerning it rather than what we perceive of it. See this volume, pp. 93-96.

5. See, for example, *The Intentions of Intentionality* (n. 2 above), pp. xiv, 116, 236.

6. See, for example, my paper, "Is Alethic Modal Logic Possible?" forthcoming in *Acta Philosophica Fennica.*

7. See, for example, *The Intentions of Intentionality* (n. 2 above), pp. 126-128; *Knowledge and the Known* (Dordrecht: Reidel, 1974), pp. 203-204.

8. See, for example, *Logic, Language-Games, and Information* (Oxford: Clarendon Press, 1973), pp. 9-12, 18-20.

9.* Human beings exist only in relation to their parents. Does it follow that they are not individuals?

10.* Mohanty's preoccupation with possible perceptions rather than possible worlds foreshadows the point I will make below in (3).

11. For related observations, see C. I. Lewis, *Mind and the World Order* (New York: Dover, 1929), p. 139; Eino Kaila, *Reality and Experience* (Dordrecht: Reidel, 1979), p. 299.

12.* Half seriously, I have sometimes used the slogan "'possible worlds' is a mass term" to drive home this point.

13. Cf. here Ronald McIntyre, "Intending and Referring," this volume, pp. 215–231, and "Husserl's Phenomenological Conception of Intentionality and Its Difficulties," forthcoming in *Philosophia,* and my comment on McIntyre in the same number.

14. See "Degrees and Dimensions of Intentionality" (n. 3 above).

15.* Contrary to what Mohanty seems to think (see, for example, his n. 5), the crucial question is not whether Frege's *Sinne* are linguistic meanings or meanings of acts (in Husserl's sense), but whether they are accessible to phenomenological reflection.

14. WHAT IS AN INTENTIONAL STATE? (SEARLE)

1.* In order to distinguish 'Intentionality' in this technical sense from the ordinary sense of the English words 'intend,' 'intention,' etc., I shall capitalize the technical occurrences.

2. For further discussion of the notion of direction of fit, see J. R. Searle, "A Taxonomy of Illocutionary Acts" in Gunderson, ed., *Language, Mind and Knowledge: Minnesota Studies in the Philosophy of Science,* VI (1975), pp. 344–369.

3.* There are some exceptions. Declarations, such as adjourning the meeting or declaring war, do not have a sincerity condition and no Intentional state is expressed by their performance.

4.* The exceptions that one can construct to this principle are cases where one dissociates oneself from one's speech act, as in, for example, 'It is my duty to inform you that p, but I don't really believe that p' or 'As your commanding officer, I order you to attack those fortifications, but I don't really want you to do it.'

5.* There are some interesting puzzling cases like doubting that p or wondering whether p. Shall we say that my doubt that p is satisfied if p? Or if not p? Or what?

6. For further discussion of the problems of fiction, see J. R. Searle, "The Logical Status of Fictional Discourse," *New Literary History* (1975).

7. "Intentionality and The Use of Language," by J. R. Searle, in A. Margalit, ed., *Meaning and Use* (Dordrecht: Reidel, 1979).

15. METHODOLOGICAL SOLIPSISM (FODOR)

I've had a lot of help with this one. I'm particularly indebted to Professors

Ned Block, Sylvain Bromberger, Janet Dean Fodor, Keith Gundersen, Robert Richardson, and Judith Thomson; and to Mr. Israel Krakowski.

1. David Hume, *A Treatise of Human Nature*, ed. L. Selby-Bigge (Oxford: Oxford Univ. Press, 1888), p. 20.

2.* I shall speak of 'type identity' (distinctness) of mental states to pick out the sense of 'same mental state' in which, for example, John and Mary are in the same mental state if both believe that water flows. Correspondingly, I shall use the notion of 'token identity' (distinctness) of mental states to pick out the sense of 'same mental state' in which it's necessary that if x and y are in the same mental state, then x = y.

3. For extensive discussion, see Jerry Fodor, *The Language of Thought* (New York: Thomas Y. Crowell, 1975); and Jerry Fodor, "Tom Swift and His Procedural Grandmother," *Cognition*, 6 (1978), pp. 229-247.

4.* This is *not*, notice, the same as saying 'formal operations are the ones that apply mechanically'; in this latter sense, *formality* means something like *explicitness*. There's no particular reason for using 'formal' to mean both 'syntactic' and 'explicit,' though the ambiguity abounds in the literature.

5. R. Descartes, *The Philosophical Works of Descartes*, vol. 1, trans. Haldane and Ross (Cambridge, England: Cambridge Univ. Press, 1967), p. 146.

6. William James, *Principles of Psychology*, vol. 1 (New York: Dover, 1890), p. 6.

7.* For elaboration of this sort of account, see Hilary Putnam, "Minds and Machines" in *Mind, Language and Reality—Philosophical Papers*, vol. 2 (Cambridge, England: Cambridge Univ. Press, 1975); it is, of course, widely familiar from discussions in artificial intelligence.

8. Terry Winograd, "Procedures as a Representation for Data in a Computer Program for Understanding Natural Language," M.I.T. A.I. Lab Tech Report 84, 1971.

9.* Some fairly deep methodological issues in A.I. are involved here. See "Tom Swift and his Procedural Grandmother," where this surface is lightly scratched.

10.* I'm told by some of my friends that this paragraph could be read as suggesting that there are two kinds of beliefs: opaque ones and transparent ones. This is not, of course, the way that it is intended to be read. The idea is rather that there are two kinds of conditions that we can place on determinations that a pair of belief tokens count as tokens of the same belief type. According to one set of conditions (corresponding to transparent taxonomy), a belief that the Morning Star is such and such counts as the same belief as a belief that the Evening Star is such and such; whereas, according to the other set of conditions (corresponding to opaque taxonomy), it does not.

11. See Jerry Fodor, "Propositional Attitudes," *Monist*, 61 (1978), pp. 501-521.

12.* I'm leaving it open that it may be to say still less than this (for example, because of problems about reference under false descriptions). For purposes of the present discussion, I don't need to run a line on the truth conditions for transparent propositional attitude ascriptions. Thank heaven, since I do not have one.

13.* It's worth emphasizing that the sense of 'behavior' *is* proprietary, and that that's pretty much what you would expect. Not every true description of an act can be such that a theory of the mental causation of behavior will explain the act under that description. (In being rude to Darcy, Elizabeth is insulting the man whom she will eventually marry. A theory of the mental causation of her behavior might have access to the former description, but not, surely, to the latter.)

Many philosophers—especially since Wittgenstein—have emphasized the ways in which the description of behavior may depend upon its context, and it is a frequent charge against modern versions of rational psychology that they typically ignore such characterizations. So they do, but so what? You can't have explanations of everything under every description, and it's a question for empirical determination which descriptions of behavior reveal its systematicity vis-à-vis its causes. The rational psychologist is prepared to bet that— to put it *very* approximately—behavior will prove to be systematic under some of the descriptions under which it is intentional.

At a minimum, the present claim goes like this: there is a way of taxonomizing behaviors and a way of taxonomizing mental states such that, given these taxonomies, theories of the mental causation of behavior will be forthcoming. And that way of taxonomizing mental states construes them nontransparently.

14.* There is an interesting discussion of this sort of case in Peter Geach, *Mental Acts* (London: Routledge and Kegan Paul, 1957). Geach says that Aquinas says that there is no 'intelligible difference' between Alfred's thought and Misha's. I don't know whether this means that they are having the same thought or that they aren't.

One might try saying: what counts for opaque type individuation is what's *in* your head, not just what's running through it. So, for example, though Alfred and Misha are both thinking, 'he feels faint,' nevertheless different counterfactuals are true of them: Misha would cash his pronoun as: 'he, Sam,' whereas Alfred would cash *his* pronoun as: 'he, Misha.' The problem would then be to decide *which* such counterfactuals are relevant, since, if we count all of them, it's going to turn out that there are few, if any, cases of distinct organisms having type identical thoughts.

I won't, in any event, pursue this proposal, since it seems clear that it won't, in principle, cope with all the relevant cases. Two people would be having different thoughts when each is thinking, 'I'm ill,' even if *everything* in their heads were the same.

15. See, especially, Nelson Goodman, *Ways of World Making* (Indianapolis: Hackett, 1978).

16.* I'm assuming, for convenience, that all the p's are such that either they or their denials are believed. This saves having to relativize to time (for example, having b and c read '. . . you believe or come to believe . . .').

17. Hilary Putnam, "The Meaning of 'Meaning'" in *Mind, Language and Reality—Philosophical Papers*, vol. 2.

18.* I blush to admit that I had missed some of these complexities until Sylvain Bromberger kindly rubbed my nose in them.

19. L. Bloomfield, *Language* (London: Allen and Unwin, 1933), pp. 139-140.

20.* It may be that Putnam *does* accept this moral. For example, the upshot of the discussion circa p. 153 of his article appears to be that a Greek semanticist prior to Archimedes *could* not (in practice) have given a correct account of what (the Greek equivalent of) 'gold' means—because the theory needed to specify the extension of the term was simply not available. Presumably *we* are in that situation vis-à-vis the objects of many of *our* thoughts and the meanings of many of our terms; and, presumably, we will continue to be so into the indefinite future. But then, what's the point of so defining psychology (semantics) that there can't be any?

21. Hartry Field, "Tarski's Theory of Truth," *Journal of Philosophy*, 69 (1972), pp. 347-375.

Index of Names

Subject Index